THE BOLSHEVIK REVOLUTION

1917–1923

A History of Soviet Russia
by Edward Hallett Carr
in Norton Paperback Editions

The Bolshevik Revolution, 1917–1923 (I)

The Bolshevik Revolution, 1917–1923 (II)

The Bolshevik Revolution, 1917–1923 (III)

A HISTORY OF SOVIET RUSSIA

THE BOLSHEVIK REVOLUTION
1917-1923

BY

EDWARD HALLETT CARR

★

VOLUME TWO

W. W. NORTON & COMPANY
New York • London

Printed in the United States of America

First published as a Norton paperback 1985
by arrangement with The Macmillan Company, New York

W. W. Norton & Company, Inc., 500 Fifth Avenue,
New York, N.Y. 10110
W. W. Norton & Company Ltd., 37 Great Russell Street,
London WC1B 3NU

ISBN 0-393-30197-4

1 2 3 4 5 6 7 8 9 0

PREFACE

OF the criticisms made by reviewers of the first volume of this work, the most cogent was the charge that I had inverted the natural order by describing the political and constitutional arrangements of the first years of the Soviet régime in advance of my treatment of the economic conditions which in large part dictated and explained them. The appearance of the second volume a year after the first will now permit of the two interconnected subjects being examined side by side ; and I am not wholly convinced that, since the awkward choice was imposed on me, I should have made things easier by embarking on the complex economic developments of the period without first setting the political framework in which they took place. Even now the picture is not complete, since the foreign relations of Soviet Russia in these years are reserved for a third volume which should be ready for publication next year.

Within the present volume awkward problems of arrangement also presented themselves. While every part of an economy is dependent on every other, it was obviously necessary here to divide the Soviet economy into its main sectors. What was less clear was the necessity of a further division by periods within the main period covered by the volume. At first sight it might have seemed preferable to discuss the development of, say, agriculture through the whole period in a single chapter. Since, however, the period included three sub-periods with markedly different characteristics — the period of the revolution itself, the period of war communism and the first stage of NEP — I finally decided on a chronological division into chapters with each sector of the economy discussed in turn in each of the three chapters devoted to these periods. The table of contents makes it easy for the reader, if he so prefers, to adopt the alternative course of pursuing the story of, say, agriculture throughout the volume without turning aside to intervening sections on industry, finance, etc.

A further problem on which a word of explanation may be required was the point at which to bring the volume to an end. The general design of this first three-volume instalment of the history was to carry it approximately up to the time when Lenin was withdrawn from the scene and the struggle for the succession began. In the first volume the creation of the USSR, the adoption of its constitution and the abolition of the People's Commissariat of Nationalities in July 1923 formed a convenient stopping-point. In the second volume the corresponding point comes slightly earlier. The culmination of the first phase of NEP was reached in the winter of 1922–1923 ; and the twelfth party congress met in April 1923 — a month after Lenin's final incapacity — under the shadow of an imminent economic crisis which was already compelling rival leaders to take up positions. In this volume, therefore, I have stopped short of the twelfth party congress except in the last chapter on " The Beginnings of Planning ". Here the discussions at the congress were a recapitulation of earlier controversies rather than the opening of a fresh debate, and have therefore been reported in this chapter.

Nearly all those whose assistance I gratefully acknowledged in the preface to the first volume have also aided me in one way or another in the preparation of its successor ; in addition to these, Mr. Maurice Dobb kindly lent me from his library some books which would otherwise have been inaccessible to me, and Mrs. Dewar of the Royal Institute of International Affairs generously allowed me to make use of the material which she has collected for a projected study of Soviet labour policies. To Mr. Isaac Deutscher I am specially indebted for putting at my disposal the notes made by him of the unpublished Trotsky archives in the Widener Library of Harvard University. To all these and others who have given me help or advice in the search for material and in the writing of the volume I should like once more to tender my sincere thanks.

I should add that a full bibliography and index to *The Bolshevik Revolution, 1917–1923* will appear at the end of its third and last volume.

E. H. CARR

June 5, 1951

CONTENTS

PART IV
THE ECONOMIC ORDER

PART IV

THE ECONOMIC ORDER

CHAPTER 15

THEORIES AND PROGRAMMES

THE teaching of Marx arose by reaction from the " utopianism " of the early socialists, who constructed ideal socialist societies out of the wealth and ingenuity of their own imagination, and did not feel it necessary to concern themselves with the question how these ideal societies of the future were to be evolved out of the existing societies. Marx's method was historical : all changes in the destinies and organization of mankind were part of an ever-flowing historical process. He made the assumption — the only postulate which he did not attempt to demonstrate — that modern society would *in the long run* always seek to organize itself in such a way as to make the most effective use of its productive resources. He started therefore from an analysis of existing society in order to show that the capitalist order, once instrumental in releasing and fostering an unprecedented expansion of the productive resources of mankind, had now reached a stage in the course of its historical development where it had become a hindrance to the maximum use of these resources and an obstacle to further progress : it was therefore bound, so long as Marx's initial postulate held good, to yield place to a new social order (which Marx called either " socialism " or " communism ") which would once more permit and promote the maximum use of productive resources. Marx's conception was political and revolutionary in the sense that he believed that the change from capitalism to socialism would involve the replacement of the bourgeoisie by the proletariat as a ruling class, and that it was inconceivable, at any rate in most countries, that this replacement could be effected without revolutionary violence. But it was also scientific and evolutionary. As the economic structure of capitalist society had grown out of the economic structure of feudal society, so by a similar process the economic structure of socialism

3

would grow out of the economic structure of capitalism. Most of Marx's writings were directed to convince his readers not that the change from capitalism to socialism was desirable — this assumption was implied in his postulate — but that it was inevitable. Marx was thus concerned throughout his life to analyse the existing capitalist order and to expose the self-frustrating and self-destructive forces at work within it rather than to depict the future socialist order which would arise out of its ruins. This latter task was still in a certain sense premature until the actual moment of the downfall of capitalism was reached. " A task presents itself ", as Marx wrote in the preface to the *Critique of Political Economy*, " only when the material conditions necessary for its solution already exist or, at any rate, are in process of arising." Marx was by temperament and conviction the sworn enemy of utopianism in any form ; and his thought was always coloured by his early polemics against the utopian socialists who entertained themselves with unreal visions of the future socialist society. Towards the end of his career, in *The Civil War in France*, he explained with contemptuous emphasis that the workers had " no ready-made utopias " and " no ideals to realize " : they knew that they would " have to pass through long struggles, through a series of historic processes, transforming circumstances and men ". This belief in the transformation of society by slow, immanent historical processes encouraged what seemed in some respects an empirical approach : you crossed your stiles when you came to them. Marx drew up no programme or manifesto of the future socialist order. Only once, in his *Critique of the Gotha Programme*, did he permit himself a momentary vision of " the highest phase of communist society " when " productive forces will reach their peak and the sources of wealth flow in full abundance ", so that " society will be able to inscribe on its banner : ' From each according to his capacities, to each according to his needs '." But, apart from the unusually eloquent terminology, this amounted to little more than a reaffirmation of Marx's basic assumption that socialism was necessary in order to release and develop the productive forces now frustrated by a degenerate capitalism ; and even here Marx had cautiously guarded himself in the covering letter to Brakke which accompanied the *Critique*. " Every step of the real movement ", he wrote, " is more important than a dozen programmes." [1] This aphorism had its dangers. It was Bernstein the revisionist who recorded Marx's (perhaps authentic) saying that " the man who draws up a programme for the future is a reactionary ",[2] and Georges Sorel the syndicalist who provided the best theoretical demonstration of the incompatibility between utopia and Marxism :

> To offer a theoretical analysis of the future economic order would be to attempt to erect an ideological superstructure in advance of the conditions of production on which it must be built : hence any such attempt would be non-Marxist.[3]

Both Bernstein and Sorel in their different ways drew from the argument the conclusion that " the movement is all, the goal nothing ". Marx would have resisted this conclusion. But his attitude lent it some support.

What Marx bequeathed to posterity was, therefore, not an economic prospectus of socialism but an economic analysis of capitalism ; his economic tools were those appropriate to the capitalist system. " Political economy ", with its familiar categories of value, price and profit, was something that belonged essentially to capitalism and would be superseded with it.[4] Under socialism even the labour theory of value would lose its meaning.[5] The very conception of economic laws operating independently of man's will belonged to the essence of capitalist society. Marx wrote repeatedly of the anarchy of production under capitalism, and argued that periodical crises were the inevitable result of relying on the blind laws of the market. In the *Communist Manifesto* he took it for granted that " the proletariat will use its political supremacy to take away all capital step by step from the bourgeoisie, centralize all elements of production in the hands of the state, i.e. of the proletariat organized as the ruling class, and increase the total of productive powers as rapidly as possible ".

---

[1] Marx i Engels, *Sochineniya*, xv, 267.
[2] Quoted in G. Sorel, *Reflections on Violence* (Engl. transl. 1916), p. 150.
[3] G. Sorel, *Décomposition du Marxisme* (3rd ed. 1925), p. 37.
[4] Engels, on the other hand, once defined " political economy in the widest sense " as " the science of the laws governing the production and exchange of the material means of subsistence in human society " (Marx i Engels, *Sochineniya*, xiv, 149) ; this phrase was frequently cited in controversies of the nineteentwenties about the continued validity of economic laws under planning.
[5] *Ibid.* xv, 273.

More than twenty years later, in *The Civil War in France*, he praised the decree of the Paris commune for the regulation of national production " on a common plan " ; and Engels looked forward to the time when the proletariat, having expropriated the bourgeoisie, would " convert . . . social means of production into social property ", and thus make possible " social production according to a previously thought out plan ".[1] Production under socialism, said Marx in *Capital*, would come under the conscious and pre-arranged control of society.[2] But Marx attempted no discussion of the conditions or of the instruments of socially planned production. All that could be learned from him on these matters had to be deduced from his analysis of the nature and consequences of capitalist production.

Of distribution and exchange [3] there was still less to be said ; the methods of social production, which determined social relations, equally determined methods of distribution and exchange.[4]

> Production, distribution, exchange and consumption . . . all form parts of a whole, differences within a unity. Production predominates over all other factors. From it the process begins each time anew.[5]

It was only " vulgar socialism " which " revolves primarily round questions of distribution ",[6] and believed that the equalization of distribution, not the socialization of production, was the goal of socialism. The *Communist Manifesto* had already proclaimed that the abolition by the communists of " bourgeois conditions of production " would also mean " the communist abolition of buying and selling ".[7] The end of capitalism would end commodity

[1] Marx i Engels, *Sochineniya*, xiv, 288-289.
[2] Karl Marx, *Das Kapital*, iii, ch. x.
[3] Marx distinguished between " distribution " (*Verteilung*) and " exchange " (*Austausch*). The former " determines the proportion (the quantity) in which products are allocated to individuals ", the latter " determines the particular products in the form of which the individual demands the share allocated to him in the distribution " ; the former represents a social, the latter an individual, decision (Marx i Engels, *Sochineniya*, xii, i, 179).
[4] Marx i Engels, *Sochineniya*, xii, i, 185.
[5] *Ibid.* xii, i, 189 : Marx added that there was none the less " a mutual interaction between the different factors " as " in every organic whole ".
[6] *Ibid.* xv, 276.
[7] All early socialists treated traders, in contrast with producers, as parasites on society : Owen in his " draft statute " of 1835 for an " Association of All Classes of All Nations " looked forward to a society " without priests, lawyers, soldiery, buyers and sellers ".

production and with it exchange in the capitalist sense. " In a collective society based on common ownership of the means of production ", wrote Marx in his *Critique of the Gotha Programme*, " producers do not exchange their products." In the eventual communist society distribution would cease altogether to be concerned with incentives to work, since material incentives would be replaced by moral incentives. But, in the transitional society which " is just emerging from capitalist society " and continues to bear the " birth marks " of its source, he envisaged a system under which the worker " receives from society a voucher that he has contributed such and such a quantity of labour (after deduction from his labour for the common fund), and draws through this voucher from the social storehouse as much of the means of consumption as costs the same quantity of labour ".[1] But these scattered *obiter dicta* only serve to show how little Marx had attempted to analyse the problems of distribution and exchange in a socialist society. Discussions about the functions of value, price and profit in a planned economy lay far ahead in the future.

A further reason which consciously or unconsciously inhibited Marx from any positive approach to the economic issues of socialism was his inability to establish precisely by whom planning in a socialist order would be done. While he was perfectly precise about the essential function of planning, he was content to assign that function to " society " as such :

> Society must calculate in advance how much labour, means of production and means of subsistence it can employ without any deduction on branches of industry which, like for example the building of railways, can for a long time, a year or more, yield neither means of production nor means of subsistence nor any use value, but withdraw labour, means of production and means of subsistence from the total annual production.[2]

Economic planning was conceived not as a function of the state, but rather as a function which would render the state superfluous. " When in the course of development class distinctions have disappeared ", declared the *Communist Manifesto*, " and all production has been concentrated in the hands of a vast association of

---

[1] Marx i Engels, *Sochineniya*, xv, 274 ; the same idea is repeated in almost identical language in Karl Marx, *Das Kapital*, iii, ch. xviii.
[2] Karl Marx, *Das Kapital*, ii, ch. xvi.

the whole nation, then public power will lose its political character ". But where in this " vast association of the nation " would the work of planning production be undertaken ? Marx never attempted to answer this question. According to one passage in *Capital*, society would itself be " organized as a conscious and systematic association ", in which the producers themselves " would regulate the exchange of products, and place it under their own common control instead of allowing it to rule over them as a blind force ".[1] While the planning and direction of economic life was clearly an integral part of socialism, Marx was content to follow the assumption made by all socialists from Saint-Simon onwards that these functions would be discharged not by the state or by any political organ, but by the producers themselves ; [2] nor did Marx's disciples before 1917 make any significant progress on these lines. Planning was taken for granted rather than discussed. The programme of the Russian Social-Democratic Workers' Party adopted by the second congress in 1903 spoke, in strict Marxist terminology, of " replacing private property in the means of production and exchange by social property and introducing planned organization of the social-productive process ".[3] But this was common form ; and nothing was done to elaborate the conception of a plan in Bolshevik literature before the revolution. On the eve of the revolution, Lenin explained the apparent lacuna by the argument which Marx himself might have used :

> In Marx there is no trace of attempts to create utopias, to guess in the void at what cannot be known. Marx formulates the question of communism in the same way as a natural scientist might formulate the question of, say, a new biological species, once we know that this has somehow come into existence and is evolving in some definite direction.[4]

Marx had left behind the conception of a socially planned economy, and his economic analysis of the capitalist order was to provide

---

[1] Karl Marx, *Das Kapital*, iii, ch. xxxix.
[2] The word used by Saint-Simon was " industriels ", which covered all those engaged in production. His disciples after his death, perhaps jealous for his somewhat uncertain reputation as a " socialist ", substituted the word " travailleurs ", speaking of " an association of the workers " (*Doctrine de Saint-Simon : Exposition, Première Année* (1830), p. 197).
[3] *VKP(B) v Rezolyutsiyakh* (1941), i, 20.
Lenin, *Sochineniya*, xxi, 482.

by process of contradiction the basis of the techniques of socialist planning.[1] But the economic policies of the transition period through which the revolution must pass in the struggle to create the socialist order had to be worked out empirically by the workers who had made the revolution.

In addition to long-term generalized indications for the development of the future socialist order, Marx made from time to time pronouncements on topical issues of economic policy ; and these had a more direct practical influence on those parties which professed to base their programmes on Marx's teaching. In the *Communist Manifesto* Marx recorded certain immediate measures which, at any rate in " the most advanced countries ", could be advocated by the proletariat as practicable reforms in existing conditions. These reforms could be achieved within the formal limits of bourgeois democracy, though Marx thought that they would inevitably tend to " outstrip themselves " and " necessitate further inroads upon the old social order ". The most important of the ten measures listed in the *Manifesto* (Marx admitted that they might vary from country to country) were the abolition of private property in land ; a progressive income-tax ; abolition of inheritance ; the centralization of credit through a national bank, and of communications in the hands of the state ; an extension of state ownership of factories and means of production ; equal obligation of all to work ; and free education and the abolition of child labour in factories " in its present form ". The theoretical objection was sometimes made that the satisfaction of these limited demands might blunt the revolutionary ardour of the proletariat by lessening their hardships, and that such demands should not be put forward by avowed revolutionaries. But in practice no party could appeal to the broad masses of the workers without a programme designed to remedy some of their immediate grievances. It became the habit of social-democratic parties, following the precedent of the *Communist Manifesto*, to distinguish between their maximum and minimum programmes, the former representing their revolutionary aspirations, the latter the immediately practicable demands which they might hope to realize even

[1] The techniques of planning as eventually adopted in the USSR were founded on the categories used by Marx in *Capital* for his analysis of the capitalist system ; but they had little or no application in the first years of the régime.

under the existing bourgeois order. One of the unforeseen effects of this division was to attract into social-democratic parties a large body of members who by conviction or temperament were more interested in the minimum than in the maximum programme; and in countries where some of the minimum demands had in fact been realized, and others seemed likely to be realized in the future, through the processes of bourgeois democracy, the parties tended more and more to relegate the demands of the maximum programme to the category of remote theoretical aims and concentrate party activities on the realization of the minimum programme. In other words, social democracy, while remaining revolutionary in theory became predominantly reformist in practice. The German Social-Democratic Party provided the classic instance of this gradual transformation.

The dissemination of Marxist doctrine in Russia presented peculiar features corresponding to the backward economic conditions and equally backward political conditions of Russian society. In the nineteenth century the conquest of the Caucasus and the opening of the Altai region in the heart of Siberia with their enormously rich mineral resources provided the material conditions for Russian industrial development and made Russia a potential industrial power. The emancipation of the serfs in 1861, a direct blow at the citadel of the Russian feudal order, marked the first introduction of modern industrial capitalism to a country where the conditions for the development of a strong independent capitalist bourgeoisie were totally lacking. The historical function of the reform, as of the enclosures in English history, was to drive from the land into the towns and factories the labour necessary for the industrialization of the national economy. But its first impact was on the status of the peasant and on the system of land tenure, whose whole future was thrown open to debate. This was the burning issue of the next thirty years. It was natural that the first Russian Marxist groups should have grown out of controversy with the *narodniks* about the destiny of the Russian peasant and Russian agriculture. Agrarian questions, though they had occupied a subsidiary place in Marx's thought, were vital for his disciples in a country where nearly 90 per cent of the population were engaged primarily in agriculture; and embarrassment was caused by the fact that Marx, in some *obiter dicta* of his later years, had appeared to take the side of the *narodniks* against the Russian Marxists.[1] The *narodniks* believed that the Russian peasant commune, the system of common land tenure with periodical redistribution of individual allotments which had prevailed under serfdom and survived its abolition, provided a basis for the principle of common ownership in a future socialist order, and that Russia thus possessed a unique opportunity of leading the world on the socialist path. But Plekhanov, the father of Russian Marxism and the founder of the first Russian Marxist group abroad, had no doubt what Marxism meant in terms of the Russian agrarian problem. Plekhanov regarded the peasant, in Russia as in the west, as a fundamentally conservative factor; " apart from the bourgeoisie and the proletariat ", he wrote in 1892 in a much-quoted passage, " we perceive no social forces in our country in which opposition or revolutionary groups could find support ".[2] He was therefore convinced that the revolution in Russia must take the course which it had followed in the west — the course laid down in the *Communist Manifesto*. The first stage would be a bourgeois capitalist revolution which would encourage the development of Russian industry and destroy such obsolete feudal systems of land tenure as the peasant commune; then, when capitalism had been triumphantly established in town and country, the moment would be ripe for its overthrow by the proletarian socialist revolution. The *narodnik* idea of proceeding to socialism through the peasant commune without the intervening capitalist stage and without the creation of a strong proletariat was pure utopia — or a cloak for reaction. Lenin appeared on the scene in the eighteen-nineties as the fervent disciple of Plekhanov. His earliest writings carried on the controversy against the *narodniks*, and passionately defended the thesis of the necessity of capitalist development in Russia.

In the middle 'nineties, when Lenin began his work, the facts were already deciding the issue in favour of the Marxists. In the eighteen-forties the acute Prussian observer Haxthausen had clearly discerned the vital rôle of serfdom in the Russian economy :

[1] See Note C : " Marx, Engels and the Peasant " (pp. 385-393 below).
[2] G. V. Plekhanov, *Sochineniya*, iii, 119.

If large-scale ownership is necessary to the progress of
civilization and of the national prosperity, which is in my
opinion incontestable, one cannot yet abolish serfdom.[1]

The emancipation undermined the equilibrium which the Russian
countryside had enjoyed at the low level of a serf economy, and
substituted no other. It benefited those capable and energetic
landowners who were able to put their estates on an efficient
capitalist basis by employing the hired labour of their former
serfs and developing large-scale production for export; the less
enterprising or less favourably placed landowners proved unable
to adapt themselves to the new conditions and sank deeper than
before into the morass of debt and inefficiency. The reform also
favoured the rise of a small number of the most efficient peasants
who could consolidate and extend their holdings and emerge from
the ruck by employing the labour of their less fortunate fellows;
but for the mass of the peasants it meant a weight of debt, harder
conditions, and new forms of exploitation which were resented
as keenly as the old. It divided the peasantry into a minority
(in some regions perhaps as large as one-fifth) of landowning
peasants, some of them employing hired labour, and a majority
of landless peasants hiring out their labour to large landowners
or well-to-do peasants. The intrusion of capitalism had introduced incipient class distinctions into the Russian countryside.[2]

Meanwhile the creation of a Russian proletariat was proceeding
apace. The first beginnings of industrialization in Russia had
followed the emancipation of the serfs. Its rapid development
after 1890 with the influx of foreign capital, provided the foundations on which the Russian Social-Democratic Workers' Party was
built: the strikes of 1896 were the real starting-point of the
proletarian movement. But the belated growth of capitalist
industry in Russia was responsible for several peculiar features,
which Lenin expressed in the dictum that in Russia " the most

[1] A. von Haxthausen, *Études sur la Situation Intérieure, la Vie Nationale,
et les Institutions Rurales de la Russie*, i (1847), 151.

[2] As Plekhanov put it, the peasantry as a whole was not a class, but an
" estate " (*sostoyanie*); the reform of 1861 divided it into two classes — the
landed " rural bourgeoisie " and the landless " poor peasants ", the exploiters
and the exploited (G. V. Plekhanov, *Sochineniya*, iii, 410). Lenin in 1905
attributed the irresolute attitude of the peasantry to its division into " petty
bourgeois " and " semi-proletarian " strata (*Sochineniya*, vi, 369-370).

modern capitalist imperialism is interwoven, so to speak, with a thick web of pre-capitalist relations ".[1] In western Europe, the industrial director or manager of the early twentieth century had evolved by a gradual and clearly traceable process from the individual entrepreneur familiar to the classical economist; the small enterprise still played an important rôle in the economy, and modern large-scale industry retained something of the material background and outlook of the past. In Russia, modern industry had sprung fully armed from the brain of western and Russian finance; [2] the motives for its development were as much political as economic; [3] it owed far more to the initiative of the state and of the banks than of the individual entrepreneur; and the proportion of large-scale enterprises was considerably higher in Russian industry than anywhere else in Europe.[4] The differences between the western and the Russian factory worker were even more noteworthy. The western factory worker still possessed some of the skills and other characteristics of the small artisan. The Russian worker was a peasant who had come from the village and might return there in slack seasons or in periods of economic depression. Legally he remained a peasant, and was differentiated from the small class of artisans who ranked in the " petty bourgeois " category. He lacked the degree of industrial skill and education which bred in the west the growing class of " labour aristocracy " interested in the profits of capitalism, and, being subject to almost unlimited exploitation, provided a fertile soil for revolutionary propaganda. Many of the differences, both in the structure of industry and in the character of the workers, were reflected in the

---

[1] Lenin, *Sochineniya*, xix, 136.

[2] According to the standard work on the subject, foreign capital investments in Russian industry before 1914 amounted to more than two milliards of rubles : of this total, 32·6 per cent was French, 22·6 per cent British, 19·7 per cent German, 14·3 per cent Belgian, and 5·2 per cent American (P.B.Ol', quoted in Y. S. Rozenfeld, *Promyshlennaya Politika SSSR* (1926), p. 44).

[3] Witte, its most powerful promoter, makes a significant comment in his memoirs : " They say I used artificial means for the development of industry. What does that stupid phrase mean ? By what means, other than artificial means, can one develop industry ? " (*Vospominaniya* (Berlin, 1922), i, 451).

[4] In 1913, 24·5 per cent of Russian industrial workers were employed in units employing more than 1000 workers and 9·5 per cent in units employing between 500 and 1000 ; the corresponding figures for Germany in 1907 had been 8·1 cent and 6·1 per cent respectively (Y. S. Rozenfeld, *Promyshlennaya Politika SSSR* (1926), p. 46).

differing political systems of western and eastern Europe. Finally the identity of the Russian factory worker and the Russian peasant meant that the interests and grievances of both reacted closely on one another, and could not for practical purposes be separated and distinguished as they habitually were in western countries.

The first programme of the Russian Social-Democratic Workers' Party was divided, in accordance with precedent, into sections containing maximum and minimum demands. But the Russian party was not exposed to the insidious danger, which had overtaken the German party, of exalting the minimum at the expense of the maximum demands — and for an obvious reason. From 1848 onwards the conception of the minimum programme coincided in the main with what might be achieved under the bourgeois revolution without straining to breaking-point the framework of the bourgeois capitalist order ; the maximum programme was that of the proletarian socialist revolution. In western Europe, where the bourgeois revolution was a *fait accompli*, the minimum programme was therefore no longer revolutionary, and was separated by this difference of principle from the revolutionary maximum programme. When the Russian Social-Democratic Workers' Party adopted its programme in 1903, the bourgeois revolution in Russia still lay in the future, and minimum and maximum programmes were therefore both revolutionary. The minimum political demands of the programme adopted by the party congress of 1903 began with the overthrow of the Tsarist autocracy and its replacement by a democratic republic.[1] The minimum economic demands which followed were, taken as a whole, equally revolutionary in the Russia of that time, though they were drafted with studied moderation and contained little that had not already been achieved, or was not on the point of achievement, in the advanced bourgeois democracies. They included the eight-hour day and the weekly rest-day ; the prohibition of night work except where technically necessary, of child labour up to 16 (with restrictions up to 18), and of the employment of women in unhealthy occupations ; state insurance against sickness and old age ; effective factory inspection ; and a number of other measures familiar in the social legislation or in the radical programmes of western countries. The agrarian section of

[1] See Vol. 1, p. 28.

the programme was particularly moderate, being confined in effect to measures designed to " remove the remnants of the régime of serfdom " and to further " the free development of the class struggle in the country ". Its principal substantive proposals were the cancellation of payments still due from the peasants in respect of their liberation and the restitution of sums already paid, the confiscation of church lands and of the imperial domains, and " the institution of peasant committees for the return to the village commoners . . . of those lands which were filched from the peasant when serfdom was abolished " (the so-called " cut-offs ").[1] Interest at the congress in the economic section of the programme was significantly absent. Neither then nor in the controversies which followed the split between Bolsheviks and Mensheviks did economic issues play a major rôle.

The Russo-Japanese war brought to a head the smouldering discontent in town and country. The revolution of 1905 was the first dramatic symptom of a spontaneous, ill-coordinated and half-unconscious fusion of the new revolt of the young factory proletariat against industrial capitalism with the age-long revolt of the Russian peasant against intolerable agrarian conditions. On Bloody Sunday, January 9, 1905, it was the urban workers who fumblingly touched off the revolution; and the mass industrial strikes of the autumn of 1905 were its most spectacular achievement. But already in February 1905 the peasants of the black-earth regions, of the Baltic provinces and of the Caucasus were in revolt; and the peasant *jacquerie* which spread all over Russia later in the year continued to flare up spasmodically in the spring and summer of 1906, long after the revolution had been extinguished in the towns and factories. What happened in 1905 confirmed the Bolshevik view on one point : the necessity for proletarian leadership in the revolution. But it showed that revolution could not be successful in Russia without active peasant support; and it showed also that the Russian peasant was open to a far more radical revolutionary appeal than was contained in the cautious agrarian chapter of the party programme.

The result of the events of 1905 was to give the peasant a wholly new importance and prominence in Bolshevik calculations.

[1] The programme of 1903 is in *VKP(B) v Rezolyutsiyakh* (1941), i, 19-23.

Already in April 1905, the third all-Bolshevik party congress in London acclaimed " the now growing peasant movement " and, while admitting that it was still " spontaneous and politically unconscious ", pronounced it worthy of social-democratic support. Going far beyond the mild prescriptions of the party programme, the congress resolution openly incited " the peasantry and the village proletariat " to a " collective refusal to pay taxes and dues, or to obey the military conscription and the orders and commands of the government and its agents ".[1] In the same month Lenin had proclaimed as the immediate goal of the revolution a " revolutionary-democratic dictatorship of the proletariat and the peasantry "; and his pamphlet *Two Tactics of Social-Democracy in the Democratic Revolution*, devoted to an elaboration of this theme, carefully distinguished between the first or bourgeois stage of the revolution, in which the proletariat would be in alliance with the peasantry as a whole, and the second or socialist stage, in which the proletariat would rally the poor peasants against the reactionary elements in the peasantry :

We support the peasant movement in so far as it is revolutionary-democratic. We prepare (yes, prepare forthwith) for a struggle with it in so far as it appears in a reactionary, anti-proletarian rôle. The whole essence of Marxism is in this dual task.[2]

But the content of the agrarian policy to be pursued at the two stages was not discussed. A Bolshevik conference in Tammerfors in December 1905 broached the question of a revision of the agrarian section of the party programme. It proposed to omit from the programme the old points about the " cut-offs " (as being too mild) and about the cancellation of redemption payments (as being now satisfied), to promise support for all revolutionary measures taken by the peasantry, including confiscation of all privately owned land, to seek to convince the peasant of the " irreconcilable opposition of his interests to those of the village bourgeoisie ", and to point the way to the goal of socialism.[3]

[1] *VKP(B) v Rezolyutsiyakh* (1941), i, 46-47.
[2] Lenin, *Sochineniya*, viii, 185-186 ; for a further analysis of Lenin's views at this time see Vol. 1, p. 55.
[3] *VKP(B) v Rezolyutsiyakh* (1941), i, 58-59 ; Krupskaya, *Memories of Lenin* [i], (Engl. transl. 1930), pp. 131-133, notes the Tammerfors conference as the occasion on which Lenin first put forward the conclusions drawn from the experience of the 1905 revolution.

One of the results of the *rapprochement* between Bolsheviks and Mensheviks in the winter of 1905-1906 was the setting up of a joint commission to collect and sift proposals for a modification of the agrarian programme,[1] to be considered by the so-called " unity " congress (afterwards numbered by the Bolsheviks as the fourth congress) which met at Stockholm in April 1906. The Stockholm congress devoted to the agrarian policy of the party the longest, fullest and most intricate discussion it ever received in social-democratic circles ; apart from the main split between Bolsheviks and Mensheviks (the latter having a small majority), both Bolsheviks and Mensheviks were divided among themselves. With few insignificant exceptions everyone agreed that the old programme was outmoded and that, in order to satisfy the peasant cravings manifested in the current disorders, something must be done about the land as a whole. The first step was relatively simple. The Bolsheviks wanted the " confiscation " of all church, imperial, state and landowners' land ; the Mensheviks wanted " alienation ", this term implying, or at any rate not excluding, compensation. But enough of the Mensheviks agreed with the Bolsheviks on this point to give them a majority ; and the word " confiscation " appeared in the resolution of the congress. Small holdings, not more precisely defined, were exempt from confiscation.

The far more delicate and controversial issue was what was to happen after confiscation. Here three broad views could be distinguished. The Mensheviks, mistrusting the authority of a centralized state, wanted to transfer the ownership of the land to the " organs of local self-government ", which would grant the use of it in perpetuity to the peasants who cultivated it ; this was the solution known as " municipalization ". The second view was represented by the draft emanating from Lenin and supported by a majority of the preparatory commission. This proposed to place the confiscated land under the control of peasant committees pending the convocation of a Constituent Assembly, whereafter, if (but only if) a fully democratic republic was established, the

---

[1] The report of the commission is in Lenin, *Sochineniya*, ix, 458-460 ; Lenin published his draft (which secured the support of a majority of the commission) with an exposition of its motives as a separate pamphlet in March 1906 (*Sochineniya*, ix, 55-76).

party would demand the abolition of private property in land and the transfer of all land to the " whole people " (or, according to another variant, to the state) ; Lenin argued that the proviso in his draft about the establishment of a fully democratic republic removed the dangers which the Mensheviks professed to see in a transfer of the land to a centralized state authority. The third group, which included a majority of the Bolsheviks, agreed with Lenin's draft on the initial stage of setting up peasants' committees, but proposed to demand at the Constituent Assembly that, after the transfer to the state of forests and mines, and to the local self-governing organs of estates " on which cultivation can be conducted in common ", the remaining land should be partitioned among the peasants in full ownership. Lenin, who had previously argued that individual peasant ownership, being essentially capitalist, represented an advance on the feudal system of large estates owned by the gentry and tilled by peasant labour,[1] now declared that, while the policy of partition was " mistaken " (since it did nothing to point the way to socialism as the ultimate goal), it was not " harmful ", whereas the policy of municipalization (which was neither capitalist nor a pointer to socialism) was " both mistaken and harmful ". He would therefore withdraw his own resolution which had no chance of success and support partition against municipalization. The whole controversy was conducted on the hypothesis of the bourgeois-democratic character of the coming revolution. Neither in his speech at the congress nor in a pamphlet in which he subsequently elaborated his argument [2] did Lenin openly state the basic objection to the advocacy of individual peasant ownership — the eventual need to reverse the process of partition when the stage of socialism was reached and to re-establish the large collective unit of production ; and nobody else was thinking so far ahead.[3] But the Bolsheviks remained in a minority. The Menshevik resolution recommending municipalization was carried as the view of the congress. An accompanying resolution on tactics did, however, open up the longer perspective, instructing the party " to warn him [i.e. the

[1] Lenin, *Sochineniya*, ix, 61.
[2] *Ibid.* ix, 149-156, 184-200.
[3] A year later Lenin wrote : " The proletariat will bring with it not the socialism of an equality of small owners, but the socialism of large-scale socialized production " (*Sochineniya*, xi, 187).

peasant] against being seduced by the system of small ownership which, so long as commodity production exists, is not able to abolish the poverty of the masses, and finally to point to the necessity of a socialist revolution as the only means to abolish all poverty and all exploitation ". A further resolution spoke of the importance of coordinating the peasant revolt " with the offensive movement of the proletariat against Tsarism ".[1]

The inadequacies of the Stockholm resolutions became apparent when they were confronted with the agrarian programme of the Social-Revolutionaries (SRs), the successors of the *narodniks* and at this time the peasant party *par excellence*. According to the programme adopted by the SR party congress in January 1906, the SRs stood for the socialization of land by way of its " removal from commercial exchange and transformation from the private property of individuals into a common national possession ". The land was to be distributed to individuals on two principles described as the " labour principle " and " equalization ", meaning an equal distribution of the land among those who worked on it, the only difficulty being that of determining the criterion by which equality should be calculated (numbers of workers in the household or number of consumers). This policy ranked the SRs with those non-Marxist socialists who believed that the essence of socialism turned not on methods of production but on equal distribution. At first sight, the SR programme did not differ sensibly from the Bolshevik draft resolution which had suffered defeat at the Stockholm congress ; this too had demanded the equal partition of the land among the peasants. But Lenin, in a long pamphlet on agrarian policy written at the end of 1907, explained both the immediate point of contact between the two positions and the ultimate and fundamental divergence :

> The idea of equality is the most revolutionary idea in the struggle with the old absolutist order in general and with the serf-owning, large landlord system of land tenure in particular. The idea of equality is legitimate and progressive in the petty bourgeois peasant in so far as it expresses the struggle with feudal serf-owning inequality. The idea of " equalization " of land tenure is legitimate and progressive in so far as it expresses

---

[1] *VKP(B) v Rezolyutsiyakh* (1941), i, 75-76 ; the debates of the Stockholm congress are in *Chetvertyi (Ob''edinitel'nyi) S''ezd RSDRP* (1934).

the striving of ten million peasants sitting on seven-desyatin allotments and ruined by the landlords for a partition [1] of serf-owning latifundia with an average area of 2300 desyatins. And at the present moment of history this idea really expresses such a striving, and gives an impetus to a consistent bourgeois revolution, while falsely wrapping this up in a misty, quasi-socialist phraseology. . . . The real content of this revolution, which the *narodnik* regards as " socialization ", will consist in the most consistent clearing of the way for capitalism, in the most decisive rooting out of serfdom. . . . The *narodnik* imagines that this " equalization " removes the bourgeois factor, whereas in fact it expresses the strivings of the most radical bourgeoisie.[2]

Thus it was possible for the Bolsheviks at this preliminary stage to make use of the SR slogan of " equalization ", and even to march in apparent alliance with the SRs on the issue of agrarian policy. But what for the SRs appeared to be the ultimate socialist goal, was for the Bolsheviks merely an incidental item in the bourgeois revolution. Once the bourgeois revolution had swept away the remnants of feudalism and serfdom in the name of the equal ownership of land by all, the split would come, since the Bolshevik conception of the socialist agrarian revolution differed root and branch from that of the SRs. But, so long as any real consideration of the agrarian policies of socialism remained premature, the dividing line between Bolsheviks and SRs could be easily blurred.

The Tsarist Government had drawn from the events of 1905-1906 the same conclusion as the revolutionaries, that the attitude of the peasant was now the focal point in the Russian situation. The constitutional manifesto of October 17, 1905, designed to placate liberal and radical elements in the cities was followed on November 3 by a further manifesto promising the peasants a remission of their outstanding redemption payments. Just a year later — the party congress at Stockholm fell in the interval — came Stolypin's famous decree of November 9, 1906, which inaugurated a new agrarian policy. The effect of the decree was twofold. Peasant communes where the habit of periodical

---

[1] Lenin adds a footnote: " Here I am speaking not of partition for ownership, but of partition for cultivation : and partition is possible — and, so long as small cultivation predominates, inevitable for some time — both under municipalization and under nationalization ".

[2] Lenin, *Sochineniya*, xi, 347.

redistribution of the land had fallen into disuse were dissolved, and the land distributed among the heads of households forming the commune.   In peasant communes where periodical redistribution was still practised, heads of households were encouraged to apply for release from the commune with a share of the communal land, and arrangements were made to facilitate such releases by a regrouping of the land.   The decree thus set out to break up the old collective system of peasant ownership and to substitute individual peasant ownership as the basis of the Russian rural economy.   Apart from legal enactments, indirect inducements were also offered, including a Peasants' Land Bank making loans on favourable terms to individual owners or would-be owners. During the ten years that followed the promulgation of the decree, more than two million households went out of the communes, the peak years of the exodus being 1908 and 1909.   The incidence of the reform was highest in the Ukraine west of the Dneiper, where about half the former communal land passed into individual ownership.   This region was the centre of the grain export trade : it was here that Russian agriculture was most profitable and most highly organized on capitalist lines.   Here too the misery of the landless peasant working as an agricultural labourer was at its most acute.   It was in this sense that Trotsky called the black-earth zone of the Ukraine " the Russian India " ; [1] from the Ukraine in the first years of the twentieth century successive waves of emigration flowed to Siberia and across the Atlantic.

While it has been customary, in view of the repressive administrative policy of the Stolypin government, to speak of the " Stolypin reaction ", this term does not properly apply to Stolypin's agrarian reform, which was a logical continuation of the course adopted with the emancipation of the serfs.   The main purpose of the emancipation had been to create a reserve of " free " labour for industrial development.   Even the countryside had been brought within the scope of a money economy ; capitalism had broken the back of the old feudal order.   The peasant commune, the last vestige of that order, now stood as a barrier to the introduction into Russian agriculture of capitalist competition and capitalist efficiency.   The Stolypin reform may have been inspired by the desire to build a bulwark against revolution through the

[1] L. Trotsky, *1905* (2nd ed. 1922), p. 18.

creation of a class of prosperous and contented peasants; but, in
so far as capitalism was an advance on feudalism, it was, as Lenin
said, " progressive in the scientific-economic sense ".[1]   On the
other hand agrarian capitalism could take two different forms:
landowners' capitalism working with hired labour and individual
peasant capitalism.   Lenin distinguished the first as the Prussian,
and the second (somewhat misleadingly) as the American, system.[2]
He denounced the Stolypin reform (also somewhat misleadingly)
as aiming at the former rather than the latter on the ground that it
was directed against the peasantry as a whole.   He denounced it
roundly as " this encouragement of robbery of the communes by
the *kulaks*, this break-up of old agrarian relations for the benefit of
a handful of well-to-do proprietors at the price of the speedy ruin
of the mass "; Stolypin was bracketed with the " black-hundred
land-owners ", and his policy described as " a policy of the utter
ruin of the peasants, of the forced smashing of the commune in
order to clear the way for capitalism in agriculture *at any cost* ".[3]
    There was some measure of truth behind these demagogic
utterances.   It had become customary in the literature of the
subject to distinguish between three categories of peasants —
the " poor peasants ", comprising some 80 per cent of the whole
number, who were landless or had holdings too small for them to
live without hiring out to others their own labour and that of their
family; the " middle peasants ", who were self-supporting on
their holdings with the labour of their family; and the " peasant
bourgeoisie " or " *kulaks* " who were prosperous enough to be
able to hire labour (though the hiring even of a single worker
would seem to have qualified for inclusion in this category).   The
purpose of the reform was to support and encourage the *kulak* or
potential *kulak* at the expense of the less energetic, less thrifty or
less fortunate mass of poor peasants, and thus create an upper
stratum of well-to-do peasants loyal to the régime: " the government ", explained Stolypin himself, " has placed its wager, not
on the needy and the drunken, but on the sturdy and the strong ".[4]
The calculation failed.   No solution could be found for the

[1] Lenin, *Sochineniya*, xi, 352.
[2] *Ibid*. xi, 348-349, 352.
[3] *Ibid*. xi, 378, xii, 123.
[4] Quoted by G. T. Robinson, *Rural Russia Under the Old Régime* (1932),
p. 194.

Russian agrarian problem — it was a dilemma which was to torment the Bolsheviks much later — which did not raise the pitiably low productivity of Russian agriculture. This could not be achieved without the introduction of modern machinery and modern techniques, which was in turn not possible on a basis of individual peasant holdings. Had Lenin been right in equating the Stolypin plan with the Prussian system, it would at least have had that essential element of efficiency which it did not in fact possess; indeed, in so far as it tended to break up large farming units and create smaller ones, it was technically regressive. As it was, Stolypin could only hope to improve the lot of a few " sturdy and strong " *kulaks* at the cost — and here Lenin was perfectly right — of a still more ruthless and unsparing exploitation of the shiftless mass of the poor peasantry. In the end, the measure which had been designed to stave off revolution made a vital contribution to the success of the revolution. By further depressing the lot of a majority of the peasants, both absolutely and in comparison with their few more fortunate fellows, it divided the peasants against themselves, and enabled the revolutionaries to make their appeal to the exploited poor against the exploiting rich even within the ranks of the peasantry. Thus Lenin the propagandist drove home throughout these years the point that the Stolypin reform spelt ruin for the mass of the peasants. But Lenin the Marxist and Lenin the Russian economist was fully aware where the ultimate solution lay :

> The landlords and the capitalists know perfectly well the enemy with whom they have to contend, feel perfectly well that *the revolution has identified* the victory of the landlords' interests with the victory of private property in land as a whole, and the victory of the peasants' interests with the abolition of private property in land as a whole, both in landlords' land and in peasants' land. . . . *In reality* the struggle is to decide whether the new Russia will be built by the landlords (and this is impossible except on the basis of private property in all kinds of land) or by the peasant masses (and this is impossible in a semi-feudal country without the destruction of private property *both* in landlords' *and* in allotment land).[1]

This is perhaps as clear a recognition as can be found in Lenin's writings at this time of the fact that the distribution of the land in

[1] Lenin, *Sochineniya*, xii, 406.

peasant holdings on a basis of equality, though a necessary intermediate step marking the bourgeois stage of the revolution, could
provide no lasting solution, and that, just as the landlords' estates
would be swept away by the bourgeois revolution, so individual
peasant holdings must one day be merged by the socialist revolution into larger economic units.

The predominant attention given at this time both by the
Russian Government and by the Russian revolutionaries to the
agrarian question is easily explained not only by the experiences
of 1905, but by the fundamental economic conditions of a country
where the peasantry formed over 80 per cent of the population and
produced 50 per cent of the national income.   More significant for
the future was, however, the rapid and continuous growth of the
industrial component in the national economy.   Between 1900 and
1913 industrial production in Russia rose by 62 per cent as against
an increase of 35 per cent in agricultural production.[1]   The same
period witnessed an extensive development of industrial and
commercial monopolies and an increasing dependence of industry
both on foreign and on Russian state investment.   Thus the
contrasts of an advanced capitalist industry functioning in a
primitive peasant environment were accentuated as the crisis of
war and revolution came nearer.   After the economic depression
of the early nineteen-hundreds the years 1908–1913 were years of
prosperity and expansion for Russian industry, and had correspondingly little to offer to revolutionary propaganda.   During
these years little fresh thought was given by Russian social-
democrats of any complexion to the industrial policies of the party.
Trotsky, inspired by the experience of the Petrograd Soviet,
continued to insist that the proletariat, in attempting to enforce
such " democratic " demands as the eight-hour day, would
inevitably be driven forward to the " socialist " policy of taking
over the factories.[2]   Lenin, too, more cautiously noted that " the
eight-hour working day and similar reforms will inevitably become
in *any* political eventuality an instrument of the forward movement " ;[3] but it is significant that this remark occurred as an

[1] P. I. Lyashchenko, *Istoriya Narodnogo Khozyaistva SSSR*, ii (1948), 349.
[2] See Vol. 1, pp. 58-59.   [3] Lenin, *Sochineniya*, ix, 197.

aside in a discussion of agrarian policy. In 1912, however, the tide of industrial unrest, which had receded after the defeat of the mass strikes of 1905, began to flow with renewed force. A serious affray in the Lena gold-field, in the course of which 500 strikers were shot down by the troops — the worst massacre since " Bloody Sunday " — opened a new period of industrial disturbances ; and a recrudescence of peasant unrest also marked the two years before the outbreak of war in 1914. The hidden forces which had made the 1905 revolution were once more seething and boiling beneath the surface. Lenin, after five years of acute depression and internecine party strife, began once more to look forward eagerly to the prospect of a troubled future.

The war of 1914 quickly revealed the inadequacy and the impotence of the Russian national economy in conditions of modern warfare. Military requirements gave an impetus to heavy industry : the two specific developments of the war years were the extension of state control over industry and the concentration of industry through the elimination of smaller and weaker concerns. But the virtual cessation of foreign supplies of machinery and specialized materials quickly brought expansion to an end even in the war industries ; and other industries soon came near to a complete standstill. At the end of 1916 it was clear that Russia's main industrial effort was exhausted. Meanwhile, agriculture had suffered more acutely than industry from the loss of its most efficient man-power to the army, and renewals of agricultural machinery and implements were no longer procurable. Production declined catastrophically, and by the winter of 1916–1917 the large cities were hungry. Industrial strikes, prompted by hunger, by increasingly hard conditions in the factories and by the evident hopelessness of the war, were the prelude to the February revolution. Lenin in Switzerland, watching all over Europe the symptoms of the death-throes of capitalism, noted that history had taken another long stride forward, but characteristically refrained from prophecy or from blue-prints of a future socialist order. During 1916 he completed his major work of the war period, *Imperialism as the Highest Stage of Capitalism*. Lenin was a true disciple of Marx ; on the eve of the revolution his contribution to the economics of socialism was a searching analysis of the economics of the latest phase of capitalist society.

Lenin's return to Petrograd on April 3, 1917, was immediately followed by the April theses, which laid down the strategy of the October revolution, proclaiming the transition from " the first stage of the revolution which has given power to the bourgeoisie " to " its *second stage*, which must give power into the hands of the proletariat and the poorest strata of the peasantry ". The economic programme was set forth in the 6th, 7th and 8th theses. Thesis 6 called for " the transfer of the centre of gravity in the agrarian programme to the Soviets of Poor Peasants' Deputies " (which, in Lenin's conception at this time, were apparently to sit separately from the Peasants' Soviets) and for " the confiscation of all land-owners' estates " : all land was to be placed at the disposal of the Soviets of Poor Peasants' and Peasants' Deputies, and large estates (of anything from 100 to 300 desyatins, according to local conditions — a low limit for the category) turned into model farms " working under the control of the poor peasants and for social account ".[1] Thesis 7 called for a single national bank controlled by the Soviets of Workers' Deputies, thesis 8 for control by the Soviets of Workers' Deputies " over the social production and distribution of products " (though this did not imply " the ' introduction ' of socialism as our *immediate* task ").[2] The greater elaboration of the agrarian thesis, as compared with those concerned with banking and with industry and trade, showed plainly where the emphasis fell in Lenin's thought. Lenin was a realist and was now thinking for the first time in the concrete terms of a Russian revolution, of a revolution in an overwhelmingly peasant country. Before leaving Switzerland he had written that the Provisional Government could not give the people bread (in the best case, it could give the people, as Germany had given, only " hunger organized with genius ") ; for bread could be obtained " only by means of measures incompatible with the sanctity of capital and land-ownership ".[3] Here, as in the not further developed hint of model farms in the 6th thesis, he was touching the nerve-centre of the Russian revolution. No bourgeois-democratic revolution, even by the most radical redistribution of

[1] The word *obshchestvennyi*, here translated " social ", is open to the same ambiguities as the corresponding substantive in the phrase " socialization of the land " : " for social account " here may mean " for common account " or " for public account ".

[2] Lenin, *Sochinemya*, xx, 88-89.   [3] *Ibid*. xx, 19.

landed property, could feed Russia : only socialism could conduct the necessary attack on landed property itself.   It would not be unfair to say that, while Trotsky deduced the necessity of a continuous transition from the bourgeois to the socialist revolution from his observation of the Petrograd proletariat in the 1905 revolution, Lenin in 1917 reached a similar conclusion through study of the fundamental problem, starkly shown up by the disintegrating process of war, how to feed the Russian people.   The two paths never quite coincided, and the premises were not identical.   But both led in 1917 to the same practical policy.

CHAPTER 16

THE IMPACT OF THE REVOLUTION

(a) Agriculture

THE precedence accorded by Lenin in the economic part of his April theses to the agrarian question was justified by the sequel, though Lenin was alone among the Bolsheviks at this time in recognizing its supreme importance. The peasantry was still an unknown quantity, and Lenin in April 1917 gave his followers an extremely cautious estimate of the prospects :

> We want the peasantry to go further than the bourgeoisie and seize the land from the land-owners, but at the moment it is impossible to say anything definite about its further attitude. . . . It is not permissible for the proletarian party to rest its hopes now on a community of interest with the peasantry. We are struggling to bring the peasantry over to our side, but to some extent it stands consciously on the side of the capitalists.[1]

Politically Lenin was right in believing that the Social-Revolutionary Party would not break with the bourgeoisie ; and the peasantry still clung to the SRs as its traditional champions. To win it from this allegiance was the condition of successful Bolshevik leadership in the revolution. Hence within the struggle of the Soviets against the Provisional Government, waged wholeheartedly and consistently by the Bolsheviks and half-heartedly and waveringly by the SRs who had a foot in each camp, a further struggle was being waged by the Bolsheviks against the SRs for the support of the peasant. This issue played its part in all the political calculations and manœuvres of the period between the February and October revolutions.

The course of the agrarian revolution in Russia illustrated Lenin's principle that the way to socialism would be " shown by the experience of millions when they take the work in hand ". The

---

[1] Lenin, *Sochineniya*, xx, 241, 245.

hopes and the excitement bred by the February revolution caused
renewed outbreaks of peasant disorder in many parts of Russia.
It is difficult to obtain any precise evidence of the nature and
extent of what took place. At the end of April 1917 Lenin noted
that " peasants are already seizing the land without compensation
or paying a quarter of the rent ", and that in the province of Penza
" peasants are taking over landlords' stock "; and the prevalence of
such occurrences [1] is attested by constant exhortations to the
peasants from the Provisional Government and its supporters to
await the decisions of the Constituent Assembly. The reply of
the Provisional Government to the disturbances was a decree
creating a hierarchy of committees to prepare the way for an
agrarian reform which could be enacted only when the Constituent
Assembly met; there were rural district land committees, popu-
larly elected, county committees, provincial committees and finally
a Chief Land Committee at the centre. The structure was thus
similar to that of the Soviets; but the peasant Soviets were still in
a rudimentary stage and lay quite outside the governmental
machine. The decree was the work of the first Minister of
Agriculture of the Provisional Government, who was a Kadet and
in principle a supporter of the nationalization of the land with
compensation. Later the land committees were captured by the
SRs and became an important instrument of their policy.

Meanwhile, the " April conference " of the Bolshevik party,
meeting at the end of that month, passed a resolution on the
agrarian question, which embodied the policy foreshadowed in the
April theses. It demanded the confiscation of all landlords',
church and state land ; the immediate transfer of all land " into the
hands of the peasantry organized in Soviets of Peasants' Deputies
or other really and fully democratically elected organs of self-
government ", and the nationalization of all land as the property of
the state, which would transfer the right of distributing it to the
local democratic organs. Lenin, in his report to the conference,
insisted that the clause providing for the transfer of land to the
organized peasantry should precede the clause providing for
nationalization on the ground that " for us it is the revolutionary

---

[1] Trotsky (*Istoriya Russkoi Revolyutsii*, i (Berlin, 1931), 429-445, ii (Berlin,
1933), ii, 5-39) gives numerous instances of peasant disturbances between
February and October 1917.

act which is important, whereas the law should be its consequence ".[1] This was the clue to the only novel point in the resolution. In opposition to the supporters of the Provisional Government, who recommended the peasants to come to a " voluntary agreement with the landlords " and threatened them with penalties for " taking the law into their own hands ", the Bolshevik resolution invited the peasants to " take over the land in an organized way, not permitting the slightest damage to property and working for an increase in production ". The Bolsheviks were thus the only party which gave its blessing to the forcible expropriation of the landlords by a peasant revolution ; it was the first step in a long and patient campaign to woo peasant support. The view that large-scale agriculture was an essential ingredient of socialism had been recognized in the April theses in the form of the proposal to turn the large estates into " model farms working . . . for social account "; and writing shortly afterwards in *Pravda* Lenin had once more presented a reasoned statement of the Bolshevik view :

> We cannot conceal from the peasants, and still less from the proletarians and semi-proletarians of the countryside that small-scale cultivation, so long as commodity markets and capitalism remain, *is not able* to deliver mankind from mass poverty, that it is necessary to *think* about a transition to large-scale cultivation for social account and to *take this in hand at once*, teaching the masses *and learning from the masses* how to make this transition by practically appropriate means.[2]

But so long as the peasant revolution still lay in the future, this still seemed a somewhat remote ideal ; and in the turbulent atmosphere of revolutionary tactics a proposition of little immediate relevance and no appeal to the peasant easily dropped into the background. The resolution of the April conference presented it in an optional and slightly attenuated form. The concluding paragraph advised the " proletarians and semi-proletarians of the countryside " to seek " the formation out of every landlord's

---

[1] Lenin, *Sochineniya*, xx, 270 ; the idea of the primacy of the revolutionary act had already been expressed by Lenin at the fourth party congress at Stockholm in 1906, when he amended the word " confiscated " in his own draft resolution to " seized " with the explanation that " confiscation is the juridicial recognition of the seizure, its confirmation by law " (*ibid.* ix, 185).

[2] *Ibid.* xx, 194.

estate of a sufficiently large model farm which would be run for the social account by Soviets of deputies of agricultural workers under the direction of agricultural experts and with the application of the best technical methods ".[1]

The " April crisis " of the Provisional Government coincided with the Bolshevik party conference. It ended with the resignation of Milyukov and the formation of a coalition government, in which all the socialist parties other than the Bolsheviks participated and Chernov, the SR leader, became Minister of Agriculture. This change saddled the SRs with full responsibility for the agrarian policy of the government, including the decision that nothing could be done in advance of the Constituent Assembly, and gave the Bolsheviks their chance. The general spread of peasant disorders over the countryside threw into relief what was now the most conspicuous and easily understandable difference between the agrarian policies of the Bolsheviks and of the coalition parties. When an All-Russian Congress of Peasants' Deputies was summoned to meet in Petrograd in May 1917, Lenin wrote an open letter to the delegates in *Pravda* in which he reduced the whole agrarian controversy to a single issue " whether the peasants on the spot should at once seize all the land without paying the landlords any rent and without waiting for the Constituent Assembly or whether they should not ".[2] And when, ten days later, Lenin himself addressed the congress as the principal Bolshevik delegate, the question of the immediate taking over of the land by the peasants was well in the forefront of the Bolshevik draft resolution and occupied a good half of Lenin's speech. He defended the party against the charge of spreading anarchy :

> The name of anarchists is reserved for those who decry the necessity of state power ; we say that it is unconditionally necessary, and not only for Russia at this moment, but even for a state making a direct transition to socialism. The firmest power is unconditionally necessary. We only want that this power should be wholly and exclusively in the hands of the majority of workers', soldiers' and peasants' deputies.

Lenin went on to constitute himself the champion of the " agricultural hired workers and poorest peasants ", whose needs would

---

[1] *VKP(B) v Rezolyutsiyakh* (1941), i, 229-230.
[2] Lenin, *Sochineniya*, xx, 350.

not be met by mere transfer of all the land to " the people ". In the first place, it was necessary that the poorer peasants should be formed into " a separate fraction or a separate group " in all peasant organizations. Secondly, every large landlord's estate (Lenin reckoned that these numbered 30,000) should be turned into a model farm " to be cultivated socially with agricultural workers and skilled agricultural experts ". Lenin reiterated once again the " socialist doctrine " that " without common working of the land by agricultural workers using the best machines under the guidance of scientifically trained agricultural experts there is no way out from the yoke of capitalism ". Nor was this a doctrinal question :

> Dire necessity is knocking at the door of the entire Russian people. This dire necessity consists in the fact that it is impossible to continue farming in the old way. If we continue as of old on our small farms, even as free citizens on free land, we shall still be faced with inevitable ruin. . . . Individual husbandry on individual plots, even though it be " free labour on free land ", offers no way out of the terrible crisis. . . . It is essential to go over to joint cultivation on large model farms.[1]

The Bolsheviks formed a small minority at the congress, which was entirely dominated by the SRs. But the occasion marked a stage in the process of driving a wedge between the mass of the peasantry and their SR patrons. The SRs stuck to their guns, and at their third party congress, which closely followed the peasants' congress, reaffirmed their condemnation of attempts to seize the land or anticipate the decisions of the Constituent Assembly.

The succession of congresses in Petrograd in the summer of 1917 compelled the SRs, fettered as they were by their participation in the Provisional Government, to show their hand more and more clearly. The first All-Russian Congress of Soviets, which met in the middle of June, had an SR majority, and its agrarian resolution was in the main an exposition of the party programme. The land was to be " taken out of commercial circulation ", that is to say, neither bought nor sold. The right of disposing of it was to be vested in " the whole people " and exercised through " democratic organs of self-government ". The right of users of the land,

---

[1] Lenin, *Sochineniya*, xx, 416-417.

" both individual and collective ", was to be guaranteed by
" special juridical norms on the principle of the equality of all
citizens ".[1] The pyramid of land committees had now been
successfully built concurrently with the peasant Soviets,[2] and they
became the mainstay of the structure envisaged by the SRs. The
elected district committees, responsible through the intermediate
organs to the Chief Land Committee in Petrograd, were to provide
for " the most speedy and final liquidation of all survivals of the
order of serfdom remaining in the countryside " and, in general, to
supervise the execution of agrarian policy.[3] The proposal for
nationalization and equal distribution of the land, recalling the
" black partition " preached by the old *narodniks*, was well calculated to conciliate peasant opinion. But the effect was negatived
by the persistence of the SRs, as members of the Provisional
Government, in denouncing the seizures of land by the peasants
in advance of the Constituent Assembly. Lenin was quick to
perceive both the general popularity of the SR programme and the
one fatal flaw in it.

The next stage was reached in August 1917. By this time the
revolution was maturing fast. Since the July days Lenin and the
other leading Bolsheviks had been either in hiding or under arrest ;
unrest was growing rapidly in town and country ; [4] the whole
machine of government was creaking under the stress of repeated
crisis. In the middle of August the journal of the All-Russian
Peasants' Congress, which was controlled by the SRs, published
what was called a " model decree " compiled from 242 demands
submitted by delegates to the first congress. The substance of
the proposals was familiar. They included the expropriation of
landowners' estates, the vesting of all property in land in the
people, prohibition of hired labour, prohibition of the buying
and selling of land, distribution of land " on a basis of equality

---

[1] *Pervyi Vserossiiskii S"ezd Sovetov* (1930), ii, 304.
[2] According to E. A. Lutsky in *Voprosy Istorii*, No. 10, 1947, p. 17, there
were, in August 1917, 52 provincial committees, 422 county committees and an
unknown number of rural district committees.
[3] *Pervyi Vserossiiskii S"ezd Sovetov* (1930), ii, 306-310.
[4] Official statistics recorded 152 cases of forcible seizure of estates by
peasants in May 1917, 112 in June, 387 in July, 440 in August, 958 in September
(*Razvitie Sovetskoi Ekonomiki*, ed. A. A. Arutinyan and B. L. Markus (1940),
p. 60).

according either to the labour standard or to the consumer standard, as local conditions shall warrant ",[1] and periodical redistribution by the organs of local self-government. Lenin, who had now become convinced that the moment for a seizure of power was near, and that, when it took place, the transition of the revolution to its socialist stage would at once begin, decided on a new tactical line. He declared that the model decree was acceptable in itself as a programme : the " self-deception of the SRs or deception by them of the peasantry " consisted in the theory that this programme could be carried out without overthrowing the capitalist régime. Hitherto, Lenin had treated nationalization of land as part of the programme of the bourgeois revolution. He now argued that, since much of the land was mortgaged to the banks, confiscation was unthinkable until " the revolutionary class has broken the resistance of the capitalists by revolutionary measures ". The 242 demands could be realized only when, under the leadership of the proletariat in alliance with the peasantry, a ruthless war was declared against capitalism.

Then [concluded Lenin] an end will be put to the reign of capital and hired labour. Then will begin the kingdom of socialism, the kingdom of peace, the kingdom of the toilers.[2]

Thus Lenin took over *in toto* the declared agrarian programme of the SRs with the vital proviso that it could be realized only as part of the revolution against bourgeois capitalism, of the proletarian socialist revolution which was about to begin.

Lenin's article on the " model decree ", written from his hiding-place in Finland and published in the semi-legal party journal *Rabochii*, which had replaced the suspended *Pravda*, did not attract widespread attention and was forgotten in the turmoil of the revolution. What Lenin did on the morrow of the revolution came as a surprise to his opponents and to many of his supporters. The two burning issues which would determine the attitude of the

---

[1] For this provision see pp. 39-40 below.
[2] Lenin, *Sochineniya*, xxi, 107-113. Lenin thus revised the view expressed by him before 1917 that the nationalization of the land was only a step in the bourgeois revolution ; nationalization was now " not only the ' last word ' of the bourgeois revolution, but also a *step towards socialism* " (*ibid.* xxi, 233).

great mass of the population, that is to say, of the peasants, to the revolution were the war and the land. What proved decisive were the two decrees submitted to the second All-Russian Congress of Soviets on October 26/November 8, 1917, and unanimously approved by it — the so-called decree on peace and the decree on land. The land decree was brief. It declared all private property in land abolished; all landlords', state, church and allotment land was placed " at the disposal of rural district land committees and of county Soviets of Peasants' Deputies pending the Constituent Assembly "; for the detailed execution of these measures the " model decree " put forward by the SRs in August (and now described by Lenin in his speech as " the expression of the unconditional will of the vast majority of the conscious peasants of the whole of Russia ") was adopted in its entirety. The small holdings of working peasants and working Cossacks were exempted from confiscation.[1] It was one of Lenin's most astute political moves, whether considered as a bid for popularity among the peasants or as the prelude to a concerted attempt to split and weaken the SRs as the major political force in the Russian countryside.

Theoretically, Lenin defended the move on two different grounds. At the outset, he defended it as a tactical necessity, a yielding to the will of the majority, even if one did not agree with it, in the belief that experience would teach wisdom. This corresponded with the view that the revolution was still at its democratic stage and not yet ripe for a full socialist programme. When the decree was submitted to the congress and voices were heard protesting that it was the work of the SRs,[2] Lenin replied :

> Does it matter whose work it is ? We, as a democratic government, cannot evade the decision of the rank and file of the people, even if we do not agree with it. In the fire of life, by applying it in practice, by carrying it out on the spot, the peasants themselves will come to understand what is right. . . . Life is the best teacher and will prove who is right; let the

---

[1] *Sobranie Uzakonenii, 1917-1918*, No. 1 (2nd ed.), art. 3 ; Lenin, *Sochineniya*, xxii, 23. The hasty character of the proceedings is exemplified by an unresolved contradiction between the main " decree on land " and the " model decree " ; the former reserved the question of compensation for the Constituent Assembly, the latter declared for confiscation without compensation.

[2] Chernov afterwards wrote indignantly that " Lenin copies out our resolutions and publishes them in the form of ' decrees ' " (*Delo Naroda,* November 17/30, 1917).

peasants starting from one end, and us starting from the other, settle this question.[1]

And three weeks later, when the SRs had been split and the coalition formed with the Left group, Lenin declared that, " on questions which concern purely SR points in the land programme approved by the second All-Russian Congress of Soviets ", the Bolsheviks would abstain from voting ; and, as an example of these specifically " SR points ", Lenin quoted " the equalization of the use of land and the distribution of land among small proprietors ".[2] Simultaneously, however, Lenin revived the argument with which he had first acclaimed the model decree in the preceding August, that the SR programme was correct in itself, but only within the framework of a socialist revolution.   Thus Lenin now invited the All-Russian Congress of Peasants' Deputies to recognize that " the complete realization of all the measures constituting the decree on land is possible only on the hypothesis of the success of the workers' socialist revolution which began on October 25 ", and to proclaim that it " whole-heartedly supports the revolution of October 25, and supports it as a socialist revolution ".[3]   Throughout this time the need to develop the large-scale unit of cultivation, on which Lenin had so vigorously insisted six months earlier, was allowed to slip imperceptibly into the background.

Practically, the result of these theoretical discussions was perhaps not very great.   Already in September 1917 Lenin had noted that " peasant revolt is flowing everywhere in a broad stream ".[4]   The October revolution broke down the last barriers which dammed the flood.   It was now the self-proclaimed government and not merely a revolutionary party which summoned the peasant to throw off the yoke : " the Soviet of People's Commissars ", ran one of its earliest pronouncements, " calls on the peasants themselves to take all power on the spot into their hands ".[5]   But the victory of the revolution quickly set in motion

---

[1] Lenin, *Socheniniya*, xxii, 23.   Lenin later developed this argument in a more finished form : " In order to prove to the peasants that the proletarians want not to order them about, not to dictate to them, but to help them and be their friends, the victorious Bolsheviks did not put *a single word of their own* into the decree on the land, but copied it word for word from the peasant ordinances (the most revolutionary, it is true) which had been published by the SRs in the SR newspaper " (*ibid*. xxiv, 641).   [2] *Ibid*. xxii, 89-90.

[3] *Ibid*. xxii, 83-84.   [4] *Ibid*. xxi, 273.

[5] *Ibid*. xxii, 53.

a struggle between the continuation of the revolutionary process to complete the destruction of the old order and the process of organization necessary to establish and consolidate the new. During the six months that followed the October revolution this struggle passed through two successive, though related, phases. In the first phase, the question was whether the seizure of landlords' estates by the peasants would follow the pattern of peasant revolt set before the revolution, with its accompanying symptoms of violence and destruction, or whether it would be carried out in an orderly and organized manner according to the prescription of the new revolutionary authorities.[1]   In the second phase, there was a revival of the fundamental conflict between the individualist currents of SR policy and the collectivist tendencies of the Bolsheviks. This conflict, which took several different forms, was temporarily suspended by the Bolshevik adoption of the SR programme in the land decree and by the subsequent coalition with the Left SRs, but quickly revived when concrete issues of agrarian policy came up for decision, and reached a turning-point when the Left SR members of the government resigned after Brest-Litovsk.

The issue between the violent or orderly seizure of land by the peasants was determined partly by the accident of local conditions and partly by the speed with which Soviet authority in general was established in the region concerned. Where the course of events varied not merely from province to province but from village to village, evidence is fragmentary and misleading. The highest degree of order and organization in the taking over of the land seems to have prevailed where agriculture was technically most advanced ; this was characteristic of regions devoted to beet cultivation, like parts of the western Ukraine and Podolia, or to large-scale cultivation of grain for export. Here agriculture was already conducted on capitalist lines with large numbers of landless peasant workers, who quickly found organized leadership.[2]   In general, the process of taking over the land was most orderly in those provinces nearest to the centre where Soviet power was

---

[1] The decree on land contained a clause warning the peasants that any damage to " confiscated property which henceforth belongs to the whole people " would be punished by a " revolutionary court " and charging county Soviets with the orderly execution of the decree.

[2] *Razvitie Sovetskoi Ekonomiki*, ed. A. A. Arutinyan and B. L. Markus (1940), p. 93.

most quickly established and the influence of the central authority most widely felt. In outlying districts conditions tended to remain anarchic and disorderly throughout the winter of 1917–1918, and violence and destruction commonly accompanied the seizure of estates by the peasants.[1] This difference became highly important during the civil war, when the Soviet forces were operating mainly in areas where the agrarian revolution had been quickly accomplished, and some measure of orderly administration was of fairly long standing, while the areas where conditions were most anarchic, and the agrarian struggle most violent and embittered, lay behind the " white " lines. But whether the taking over was orderly or violent depended almost entirely on the impulse and initiative of the men on the spot ; the central authority had little or no voice in the matter. " The business of liquidating the landlords' power was carried out by the peasant masses, by the local organs ", records the first People's Commissar for Agriculture ; " these were the real apparatus of the People's Commissariat ".[2]

The second phase, which overlapped the first in time, was concerned with the division of the land after the process of nationalization or seizure had taken place, and drove a broad wedge between the Bolsheviks and their SR allies. Bolsheviks and SRs had been in whole-hearted agreement about the expropriation without compensation of the former landlords. So long as this was the main point at stake, the interest of all the peasants was the same. Once this was achieved, different categories of the peasantry had different aims and ambitions ; and here, broadly speaking, the SRs took the side of the relatively well-to-do and well-established peasants cultivating their own land individually

[1] E. A. Lutsky in *Izvestiya Akademii Nauk SSSR; Seriya Istorii i Filosofii*, v (1948), No. 6, pp. 510-514, shows from local records that in the provinces of Tver and Ryazan, where Soviet authority was established immediately after the October revolution, the transfer of land to the peasants took place in the majority of cases in an orderly manner, whereas in the more remote province of Tambov, where Soviet authority was established only at the end of January 1918, " the liquidation of landlords' property took place to a considerable extent in the form of spontaneous sackings of the estates ". According to an official of Narkomzem, disturbances occurred mainly in the black earth region of the Ukraine and the middle Volga, where land hunger was most acute (*O Zemle*, i (1921), 20).

[2] V. P. Milyutin, *Agrarnaya Politika SSSR* (2nd ed., 1927), p. 60 ; another commentator speaks of " agrarian local ' self-determination ' " (S. N. Prokopovich, *The Economic Condition of Soviet Russia* (1924), p. 68).

or in communes, and the Bolsheviks championed the poor peasants who were landless or whose miniature holdings were not sufficient to support them without hiring themselves out to others. This distinction had to some extent already been reflected in the clash between SRs and Bolsheviks in the issue of the orderly or " spontaneous " transfer of the land to the peasants. The poor and landless peasants were more likely to engage in the violent and revolutionary break-up of the landlords' estates than the more prosperous peasants whose own small possessions might suffer in any widespread and spontaneous outbreak of peasant disorder. In this sense the SRs — and especially the Right SRs — were a less revolutionary party than the Bolsheviks, and had an analogy with the Mensheviks who represented the skilled groups of workers in the towns. The history of agrarian policy from October 1917 to June 1918 was expressed, first, in the split between Right and Left SRs, the latter standing for the interests of a more depressed stratum of the peasantry than the former, and then in the split between Left SRs and Bolsheviks who alone were prepared to carry to its conclusion the radical policy of supporting the poor peasant against the *kulak*.

The taking over by the Bolsheviks of the main parts of the SR agrarian programme had been facilitated by the fact that the programme contained several points which were subject to different interpretations even among the SRs themselves. When the SR model decree incorporated in the Bolshevik decree on land of October 26/November 8, 1917, defined the equal utilization of land as meaning its equal distribution among those who worked on it " according either to the labour standard or to the consumer standard ", it evaded the most conspicuous of these differences. That " equal distribution " meant distribution to those working on the land had been assumed by all. But was equality calculated on the basis of the number of actual workers (and if so, did women and adolescents count as full workers), or on the basis of the number of mouths to be fed (including young children, the old and the disabled) ? The first alternative rested on the conception that every man was entitled to as much land as he could effectively work, the second on the conception that he was entitled to as much land as was necessary to feed himself and his family. The two conceptions, both reasonable in themselves and both firmly

rooted in revolutionary tradition, did not coincide ; nor was there
any guarantee that sufficient land would be available everywhere
to satisfy either of these ideal demands. This question never
became a formal issue between the SRs and Bolsheviks because
there was no uniform answer to the question what category of
peasants would be favoured by what solution. But, once the
question was left to be determined locally, everything depended
on the character and bias of the authority which would decide it.
A second difference of interpretation arose over the provision of
the model decree that " intensively cultivated estates " (meaning
" gardens, plantations, nurseries, etc."), together with stud-farms
and breeding establishments, should be handed over for the
" exclusive use *of the state or of the communes*, according to their
size and importance ". Here the Bolsheviks, who stood in principle for large-scale cultivation and centralized control, were likely
in the long run to take a different view from most SRs, both about
what should be included in the category of " intensively cultivated
estates " (did these cover all land devoted to such " industrial "
crops as beet, flax and cotton ?) and about what authority should in
practice manage them. The third and most crucial difference
turned on the question what land was in fact to be distributed.
The model decree appeared to make it clear that peasants' holdings
as well as landlords' estates were to be thrown into the common
pool for " equal " distribution ; only the " inventory " of " peasants with small holdings " was declared exempt. But, when the
issue took concrete shape, the Right SRs, representing the interests
of the well-to-do peasants, began to retreat from this position and
to argue that land already in individual or collective peasant
ownership was untouchable, and that the principle of equality
applied only in so far as it could be realized by the distribution of
the confiscated landlords' estates to poor or landless peasants.[1]

---

[1] In general the SRs moved steadily to the Right in the period of the Provisional Government, in which from May 1917 they held the Ministry of Agriculture. The last SR Minister of Agriculture, Maslov, reached a compromise with
the Kadets on a proposal by which compensation would be paid to expropriated
landlords out of rents payable by peasants to whom the confiscated estates were
distributed. This was denounced by Lenin (*Sochineniya*, xxi, 357-361) as a
" new betrayal of the peasants by the party of the SRs ". A hostile but well-
documented account of the attitude of the SRs to the agrarian question between
the February and October revolutions is in E. A. Morokhovets, *Agrarnye
Programmy Rossiiskikh Politicheskikh Partii v 1917 g.* (1929), pp. 103-116.

Here the interests of different categories of peasants were plainly irreconcilable ; and this was the rock on which the fundamental breach occurred between Right and Left SRs and, eventually, between Left SRs and Bolsheviks. Meanwhile, since so many vital points were left open by the decree for practical interpretation on the spot, the control of the district land committees charged with the execution of the decree was all-important, and remained for the present predominantly in SR hands. Relations between the land committees and the Soviets of Peasants' Deputies, which Lenin pointedly described to a delegation of peasants as the " plenipotentiary organs of state power in the localities ",[1] were enveloped in the constitutional haze characteristic of most enactments and pronouncements of this period.

The situation was far too delicate to allow the Bolsheviks, whose independent power in the countryside was still negligible, to break with the SRs ; and when the Chief Land Committee, which was controlled by Right SRs, issued on October 31/ November 13, 1917, a statement refusing to recognize the validity of the land decree, no action was taken against it.[2] A few days later, when Milyutin, the first People's Commissar for Agriculture, resigned, Lenin, already feeling his way towards a split between the two wings of the SRs, publicly offered the post to Kolegaev, the principal spokesman of the Left SRs on agrarian affairs.[3] The offer was rebuffed. But less than a fortnight later Lenin's policy of splitting the SRs had succeeded, the coalition between Bolsheviks and Left SRs had been formed, and Kolegaev was People's Commissar for Agriculture. The Left SRs, unlike the Right SRs, recognized the land decree of October 26/November 8, 1917. So much had been gained. But Milyutin during his brief tenure of office had had little time to organize the People's Commissariat of Agriculture (Narkomzem),[4] which remained under Kolegaev, in

[1] Lenin, *Sochineniya*, xxii, 52 ; to mark its authoritative character, Lenin's statement was also published in *Sobranie Uzakonenii, 1917–1918*, No. 2, art. 24.

[2] *Volya Naroda*, October 31, 1917, quoted in *Voprosy Istorii*, No. 10, 1947, p. 19.

[3] *Protokoly Zasedanii VTsIK 2 Sozyva* (1918), p. 29.

[4] " In the first days the People's Commissariat of Agriculture had no centralized organization ; all relations and all the work were conducted in Smolny " (V. P. Milyutin, *Agrarnaya Politika SSSR* (2nd ed., 1927), p. 60 ; Milyutin also speaks of " sabotage " and the " resistance of officials ".

personnel and in outlook, a lineal descendant of the SR Ministry of Agriculture under the Provisional Government. A further decree and instruction of December 13/26, 1917, reaffirmed in essentials the SR policy. The land committees were once more declared competent to " carry into effect the agrarian laws already issued or to be issued in the future ". It was specifically laid down that " lands under special cultivation or of industrial importance . . . as well as scientific demonstration farms and the lands of agricultural and other educational institutions " were to be exempt from partition and placed under the management of the land committees ; all other lands were to be distributed on " equality-labour " principles, not further defined.[1] A week later the council of the Chief Land Committee, which still refused to recognize the land decree, was dissolved by decree of Sovnarkom.[2] This act, by cutting off the committees from independent representation at the centre, was a first step towards curtailing their prestige and power and subordinating them to the local Soviets.

The next important turning-point came in January 1918 with the dissolution of the Constituent Assembly and the meeting of the third All-Russian Congress for Soviets. Soviet authority had now been established throughout northern and central Russia and on the Volga and was penetrating rapidly into Siberia. Everywhere the expropriation of the landlords had been completed or was in course of completion. But, since the necessity of awaiting the verdict of the Constituent Assembly had hitherto been accepted by all, the process of redistribution had not yet begun and everything turned on the control of the county and district land committees or land sections of the local Soviets. Here the situation was still far from reassuring for the Bolsheviks. Even at the centre, the coalition between Left SRs and Bolsheviks was by no means whole-hearted. When the third All-Russian Congress of Soviets met to confirm the dissolution of the Constituent Assembly, the old All-Russian Congress of Peasants' Deputies, though formally merged in the larger entity, attempted to maintain a shadowy independent existence as a " peasant section " of the All-Russian Congress of Soviets. In the country, the coalition was still largely ineffective ; the land committees continued to be

[1] *Sobranie Uzakonenii, 1917–1918*, No. 7, art. 105.
[2] *Voprosy Istorii*, No. 10, 1947, p. 38.

dominated by SRs who were more or less openly hostile to the Bolsheviks. A congress of delegates of land committees assembled in Petrograd simultaneously with the third All-Russian Congress of Soviets. Though three-quarters of the delegates purported to be Left SRs, they adopted a hostile attitude towards the All-Russian Congress of Soviets, agreeing at first to deal only with its " peasant section ". Kolegaev worked feverishly as an intermediary, and Lenin addressed the delegates.[1] The approval of the congress was at last secured for a draft law " On the Socialization of the Land " which was designed to tackle the vexed question of land distribution and was hastily submitted to the last session of the third All-Russian Congress of Soviets on January 18/31, 1918. The late stage at which the draft was submitted prevented its discussion by the congress. It was approved in principle and handed over to VTsIK for detailed elaboration.[2] The same congress had already laid down in the Declaration of Rights of the Toiling and Exploited People the two main planks of Bolshevik agrarian policy : " private property in land is abolished " and " model estates and agricultural undertakings are declared a national possession′".

The final text of the law " On the Socialization of the Land ", promulgated by a calculated coincidence on February 19, 1918, the 57th anniversary of Alexander II's decree emancipating the serfs,[3] represented up to a certain point a conflation of the views of the Bolsheviks and those of the SRs. Article 9 entrusted the distribution of agricultural land to " the land sections of the village, district, county, provincial, regional and federal Soviets ", thus either superseding the old land committees or transforming them into departments of the Soviets ; since the Right SRs had continued to dominate the structure of the land committees, this measure was as acceptable to the Left SRs as to the Bolsheviks,

---

[1] Information about the proceedings of this congress drawn from the contemporary press and from unpublished archives will be found in *Voprosy Istorii*, No. 10, 1948, pp. 29-30, and *Izvestiya Akademii Nauk SSR: Seriya Istorii i Filosofii*, vi (1949), No. 3, p. 231 ; an unsatisfactory press account of Lenin's speech, the only surviving record of it, is in *Sochineniya*, xxii, 252-253.

[2] *Tretii Vserossiiskii S″ezd Sovetov* (1918), p. 86.

[3] *Sobranie Uzakonenii, 1917-1918*, No. 25, art. 346 ; further negotiations between the closing of the congress on January 18/31, 1918, and the promulgation of the law nineteen days later are described in *Voprosy Istorii*, No. 10, 1948, pp. 32-33.

though the latter, being in control of the Soviet machinery as a whole, ultimately reaped the benefit of it. This was perhaps the provision in the new law which proved in the long run most advantageous to the Bolsheviks. But Lenin could also point with pride to article 11, which defined the purposes of a socialist agrarian programme in the following terms :

(a) To create conditions favourable to the development of the productive forces of the country by increasing the productivity of the soil, by improving agricultural technique, and finally by raising the general level of agricultural knowledge among the toiling masses of the agricultural population ;

(b) To create a reserve fund of agricultural land ;

(c) To develop agricultural enterprises such as horticulture, apiculture, market gardening, stock raising, dairying, etc. ;

(d) To hasten in different regions the transition from less productive to more productive systems of land cultivation by effecting a better distribution of the agricultural population ;

(e) To develop the collective system of agriculture, as being more economic in respect both of labour and of products, at the expense of individual holdings, in order to bring about the transition to a socialist economy.[1]

Thus, side by side with SR principles of " black partition ", the Bolshevik principle of collective agriculture, momentarily shelved in the land decree of October 26/November 8, 1917, was also clearly established and recognized in the new law.

These Bolshevik pronouncements were, however, rather in the nature of accretions to a law whose " ' soul ' ", as Lenin afterwards said in inverted commas, was " the slogan of the equal use of the land ".[2] What the law did was, by attempting to apply this slogan, to demonstrate its chimerical character. The fundamental SR principles were fully accepted. " The right to use the land belongs to him who cultivates it with his own labour ", declared article 3 ; and article 52 expressly described the employment of hired labour as " not permitted by the law ". " The distribution of land among the toilers ", ran article 12, " should be made on an

---

[1] *Sohranie Uzakonenii, 1917–1918*, No. 25, art. 436. On two occasions later in 1918 Lenin referred with particular satisfaction to this article (*Sochineniya*, xxiii, 397, 425-426) ; he even boasted, with some exaggeration, that in this decree " the Soviet power gave *direct* preference to communes and associations, putting them in the first place " (*ibid.* xxiii, 399).

[2] *Ibid.* xxiii, 398.

equal basis and according to capacity to work on it. . . . Care
should be taken that no one should have more land than he can
work, or less than he needs for a decent existence." The application of this maxim meant, according to article 25, that " the area
of land allocated to individual holdings . . . must not exceed the
limits of the consumer-labour standard " ; and a detailed " instruction " was appended on the way to calculate this standard. The
appropriate size of a given holding was to be determined by an
elaborate calculation which took into account both the number of
" worker units " on it (a man counting as one, a woman as 0·8,
boys of 16–18 as 0·75, girls as 0·6 and children of 12–16 as 0·5) and
the number of " bread-eaters ". The assumption seems to have
been made that, where holdings fell short of this standard, the
deficiency could be made good out of the " land reserve " created
by the confiscation of landlords' estates, and that, where this was
impossible, there would have to be a migration of families to
some other zone. But none of the practical difficulties of application was worked out or even considered. The question of levelling
down peasant holdings in excess of the standard was passed over
in silence, though another section of the law contained the provision that " surplus revenue derived from the natural fertility of
the soil or from the proximity of a market is to be handed over
to organs of the Soviet Government, which will use it for the
social good ". The law contained several provisos for adapting
its stipulations to particular local conditions.

The law " On the Socialization of Land " was afterwards
criticized by Lenin on the theoretical ground that, while the
slogan of equal distribution had " a progressive and revolutionary
significance in the bourgeois-democratic revolution ", it had no
relevance to the socialist revolution and was accepted by the
Bolsheviks only as a necessary step in revolutionary development
and as something which most of the peasants wanted at the time.

We Bolsheviks shall *help* the peasantry [he wrote] to outlive
petty bourgeois slogans, to *make the transition* as rapidly and
easily as possible to socialist slogans.[1]

A more immediate practical criticism of the law might have been
that the extreme vagueness of its terms left almost every doubtful
point open to local interpretation and ruled out any prospect of

[1] *Ibid.* xxiii, 398.

uniformity in the application of the principles laid down by it. Yet the wide diversity of conditions, both economic and social, in different parts of the former Tsarist empire made any kind of uniform agrarian legislation a hazardous undertaking. It was clear that at this time, and on so burning an issue as the disposal of the land, no central authority without strong powers of enforcement (which the Bolsheviks did not possess) could have imposed its decision even on such parts of the Russian countryside as accepted Soviet rule. How the land was distributed depended on the collective will of the peasants concerned or on the decision of such local authorities as they recognized. What was handed down from Moscow was accepted in so far as it seemed reasonable and corresponded to the peasants' own conception of what the revolution should bring them ; and this conception, as Lenin knew, stood far nearer to the " equal distribution " of the SRs than to the collectivism which the Bolsheviks recognized not merely as the ultimate goal, but as the ultimate necessity, for Russian agriculture.

During the spring and early summer of 1918 a redistribution of the land took place in the central, north-western and north-eastern provinces of European Russia and throughout the Volga basin — 28 provinces in all — where the Soviet power was securely established.[1] But the actual process bore little relation to the law just promulgated, and was as confused, as varied and as difficult to follow as the taking over of the land from the landlords during the preceding winter.

> Socialization was not carried out on a national scale [wrote an official of Narkomzem]. . . . In practice the land was simply seized by the local peasants and no attempt was made by them to migrate from places where land was scarce to places where it was more abundant. Equal distribution of the land within the villages took place everywhere, but equalization between rural districts was less frequent. Still less frequent were cases of equal distribution between counties and provinces.[2]

---

[1] *Voprosy Istorii*, No. 11, 1947, pp. 6-8, gives a detailed list of the twenty-eight provinces. Distribution seems also to have taken place in parts of Asiatic Russia ; but here the process was less regular, and detailed records are not available.

[2] *O Zemle*, i (1921), 24-25. According to *Voprosy Istorii*, No. 11, 1947, p. 14, " the fundamental organ which decided practical questions of the distribution of land between districts and villages was the county land section " ; it would seem that little effective part was played by the higher organs.

Distribution by number of consumers was more common in the land-hungry central and Volga provinces, distribution according to labour capacity in the less densely populated provinces of northern Russia and in the Siberian steppes. The system of communal holdings with periodical redistribution was not affected by the reform; indeed, if the prohibition on the hiring of labour and on the leasing of land was to be enforced, periodical redistribution to take account of changing family situations was a clear necessity. The evil of dispersed holdings was aggravated rather than relieved; extreme cases are quoted in which peasants received allotments 70 or 80 versts from their homes.[1] Some accounts speak of the smoothness with which the process of distribution was carried out by the peasants, thanks to their experience of periodical redistribution in the peasant communes, and others of open clashes between *kulaks* and poor peasants.[2] These differing pictures were all true; the difficulty arises in attempting to establish any kind of proportion or general perspective. Of the confiscated land 86 per cent is said to have been distributed to peasants, 11 per cent going to the state, mainly in the form of Soviet farms, and 3 per cent to agricultural collectives. The average increase in the peasant holding varied from district to district between one-quarter and three-quarters of a desyatin.[3] But the application of equality was not merely confined within narrow limits : it was also not uniform. Sometimes all land in the village or district was brought into the pool for redistribution, sometimes only the confiscated landlords' land. Sometimes distribution was made on the basis of the number of " consumers " or bread-eaters, sometimes of the number of workers or of their supposed capacity to work (cases were recorded in which land was distributed only to peasants who were in possession of seed). Broadly speaking, the Bolsheviks supported distribution of all land, and reckoning by number of consumers, both of which were calculated to favour the poor and landless; the SRs sought to restrict distribution to landlords' land, and to distribute according

---

[1] *O Zemle*, i (1921), 160.

[2] See the accounts quoted in Bunyan and Fisher, *The Bolshevik Revolution, 1917-1918* (Stanford, 1934), pp. 679-683.

[3] *Otchet Narodnogo Komissariata Zemledeliya IX Vserossiiskomu S"ezdu Sovetov* (1921), p. 6; the percentages are repeated with a trivial variation in *O Zemle*, i (1921), 23.

to capacity to work, these methods favouring the well-to-do peasants.[1] It would seem probable, both on general grounds and owing to the preponderance of SRs in most of the organs concerned with the redistribution, that the poor peasants fared on the whole less well than their more prosperous neighbours.

The ratification of the Brest-Litovsk treaty led to the resignation of the Left SR members of Sovnarkom in March 1918; and Kolegaev was succeeded as People's Commissar for Agriculture by Sereda, a Bolshevik. This step did not immediately weaken the predominance of the Left SRs in the local land committees, so that the process of redistribution was probably not affected. The Left SRs also retained their membership of VTsIK;[2] and, though a determined attempt to retain their control of Narkomzem even after Kolegaev's resignation was defeated,[3] the change in the composition and outlook of the commissariat, hitherto manned almost exclusively by SR officials, was only gradual. As late as May 1918 Sverdlov still had reason to complain that " the leading rôle in the rural district Soviets is played by the *kulak*-bourgeois element ".[4] Moreover the writ of the central government still scarcely ran in the country areas. It was the period when local Soviets still interpreted the slogan, " All power to the Soviets ", in the sense of their own absolute sovereignty — or, at any rate, of their own discretion to apply or ignore the instructions of a central authority. No attempt to establish such authority was likely so long as policy at the centre was controlled by SRs, whether of the Right or of the Left; this was the price that had to be paid for the coalition with the Left SRs.

[1] Instances of these different practices will be found in *Razvitie Sovetskoi Ekonomiki* (ed. A. A. Arutinyan and B. L. Markus, 1940), pp. 94-95, and in *Izvestiya Akademii Nauk SSSR: Seriya Istorii i Filosofii*, vi (1949), No. 3, pp. 231-235: both these accounts are based in part on unpublished archives.

[2] Complaints were, however, heard that the peasant section of VTsIK was henceforth no longer consulted on major issues (*Protokoly Zasedanii VTsIK 4ᵍᵒ Sozyva* (1920), pp. 403-404), and deliberately starved of funds (*Pyatyi Vserossiiskii S"ezd Sovetov* (1918), pp. 53-54).

[3] The Left SR demand was considered and rejected by the party central committee on May 3, 1918 (*Leninskii Sbornik*, xxi (1933), 147): it was only after the July rising that most of the Left SR officials were ousted from Narkomzem.

[4] *Protokoly Zasedanii VTsIK 4ᵍᵒ Sozyva* (1920), p. 294.

What now made active intervention from the centre imperative — and heralded the final downfall of the coalition — was an acute emergency of which the Bolsheviks could not fail to be increasingly conscious : the food shortage in the capital. Lengthening bread queues in Petrograd in the first weeks of 1917 had been an important contributory factor to the February revolution; the harvest of 1917 had reflected the absence of men at the front and was below standard; transport and economic organization continued to deteriorate; and after the October revolution, the Ukraine, Russia's richest granary, passed out of the control of the central authority. Deficiencies were officially attributed to speculators and rich peasants who were withholding stocks of grain from the market. This was a part, though only a part, of the truth; but it was the only part which held out any hope of a remedy before the next harvest still six months away. In January 1918 the food situation was once more anxious both in Petrograd and in Moscow. At a conference between the presidium of the Petrograd Soviet and representatives of the supply departments Lenin advocated " mass searches " of all storehouses and goods yards, and the shooting on the spot of speculators found to be holding up grain supplies.[1] The People's Commissar for Supply proposed both to send armed detachments into the villages to extract the grain by force and to stimulate the exchange of products between town and country.[2] Both expedients were tried in the next few months, and both failed. At the height of the Brest-Litovsk crisis it was not easy to organize armed detachments to send into the villages, and some of those that went encountered bitter resistance. Measures to promote trade and exchange were equally ineffective, partly because there was also a shortage of such goods as the peasants might want to buy and partly because, as Lenin explained, the well-to-do petty bourgeois peasant had his little stock of money and was under no pressure to sell.[3] The country was in passive revolt against the town. The cardinal problem of a proletarian revolution in a predominantly peasant economy was already rearing its head. It would be difficult to surpass the picture of administrative helplessness presented to the fifth All-

[1] Lenin, *Sochineniya*, xxii, 243.
[2] *Izvestiya*, January 18/31, 1918.
[3] Lenin, *Sochineniya*, xxii, 515.

Russian Congress of Soviets, in the summer of 1918, by the People's Commissar for Supply :

> We received no information about consignments and loads despatched, about the fulfilment of our orders, in a word, complete, terrible chaos reigned in the whole business. . . . When consignments passed through stations, completely unknown persons appeared who thought they had the right to uncouple wagons, to reload consignments, etc. . . . And at the same time we encountered the fiercest resistance of the population which was unwilling in any event to give up the grain. Among the many facts which we learned, we came to the conclusion that the measure on which we had staked so many hopes, namely, exchange of goods, was not likely to prove particularly useful. Many cases occurred in our experience where the peasants, seeing that we had no goods, declared : " We will not give grain without goods ". But when we brought the goods, we did not get the grain and they distributed the goods among themselves.[1]

But even before this the situation had become desperate. The attempt to overawe or persuade the peasants as a single group had brought no substantial results ; and almost, it seemed, as a last throw, the government was driven back to an expedient which had, after all, been an essential element of the Bolshevik programme ever since Lenin wrote in 1905, in *Two Tactics of Social-Democracy in the Democratic Revolution*, of the two stages in the revolution in the countryside.[2] Now, in the spring of 1918, the sequence there foreshadowed could be realized. The proletariat had completed the first stage of the revolution by marching, in alliance with the peasantry as a whole, against the feudal landlords. The time was ripe for the second stage of the revolution, when the proletariat would split the peasantry in two and march with the " semi-proletarian " poor peasants against the petty bourgeois *kulaks*. " We are convinced ", Lenin told a peasant gathering in Moscow on February 14, 1918, " that the working peasantry will declare unsparing war on its *kulak* oppressors and help us in our struggle for a better future for the people and for socialism." [3] Three weeks later at the party congress which decided on the ratification of the Brest-Litovsk treaty he added more specifically :

[1] *Pyatyi Vserossiiskii S"ezd Sovetov* (1918), pp. 141-142.
[2] See Vol. 1, p. 55.   [3] Lenin, *Sochineniya*, xxii, 253.

The agrarian question will have to be transformed in the sense that we see here the first steps of a movement by the small peasants, who want to come over to the side of the proletariat, who want to help it in the socialist revolution, to undertake, in spite of all their prejudices, in spite of all their old beliefs, the task of making the transition to socialism. . . . The peasantry, not in words but in deeds, has shown that it wants to help and is helping the proletariat, which has conquered power, to realize socialism.[1]

In May 1918 he was again emphasizing that the petty bourgeois element in the countryside could be held in check only " if we organize the poor, i.e. the majority of the population or the semi-proletarians, around the conscious proletarian vanguard ".[2] The failure of the Bolsheviks in the first six months of the revolution to make any serious move towards the realization of this policy was the symptom of their weakness in the rural areas — the weakness which had forced them into a political coalition with the Left SRs. Only under the compulsion of impending hunger in the towns did they at length turn their active attention to the measures necessary to establish their power in the country.

The new Bolshevik policy for the countryside was started in earnest in May 1918. On May 9 VTsIK gave its approval to a " decree to confer on the People's Commissariat of Supply Extraordinary Powers for the Struggle with the Rural Bourgeoisie which Conceals Grain Stocks and Speculates in them ". The theme announced in the lengthy title of the decree was developed in a rhetorical preamble :

At a moment when the consuming provinces are hungry, the producing provinces at the present time still hold vast stocks of grain from the 1916 and 1917 harvests which has not even been thrashed. The grain is in the hands of the rural *kulaks* and rich peasants, in the hands of the rural bourgeoisie. Well fed and secure, having amassed enormous sums of money gained during the war years, the rural bourgeoisie remains obstinately deaf and unsympathetic to the cries of the workers and poor peasants, and refuses to bring the grain to the collecting points in the calculation that it will force the state into even new increases in bread prices.

The concrete provisions of the decree were not very impressive. It called on " all workers and landless peasants " for an " unsparing

[1] *Ibid.* xxii, 356-357.   [2] *Ibid.* xxii, 515.

struggle " against the *kulaks*, threatened severe penalties for those who concealed grain stocks or used them to distil spirit, and gave to the People's Commissariat of Supply (Narkomprod) authority to overrule any decisions of local food authorities or dissolve and reorganize such authorities and to " apply armed force in the event of resistance being offered to the removal of grain or other natural products ". There was little pretence in the decree that anything but force would serve the purpose in hand : " to the constraint put by the possessors of grain on the hungry poor the answer must be constraint imposed on the bourgeoisie ".[1]

The new line once adopted was pursued with vigour. A few days later a representative of the Putilov factory visited Lenin in Moscow to lay before him the plight of the Petrograd workers. Lenin's reply was a telegram in which he urged the workers to " save the revolution by enrolling in the food detachments organized by the Commissariat of Supply ",[2] and a letter to the Petrograd workers " On the Famine " which contained his fullest exposition of the new tactics. He contrasted the open opposition of the Right parties, including the Right SRs, to the Soviet power with the " characterless " attitude of the Left SR party, which " ' protests ' against the food dictatorship, allows itself to be intimidated by the bourgeoisie, fears the struggle with the *kulak*, and tosses hysterically from side to side, advising an increase in fixed prices, permission for private trade and so forth ". The letter ended with a return to first principles :

> One of the greatest, the indestructible tasks of the October, Soviet, revolution is that the outstanding worker, *as the mentor* of the poor peasant, *as the leader* of the toiling rural masses, *as the builder of the labour state*, should go to the " people ". . . . We need a mass " crusade " of outstanding workers to every corner of this vast country. We need ten times more *iron detachments* of the conscious proletariat unreservedly devoted to communism. Then we shall conquer famine and unemployment. Then we shall succeed in making the revolution the real ante-chamber of socialism.[3]

---

[1] *Sobranie Uzakonenii, 1917–1918*, No. 35, art. 468 ; it was dubbed by its opponents the " food dictatorship decree " and afterwards commonly referred to by this name.

[2] Lenin, *Sochineniya*, xxiii, 524-525 ; for Lenin's original draft see *ibid.* xxiii, 25.   [3] *Ibid.* xxiii, 26-31.

The *narodnik* " going to the people " fifty years earlier had been the movement of the radical intelligentsia to lead the peasantry in revolt against the feudal landlord. The Bolshevik going to the people was to be a movement of the socialist proletariat to lead the poor peasant in revolt against the bourgeois *kulak* and thus pave the way for the victory of the socialist revolution. The dual function of these " iron detachments " of workers was apparent in a further decree of May 27, 1918, which gave to Narkomprod a monopoly over the distribution of all "objects of prime necessity ". The detachments, " recruited primarily in the consuming regions ", were to be attached to the local organs of Narkomprod in order to assist in the collection of supplies. But they were also to be used " for purposes of organization, instruction and agitation ", and their " chief task " was declared to be " the organization of the working peasantry against the *kulaks* ".[1]

When these decrees were issued, the clouds of civil war were darkening on all sides. The first open outbreaks occurred almost at the moment of Lenin's letter to the Petrograd workers. The civil war hastened the adoption throughout the whole field of economic policy of a series of measures which came to be known as " war communism ". But the changes had to some extent been prepared by what went before ; and nowhere was this more marked than in agrarian policy, where the threat of hunger had already begun to shape those forms of organization which the emergency of the civil war was to complete. The foundation of " war communism " in agriculture was laid by the issue of the decree of June 11, 1918, establishing the famous " committees of poor peasants " (Kombedy) — " rural district and village committees of poor peasants organized by the local Soviets of Workers' and Peasants' Deputies with the immediate participation of the organs of supply and under the general direction of the People's Commissariat of Supply ". The whole rural population was eligible to elect, or be elected to, these committees with the exception of " known *kulaks* and rich peasants, landlords, those having surpluses of grain or other natural products and those having trading

---

[1] *Sobranie Uzakonenii, 1917-1918*, No. 38, art. 498 ; for the decree in general see p. 123 below. A supplementary decree was issued a few days later " On the Method of Delivery of Grain to the State " (*ibid.* No. 38, art. 502).

or manufacturing establishments employing the labour of poor
peasants or hired labour ".[1] They were to be instruments for the
extraction of grain surpluses from " the *kulaks* and the rich ",
for the distribution of grain and articles of prime necessity
and in general for the execution on the spot of the agricultural
policies of the Soviet Government. The poor peasants were to be
rewarded for their services by obtaining allocations of grain from
the quantities seized, free till July 15, at a discount of 50 per
cent on the fixed prices till August 15, and thereafter at 20 per
cent discount, and by similar discounts on the prices of other
necessaries.[2]

All the evidence confirms the high importance which Lenin,
in particular, ascribed to this measure. It was a measure of
political expediency. Stolypin, in seeking to find means to
increase the productivity of Russian agriculture, had been also —
and perhaps primarily — concerned to mould his reforms in such
a way as to win the loyalty of the favoured section of the peasantry
for the régime. A similar motive lay behind the Bolshevik appeal
to the poor peasant. But it was also a measure of socialist principle. The bourgeois line was clear enough :

They tell us : It is not necessary to have special prices, fixed
prices, grain monopolies. Trade as you please. The rich will
earn still more, and, as for the poor dying, well, they have always
died of hunger. But a socialist cannot reason like that.[3]

The rich peasant who produced the surpluses was interested in
high and unrestricted grain prices. The poor peasant who did
not even produce enough for his own consumption and had to

[1] An account given some time later to a British traveller described the method
of election : " A meeting of all the village was called at which the chairman
[of the village Soviet] read out a list of candidates for the ' committee of poverty '.
Each name, as it was read, was discussed, and several candidates were rejected
as not being ' poor '. The voting was by show of hands. About 40 were elected,
with a ' praesidium ' of three " (*British Labour Delegation to Russia, 1920 :
Report* (1920), p. 134). Zinoviev, desiring a few months afterwards to discredit
the committees, told the sixth All-Russian Congress of Soviets that there was
no " genuine elective principle " about their appointment : " they were
nominated by representatives of the executive committee [of the Soviet] or of
the party organization coming together " (*Shestoi Vserossiiskii Chrezvychainyi
S"ezd Sovetov* (1919), pp. 87-88).
[2] *Sobranie Uzakonenii, 1917-1918*, No. 43, art. 524.
[3] Lenin, *Sochineniya*, xxii, 126.

live by hiring out his labour was interested in low and fixed prices. This measure was a declared choice between bourgeois and socialist policies. Finally, Lenin felt that the step was above all significant as marking the final and decisive stage in the transition from the bourgeois to the socialist revolution. This transition had long ago been effected by the workers in the towns. But in the country, so long as the peasantry remained united for the expropriation of the feudal landowners, the revolution had not emerged from its bourgeois-democratic phase. It was when the peasantry split, and the poor peasants, linked with the industrial workers and led by them, took the offensive against the petty bourgeois kulaks that the socialist revolution in the countryside could be said to have begun. " It is only in the summer and autumn of 1918 ", wrote Lenin at this time, " that our countryside is itself experiencing its October (i.e. proletarian) revolution."¹ And a little later he described the creation of the committees of poor peasants as " a turning-point of gigantic importance in the whole course of development and building of our revolution " and as the step by which " we passed the boundary which separates the bourgeois from the socialist revolution ".²

Thus the impact of hunger and civil war had thrust the Soviet régime along a path of expediency which seemed also the path of socialism. This dual character of measures which were taken to meet an inescapable emergency and were at the same time the expression of communist principles was the essence of what came to be known later as " war communism ". The coincidence was not accidental, and was accepted by the Bolsheviks as an expression of the Marxist thesis that the principles enunciated by communists were scientifically deducible consequences of an objective situation.

(b) Industry

Industrial policy had not seemed to Bolshevik thinkers to offer the same difficulties as agrarian policy. The socialist revolution, led by the proletariat, might find it an embarrassing task to elaborate and impose an agrarian policy which did not contradict its own principles and, at the same time, did not

¹ Ibid. xxiii, 393.   ² Ibid. xxiii, 420.

antagonize the peasantry.   But industrial policy was straightforward enough : the control of industry would naturally be taken
over by the workers acting on their own behalf and in their own
name.   The party conference of April 1917, adding little on this
point to the bare outline of the April theses, advocated among its
" immediate measures " the " establishment of state control . . .
over the most powerful syndicates of capitalists " ; [1] and Lenin,
defending this resolution, declared that, when these had been
taken over and brought under the control of the Soviets, " Russia
will have set one foot in socialism ".[2]   In practice the issue proved
less simple.   The Bolsheviks had somewhat the same experience
in the factories as on the land.   The development of the revolution
brought with it a spontaneous taking over not only of the land by
the peasants, but of factories by the workers.   In industry as in
agriculture, the revolutionary party and, later, the revolutionary
government, were carried along by a movement which was in many
respects embarrassing to them, but which, as a main driving force
of the revolution, they could not fail to endorse.

In Russia as in the other belligerent countries, the war, after an
initial period of confusion, provided a temporary stimulus to
industrial production.   But in Russia, with its scanty industrial
equipment, isolation from major sources of supply, low productivity of labour, and weak industrial and political organization, the
response was feebler than elsewhere, and the peak more quickly
reached.   By 1916, under the influence of war weariness, shortage
of essential supplies and wear-and-tear of plant and machinery,
production had begun to fall off.   The February revolution intensified every adverse factor.   Shortages of all kinds became chronic ;
and cases occurred of the closing of factories for lack of raw
materials.   These conditions gave a fresh impetus to the usual
war-time movement for nationalization and state control.   An
early act of the Provisional Government was to establish a standing
" conference on the development of the productive forces of
Russia ".   In June 1917 this was replaced by an Economic Council
and a Chief Economic Committee, whose functions were " to
work out a general plan of organization of the national economy
and of labour, and also to elaborate draft laws and take general

[1] *VKP(B) v Rezolyutsiyakh* (1941), i, 237.
[2] Lenin, *Sochineniya*, xx, 282.

measures for the regulation of economic life ".[1]   The Economic
Council was a large deliberative assembly; the Chief Economic Committee provided the nucleus of a small planning
department.   But, under the rule of the Provisional Government, neither possessed or was likely to possess the power or
initiative to arrest the cumulative process of economic decline and
disintegration.

More important than these palpably half-hearted approaches
to war-time planning was the stimulus given by the February
revolution to the workers' movement.   Workers' committees
quickly sprang up in the factories, and received legal recognition
in a decree of the Provisional Government of April 22, 1917, as
entitled to represent the workers in their dealings with employers
and with the government.[2]   The first demands were for the eight-
hour day and for increased wages.   But these demands soon culminated in more or less organized attempts by the workers,
sporadic at first, but becoming gradually more frequent, to interfere with managements and themselves take possession of factories.
This, as Trotsky had specifically foreseen in 1905, was the inevitable reaction of the workers in a revolutionary situation to refusals
of their demands, and defied any attempt to limit the revolution to
a bourgeois-democratic framework.   Employers sometimes submitted and came to terms with the factory committees, but more
often retaliated by declaring lock-outs and closing down their
factories.[3]   The Bolsheviks did everything to encourage the rising
tension.   The mounting tide of anarchy in the factories served
their revolutionary purposes.   They could not have dammed it
even if they had desired to do; but they could partly steer it
so long as they were prepared to ride with it.   It was this situation which involved them in accepting and acclaiming as their

[1] *Sobranie Uzakonenii i Rasporyazhenii Vremennogo Pravitel'stva, 1917,*
No. 182, art. 1015.
[2] S. Zagorsky, *State Control of Industry in Russia during the War* (Yale,
1928), p. 173.
[3] A general account of the factory committee movement between February
and October 1917 is in *Voprosy Istorii,* No. 10, 1947, pp. 40-64.   G. Tsyperovich,
Syndikaty i Tresty v Rossii (3rd ed., 1920), p. 145, speaks of an " artificial curtailment of production " and " mass closing of enterprises " by employers before
October 1917 ; according to statistics quoted in V. P. Milyutin, *Istoriya
Ekonomicheskogo Razvitiya SSSR* (2nd ed., 1929), p. 45, 568 enterprises employing over 100,000 workers were closed between March and August 1917, the
number increasing from month to month.

own practices which were anarchist and syndicalist rather than Bolshevik.

What, however, nobody had foreseen was that the seizure of factories by the workers was in the long run even less compatible than the seizure of land by the peasants with the establishment of a socialist order. The difficulty was masked for some time by the ambiguous and equivocal phrase " workers' control ". When Lenin argued in April 1917 that the sugar syndicate should pass " into the hands of the state, under the control of the workers and peasants ",[1] he was giving a concrete instance of the principle of " Soviet " or " state " control laid down in the April theses and in the resolution of the April conference. The second part of the phrase was merely a gloss on the first; the " workers and peasants " were those through whom, and in whose name, the state would act. When, a few weeks later, a decision of the Provisional Government to set up a committee to establish " social control " over industrial enterprises provoked Lenin into the assertion that " consciousness is growing in workers' circles of the necessity of *proletarian* control over factories and syndicates ", and that only proletarian control could be effective,[2] he did not admit — and perhaps scarcely realized — that he was saying anything new, or that the demand " in workers' circles " was for anything different from what he had already advocated. A few days later, in the middle of May 1917, Lenin further elaborated his ideas on " control ". Soviets or congresses of bank employees should work out plans for the creation of a single state bank and for the exercise of the " most precise control "; Soviets of employees in syndicates and trusts should similarly work out measures of control over their institutions; the right of control should be accorded not only to all Soviets of Workers', Soldiers' and Peasants' Deputies, but to workers' Soviets in each large factory and " to the representatives of each large political party ".[3] But from these apparently drastic recommendations two points emerged. In the first place, the insistence in this context on publicity of accounts shows that Lenin was thinking of control through book-keeping over financial and commercial decisions, not of control over the technical processes either of manufacture or of factory organization : these issues simply did not arise for him

[1] Lenin, *Sochineniya*, xx, 211.   [2] *Ibid.* xx, 348.   [3] *Ibid.* xx, 377.

at the present stage.[1] Secondly, it would appear that Lenin was thinking in terms of " political " action by the Soviets in their capacity as repositories and agents, central and local, of state power, not of " direct " action by Soviets as representing the professional interests of the workers in a particular factory, industry or branch of administration. This distinction between " political " and " direct " action was important both in theory and in practice. In theory it divided the communists, who believed in the organization of economic power through a centralized political authority exercised by the workers as a whole, from the anarchists and syndicalists, who believed that the direct and spontaneous economic initiative of the workers was the ultimate form of all effective revolutionary action, and the alternative to a centralized political authority which was bound to degenerate into despotism. In practice, the distinction was between the Bolshevik leaders, who were planning the major strategy of revolution on the hypothesis of a disciplined and orderly organization of workers, and the workers in the factories, who, weighed down by the oppressive hardships of their daily life and fired by revolutionary enthusiasm to throw off the yoke of their own capitalist employers, took piecemeal action as opportunity offered without regard to the policies or arguments of the leaders at party headquarters. Since all Soviets were Soviets of Workers or Workers' Deputies, the line between " political " action and " direct " action taken by them or in their name was easily blurred ; the Soviets, as has already been noted, had in them a marked syndicalist strain.[2] Lenin, in his enthusiasm for the Soviets and for the principle of administrative control exercised by the workers themselves, had still further blurred the line by his utterances of April and May 1917. But the potential antithesis in industrial policy between " state control " and " workers' control ", which matched the antithesis in agrarian policy between state farms and peasant proprietorship, was real enough. If " workers' control " meant direction by the central congress of Soviets and by its executive committee, it was no more than a synonym for

[1] Until, much later, he became a fervent advocate of electrification, Lenin showed no interest in the technical processes of industry ; while he thoroughly understood the political mentality of the factory worker, he knew less of the daily working life of the factory worker than of the peasant.

[2] See Vol. 1, p. 128.

nationalization and state control under a " workers' and peasants' government ".   If on the other hand workers' control meant control by works committees or factory Soviets, it was something quite different, and this something might easily conflict not only with state control, but with any policy of " planning " to end the capitalist anarchy of production.   There was justice in the comment made later by one of the leaders of Bolshevik economic policy :

> If one asks oneself how our party before October 25 conceived the system of workers' control as a whole and on the basis of what economic order we meant to construct it, we shall nowhere find a clear answer.[1]

The first test came at a conference of more than 400 representatives of " factories and works committees " of the Petrograd region which met in Petrograd on May 30, 1917.   Lenin prepared for the conference a draft resolution which was approved by the central committee of the party and by the predominantly Bolshevik organizing bureau of the conference.   The resolution, which constituted the most important Bolshevik pronouncement before the revolution on the organization of industry, was built up on the thesis of " workers' control ", apparently the first use of this now popular slogan in a party document.   Having referred to " the complete dislocation of the whole of economic life in Russia " and the approach of " a catastrophe of unheard of dimensions ", it continued :

> The way to avert a catastrophe is to establish a real workers' control over the production and distribution of goods.   To establish such control it is necessary, first, to make certain that in all the basic institutions there is a majority of workers, not less than three-fourths of all the votes, and that all owners who have not deserted their business, as well as the scientifically and technically trained personnel, are compelled to participate ; secondly, that all the shop and factory committees, the central and local Soviets of Workers', Soldiers' and Peasants' Deputies, as well as trade unions, be granted the right to participate in such control, that all commercial and bank accounts be open to their inspection, and that the management be compelled to supply them with all the data ; and, thirdly, that the represen-

[1] N. Osinsky [Obolensky], *Stroitel'stvo Sotsializma* (1918), p. 34.

tatives of all the more important democratic and socialist parties be granted the same right. Workers' control, already recognized by the capitalists in a number of cases where conflicts arise, should be immediately developed, by way of a series of carefully considered and gradual, but immediately realizable, measures, into complete regulation of the production and distribution of goods by the workers.

The resolution went on to speak of the need of an " all-state organization " for the purpose of " the organization on a broad regional and finally all-state scale of the exchange of agricultural implements, clothing, boots and similar goods ", for " general labour service " and for a " workers' militia ". It was presented to the conference by Zinoviev. It received 290 votes at a first reading and, after minor amendments by a drafting committee, was declared carried by a majority of 297 to 21, with 44 abstentions. The conference was the first major representative body which had yielded an impressive Bolshevik majority and was significant on that account.[1]

The structure and tactics of the resolution were an excellent example of Lenin's political genius. He welcomed with open arms the spontaneous revolutionary movement for workers' control ; he even appeared to encourage it by extending it to the largest possible number of workers' organizations — factory committees, local and central Soviets, trade unions and " democratic and socialist parties " were all named in the resolution ; and, in so doing, he implicitly brought to light the anarchic implications of workers' control, as commonly conceived and practised, and pointed the way to the " carefully considered and gradual " measures which would be necessary to bring about " the complete regulation of the production and distribution of goods by the workers ". For Lenin the resolution was not only a tactical manœuvre, but an educational process. At the conference he was content to deliver one of the subsidiary speeches in which he observed that " in order to realize genuine control over industry, it must be workers' control ", but qualified this to mean " that a majority of workers should enter all responsible institutions and that the administration should render an account of its actions

---

[1] Lenin's original draft is in *Sochineniya*, xx, 422-424 ; for the proceedings of the conference see *Oktyabr'skaya Revolyutsiya i Fabzavkomy* (1927), i, 63-137.

to all the most authoritative workers' organizations ".[1] Lest the moral should be lost, he stressed it in an article in *Pravda* more explicitly and more distinctly than he had ventured to do at the conference : it was necessary " that the organization of control and management, being an organization ' on an all-state scale ', should be directed by the Soviets of Workers', Soldiers' and Peasants' Deputies ".[2] Not all of those who voted for the resolution would, however, have accepted this interpretation.

A month later a new factor was introduced in the form of an all-Russian conference of trade unions. The Russian trade unions had first emerged as an active force in the revolution of 1905, and after ten years of virtual extinction, had once more been brought to life by the February revolution.[3] The conference of June 1917 had a large SR and Menshevik majority, illustrating once again the tendency of the organized labour *élite* to be less radical and revolutionary than the rank and file ; and it showed no disposition to palter with the " economic anarchy " of the factory committees. While paying lip-service to the principle of such committees, the conference wished to make them the organs of a centrally determined trade union policy, and thought that the committees should be elected under trade union supervision from lists drawn up by the trade unions. The most important achievement of the conference was to lay the foundation of a central trade union organization. It elected for the first time an All-Russian Central Council of Trade Unions, composed proportionally of members of all parties represented at the conference ; the Bolshevik members were Shlyapnikov and Ryazanov. More important still, it appointed a secretary in the person of Lozovsky, one of the *Mezhraiontsy* who were to join the Bolshevik party a few weeks later.[4] Lozovsky was an able and ambitious intellectual who, in the next few years, played an influential rôle in the destinies of the trade union movement. But for the moment the trade unions counted least of any of the groups or organizations claiming in one

---

[1] Lenin, *Sochineniya*, xx, 459 ; only a short newspaper report of the speech has survived.
[2] *Ibid.* xx, 472.
[3] The rôle of the trade unions and the Bolshevik attitude towards them will be discussed in the next section (see pp. 101-103 below).
[4] The conference was fully reported in *Izvestiya* of July 2, 1917 ; no official record is known to exist.

capacity or another to represent the workers. Most of them were dominated by the Mensheviks and by a Menshevik outlook. They played no part in the preparation of the October revolution; some of them actually denounced it. The central council set up by the June conference had neither the resources nor the organization which would have enabled it to give a lead. According to a gloomy picture afterwards painted by Lozovsky, it had only one organizer to send to the provinces and had only managed before the October revolution to publish two numbers of its monthly journal.[1]

The factory committees had, on the other hand, gone from strength to strength. The conference of the Petrograd factory committees in May 1917 was only the first of four such conferences held between May and October; and the last of these was followed by a larger and more representative assembly which, sitting for a week on the eve of the October revolution, declared itself the " first all-Russian conference of factory committees " and set to work to create a central organization for the committees.[2] This ambition threatened an immediate clash with the central council of the trade unions, and the issue between the two rival organizations was hotly debated. The Bolsheviks, who had a clear majority at the conference, were themselves divided, standing midway between the SRs and anarchists, who upheld the independence of the factory committees, and the Mensheviks, who stood for orderly trade union organization. This uncertainty left its mark on the resolutions adopted by the conference. The blessing given to " workers' control on an all-state scale " was equivocal; and similar doubts attached to the distinction between " control over the conditions of labour ", which was to be carried out " under the leadership of the trade unions ", and " control over production ", which was by implication left to the committees. A central organ, whose function was boldly described as " the regulation of the national economy ", was to be elected by the all-Russian organiza-

[1] *Pervyi Vserossiiskii S"ezd Professional'nykh Soyuzov* (1918), pp. 34-36; a Menshevik delegate at the first All-Russian Congress of Trade Unions in January 1918 said that for the previous six months the central council " has done absolutely nothing " and that Lozovsky was its " one active worker " (*ibid.* p. 52).

[2] Reports of all these conferences are in *Oktyabr'skaya Revolyutsiya i Fabzavkomy* (2 vols., 1927).

tion of the factory committees, but was to work as a section of the
All-Russian Central Council of Trade Unions.[1]

In the turmoil of the last months before the revolution, these
differences and rivalries mattered little. Attacks by workers on
factories and factory managements heightened the revolutionary
tension, and hastened the process of economic dislocation. Lenin
welcomed these acts as signs of the times, and continued to
commend " workers' control ". In a pamphlet entitled *The
Impending Catastrophe and How to Combat It*, written early
in September 1917 but not published till some weeks later, he
propounded his first vague outline of an industrial policy. What
was required to combat the threat of famine, he wrote, was
" control, inspection, accounting, regulation on the part of the
state, the establishment of a correct distribution of the labour
forces engaged in the production and distribution of goods, a
husbanding of national resources, a cessation of all wasteful
expenditure of resources, an economy in the use of them " ; and
he added that the existing coalition government of Kadets, SRs
and Mensheviks would never take such measures " for fear of
trenching on the omnipotence of the landowners and capitalists,
on their extravagant, unheard of, scandalous profits ".[2] Lenin
demanded five concrete measures : the nationalization of banks,
which could be achieved by a stroke of the pen ; the nationalization of the great " trading and industrial syndicates (sugar, coal,
iron, oil, etc.) " and the establishment of state monopolies, which
could also be easily achieved, since monopolies had already, in
effect, been created by capitalism ; the abolition of commercial
secrecy ; the forced unification of small enterprises, since this
would facilitate both efficient production and control ; and the
" regulation of consumption " by fair and effective rationing. In
this scheme of things workers' control had its place. Lenin
thought it would be a good idea to call the workers and employers

---

[1] *Oktyabr'skaya Revolyutsiya i Fabzavkomy* (1927), ii, 186-188, 193 ;
Ryazanov, who had argued for the complete amalgamation of the committees
with the trade unions (*ibid.* ii, 191-192), later described this resolution as " a
death sentence " on the factory committees, which had " yielded to the trade
unions the whole domain of leadership to improve the condition of the working
class ", but admitted that the committees themselves did not accept this interpretation of it (*Pervyi Vserossiiskii S"ezd Professional'nykh Soyuzov* (1918),
pp. 233-234).   [2] Lenin, *Sochineniya*, xxi, 160.

together " into conferences and congresses ", and to " hand over
to them such-and-such a percentage of the profits on condition that
they would carry out a general control and increase of production ".
This would mean " control *over* landowners and capitalists *by*
workers and peasants ".[1] But Lenin was here talking — mainly
for propaganda purposes — of measures theoretically open to the
Provisional Government even within the framework of a bourgeois revolution. He had not yet faced the issue of workers'
control in a future socialist order.

A few weeks later Lenin wrote a far more important pamphlet,
Will the Bolsheviks Retain State Power ?, in which he dealt for the
first time in detail with economic policy after the revolution. He
repeated his points about the nationalization of the banks and the
big syndicates and the " compulsory trustification " of small
enterprises. He introduced the word " plan ", a little hesitatingly
at first, and declared for " the centralism and the plan of the
proletarian state ".[2] This first outline of Lenin's philosophy
(it was hardly yet a policy) of planning was coupled with a vigorous
assertion of the rights of workers' control :

> The chief difficulty of the proletarian revolution is the
> realization on a nation-wide scale of the most precise conscien-
> tious accounting and control, of *workers' control* over the pro-
> duction and distribution of goods.

But Lenin, rebutting once again the charge of syndicalism, went
on to reaffirm in clear and unmistakable terms the interpretation
he had given of the phrase after the May conference :

> When we say " workers' control ", placing this slogan *side
> by side* with the dictatorship of the proletariat, and always *after*
> it, we thus make clear what state we have in mind. The state
> is an organ of the rule of a class. Which class ? If the bour-
> geoisie, then this is just the Kadet-Kornilov-Kerensky state-
> hood, under which the working people of Russia have been
> suffering for over half a year. If the proletariat, if we have in
> mind a proletarian state, i.e. the dictatorship of the proletariat,
> then workers' control *can* become a national, all-embracing,
> omnipresent, most exact and most conscientious *accounting* of
> production and distribution of goods.[3]

[1] *Ibid.* xxi, 164-179.
[2] *Ibid.* xxi, 269-270 ; the passage is further quoted and discussed on p. 363
below.   [3] *Ibid.* xxi, 259.

And he added that the existing state machinery of accounting and control would not, like the " oppressive " parts of the state machine, have to be destroyed by the revolution : it would simply be taken out of the hands of the capitalists and subordinated to the " proletarian Soviets ".[1] Thus " workers' control " was equated with control by " proletarian Soviets " and the fine distinction between Soviets of workers acting in a political and in a professional capacity was not drawn. Finally in *State and Revolution* Lenin resolved the whole antithesis with a magnificent sweep of the pen :

> Here *all* citizens are transformed into hired servants of the state such as are the armed workers. *All* citizens become employees and workers of *one* all-national state " syndicate ". The essential is that they should work equally, observe the correct norms of work, and receive equally. The accounting and control of this has been extraordinarily *simplified* by capitalism and reduced to extremely simple operations of observation and registration accessible to every literate person, to a knowledge of the four rules of arithmetic and to the issue of the appropriate vouchers.[2]

There could be no antithesis between state control and workers' control once state and workers were one and the same. There are few better examples of Lenin's extraordinary skill in reconciling the obstinate pursuit of an ultimate objective which he recognized as necessary with the satisfaction of an immediate popular demand in apparent conflict with that objective.

The history of industrial policy in the first months of the revolution followed closely the evolution of Lenin's thinking in the immediately preceding months, passing through " workers' control " to " planning ". The commentator who placed " workers' control " side by side with " land " and " peace " as the " most popular and widely current slogans of the October revolution "[3] exaggerated only in so far as the number of factory workers interested in workers' control was far smaller than the number of

---

[1] Lenin, *Sochineniya*, xxi, 260.
[2] *Ibid*. xxi, 440 ; the conception of the workers' state as "one vast syndicate" is repeated from *ibid*. xxi, 437.
[3] *Narodnoe Khozyaistvo*, No. 1-2, 1919, p. 23.

those interested in peace or the acquisition of land. " We shall establish genuine workers' control over production ", announced Lenin in his first speech to the Petrograd Soviet on the afternoon of October 25/November 7, 1917; and workers' control was named among the purposes of the new régime both in the resolution passed on that occasion and in the proclamation of the second All-Russian Congress of Soviets on the next day.[1] It had been intended that the congress should pass a decree on the subject simultaneously with the decrees on land and peace ; and Milyutin had even been instructed some days earlier by the party central committee to prepare a draft.[2] But the complexity of the question was perhaps revealed in the process of drafting. Nothing transpired at the congress, and a week later *Pravda* published a draft decree from Lenin's pen. This provided that workers' control was to be organized in each factory after the manner of the Soviets either " directly, if the enterprise is small enough to make this possible ", or, in other cases, " through elected representatives ". Decisions of the organs of workers' control were binding on employers, and could be overruled only by " the trade unions and congresses " (whether congresses of trade unions or Soviets is not clear). Both employers and representatives of workers' control in enterprises of state importance were responsible to the state " for the strictest order, discipline and maintenance of property ".[3] The conception was that already elaborated by Lenin in *Will the Bolsheviks Retain State Power?* It was assumed without question that the employers and technical staffs would continue to operate their enterprises under the vigilant eye of " workers' control ".

It was at this point that the intervention of the trade unions became decisive. The October conference of the factory committees had revealed the interest of the trade union central council in curbing the anarchic tendencies of workers' control ; the same interest was now shared in even larger measure by a revolutionary government struggling to maintain and organize the essential processes of production. Thus, in the controversy behind the scenes which followed the publication of Lenin's draft, the trade unions became the unexpected champions of order, discipline and

---

[1] Lenin, *Sochineniya*, xxii, 5-6, 11.
[2] *Ibid.* xxii, 575, note 7.   [3] *Ibid.* xxii, 25-26.

centralized direction of production; and the revised draft decree, finally presented to VTsIK on November 14/27, 1917, was the result of a struggle between trade unions and factory committees, which repeated the struggle at the October conference.[1] The draft decree opened with the ingenuous statement that workers' control was instituted " in the interests of planned regulation of the national economy ". It repeated the provisions of Lenin's original draft on the binding character of decisions of the workers' representatives and the responsibility of owners and workers' representatives to the state. But it improved on his borrowing from a Soviet model by setting up a whole new and complicated machinery of workers' control in exact imitation of the political system of the Soviets. Factory committees or councils became responsible to a higher council of workers' control for the whole locality — city, province or industrial region — and these local councils were responsible to an All-Russian Council of Workers' Control which was eventually responsible to a congress of councils of workers' control. The decree concluded by promising, as a sop to the critics, that " an ordinance about relations between the All-Russian Council of Workers' Control and other institutions organizing and regulating the national economy will be issued separately ". In the debate in VTsIK its sternest critic was Lozovsky, the spokesman of the trade unions :

> The fundamental defect of this project is that it stands outside all connexion with the planned regulation of the national economy and dissipates control over production instead of concentrating it. . . . It is necessary to make an absolutely clear and categorical reservation that the workers in each enterprise should not get the impression that the enterprise belongs to them.

He would, however, vote for the decree on the understanding that " the trade unions will come into the organs set up by the decree in order to establish control in a manner consonant with the interests of the working class ". Milyutin, the *rapporteur* of the decree, who was afterwards himself a strong " nationalizer ",

[1] A. Lozovsky, *Rabochii Kontrol'* (1918), p. 20. A reviewer of this pamphlet in *Vestnik Narodnogo Komissariata Truda*, No. 2-3 (February-March), 1918, pp. 385-387, accuses Lozovsky of exaggerating both the harm done by " workers' control " and the extent of the mutual hostility between factory committees and trade unions ; in practice the fusion did not prove difficult to effect.

explained somewhat apologetically that " life overtook us " and that it had become urgently necessary to " unite into one solid state apparatus the workers' control which was being operated on the spot ", so that legislation on workers' control which should logically have fitted into the framework of an " economic plan " had had to precede legislation on the plan itself.[1] In fact, workers' control as originally conceived and as widely practised at this time found hardly any support in VTsIK. One speaker referred to the cleavage between those who wished to expand the framework of workers' control and those who sought to narrow it. But those who paid most lip-service to workers' control and purported to " expand " it were in fact engaged in a skilful attempt to make it orderly and innocuous by turning it into a large-scale centralized public institution. The decree was approved by VTsIK by a majority of 24 votes to 10 and promulgated on the following day.[2]

Life continued to " overtake " the legislators ; and the carefully thought-out decree of November 14/27, 1917, had no practical outcome.[3] The spontaneous inclination of the workers to organize factory committees and to intervene in the management of the factories was inevitably encouraged by a revolution which led the workers to assume that the productive machinery of the country now belonged to them and could be operated by them at their own discretion and to their own advantage. What had begun to happen before the October revolution now happened more frequently and more openly ; and for the moment nothing would have dammed the tide of revolt. But actual events varied from factory to factory, so that no complete or uniform picture can be obtained. Most frequently the employers prepared to close the factory and lock out recalcitrant workers. This was the contingency which the Soviet Government feared most : Lenin's draft decree on workers' control contained a clause prohibiting any " stoppage of an enterprise or of production " without the

[1] *Protokoly Zasedanii VTsIK 2 Sozyva* (1918), p. 60.
[2] The debate is in *ibid.*, pp. 60-62, the decree in *Sobranie Uzakonenii, 1917-1918*, No. 3, art. 35.
[3] The All-Russian Council of Workers' Control met only once, as Ryazanov stated in January 1918 (*Pervyi Vserossiiskii S"ezd Profsoyuzov* (1918), p. 234). or never met at all, as the same speaker stated four months later (*Trudy I Vserossiiskogo S"ezda Sovetov Narodnogo Khozyaistva* (1918), p. 104) ; according to another version it " attempted to meet ", but failed to get a quorum (*ibid.* p. 72).

consent of the workers' representatives.[1] Sometimes a more or less uneasy bargain was struck between management and workers permitting the work to continue; sometimes this collaboration took embarrassing forms, as when employers and workers in a particular industry combined to obstruct government orders to close down or concentrate factories engaged in the production of munitions, or, more unexpectedly still, came to an agreement not to apply the decree prohibiting night work for women.[2] Most often the factory committees simply took over the factories in the name of the workers. Left to themselves the workers could, in the nature of things, rarely provide the technical skill or industrial discipline or knowledge of accountancy necessary for the running of a factory. Cases occurred in which the workers, having taken over a factory, simply appropriated its funds or sold its stocks and plant for their own advantage.[3] A button factory in Moscow, where a committee of workers took possession and the former manager was condemned to three months' imprisonment for sabotage, had to close down after a fortnight's struggle owing to the inability of the committee to manage it; and instances were quoted in which workers or factory committees, having evicted the managers, later went to them and begged them to return.[4] In the spring of 1918, when workers' control was already discredited, a speaker at the first All-Russian Congress of Councils of National Economy gave an understanding account of some of the conditions which had produced it:

> Those who work in these enterprises can say that the fault did not lie only in the workers, in the fact that the workers took to " holding meetings ", but in the fact that the personnel of the enterprises, the managing staff, folded its hands because the old stick had fallen from them — the stick with which it used to drive the workers — and it had none of the other means which the western European bourgeoisie has of making the worker work. . . . All these conditions confronted the working class with the insistent task of management, and it had to be taken in

[1] An article in *Izvestiya* of November 23/December 6, 1917, described workers' control as necessary " to paralyse the activity of the lock-outists " and argued that, without this decree, " the ruin of the country and the revolution threatened ".

[2] *Pervyi Vserossiiskii S"ezd Profsoyuzov* (1918), pp. 175, 194.

[3] G. Tsyperovich, *Syndikaty i Tresty v Rossii* (3rd ed., 1920), p. 157.

[4] A. Lozovsky, *Rabochii Kontrol'* (1918), pp. 33-34.

hand. Of course, the working class took it in hand clumsily. That is understandable. They chased out the old directors and technicians, perhaps because these people had treated them badly in the past, though cases are known of kindly treatment of decent managing personnel in enterprises.[1]

The conception of workers' control spread even to the civil service. Among the curiosities of the welter of decrees issued in the first month of the revolution were two abolishing the Soviets of employees which had taken control of the People's Commissariat of Posts and Telegraphs and of the Admiralty.[2] On the railways yet another situation arose. Workers and technical staffs combined to take over and operate the railways, and for a long period obstinately set all external authority at defiance.[3]

How far such conditions were general through Russian industry is difficult to ascertain. Ryazanov, a sworn enemy of the factory committees, said in January 1918 that they were never effective outside Petrograd, and there only in the metallurgical industry.[4] But this was certainly an under-statement even at that date ; and the metal workers in Petrograd were the revolutionary *élite* of the proletariat, so that what was done there in the first weeks of the revolution was likely to be imitated elsewhere later. Even before the October revolution conditions in Petrograd, the creaking centre of Russia's war industry, were particularly acute : now dislocation spread from the centre outwards. This process cannot be attributed exclusively, or mainly, to workers' control. It had been set in motion, long before the revolution, by such factors as shortage of raw materials, neglect of machinery and plant, and the general weariness and demoralization begotten of the war. The revolution reinforced all these adverse factors and speeded up the process. But the onset of industrial chaos,

[1] *Trudy 1 Vserossiiskogo S"ezda Sovetov Narodnogo Khozyaistva* (1918), pp. 339-340.
[2] The first, though published as a decree (*Sobranie Uzakonenii, 1917–1918*, No. 3, art. 30), took the form of an appeal issued on November 9/22, 1917, by the " People's Commissar for the Ministry [*sic*] of Posts and Telegraphs " to all postal and telegraph employees to stop sabotage. It concluded : " I declare that no so-called initiatory groups or committees for the administration of the department of posts and telegraphs can usurp the functions belonging to the central power and to me as People's Commissar ". The decree dissolving the Admiralty Soviet was dated Nov. 28/Dec. 11, 1917 (*ibid.*, No. 4, art. 58).
[3] See Note D : " Workers' Control on the Railways " (pp. 394-397 below).
[4] *Pervyi Vserossiiskii S"ezd Professional'nykh Soyuzov* (1918), p. 234.

radiating from the capitals throughout Soviet territory, defies any precise record. In some areas and in some factories the revolution was slow to penetrate, and work for a time went on much as before. The Coats cotton-thread factory in Petrograd worked without trouble at full pressure till the end of February 1918, when it was brought to a standstill by the abnormal accumulation of stocks, due to a breakdown in the distributive machinery through the failure of communications and transport.[1] Where the whole economic organism was in decay, sound spots could not long resist the general contagion.

The process of disintegration went on partly as a result of Bolshevik action, and partly in spite of Bolshevik attempts to check it. This dual attitude was readily explicable. Up to a point the economic breakdown was an indispensable part of Bolshevik policy. The smashing of the economic, as well as of the political, machinery of bourgeois rule was an indispensable condition of the victory of the revolution; and as a weapon of destruction workers' control rendered indisputable service to the revolutionary cause. To break down was essential as a preliminary to building up.[2] But, once a certain point had been reached (and it was an " ideal " point which could not be precisely defined in time), continued destruction threatened the existence of the régime. The notion that the problems of production and of the relations of classes in society could be solved by the direct and spontaneous action of the workers of individual factories was not socialism, but syndicalism. Socialism did not seek to subordinate the irresponsible capitalist entrepreneur to an equally irresponsible factory committee claiming the same right of independence of the actual political authority; that could only perpetuate the " anarchy of production " which Marx regarded as the damning stigma of capitalism. The fatal and inevitable tendency of factory committees was to take decisions in the light of the interests of the workers in a particular factory or in a particular region. The essence of socialism was to establish an economy planned and carefully coordinated by a central authority in the common interest of all.

Workers' control as a form of organization scarcely outlived

---

[1] *The Lansing Papers, 1914-1920*, ii (Washington, 1940), 369.
[2] This idea was later developed at length by Bukharin (see p. 197 below).

the first few weeks of the revolution.   When the attempt made in the decree of November 14/27, 1917, to institutionalize it, and thus neutralize its centrifugal effects, ended in failure, and the decree became a dead letter, some other means had to be found of setting constructive forces in motion.   The instrument chosen for the purpose was the Supreme Council of National Economy, which was set up, without any very clear conception of its functions, in December 1917, and became in the next two years the main focus for the centralization and administration of industry.   On the side of labour the corresponding functions were performed by the trade unions, whose jealousy of workers' control had brought them into close alliance with the economic organs of the state; this process was in full swing when the first All-Russian Congress of Trade Unions met in January 1918.[1]

The creation of a body variously described as a Supreme Economic Conference or a Council of National Economy seems to have been mooted in the first days of the revolution.   On November 17/30, 1917, three days after the decree on workers' control, Sovnarkom issued a decree formally dissolving the Provisional Government's Economic Council and Chief Economic Committee, and handing over their effects " provisionally, pending the creation of a Council of National Economy, to the representatives of Sovnarkom for the organization of the Supreme Economic Conference ".   These representatives appear to have been Obolensky, Smirnov and Saveliev : to them were now added Bukharin, Larin and Milyutin.[2]   Ten days later Lenin complained that " the economic conference has not hitherto received sufficient attention ", and protested in vain against a proposal to distract Bukharin from this major task by appointing him to the editorial board of *Pravda*.[3]   On December 1/14, 1917, Lenin spoke in VTsIK in favour of a draft decree proposed by Bukharin for the

---

[1] The further development of the trade unions will be discussed in the following section (see pp. 105-108 below).

[2] *Sobranie Uzakonenii, 1917-1918*, No. 3, art. 38 ; Lenin, *Sochineniya*, xxii, 588 ; *Narodnoe Khozyaistvo*, No. 11, 1918, p. 12.   According to Larin, (*ibid.* p. 16), Lenin said to him a few days after the revolution : " You have studied the questions of the organization of the German economy, the syndicates, trusts and banks ; study this for us ".

[3] Lenin, *Sochineniya*, xxii, 107.

creation of a Supreme Council of National Economy;[1] and on December 5/18, 1917, the decree was issued.[2] The decree on workers' control had defined the purpose of workers' control as being " the planned regulation of the national economy ". The decree of December 5/18, 1917, described the purpose of the Supreme Council of National Economy (Vesenkha for short) as being " to organize the economic activity of the nation and the financial resources of the government ". The new organ was to " direct to a uniform end " the activities of all existing economic authorities, central and local, including the All-Russian Council of Workers' Control; it was to be composed of the members of the All-Russian Council of Workers' Control, of representatives of all the People's Commissariats, and of experts nominated in a consultative capacity. It thus replaced, absorbed and superseded the machinery of workers' control; as Lenin noted a few weeks later, " we passed from workers' control to the creation of the Supreme Council of National Economy ".[3] In some cases there was apparently even continuity of organization : the Petrograd regional council of workers' control — perhaps one of the few firmly established organs of workers' control — transformed itself into the Petrograd regional council of national economy.[4]

Much had, however, been learned during the three weeks since the decree on workers' control. The new decree conferred on Vesenkha powers to confiscate, acquire, sequester or forcibly syndicalize all branches of production or commerce; it was instructed to centralize and direct the work of all economic organs of the administration; and all draft economic laws and decrees were to be submitted to Sovnarkom through it. Current work was to be coordinated by a bureau of fifteen members. Obolensky was appointed president of Vesenkha with the rank and title (which

[1] Lenin, *Sochineniya*, xxii, 108 ; the records of this meeting of VTsIK are unfortunately missing. Larin (*Narodnoe Khozyaistvo*, No. 11, 1918, p. 17) records that the decree was drafted by Bukharin ; Bronsky (*Trudy I Vserossiiskogo S"ezda Sovetov Narodnogo Khozyaistva* (1918), p. 162) attributes it to Bukharin, Saveliev and himself.
[2] *Sobranie Uzakonenii, 1917–1918*, No. 5, art. 83.
[3] Lenin, *Sochineniya*, xxii, 215.
[4] *Narodnoe Khozyaistvo*, No. 11, 1918, p. 8 ; Rykov later said that Vesenkha " arose out of the Petrograd factory committees " (*Tretii Vserossiiskii S"ezd Professional'nykh Soyuzov* (1920), i (Plenumy), 7).

quickly fell out of use) of People's Commissar for the Organization and Regulation of Production. The first bureau of Vesenkha included the names of Bukharin, Larin, Milyutin, Lomov, Saveliev, Sokolnikov and Shmidt.[1] The premises of the old Chief Economic Committee were duly taken over. But the existing staff walked out; and Vesenkha inherited nothing from its predecessor but the office furniture and a few files and books.[2] While every project of the infant régime was at this time vague and chaotic, Vesenkha was evidently conceived as the central planning and directing organ of the economic life of the country. Lenin described it, on the eve of its birth, as " the fighting organ for the struggle with the capitalists and the landlords in the economic sphere, just as Sovnarkom is in politics ".[3] How undefined and far-reaching its potential functions were is shown by the juxtaposition of " demobilization " and " finance " with " fuel " and " metals " in the initial list of departments into which it was divided. The first assignment of its president, Obolensky, was to supervise the taking over of the State Bank.[4] Its first recorded decrees (for it assumed a legislative power not formally conferred on it) were a regulation for the supply of electricity during prohibited hours to government headquarters in Smolny[5] and a set of rules and principles governing foreign trade policy.[6]

It was, therefore, no part of the original design which soon made Vesenkha the main instrument of Soviet industrial policy to the virtual exclusion of other functions. But this course was set, more or less by accident, at the first meeting of the bureau of Vesenkha on December 14/27, 1917. It was an eventful day. The private banks had been occupied that morning by Red Guards, and VTsIK later in the day passed its decree nationalizing them.[7] Lenin attended the meeting of the Vesenkha bureau, and introduced a draft decree for the nationalization not only of the banks, but of all industrial enterprises.[8] There is no formal record of the

[1] *Sobranie Uzakonenii, 1917–1918*, No. 9, art. 129 : *Bol'shaya Sovetskaya Entsiklopediya*, xiii (1929), 561, art. VSNKh.
[2] *Narodnoe Khozyaistvo*, No. 11, 1918, pp. 11-12.
[3] Lenin, *Sochineniya*, xxii, 108.
[4] *Narodnoe Khozyaistvo*, No. 11, 1918, p. 12.
[5] *Sobranie Uzakonenii, 1917–1918*, No. 10, art. 158.
[6] *Ibid.* No. 10, art. 159 ; see further pp. 127-128 below.
[7] See pp. 135-136 below.
[8] Lenin, *Sochineniya*, xxii, 139-141.

occasion. According to Obolensky, only Lozovsky and Ryazanov openly contested Lenin's proposals. But most of those present regarded them as impracticable,[1] and the draft decree remained unpromulgated and unpublished. On December 20, 1917/ January 2, 1918, came a decree by which Vesenkha assigned to itself control over all government financing of industry and over all wages paid by state institutions, which were to be coordinated by the " state planning section " of Vesenkha.[2] The decree, like so many others of the period was a dead letter, and is of interest only as proving that somebody in Vesenkha — probably Larin — was already thinking far ahead of the time. It was still a far cry not only to a comprehensive economic plan, but to a general and effective nationalization of industry.

A few days later came the first public meeting of Vesenkha, of which a graphic account has been left by a foreign eye-witness.[3] Some twenty persons gathered round a table in an unheated room half empty of furniture : they included representatives of the trade unions, workers from factory committees, several People's Commissars, and a few engineers from the railways and the metal works as " specialists " — " a very mixed company ". Obolensky made a speech in which he spoke of the inadequacy of the decree on workers' control, and the need to coordinate the efforts of factory committees and trade unions with the central political authority of the Soviets. Various practical difficulties were mooted and discussed. The meeting approved a plan to create special commissions — the future *glavki* and " centres " — for different branches of industry, and a decree, which was issued on December 23, 1917/January 5, 1918, setting up a network of subordinate local organs. The decree provided for the establishment in each region of a Council of National Economy (Sovnarkhoz) under the supervision of Vesenkha. Each regional Sovnarkhoz was a replica in miniature of Vesenkha at the centre. It was to be divided into fourteen sections for different branches of production, and was to contain representatives of local institutions and organizations : the number of these representatives was to be determined

[1] *Narodnoe Khozyaistvo*, No. 11, 1918, pp. 11-14.
[2] *Sobranie Uzakonenii, 1917-1918*, No. 11, art. 167.
[3] M. Philips Price, *My Reminiscences of the Russian Revolution* (1921), pp. 213-215.

by the Soviet (presumably the corresponding regional Soviet) of Workers', Soldiers' and Peasants' Deputies.[1] It was open to regional Sovnarkhoz to create provincial and local Sovnarkhozy responsible to it and exercising the same functions in smaller units : these incorporated the corresponding organs of workers' control where the latter had come into being.[2] The whole system, which was further formalized at the first All-Russian Congress of Councils of National Economy in May 1918,[3] was designed as an economic replica of the political structure of Soviets of Workers' and Peasants' Deputies with its pyramid of ' congresses. But this parallelism, resting on the unreal conception of a division of competence between political and economic authorities,[4] was quite ineffective. At the highest level Vesenkha could never aspire to be an economic Sovnarkom ; and the provincial and local Sovnarkhozy could make no headway against the political Soviets. The idea of economic Soviets was still-born. What had been created was a central economic department with local offices.

The elaborate organization provided for in this decree still bears the marks of the original intention to exercise a general supervision over every aspect of economic activity. But this intention soon faded. The planning of national economy as a whole remained a remote ideal. Agricultural policy depended on a delicate balance between Left SRs and Bolsheviks ; financial policy had in the main been settled before Vesenkha came into existence, and remained the preserve of the People's Commissariat of Finance ; trade was still treated as a subsidiary function of production. The real gap, once workers' control had proved its inadequacy, was in industrial policy. Here planning and organization were a crying need ; and the functions of Vesenkha were

[1] *Sobranie Uzakonenii, 1917–1918*, No. 13, art. 196.
[2] In the provinces little or no distinction seems to have been drawn between the Sovnarkhozy, the economic sections of local Soviets and the local organs of workers' control (where these existed) : in Nizhny Novgorod the same body did duty for all three (*God Proletarskoi Diktatury* (Nizhny Novgorod, 1918), pp. 28-31) ; another example is quoted in *Trudy I Vserossiiskogo S"ezda Sovetov Narodnogo Khozyaistva* (1918), p. 219).
[3] *Ibid.*, pp. 485-488
[4] Lenin, in his opening speech at the first All-Russian Congress of Councils of National Economy, developed the theme that Vesenkha was destined " alone among all state institutions to keep a permanent place for itself ", since it would survive as an " administration " under socialism when the political organs of government had died away (*Sochineniya*, xxiii, 36).

gradually narrowed down to the filling of this gap. The organization for which Vesenkha made provision in its decree of December 23, 1917/January 5, 1918, included " special commissions for each branch of industry ". On the other hand most of the major Russian industries had created for themselves during the war, with official encouragement and support, central agencies claiming more or less effectively to speak for the industry as a whole, to coordinate its output and to regulate its sales. During the first weeks of the revolution the question constantly arose of the relations of such agencies to the Soviet power ; in a few industries the trade unions were also strong enough to play a part, though nowhere except in the railways, which were already state-owned, was their rôle decisive. Sometimes, no doubt, Vesenkha attempted to ride rough-shod over the industrialists. A delegate at the first All-Russian Congress of Councils of National Economy in May 1918 conjured up a picture of a " sort of *bohème* " in which " a tailor will be put at the head of a big metallurgical concern, and a painter at the head of textile production ".[1] Such things occurred, and were sometimes justified by the theories which had been preached by Lenin in *State and Revolution* and were now being busily disseminated by Bukharin. But they were most likely to occur where the employers and managers openly practised resistance or sabotage or simply abandoned their factories. The more common state of relations between surviving capitalist organs and the instruments of the new power seems to have been an uneasy, distrustful and quasi-hostile cooperation. Early appointments to Vesenkha may have been based on the qualification of party allegiance. But it is on record that both the economic committee of the Moscow regional Soviet and the first Kharkhov regional Sovnarkhoz contained representatives of the entrepreneurs.[2]

The gradual concentration in the hands of Vesenkha, in the first winter of the revolution, of a centralized control over industry may be illustrated from what happened in the two largest Russian industries — metals and textiles. In both cases the control was built on foundations laid before the revolution. The metallurgical industry was the most highly organized unit in the Russian econ-

[1] *Trudy I Vserossiiskogo S"ezda Sovetov Narodnogo Khozyaistva* (1918), p. 71.
[2] *Bol'shaya Sovetskaya Entsiklopediya*, xiii (1929), 559-560, art. VSNKh.

omy; the first selling organization for the industry as a whole, Prodamet by name, had been created as early as 1902. War demands brought about the creation in 1915 of an official committee for the distribution of metals called Rasmeko. One of the first acts of Vesenkha was to transform Rasmeko into an executive organ of its metals section and to assign to it the task of fixing prices for metals.[1] By March 1918 the mining and metallurgical section of Vesenkha, built on these pre-revolutionary foundations, was an active organization with a headquarters staff of 750.[2]

The textile industry was the oldest large-scale industry in Russia. It was unique in having virtually all its factories in the central region, so that the whole industry was concentrated in the area under Soviet control; it was, however, soon to be cut off from its main native supplies of raw material in Turkestan. The fact that few textile factories were among those nationalized in the first period [3] suggests that the employers were less intransigent than in some other industries. The Provisional Government, in agreement with the textile industry, had set up an organization under the name of Tsentrotkan' with its headquarters in Moscow and with the ostensible purpose of facilitating the better distribution of supplies. On December 16/29, 1917, a decree instructed the economic section of the Moscow Soviet to reorganize Tsentrotkan' in such a way as " to keep account of all textile manufactures, to sequester them for state ownership and to distribute them through the general state organization of the People's Commissariat of Supply ".[4] In all probability nothing was achieved by this decree except to lay the tentative foundations of an organization in which the Soviet power could find some common ground with the industrialists. At the end of January 1918 the trade union of textile workers held a congress, certainly not without official

---

[1] *Sobranie Uzakonenii, 1917–1918*, No. 10, art. 149; a few days earlier a decree of similar tenor had been issued by the People's Commissariat for Trade and Industry (*ibid.* No. 10, art. 155), which, however, soon abandoned to Vesenkha any claim to concern itself with industrial organization.

[2] *Byulleteni Vysshego Soveta Narodnogo Khozyaistva*, No. 1, April 1918, p. 42.

[3] According to V. P. Milyutin, *Istoriya Ekonomicheskogo Razvitiya SSSR* (2nd ed., 1929), p. 112, the textile industry accounted for only 5 per cent of all concerns nationalized before June 1, 1918.

[4] *Sobranie Uzakonenii, 1917–1918*, No. 9, art. 137.

encouragement, and passed a resolution in favour of creating a
central organization, which it called Tsentrotekstil, to control
the industry.[1] Finally in March 1918 Vesenkha created a central
organ for the textile industry which, while taking the name proposed by the workers, was evidently a combination of Tsentrotekstil and Tsentrotkan'. The new Tsentrotekstil was described
in its statute as " a state organ unifying and directing the whole
activity of the industry ". It was to be composed of 30 workers
in the industry, 15 engineers and managers (these were referred to
by a locution familiar in Tsarist times as the " assessed " or " tax-
paying " group) and 30 representatives of various official or semi-
official bodies : the executive organ was to be a bureau of eleven.[2]
The threatened shortage of raw materials (which became acute in
the autumn of 1918) may have helped to promote a comparatively
high degree of cooperation in this industry between managers,
workers and the Soviet power.

The metallurgical and textile industries help to illustrate the
process by which Vesenkha began in the first months of 1918 to
build up a system of unified administration for particular industries. During 1915 and 1916 the Tsarist Government had set up
central organs, sometimes called " committees " and sometimes
" centres ", for many industries producing commodities directly
or indirectly necessary for the prosecution of the war,[3] and by
1917 these central organs, which were generally composed of
representatives of the industry concerned and exercised regulatory
functions of a rather undefined character, had spread over almost
the whole field of industrial production. During the first half of
1918 Vesenkha gradually took over these bodies, or what was left
of them, and converted them, under the name of *glavki* (chief
committees) or *tsentry* (centres), into administrative organs
subject to the direction and control of Vesenkha. The chief
committee for the leather industry (Glavkozh) was set up in
January 1918.[4] This was quickly followed by chief paper and

[1] *Narodnoe Khozyaistvo*, No. 10, 1918, p. 32 ; No. 11, 1918, pp. 43-46.

[2] *Ibid.* No. 2, 1918, pp. 43-44.

[3] S. Zagorsky, *State Control of Industry in Russia during the War* (Yale,
1928), p. 129, records the setting up of committees for the cotton, wool, leather,
flax and paper industries.

[4] *Narodnoe Khozyaistvo*, No. 11, 1918 p. 18 ;   *Trudy I Vserossiiskogo
S"ezda Sovetov Narodnogo Khozyaistva* (1918), p. 95.

sugar committees, and soap and tea " centres "; these together with Tsentrotekstil were all in existence by March 1918.[1] These organs could scarcely have come into being except on foundations already laid before the revolution or without the collaboration of the managerial and technical staffs of the industries. The journals which many of them published in the spring and summer of 1918 had, behind their official aspect, much of the character of the old trade journals. It might have looked for the moment as if the Russian economy, following the model set up in Germany during the war, was on its way towards a compromise between industry and the new state power on the basis of concentration and self-administration under broad state supervision exercised by Vesenkha. How far this supervision was effective is a question to which no clear and uniform answer can be given. But in so far as it was effective, it was the product of cooperation rather than of constraint. At a time when the Russian economy, shattered by war and revolution, was plunging downward into a gulf of anarchy and disintegration, a certain tacit community of interests could be detected between the government and the more sensible and moderate of the industrialists in bringing about a return to some kind of orderly production.[2]

Extensive nationalization of industry was thus no part of the initial Bolshevik programme; and, though powers had been conferred on Vesenkha to " confiscate, requisition or sequester ", the first steps towards nationalization were halting and diffident. The nationalization of industry was treated at the outset not as a desirable end in itself but as a response to special conditions, usually some misdemeanour of the employers; and it was applied exclusively to individual factories not to industries as a whole, so that

---

[1] *Byulleteni Vysshego Soveta Narodnogo Khozyaistva*, No. 1, March 1918, p. 28; the decree setting up the chief sugar committee (Glavsakhar) is in *Sobranie Uzakonenii, 1917-1918*, No. 29, art. 377; particulars of the setting up of the tea centre (Tsentrochai) are in *Izvestiya Tsentrochaya*, No. 1, April 25, 1918.

[2] *Narodnoe Khozyaistvo*, No. 3, 1918, pp. 7-12, published an article by a " specialist " named Makevetsky, an expert on poison gas and a former instructor at the Technological Institute, arguing that the progress and efficiency of the Russian chemical industry could be assured only by acceptance of state control, and advocating nationalization of the industry; V. N. Ipatieff, *The Life of a Chemist* (Stanford, 1946), p. 237, records the formation of Glavkhim, the chief committee for the chemical industry, out of the chemical committee of Chief Artillery Administration of the Tsarist Ministry of War.

any element of planning was quite absent from these initial measures. Two epithets were used in Soviet literature to describe the nationalization policy of this early period. It was " punitive ",[1] meaning that its motive was to defeat or punish the resistance or sabotage of the capitalists ; and it was " spontaneous ",[2] meaning that it was mainly the result of action by workers on the spot, not by the central authority. Ample evidence can be found to justify both descriptions.

The " punitive " character of early nationalization is illustrated by the fact that the first nationalization decrees, whether issued by Sovnarkom or by Vesenkha, always cited the reasons provoking or justifying nationalization. Refusal to submit to workers' control was the reason most commonly given.[3] But an electric lighting company was nationalized because, in spite of government subsidies, the management had brought the enterprise to " complete financial ruin and disputes with employees ".[4] The Putilov works in Petrograd were taken over owing to their " indebtedness to the treasury " ; another large metallurgical concern was nationalized " in view of the declaration by the management of its intention to wind up the affairs of the company ".[5] Another iron and steel works producing nails was nationalized " in view of the company's inability to continue operating the plant and of its importance to the government ".[6] The Declaration of Rights of the Toiling and Exploited People adopted by the third All-Russia Congress of Soviets in January 1918 proclaimed all factories, mines and transport state property. This, though a statement of principles

---

[1] V. P. Milyutin, *Istoriya Ekonomicheskogo Razvitiya SSSR* (2nd ed., 1929), p. 137 ; Lenin at the third All-Russian Congress of Soviets in January 1918, denouncing the capitalist enemies of the régime, described " the nationalization of the banks and the confiscation of their property " as measures " to reduce them to obedience " (*Sochineniya*, xxii, 210).

[2] *Trudy I Vserossiiskogo S"ezda Sovetov Narodnogo Khozyaistva* (1918), p. 92 ; *Za Pyat' Let* (1922), p. 238 : for the Russian word *stikhiinyi*, see Vol. 1, p. 15, note 1.

[3] Early examples will be found in *Sobranie Uzakonenii, 1917–1918*, No. 4, art. 69 ; No. 6, art. 95 ; No. 13, arts. 190, 191, 192 ; according to V. P. Milyutin, *Istoriya Ekonomicheskogo Razvitiya SSSR* (2nd ed., 1929), p. 115, 70 per cent of all nationalizations in this period were due to employers either refusing to accept workers' control or abandoning their factories.

[4] *Sobranie Uzakonenii, 1917–1918*, No. 9, art. 140.

[5] *Sbornik Dekretov po Narodnomu Khozyaistvu* (1918), pp. 270-271.

[6] *Sobranie Uzakonenii, 1917–1918*, No. 9, art. 130.

rather than a legislative act, marked a more decisive movement of
opinion ; and from this time nationalization decrees ceased as a
rule to offer any reason for the act.[1] The "spontaneous" element in
early nationalization was even more conspicuous than its punitive
character. The nationalization decrees issued by Sovnarkom and
Vesenkha related mainly to enterprises in Petrograd and to a few
well-known provincial concerns with offices in the capital. But a
much greater number of large and small enterprises up and down
the country were nationalized by regional or local Soviets or
Sovnarkhozy or other local organs, or by the workers themselves
with or without the covering approval of the local Soviets.[2]
Sometimes nationalizations by local Soviets went hand in hand with
claims for political autonomy. When immediately after the revolution a commission was sent to Turkestan to organize supplies of
cotton for the textile factories of Moscow and Petrograd, it discovered that the Turkestan Soviet and Sovnarkom had already
nationalized the local cotton industry.[3] Exactly what happened
over the vast expanse of Soviet territory defies any precise computa-
tion.[4] But everything goes to show that the disorderly procedure
of workers' control was a main source of nationalization in the
winter of 1917–1918, and that regional and local Soviets and
Sovnarkhozy more often issued decrees covering action taken
by the workers themselves than decrees proceeding from their
own initiative. Nationalization, as Rykov afterwards said, " went
on without any regard for questions of supply or for economic

---

[1] See *ibid.* No. 27, arts. 350, 351, 354–360, for a series of nationalization
decrees issued in February and March 1918.
[2] An early decree concerned primarily with food supplies had incidentally
given to local Soviets the right to sequester " all trading and industrial enterprises " (*Sobranie Uzakonenii, 1917–1918*, No. 1 (2nd ed.), art. 9) ; but questions
of legality counted for little at this time.
[3] *Trudy I Vserossiiskogo S"ezda Sovetov Narodnogo Khozyaistva* (1918), p. 97.
[4] According to statistics quoted in V. P. Milyutin, *Istoriya Ekonomicheskogo
Razvitiya SSSR* (2nd ed., 1929), p. 113, out of 521 enterprises nationalized
before June 1, 1918, 50 per cent had been nationalized by regional Sovnarkhozy,
25 per cent by lower Sovnarkhozy or Soviets, and only 20 per cent by Sovnarkom
or Vesenkha. But these statistics, though no doubt fairly complete for the
higher authorities, were certainly quite unreliable for nationalizations at a lower
level ; nor can any statistics show what proportion of formal nationalizations
were the product of " spontaneous " action by the workers. Rykov commented
on the unreliability of statistics of nationalization : " Several figures have been
given and nobody knows how accurate those figures are " (*Trudy I Vserossiiskogo
S"ezda Sovetov Narodnogo Khozyaistva* (1918), p. 92).

considerations; it arose simply from the direct necessities of the struggle with the bourgeoisie ".[1] It was characteristic of this haphazard process of " punitive " or " spontaneous " nationalization that it applied only to individual enterprises. With the exception of the merchant fleet, which was already organized as a single unit, and was taken over by a decree of January 1918,[2] the first nationalization of an industry as a whole was the nationalization of the sugar industry in May 1918, followed by that of the oil industry in the following month.[3] Yet it was clear that so long as the factory rather than the industry was the unit of nationalization, the syndicalist tendencies inherent in workers' control had not been fully overcome. In a community which sought to organize itself on socialist rather than syndicalist lines, the fate of a particular factory or enterprise could not be determined exclusively, so to speak, on its merits. The whole industry or branch of production, and ultimately the whole national economy, must be considered as a single entity.

The Brest-Litovsk treaty had the effect of a severe shock to the whole Soviet organization. It had thrown a harsh searchlight on a picture of almost total helplessness and disintegration, and called an abrupt halt to the economic policies of drift and compromise which had characterized the past three months. At the moment of the signature of the treaty, major emphasis was still being laid on the need to create a new army for the " defence of

---

[1] *Trudy I Vserossiiskogo S"ezda Sovetov Narodnogo Khozyaistva* (1918), p. 92.
[2] *Sobranie Uzakonenii, 1917–1918*, No. 19, art. 290.
[3] *Ibid.* No. 34, art. 457; No. 45, art. 546. Both these industries were in a specially precarious state owing to the German occupation of the Ukraine. An apparent exception to the statement in the text is the nationalization of match and candle factories by decree of March 7, 1918 (*ibid.* No. 29, art. 385). This was an anomalous case. The purpose of the decree was to create a state monopoly over the distribution of certain primary commodities (rice, pepper and coffee were also included). The " nationalization " of match and candle factories was incidental to this purpose ; and, in spite of the term used, they were placed under the control not of Vesenkha (which issued the decree) or of any other state organ, but of the central council of cooperatives (Tsentrosoyuz). At the first All-Russian Congress of Councils of National Economy in May 1918 it was specifically stated that Vesenkha had up to that time nationalized only two industries as a whole : water transport and the sugar industry (*Trudy I Vserossiiskogo S"ezda Sovetov Narodnogo Khozyaistva* (1918), p. 93).

the socialist fatherland " and on the sure prospect of the coming
international revolution : these were still the keynotes of the
resolution of the seventh party congress which approved the
ratification of the treaty of March 8, 1918. Exactly a week later
the resolution of the fourth All-Russian Congress of Soviets which
formally ratified the treaty repeated these *motifs*, and prefaced
them with a new one — the need for a decisive turn in economic
policy :

> The congress most insistently draws the attention of all
> workers, soldiers and peasants, of all the toilers and the oppressed
> masses to the main current and indispensable task of the present
> moment : the raising of the activity and self-discipline of the
> workers, the creation everywhere and in all directions of strong,
> solid organizations covering as far as possible all production
> and all distribution of goods, a relentless struggle with the chaos,
> disorganization and disintegration which are historically inevit-
> able as the consequence of a devastating war, but are at the same
> time the primary obstacle to the final victory of socialism and the
> reinforcement of the foundations of socialist society.[1]

The time had come to take account of the immense economic
losses, not indeed caused, but registered, by the Brest-Litovsk
treaties. They amounted to 40 per cent of the industry and of the
industrial population of the former Russian Empire, 70 per cent
of the iron and steel production, and 90 per cent of the sugar.[2]
Drastic expedients were necessary to snatch the country back
from the jaws of ruin. The mere fact that the German ordeal had
somehow been survived bred, on the other hand, a certain qualified
optimism. The disorders of the past few months could legitimately be ascribed in part to the horrors of war ; and these were
for the moment at an end. For the first time the Soviet republic
was free from the immediate preoccupation of foreign invasion.
Industrial reconstruction was the first and foremost task of the
" breathing-space ".

The new turn of policy was accompanied by important changes
at Vesenkha. Its first president Obolensky seems to have been

---

[1] *S"ezdy Sovetov RSFSR v Postanovleniyakh* (1939), p. 69.
[2] These figures were given by Radek in a report to the first All-Russian
Congress of Councils of National Economy in May 1918 (*Trudy I Vserossiiskogo
S"ezda Sovetov Narodnogo Khozyaistva*, p. 15) ; more detailed calculations of
the losses involved are made in *Na Novykh Putyakh* (1923), iii, 161-163.

dropped almost at once.[1]   He, Bukharin and Lomov all participated in the debates of the party central committee as active
opponents of the Brest-Litovsk treaty; and on their defeat they
withdrew from the bureau of Vesenkha and from all responsibility
for its policy.[2] This opened the way for Larin and Milyutin, who
became the most influential figures at Vesenkha headquarters;
Larin was at one time expected to succeed to the presidency.[3]
Larin, a former Menshevik, was a student and admirer of the
state-inspired industrial concentration and planned economy of
war-time Germany.   Milyutin, though always a Bolshevik, was
no uncompromising extremist, as his resignation over the issue of
a coalition in November 1917[4] had shown.   Both Larin and
Milyutin now came forward as practical business men concerned
primarily to arrest the disastrous fall in production.   Both were
strong planners and centralizers.   The policy which they represented was a reaction against the excesses of workers' control and
" spontaneous " nationalization, and secured for a time the support
of Lenin.

The first unmistakable step along the new path was a decree
issued by Vesenkha on March 3, 1918 — the date of the signature
at Brest-Litovsk — over the signature of Larin.   This decree
contained a clear recognition of the functions of technical management in industry and at the same time attempted to lay the
foundations of a complete system of central supervision and control.
Each " central direction " (the *glavk* or centre) was to appoint to
every enterprise belonging to the industry under its care a commissioner, who would be the government representative and super-
visor, and two directors, one technical, the other administrative.
The administrative director was subject to the decisions of an

---

[1] In January 1918 Obolensky was sent to Kharkov to prepare for the
nationalization of the Donetz mines (*Narodnoe Khozyaistvo*, No. 11, 1918, p. 14);
in March 1918 he reported to the plenum of Vesenkha in favour of nationalization of the Donetz mines (*Byulleteni Vysshego Soveta Narodnogo Khozyaistva*,
No. 1, April 1918, pp. 34-41).

[2] The first number of the journal of Vesenkha *Narodnoe Khozyaistvo*,
bearing the date March 1918, came out under the responsibility of an editorial
board consisting of Obolensky, Lomov and Smirnov; from the second number
(April 1918) onwards, Milyutin became the editor.

[3] See a statement by Saveliev, who was acting president after Obolensky's
departure, recorded in Bunyan and Fisher, *The Bolshevik Revolution, 1917-1918*
(Stanford, 1934), p. 624.

[4] See Vol. 1, p. 109.

" economic administrative council " composed of representatives
of the workers, employers and technical personnel of the enterprise,
as well as of the trade unions and local Soviet organs.   The technical administrator could be overruled only by the government
commissioner or by the " central direction " of the industry.   The
decree laid down the principle that " in nationalized enterprises
workers' control is exercised by submitting all declarations and
decisions of the factory or shop committee or of the control
commission to the economic administrative council for approval " ;
and there was a provision that not more than half the members of
the administrative council should be workers or employers.[1]   At a
session of Vesenkha which opened on March 19, 1918, Milyutin
introduced the main report by declaring that " the dictatorship of
the proletariat has made inevitable a change of our whole economic
policy from top to bottom ".   He made a guarded attack on the
" inadequacies " of workers' control and nationalization as hitherto
applied :

> Nationalization has proceeded either from below, being
> carried out by regional, or often by local, Soviets of Workers',
> Soldiers' and Peasants' Deputies, or from above, from here,
> by Sovnarkom or Vesenkha.   But the defect in this system of
> nationalization has been that there was no general plan.   The
> whole process was dictated from without by the economic
> situation and by the facts of the class struggle.   At the present
> time the state has to finance our industry, and in reality both
> nationalized enterprises and private enterprises are now for the
> most part maintained by the state treasury.   For this reason it
> would really be difficult in this respect to draw a picture which
> distinguished nationalized from non-nationalized enterprises in
> the matter of their financial indebtedness to the state ; and for
> this reason we are faced in the future with the necessity of
> administering those factories, workshops, etc., which are not yet
> nationalized, and with *carrying on to its completion the nationaliza-
> tion of industry.*

The corollary of this was the abandonment of the " punitive "
system of nationalization for " a system of planned nationalization ", adequately prepared and covering the whole of any given
industry.   Such further nationalization must be linked with an
" increase in productivity ".   Larin also declared — a view then

[1] *Sbornik Dekretov i Postanovlenii po Narodnomu Khozyaistvu* (1918),
pp. 311-315.

as novel as it may in retrospect appear obvious — that the function of Vesenkha was " to increase the quantity of useful objects produced in the country " ; and he was far in advance of the time in putting forward three ambitious projects of public works — the intensive equipment of the Kuznetsk mines in central Siberia, the electrification of industry in Petrograd, and irrigation in Turkestan.[1] Plans to develop mining and industry in Siberia to replace the lost industrial regions of the Ukraine and south-eastern Russia were much canvassed in the opening of 1918, but were quickly interrupted by the civil war; the same reason made the Turkestan project impracticable. The electrification of industry was the germ of an idea which became fruitful later, and occupied an honourable place in the history of Soviet planning. But for the moment Larin was building castles in the air.

The issue round which acute controversy flared up in the brief interval of external tranquillity after Brest-Litovsk was the relation of the revolutionary government to the former leaders of capitalist industry. Lenin's conception of " state capitalism " as a régime which would leave owners in possession and management of their industrial enterprises while subjecting them to general state supervision and direction had not been discarded. Dealings between Vesenkha and the industrialists had been encouraged; and it was not surprising that negotiations should have been opened with Meshchersky, a prominent iron and steel magnate, whose group owned the principal locomotive and wagon-building works in the country, for the future organization of the industry. In March 1918 Meshchersky put forward an ingenious proposal under which his group would hold half the shares in a new metallurgical trust and the state the other half, the group undertaking the management of the trust on behalf of the partnership.[2] By a narrow majority Vesenkha decided to negotiate on this basis.[2] About the same time Stakheev, another industrialist, made a

---

[1] Milyutin's two speeches are in V. P. Milyutin, *Istoriya Ekonomicheskogo Razvitiya SSSR* (2nd ed., 1929), pp. 130-141, Larin's report in *Byulleteni Vysshego Soveta Narodnogo Khozyaistva*, No. 1, April 1918, pp. 23-34 ; no official record of the proceedings seems to have been published. Milyutin's speech included a section on labour policy, for which see pp. 109-110 below.

[2] According to an account in *Narodnoe Khozyaistvo*, No. 11, 1918, p. 22, the decision was taken by a majority of only one at a meeting of the presidium of Vesenkha " with some leaders of Sovnarkom ".

proposal to form a trust for the iron and steel industry of the Urals, 200 million rubles of the share capital to be subscribed by his group, 200 millions by the state, and 100 millions by unnamed American capitalists. An alternative proposal was for the state to subscribe the whole capital, and for the Stakheev group to manage the trust on behalf of the state.[1]

These schemes, of which the Meshchersky project was the more serious, soon encountered stiff political opposition. The Left group, which had been defeated on the ratification of the Brest-Litovsk treaty, now took the field under the leadership of Bukharin and Radek on a broad economic front. On April 4, 1918, a series of theses were presented by this group to a party meeting ; these were published a fortnight later in the first number of the short-lived journal *Kommunist*.[2] Lenin, who was present at the meeting, read a set of counter-theses : these were not published at the time, but were evidently part of a first draft of an extensive article entitled *Current Tasks of the Soviet Power* which, having received the endorsement of the central committee of the party — an unusually solemn formality — appeared in *Izvestiya* on April 28, 1918.[3] On the following day a major public debate on the question was opened by Lenin in VTsIK, Bukharin speaking on behalf of the Left group ; and on May 3 VTsIK adopted six theses on the *Current Tasks of the Soviet Power* which were a full endorsement of Lenin's position.[4] Not content with this formal victory, Lenin harried his defeated rivals in a lively pamphlet, *On " Left " Infantilism and the Petty-Bourgeois Spirit*, which marked the end of the controversy and provided the most finished analysis of Lenin's economic outlook at this time.

Both sides agreed that a turning-point had been reached. The

[1] G. Tsyperovich, *Syndikaty i Tresty v Rossii* (3rd ed. 1920), pp. 161-162.

[2] See Vol. 1, pp. 188-189 ; the theses are reprinted in Lenin, *Sochineniya*, xxii, 561-571.

[3] *Ibid.* xxii, 439-468 ; a fragment of the original draft, written at the end of March and differing widely in form from the final text, has been preserved, *ibid.* xxii, 412-425 ; the approval of the central committee is recorded, presumably from unpublished party archives, *ibid.* xxii, 620, note 177. *Kommunist*, No. 1, April 20, 1918, p. 13, reproached Lenin with failure to publish his counter-theses.

[4] *Protokoly Zasedanii VTsIK 4ᵍᵒ Sozyva* (1920), pp. 206-238 ; Lenin's two speeches (the second a reply to Bukharin) are also in *Sochineniya*, xxii, 471-498, the six theses *ibid.* xxii, 499-501.

revolution had triumphed over its enemies at home, the power of the bourgeoisie had been crushed, and the bourgois administrative machine, political and economic, smashed; the destructive phase of the revolution was complete. But on how to proceed to the constructive phase opinions were radically divided. The members of the Left group stood at the opposite pole to those who, before and after October 1917, had been sceptical of the possibility of an immediate transition to the socialist revolution; they, on the contrary, maintained that the socialist revolution had been accomplished and were impatient to garner its refreshing fruits. They shrank from producing any concrete programme, and remained essentially an opposition group. But the principle at stake was clear. The programme of the proletarian revolution was being side-tracked in the interests of the consolidation of the new state power. Just as the cause of international revolution had been sacrificed at Brest-Litovsk to " the protection and reinforcement of what is left of the Soviet state ", so in the economic sphere " all forces will now be directed to the reinforcement and development of productive capacity, to organic construction, involving a refusal to continue the break-up of capitalist productive relations and even a partial restoration of them ". The argument continued :

> Instead of advancing from partial nationalization to a general socialization of large-scale industry, agreements with " captains of industry " must lead to the formation of big trusts directed by them and embracing basic industries, which from an outside view may have the appearance of state undertakings. Such a system of organized production creates a social base for the evolution of state capitalism and constitutes a transitional stage towards it.

The same criticism was echoed by the Menshevik press, which complained that " a policy of the creation of industrial trusts is being carried on under the flag of the nationalization of industry ".[1] Lenin's new insistence on central organization and the measures proposed by him to realize it were dismissed as being a retreat from socialism into state capitalism.

In the middle of April 1918, while this controversy was at its height, the decision was taken to reject the Meshchersky project.[2]

[1] Quoted in Lenin, *Sochineniya*, xxii, 523.

[2] Few details about the Meshchersky negotiations were ever disclosed. A speaker at the first All-Russian Congress of Councils of National Economy

What part the opposition played in forcing this decision is not certain; according to one version it was dictated by the discovery that the majority of the shares in the Meshchersky group had passed into German hands.[1] But the discussion of principle continued without reference to this decision. Lenin's rebuttal of the attack of the Left opposition was characteristic and significant. Since April 1917 he had preached, against those who sought to confine the revolution within a narrow bourgeois framework, the doctrine of the immediate transition from the bourgeois to the socialist revolution. But he had guarded himself carefully about the time and the conditions in which socialism could be attained. " Not the ' introduction ' of socialism as our *immediate* task ", he had said in the April theses, " but immediate transition merely to *control* by the Soviet of Workers' Deputies over the social production and distribution of products." In *State and Revolution* written on the eve of the October revolution he had spoken, with one eye on war-time Germany, of " the epoch of the growth of monopoly capitalism into state monopoly capitalism ", though he had denounced the heresy that this state monopoly capitalism could be called " state socialism " ; it was not socialism, but it was a step on the road to socialism.[2] This conception of a highly concentrated and monopolistic economy operated by capitalists nominally under private ownership, but under close state supervision, was what Lenin meant by " state capitalism ". The attempt to realize it immediately after the revolution under a system of workers' control had broken down, partly owing to the refusal of the capitalist employers to play their expected part.[3]

alleged that the Bolsheviks had " spent four whole months learning and taking lessons from that pretty good trust-operator, Meshchersky " ; according to Rykov, a scheme was negotiated by Meshchersky with Larin, but rejected by a majority of the presidium of Vesenkha (*Trudy I Vserossiiskogo S"ezda Sovetov Narodnogo Khozyaistva* (1918), pp. 72, 112). According to an article by Osinsky (Obolensky) in *Kommunist*, No. 2, April 27, 1918, p. 17, Lenin had supported the scheme at the party discussion on April 4, saying that he was perfectly ready to give Meshchersky a " bribe " of 200-250 million rubles if the group would undertake the organization of a great metallurgical trust.

[1] G. Tsyperovich, *Syndikaty i Tresty v Rossii* (3rd ed. 1920), p. 165.

[2] Lenin, *Sochineniya*, xxi, 391, 416.

[3] Oddly enough this was long felt as a grievance against them ; " the capitalist class ", said Shlyapnikov indignantly at the first All-Russian Congress of Trade Unions, " renounced the organizing rôle in production assigned to it " (*Pervyi Vserossiiskii S"ezd Professional'nykh Soyuzov* (1918), p. 2).

But far greater success, in spite of the failure of the Meshchersky negotiations, had attended the policy of organizing a series of great industrial monopolies under the control and direction of Vesenkha.[1] This was not socialism but a step on the road to it. Lenin had never disputed the contention, dear to the hearts of the Mensheviks, that Russia must cease to be backward before she could become socialist. The problem was rendered acute by the failure of the German and western European proletariats, contrary to all Lenin's calculations, to come to the aid of the Russian revolution. Backward Russia must complete her bourgeois revolution, must modernize herself by her own exertions, pending the arrival of help from Europe.

It followed that Lenin could accept the imputation of " state capitalism ", not as an accusation but as a panegyric. In the debate in VTsIK he ironically turned the tables on his opponents :

> Evolution towards state capitalism — there is the evil, there is the foe against whom we are invited to struggle.
> And yet when I read these references to such enemies in the paper of the Left communists, I ask : What has happened to these people, how can they through poring over extracts from a book forget reality ? Reality says that state capitalism would be for us a step forward. If we in Russia in a short space of time could get state capitalism, that would be a victory. How could they fail to see that the small proprietor, small capital, is our enemy ? How could they see the chief enemy in state capitalism ?[2]

In *On " Left " Infantilism and the Petty-Bourgeois Spirit* he developed the idea with equal emphasis and in greater detail. Russia was a cockpit in which various forms of production were struggling with one another. But it was essential to recognize which were enemies and which were allies :

> It is not state capitalism which is struggling here against socialism, but the petty bourgeoisie plus private commercial capitalism which are struggling together as one man both against state capitalism and against socialism.[3]

[1] Kritsman, an able exponent of the economic theories of this period, wrote of Vesenkha as being " the heir and successor (in the matter of uniting the national economy) of the organs of finance capital " (Y. Larin i L. Kritsman, *Ocherk Khozyaistvennoi Zhizni i Organizatziya Narodnogo Khozyaistva Sovetskoi Rossii* (1920), p. 122).

[2] Lenin, *Sochineniya*, xxii, 481.   [3] *Ibid.* xxii, 514.

State capitalism is thus not only the stepping-stone to socialism, but the ally of socialism as the enemy of its enemies.

The foreign country on which the vision, not only of Lenin the revolutionary, but of Lenin the statesman, continued to be focused was Germany. Lenin's interest in the German war economy began to bear fruit. The Brest-Litovsk treaty was still unratified when he turned eagerly to this theme :

> Yes, learn from the German ! History proceeds by zigzags and crooked paths. It happens that it is the German who now, side by side with bestial imperialism, embodies the principles of discipline, of organization, of solid working together, on the basis of the most modern machine industry, of strict accounting and control.
> And this is precisely what we lack. This is precisely what we need to learn.[1]

He devoted a whole chapter of On " Left " Infantilism and the Petty-Bourgeois Spirit to Germany as the " most concrete example of state capitalism " and the " ' last word ' in contemporary large capital technique and planned organization ". The only fault of German state capitalism was that its state was the state of " junker-bourgeois imperialism ". Put in its place the " Soviet, i.e. proletarian, state ", and " you will get the complete sum of the conditions which socialism offers ". History had played a strange trick. It had given birth at the beginning of 1918 to " two separate halves of socialism, side by side, like two chickens to be in one shell " — the one in Germany, the other in Russia. The political revolution had occurred in Russia ; the economic organization was in Germany. Both were necessary for the attainment of socialism. The task of Russian socialists, pending the outbreak of the German revolution, was " to study the state capitalism of the Germans, to adopt it with all possible strength, not to spare dictatorial methods in order to hasten its adoption even more than Peter hastened the adoption of westernism by barbarous Russia,

---

[1] Ibid. xxii, 378. Bronsky, who went to Berlin to conduct economic negotiations with Germany after Brest-Litovsk, related that, when he explained Soviet economic policy to German officials, they replied : " What you plan is being carried out by us ; what you call ' communism ' we call ' state control ' " (Trudy I Vserossiiskogo S"ezda Sovetov Narodnogo Khozyaistva (1916), p. 157). Lenin would have accepted the comparison, but never called it either communism or socialism.

not shrinking from barbarous weapons to fight barbarism ".[1] It seems to be the only admiring reference to Peter the Great — or perhaps to any other Russian Tsar — in Lenin's works. Lenin thus distinguished quite sharply between the first and second periods of the revolution. The business of " crushing the resistance of the exploiters " had in the main been accomplished " in the period from November 7 (October 25) 1917 down to (approximately) February, 1918 ". On the other hand "our work of organizing proletarian accountancy and control has, plainly and obviously for every thinking man, *fallen behind* the immediate task of expropriating the expropriators ". What lay ahead in the next period was " the radical task of creating a higher social order than capitalism " ; and this meant " to raise the productivity of labour, and in connexion with this (and for this) to organize it more highly ". For the first period the slogan, " Loot what has been looted from you ", was perfectly correct ; in the second the motto ought to be, " Keep account of what has been looted, and do not allow it to be dissipated, and if any one tries to appropriate it directly or indirectly for himself such disturbers of discipline should be shot ".[2] In the first period it had been important to stress socialist hostility to the state, the need to smash the bourgeois state machine : this he had emphasized in *State and Revolution*. But when Bukharin reviewed *State and Revolution* in *Kommunist* in April 1918, he had quoted only " what is already . . . obsolete, what is the affair of yesterday " ; he had been silent about the task of tomorrow, about " everything that concerns accounting, control and discipline ".[3] In the first period, " workers' control " had been the prevalent slogan ; now this was forgotten in the new emphasis on organization as the road to socialism :

In the Tsar's day we organized thousands, and in Kerensky's hundreds of thousands. That is nothing, that does not count

---

[1] Lenin, *Sochineniya*, xxii, 516-517 ; in quoting this passage nearly three years later Lenin deliberately or accidentally omitted the reference to Peter (*ibid.* xxvi, 326).

[2] *Ibid.* xxii, 493. There is no terse idiomatic English translation of the famous phrase, *Grab' Nagrablennoe* ; Lenin here calls it the equivalent of " the expropriation of the expropriators ", but " without Latin words ".

[3] *Ibid.* xxii, 489 ; the reproach against Bukharin, who had attempted to discredit Lenin's present attitude by recalling the anti-state views of *State and Revolution*, was repeated in On " *Left* " *Infantilism and the Petty-Bourgeois Spirit* (*ibid.* xxii, 527-528).

in politics. That was preparatory work. That was the preparatory class. Until the vanguard of the workers learn to organize
tens of millions, they are not yet socialists and not creators of
the socialist society, and will not acquire the necessary experience of organization. The road of organization is a long road,
and the tasks of socialist construction demand persistent prolonged work and corresponding experience, of which we have
not enough. Even the next immediately following generation,
better developed than ours, will scarcely effect the full transition
to socialism.[1]

Lenin at this time drove home the importance of organization in
terms that were perhaps intentionally hyperbolic. If a merchant
told him that there had been an improvement on some railway,
" such praise seems to me a thousand times more valuable than
twenty communist resolutions ". The railways were the " key ",
were " one of the manifestations of the most palpable link between
town and country, between industry and agriculture, on which
socialism is entirely based ".[2] Here can be seen a foretaste of the
way in which two years later Lenin's imagination was to be captured by the panacea of electrification.

In May 1918 a halt was called to the controversy about the
organization of industry, which ended without a decisive victory
for either side. On the one hand, the proposal for a deal with the
capitalists was rejected, and not renewed; the possibility of a
compromise with the industrialists under the banner of " state
capitalism " had disappeared. On the other hand, the plea of the
Left opposition for local autonomy and " workers' control "
received short shrift: organization and centralization were the
mottoes of the day. The rejection of the Meshchersky plan was
followed by a conference of the metallurgical industry called by
Vesenkha in Moscow in the middle of May to discuss nationalization. The conference was composed mainly of representatives of
the workers and technical staffs of the enterprises concerned, and
was presided over by Larin. A letter was read to the conference
from Lenin, who in the name of Sovnarkom declared in favour
of nationalization on the understanding that this implied the

---

[1] Lenin, *Sochineniya*, xxii, 487.   [2] *Ibid.* xxii, 494.

unification of the different enterprises under a single administration including engineers and specialists, and that regulations should be adopted providing for " strict labour discipline ". The technicians abstained from voting, but did not otherwise obstruct the proceedings. The logic of the situation was imperative : once the Meshchersky project of half-and-half nationalization was rejected, full nationalization was the only conceivable alternative. The result of the conference was a resolution endorsing " the immediate nationalization of the factories and the establishment of unification " ; and a temporary committee was appointed, under the aegis of Vesenkha to organize the " united state metallurgical factories " (Gomza) — the first and largest of the trusts set up by Vesenkha in pursuance of Lenin's principle of " enforced trustification ".[1] A fortnight earlier a decree of Sovnarkom had nationalized the sugar industry [2] — the first industry other than transport to be dealt with as a single entity.

The first All-Russian Congress of Councils of National Economy assembled in Moscow on May 26, 1918. It was planned as a kind of economic parliament. Rather more than 100 voting delegates were drawn from Vesenkha and its *glavki* and centres, from regional and local Sovnarkhozy or other economic organs, and from the trade unions ; in addition there were nearly 150 nonvoting delegates.[3] Rykov, who had recently been appointed president of Vesenkha,[4] presided at the congress. The voices of the Left opposition were once again raised. Bukharin, whose function was the formal one of bringing greetings to the congress from the central committee of the party, observed a little tartly that there were some who, " instead of raising the banner ' forward to communism ', raise the banner 'back to capitalism ' ". Obolensky feared that under the new dispensation " the keys of production remain in the hands of the capitalists ". Lomov, who reminded the congress that the phrase about learning socialism from the

---

[1] Lenin, *Sochineniya*, xxiii, 22 ; for accounts of the conference see *ibid.* xxiii, 538-539, note 4, and J. Bunyan, *Intervention, Civil War, and Communism in Russia* (Baltimore, 1936), pp. 379-381.

[2] *Sobranie Uzakonenii, 1917-1918*, No. 34, art. 457.

[3] *Trudy I Vserossiiskogo S"ezda Sovetov Narodnogo Khozyaistva* (1918), pp. vi-x, 82 (where there is an obvious misprint in the total number of delegates).

[4] Rykov's unimpeachable Bolshevik record and colourless opinions probably secured him preference over Larin, an ex-Menshevik ; Larin and Milyutin remained directors of the " economic policy section " of Vesenkha.

capitalists had been coined in the eighteen-nineties by the " quasi-Marxist " (and present bourgeois) Struve, fought a rear-guard action in defence of workers' control, and struck the note which was to become characteristic of all opposition groups for several years to come :

> We are by every means — by nationalization, by centralization — strangling the forces of our country. The masses are being cut off from living creative power in all branches of our national economy.[1]

But the hard fact of the practical need to increase and organize production at whatever theoretical sacrifice dominated the congress. Milyutin, making the principal report, was criticized not so much for his proposals as for his optimistic estimates of the future ; and Rykov, as president of Vesenkha, came out for a thorough-going policy of nationalization. The haphazard methods hitherto pursued had been neither an effective antidote to economic anarchy nor an effective contribution to the building of socialism. The nationalization of separate enterprises was not socialism ; if anything, it was syndicalism. Even the nationalization of industries was not enough.

> I have always thought [said Rykov] that it was possible to organize a socialist *society* provided that there was an international socialist revolution ; but to organize a socialist *branch of industry*, to socialize a particular factory or works — excuse me, but hitherto no socialist has ever made such proposals, or can make them.[2]

But while the pure doctrine of the incompatibility of an economy half socialist, half capitalist, was thus uncompromisingly proclaimed, it was also necessary to admit that " we are in a position to nationalize, and to administer nationalized enterprises, only in a part of industry ", and it would therefore be necessary to begin with the most important.[3] The key resolution of the congress struck this comparatively modest note :

> In the sphere of the organization of production it is indispensable to complete the work of nationalization, and from the

---

[1] *Ibid.* pp. 7, 63, 73, 75.   [2] *Ibid.* p. 98.   [3] *Ibid.* p. 113.

process of nationalizing separate enterprises (of which 304 have been nationalized and sequestered) to pass over to the consistent nationalization of branches of industry, and, as one of the first priorities, of the metal-working, machine-building, chemical, oil and textile industries. The process of nationalization should lose its incidental character and be carried out exclusively either by Vesenkha or by Sovnarkom at the instance of Vesenkha.[1]

The congress also adopted resolutions on trade, finance and labour discipline. There was even an agrarian section which passed resolutions, including one on the desirability of communal farms; but the full congress had no time to consider these.[2] The general effect of the proceedings was both to narrow and to strengthen the authority of Vesenkha. Its concentration on the organization of industry as its principal function was confirmed, and within this field it became supreme.[3] A concerted Soviet industrial policy became possible for the first time in May 1918, though shortage of resources, and above all of qualified personnel, continued to militate against the effective execution of policy.

Events were soon, however, to force the pace. Even while the first All-Russian Congress of Councils of National Economy was in session in Moscow, the Czech legions were taking up arms in the Urals; the month of June saw the rapid development of civil war and the beginnings of allied intervention. All this was calculated to produce an increase of nervous tension in Moscow and an urgent need for stricter organization and control of industry. But the immediate impulse to action came from another quarter. The German occupation of the Ukraine after Brest-Litovsk had quickened German interest in Russian resources; and shares in Russian heavy industry were apparently being bought on a large scale by German groups. If this process went on, an important part of

---

[1] *Trudy I Vserossiiskogo S"ezda Sovetov Narodnogo Khozyaistva* (1918), p. 473.

[2] *Ibid.* pp. 273-274, 460-463.

[3] The rise of Vesenkha was achieved in part at the expense of the People's Commissariat of Trade and Industry which, evicted from the field of industrial policy, found its functions confined mainly to the control of foreign trade. The evolution of this commissariat was described by the deputy commissar Bronsky at the first All-Russian Congress of Councils of National Economy in May 1918 (*Ibid.* pp. 161-162). Vesenkha even set up a foreign trade section with a staff of 39 (*Narodnoe Khozyaistvo*, No. 1, 1918, p. 11); but there is little evidence of its activity in this field.

Russian industry would pass into German ownership, and German diplomatic intervention against nationalization was to be feared. According to some reports, the German Ambassador at Moscow, Mirbach, had already received instructions to protest.[1]

These fears led to dramatic action. On June 28, 1918, after an all-night sitting, Sovnarkom issued a decree nationalizing every important category of industry. The aims of the decree, as stated in a short preamble, were " a decisive struggle against disorganization in production and supply " and " the strengthening of the dictatorship of the working class and of the poor peasantry " — an attempt to establish a rather illusory parallel between it and the institution of committees of poor peasants as an instrument of agrarian policy. The industries, whose total assets were now declared " the property of the Russian Socialist Federal Soviet Republic " were the mining, metallurgical, textile, electrical, timber, tobacco, resin, glass and pottery, leather and cement industries, all steam-driven mills, local utilities and private railways, together with a few minor industries. But after this brave beginning the makers of the decree showed a keen consciousness of the distinction, on which both Lenin and Rykov had in their turn insisted, between nationalizing an enterprise and administering it when nationalized. The task of " organizing the administration of nationalized enterprises " was entr·sted " as a matter of urgency " to Vesenkha and its sections. But, until such time as Vesenkha issued specific instructions regarding individual enterprises covered by the decree, such enterprises would be regarded

---

[1] No proof appears to exist of projected German action ; but that fear of such action was the motive of the hasty issue of an omnibus decree is confirmed by two independent witnesses (M. Philips Price, *My Reminiscences of the Russian Revolution* (1921), pp. 285-286 ; S. Liberman, *Building Lenin's Russia* (Chicago, 1945), pp. 24-26). Radek, at the first All-Russian Congress of Councils of National Economy a month earlier, had spoken of the need to " buy out the shares of German citizens in Russian enterprises ", and complained that the bourgeoisie was " trying by all means to sell its shares to German citizens, and trying to obtain German legal support by all sorts of forgeries and all sorts of fictitious deals " (*Trudy I Vserossiiskogo S"ezda Sovetov Narodnogo Khozyaistva* (1918), p. 16). Bronsky (quoted in Y. S. Rozenfeld, *Promyshlennaya Politika SSSR* (1926), pp. 99-100) gives a somewhat different version. Since the conclusion of the Brest-Litovsk treaty, negotiations with the German Government had been proceeding in Berlin (Bronsky was head of the Soviet delegation) to fix *inter alia* a lump sum compensation for German properties seized in Russia : the Soviet Government was anxious to get as many properties as possible nationalized before the agreement was concluded.

as leased rent-free to their former owners, who would continue to finance them and to draw revenue from them; and directors and staff were forbidden under penalties to abandon their posts.[1] The decree of June 28, 1918, thus maintained the distinction between the legal transfer of ownership to the state, which did not by itself entail any practical consequences, and the practical assumption by the state of responsibility for administration. The first step had now been hastily completed, so far as major industries were concerned, under the threat of German intervention. The second step was pushed forward — and probably at a much more rapid rate than the makers of this decree contemplated — by the civil war.

(c) Labour and the Trade Unions

The Marxist programme constituted what was fundamentally a " labour " policy. It drew the logical deductions from the theory that labour is the sole source of value; and it made the proletariat the main instrument and the main beneficiary of the coming revolution. If it sometimes seemed indifferent to the demands which normally figured in " labour " platforms, this was because these demands presupposed acceptance of the capitalist system and were relevant only for so long as that system continued to exist. Hence such demands could be only secondary; the main purpose of the workers must always be the overthrow of capitalism, not the improvement of their own position within it. The items which figured as the minimum demands of the workers in the *Communist Manifesto* and in later party programmes inspired by it were important not so much for their own sake, but as means to a revolutionary end. What happened to parties which concentrated exclusively or excessively on these minimum demands was shown by the example of the " revisionists " in Germany and of the " Economists " in Russia. Having these examples in mind, the Bolsheviks were unlikely to forget that they were a revolutionary and not a " reformist " party; their labour policy had to be considered in the light of this criterion. On the other hand, they could not disinterest themselves in the practical demands of the workers which might receive some measure of satisfaction even

---

[1] *Sobranie Uzakonenii, 1917–1918*, No. 47, art. 559.

under bourgeois rule. The party programme adopted by the second congress in 1903 contained demands for the eight-hour day, the weekly rest day and other familiar points of a labour programme.

The same element of uncertainty and compromise was present in the Bolshevik attitude to the trade unions. The First International had picked its way delicately between those of its members (mainly the English group) who thought trade-unionism all important and those (mainly French and German) who were inclined to dismiss it as irrelevant to the revolutionary struggle. A resolution passed by the Geneva congress in 1866 recognized that trade unions were necessary and vital " so long as capitalism exists ", but warned them against the pursuit of " narrow " aims and urged them to " strive for the general liberation of the oppressed millions of working people ".[1] This resolution was quoted by Lenin in 1899 in the protest against the so-called *credo* of the Economists, who would have confined the activity of the working class to the " economic struggle " of trade-unionism.[2] Tradition was preserved in the habit of Lenin and other Bolshevik writers of using the phrase " trade-unionism " (in English) in a pejorative sense. In *What is to be Done?* Lenin wrote that the Economists " constantly lapse from social-democracy into trade-unionism ", argued that " the political struggle of social democracy is far broader and more complex than the economic struggle of the workers with the employers and with the government ", and thought that social-democrats, while they should work in the unions, should make no attempt to build up social-democratic trade-unions.[3] The principle of " non-party " unions was upheld by Bolsheviks and Mensheviks alike at the fourth party congress in

---

[1] The resolution was based on an " instruction " to the delegates of the central council written by Marx, who was not present at the congress. The " day-to-day activity " of the trade unions in the struggle against employers was recognized as " not only legitimate, but indispensable ". On the other hand, " if the trade unions are necessary for partisan warfare between capital and labour, they are still more important as *an organizing force for the destruction of the very system of hired labour and the power of capital* " : their chief task could be nothing short of the " complete liberation " of the working class (Marx i Engels, *Sochineniya*, xiii, i, 201-202).

[2] Lenin, *Sochineniya*, ii, 480-482 ; for the controversy with the Economists see Vol. 1, pp. 10-12.

[3] *Ibid.*, iv, 447-448.

Stockholm in 1906, and embodied in the resolution of the congress.[1]
The London congress of 1907, while reaffirming this resolution,
drew attention to the need for " ideological leadership of the social-
democratic party in the trade unions ";[2] and later in the year
Lenin announced his conversion to the view that the neutrality
of the trade unions was " *in principle* indefensible ".[3] In the next
year the central committee rallied to this thesis, which henceforth
took its place as accepted party teaching.[4] The tendency to treat
the trade union movement as ancillary to the party and an instrument of party policy was inherent in Bolshevik doctrine, and was
strengthened by every move to promote more active participation
by the party in the unions.[5]

The Bolshevik attitude to labour policy and the trade unions
reflected Russian conditions. Before 1905 no programme for the
improvement of labour conditions offered any prospect of success,
and only an embryonic trade union movement existed. Serious
strikes occurred, but these were sporadic and spontaneous out-
bursts of revolt against intolerable hardships. In 1905 the recalcitrant workers organized themselves not in trade unions but in
Soviets — bodies which had from the first a political and revolutionary complexion. The first Russian trade union conferences
were held in 1905 and 1906 ; but, in the period of repression which
followed, the trade unions suffered scarcely less than the political
parties of the Left. The February revolution of 1917 brought a
revival of the trade unions and a large accession of membership.
The rôle of the trade unions in the period between the February
and October revolutions has already been described.[6] The sixth
party congress of August 1917, in its resolution " On the Economic
Situation ", referred to the trade unions, the factory committees and
the Soviets of Workers' Deputies as " workers' organizations "
without attempting to distinguish between their character and
functions.[7] But the trade unions were eclipsed in the conscious-

[1] *VKP(B) v Rezolyutsiyakh* (1941), i, 79-80.
[2] *Ibid.* i, 108.   [3] Lenin, *Sochineniya*, xii, 66.   [4] *Ibid.* xii, 138.
[5] It was significant that in Great Britain, where the trade unions were older
than the Labour Party, any move for closer relations between them meant more
effective control over the party by the unions, and that in Germany, where they
had grown more or less simultaneously, prolonged rivalry ended in a doctrine
of equal partnership ; the Bolshevik view was at the opposite extreme to the
British.   [6] See pp. 62-63 above.
[7] *VKP(B) v Rezolyutsiyakh* (1941) i, 257.

ness of the most radical and active of the workers by the power of the Soviets ; [1] and, as between the trade unions and the factory committees, the Bolsheviks down to the moment of the October revolution had every motive to support the committees, which were revolutionary in outlook and contained a Bolshevik majority, against the trade unions, which stood for the orderly organization of labour and were predominantly Menshevik.

The turning-point in the Bolshevik attitude came quickly after the victory of the Soviet power.   The Russian trade unions, born late in the day and in established conditions of large-scale industrial organization, had tended to grow up on the basis not of individual trades and crafts, but of industries as a whole.   Most Russian trade unions were for this reason not only more comprehensive and more generalized in their membership than their western counterparts, but more disposed to regard themselves as representatives of the workers as a whole rather than of a particular

[1] An important reason why, both before and after October 1917, the Soviets were bound to count for more than the trade unions was that they represented the soldiers (i.e. the peasants) as well as the workers.   Zinoviev at the first All-Russian Congress of Trade Unions in January 1918, contrasting the Soviets of 1917 with those of 1905, noted that " their strength consists in the fact that the soldiers united with the workers " (*Pervyi Vserossiiskii S"ezd Professional'nykh Soyuzov* (1918), p. 72).   But the sense of a certain overlap between the Soviets and the trade unions was a foretaste of the dilemma of the trade unions under socialism : where the organs of government were professedly representative organs of the workers, what place was left for trade unions of the conventional kind ?   Conversely, the Mensheviks, asserting the exclusive claim of the trade unions to represent the workers, logically denied that the Soviets represented the workers (see the Menshevik resolution at the second All-Russian Congress of Trade Unions referred to on p. 200 below).   Jealousy between Soviets and trade unions still persisted, at any rate locally, as late as the winter of 1920-1921 ; during the trade union controversy at that time, the view was widely held, according to Zinoviev, in provincial party circles that the existence of the Soviets made trade unions superfluous (*Partiya i Soyuzy*, ed. G. E. Zinoviev (1921), pp. 3-4).   Among the champions of this view was Myasnikov (*ibid.* pp. 282-287), who was expelled from the party a few months later (see Vol. 1, pp. 207-208).   The same issue arose when Soviets were set up in Germany in November 1918.   At the founding congress of the German Communist Party in December 1918 one delegate proposed the slogan, " Get out of the trade unions ", and even Rosa Luxemburg thought the trade unions were destined to disappear, being replaced by Councils of Workers' and Soldiers' Deputies and by the factory committees (*Bericht über die Verhandlungen des Gründungparteitages der KPD* (1919), pp. 16, 80) ; the Left wing of the German Independent Social-Democratic Party also argued at this time that the trade unions must be absorbed into the system of Councils of Workers' Deputies (E. Prager, *Geschichte der USPD* (1922), p. 192).

professional group.[1]   This tradition, encouraged by the quasi-
revolutionary situation in which the Russian trade unions had been
compelled to operate, fitted in perfectly with the new constructive
needs of Soviet policy.   In the first place, the revolutionary
government hastened to enact such measures of labour legislation
as had long been familiar in western democratic countries, though
without much regard to their practicability in existing Russian
conditions.   Four days after the revolution a decree was issued
establishing the principle of the 8-hour day and the 48-hour week,
placing limitations on the work of women and juveniles and forbidding the employment of children under 14.[2]   Provision for
social insurance against unemployment and sickness was made in
decrees of December 11/24, 1917, and December 22, 1917/January
4, 1918.[3]   To carry out this policy of " protective " labour legislation was impossible without the cooperation of a central organ
representative of the workers.   The trade unions stepped into the
breach, and their position was correspondingly strengthened.   In
default of other machinery, they were charged with the administration of social insurance under the decrees of December 1917.[4]
Secondly, the Soviet Government now urgently needed a counter-
weight to the growing anarchy of the factory committees and
workers' control, and found it in an organization which claimed to
represent the general, as against the sectional, interests of the
working class.   Here, too, the trade unions came triumphantly
into their own.   The subordination of the factory committees to
orderly trade union organization became the goal of Soviet, as
well as of trade union, policy.

[1] Tomsky told the visiting British Labour delegation in 1920 : " Our tactics
differ entirely from those adopted in England or the United States.   In those
countries the unions are trying to improve conditions for their own members
only ; here we are trying to improve conditions for the entire working class "
(*British Labour Delegation to Russia, 1920 : Report* (1920), p. 118).

[2] *Sobranie Uzakonenii, 1917–1918*, No. 1 (2nd ed.), art. 6.   A year later
Narkomtrud issued an instruction requiring the enforcement of the parts of
this decree limiting the working day of juveniles and forbidding the employment
of children, which had admittedly not been carried out ; at the end of 1918 a
further decree was issued prohibiting the employment of children (*Sobranie
Uzakonenii, 1919*, No. 1, art. 7).   Such prohibitions were of little effect in the
period of acute labour shortage in the civil war.

[3] *Sobranie Uzakonenii, 1917–1918*, No. 8, art. 111 ; No. 13, art. 188.

[4] Even earlier the trade unions had acquired the beginnings of an official
status by the admission of 50 trade union representatives to the expanded
VTsIK (see Vol. I, p. 111).

The new alliance between government and trade unions was publicly sealed at the first All-Russian Congress of Trade Unions which met in Petrograd in January 1918 at the moment of the dismissal of the Constituent Assembly. The success of the October revolution had affected the political complexion of the unions : out of a total of 416 voting delegates 273 were Bolsheviks and 66 Mensheviks.[1] The future relation between government and trade unions at once became the cardinal issue of the congress and the subject of its most stubborn debates. It was complicated by the attitude of Lozovsky, who, while championing the alliance between government and unions for the purpose of overcoming the anarchy of workers' control, had spoken and written with his customary vigour on the need to keep the trade unions wholly independent of the organs of political authority, and had resigned, or been expelled, from the Bolshevik party. Ryazanov, the other leading Bolshevik in the central council of the trade unions, retained his party membership, but was known to hold opinions not far removed from those of Lozovsky. At the congress Zinoviev, who appeared as principal delegate of the Bolshevik party, attacked the " independence " of the trade unions : this slogan, which had formerly meant independence from the bourgeoisie, could mean nothing under a workers' government except the right to " support saboteurs ". The trade unions had already become a part of the Soviet power by sending their delegates to VTsIK. On the other hand, Zinoviev disclaimed any intention to ban strikes (the issue of nationalized industries had scarcely yet arisen) ; the government would even make a contribution to strike funds. The chief Menshevik spokesmen, Maisky and

---

[1] *Pervyi Vserossiiskii S"ezd Professional'nykh Soyuzov* (1918), p. 338. The process by which Bolshevik control was secured varied from union to union and would require a separate study. In some cases the rank and file of the unions was predominantly Bolshevik in sympathy from the start : at the founding congress of the All-Russian Metal Workers' Union in January 1918 there were 75 Bolshevik delegates, 20 Mensheviks, 52 non-party delegates and a handful of Left SRs and other small groups (*Professional'nye Soyuzy SSSR*, ed. Y. K. Milonov (1927), p. 119) ; at the first All-Russian congress of textile workers in the same month 52 per cent of the delegates were Bolsheviks (*ibid.* p. 135). On the other hand, it was not till March 1918 that a majority was secured, by more or less high-handed means, in the Postal and Telegraph Workers' Union (*ibid.* pp. 325-326), where the course of events was broadly similar to that in the railwaymen's union (see pp. 394-395 below) ; and the printers' union long remained a Menshevik stronghold.

Martov, argued that, since the revolution was a bourgeois-democratic revolution and could not be anything more, the trade unions had still to perform their customary functions in complete independence of the state. Lozovsky, having defended his attitude since the October revolution, cleverly took a middle position. He dissociated himself strongly from the views of Zinoviev, deprecating the idea that the unions should forthwith become " organs of state " whose decisions would be " carried out by compulsion ". But he accepted the conclusion also implicit in the argument of the Mensheviks that, once socialism was achieved, the objection to the absorption of the unions into the state machine would disappear. The main congress resolution, while hailing the revolution as the " socialist revolution ", reflected a degree of compromise with Lozovsky's more cautious views in regard to the time-table :

> In their developed form the trade unions should, in the process of the present socialist revolution, become organs of socialist power. . . . In consequence of the process thus foreshadowed, the trade unions will inevitably be transformed into organs of the socialist state, and for those employed in industry participation in the trade unions will be part of their duty to the state.[1]

The first All-Russian Congress of Trade Unions thus virtually settled the principle of the subordination of the trade unions to the state, which now remained uncontested, except by the Mensheviks, for nearly three years. But the fundamental question of labour policy in a socialist economy had been barely skimmed. The resolution declared that the unions " must undertake the chief burden of organizing production and of rehabilitating the country's shattered productive resources " ; and it was in this spirit that it listed " the most urgent tasks " of the unions as being " energetic participation in all central bodies regulating output, the organization of workers' control, the registration and redistribution of the labour force, the organization of exchange between town and country, active participation in the demobilization of industry, the struggle against sabotage, the enforcement of the general obligation to work etc." [2] The factory committees were once again a bone of contention. One anarchist delegate

---

[1] *Pervyi Vserossiiskii S"ezd Professional'nykh Soyuzov* (1918), pp. 38, 73-75, 97-98, 364-365.   [2] *Ibid.* p. 364.

described them as " cells of the coming socialist social order, the order without political power "; another referred to the trade unions by way of contrast as " living corpses ". But the congress had little difficulty in passing a resolution which proclaimed that " factory and workshop committees should become local organs of the corresponding trade unions ".[1] The incorporation of the factory committees in the centralized trade union system meant that the particular interest of small groups of workers must yield place to the general interest of the proletariat as a whole; and it could not be denied that the general interest in the winter of 1917–1918 and for many years after consisted primarily in " organizing production " and " rehabilitating the country's shattered resources ". Much was omitted from that argument. But within its limits it was valid. One corollary of the acceptance of this rôle by the trade unions was the striking of a close alliance between the central council of trade unions and Vesenkha. Both had suffered from the factory committees; both had the same belief in centralization; and both upheld the cause of industrial production against the claims of other sections of the economy. If in capitalist countries employers and trade unions sometimes discovered a common interest against the consumer or against the agriculturalist, this common interest was reflected in Soviet Russia in the relation between these two important organs. By March 1918 the fusion between Soviet and trade union organs and functions had progressed far. Most of the officials of the People's Commissariat of Labour (Narkomtrud), as well as its regional and local representatives (the so-called " labour commissars "), were now nominated by the trade unions; and, according to an article by Shmidt in the official journal of Narkomtrud, " the whole question is how most practically to carry out the fusion which must come about between the All-Russian Central Council of Trade Unions and the People's Commissariat of Labour ".[2]

The congress with its Bolshevik majority had elected a new All-Russian Central Council of Trade Unions with Zinoviev as president and Shmidt as secretary in place of the errant and not yet penitent Lozovsky. Zinoviev, however, was too much occupied with other functions, and in March 1918, when the headquarters of

[1] *Ibid.* pp. 85, 101, 374.
[2] *Vestnik Narodnogo Komissariata Truda*, No. 2-3, 1918, pp. 27-28.

the council moved with the government to Moscow, was succeeded by Tomsky, a Bolshevik worker who remained the dominant figure in the Soviet trade union movement for ten years and did much to build up its prestige. From January onwards the trade unions acquired recognition as the agents and executors of a labour policy in the framing of which they could exercise a consultative voice. It was readily accepted that the main immediate object of that policy, and therefore of the trade unions, must be to organize and increase production. It was more slowly realized that the condition of increased production — or of a stay in its rapid decline — was the organization of labour and the enforcement of labour discipline, and that this would therefore prove to be the major task of the trade unions in the years ahead.

The acceptance of this uncongenial principle came in a roundabout way. As early as May 1917 Lenin had spoken at the All-Russian Peasants' Congress of the eventual need for " labour service " to recruit workers for large-scale agricultural units.[1] In September 1917 he had written in more general language that " life ", in passing beyond the capitalist framework, had placed " universal labour service " on the order of the day.[2] On the eve of the revolution, in a striking passage of *Will the Bolsheviks Retain State Power?*, he noted with satisfaction that " the grain monopoly and bread cards have been created not by us, but by the capitalist state at war " : the capitalist state had also created " universal labour service within the framework of capitalism, that is to say, military penal servitude for the workers ". These were all ready-made implements which the workers would take over and apply to the capitalists — " *and to the rich* in general ", added Lenin. The French revolution had guillotined its enemies ; the proletarian revolution would compel them to work for it. " He that does not work, neither shall he eat ", quoted Lenin, adding that this was " the fundamental, primary and principal rule which the Soviets of Workers' Deputies can and will put into effect when they become the rulers." [3] The implied hope that, if compulsion were applied to the capitalists, it would not be required for the workers did not long survive the victory of the revolution. But to

[1] Lenin, *Sochineniya*, xx, 417: the term " labour service " (*trudovaya povinnost'*) was framed on the analogy of " military service " (*voennaya povinnost'*) and always carried the connotation of compulsion.

[2] *Ibid.* xxi, 233.   [3] *Ibid.* xxi, 263-264.

abandon it publicly was not easy. When labour exchanges were set up by a decree of January 1918 it was made obligatory for employers to engage labour exclusively through them, but the only formal obligation placed on the worker was to register at the exchange if unemployed.[1] Shmidt spoke at the congress of January 1918 of those guilty of " sabotage " and " opposition to the policy pursued by the working class in the person of its governmental representatives ", and thought that " we shall not be able to avoid using power to compel them to do the work which they have to do ".[2] In an article written in the same month Lenin once more quoted " he that does not work, neither shall he eat " as " the *practical* creed of socialism ", and slipped in " workers who slack at their work " among the categories of misdemeanants who deserved to be " put in prison ".[3] But the article was put aside and not published; and the issue remained in abeyance for another two months.

The Brest-Litovsk crisis and the drive to halt the galloping decline in industrial production made the question of labour discipline and labour incentives inescapable. The seventh party congress, which decided early in March 1918 on acceptance of the treaty, demanded " the most energetic, unsparingly decisive, draconian measures to raise the self-discipline and discipline of workers and peasants "; [4] and the fourth All-Russian Congress of Soviets which formally ratified it a week later also advocated the " raising of the activity and self-discipline of the workers ".[5] The issue was broached in a report to a session of Vesenkha by Milyutin who spoke of " the question of labour service, labour service in the broad sense of the term, not the kind of labour service which has been applied in the west,[6] not the kind of service which is thought of here by the masses and which says

---

[1] *Sobranie Uzakonenii, 1917-1918*, No. 21, art. 319.
[2] *Pervyi Vserossiiskii S"ezd Professional'nykh Soyuzov* (1918), p. 108.
[3] Lenin, *Sochineniya*, xxii, 166-167.
[4] *VKP(B) v Rezolyutsiyakh* (1941), i, 278.
[5] *S"ezdy Sovetov RSFSR v Postanovleniyakh* (1939), p. 69.
[6] Larin had just published a pamphlet on the subject *Trudovaya Povinnost' i Rabochii Kontrol'* (1918) which drew extensively on the experience of labour mobilization in war-time Germany; a leading article on the pamphlet in the official *Vestnik Narodnogo Komissariata Truda*, No. 2-3, 1918, pp. 385-387, was evidently concerned to remove the unfortunate impression which might be made by this precedent.

that all must be put to work, but labour service as a system of labour discipline and as a system of the organization of labour in the interests of production ". Such a scheme, he added, could be " based only on the independence and iron self-discipline of the masses of the working class ".[1] But it was the central council of trade unions which ultimately took over the responsibility, and on April 3, 1918, issued a " regulation " on the whole question — the first detailed pronouncement of the régime on discipline and incentives for labour, and on the functions of the trade unions in regard to them. In conditions of " economic disintegration " which threatened to bring about " the extinction of the proletariat, the trade unions saw themselves obliged to " apply all their efforts to raise the productivity of labour and consistently to create in factories and workshops the indispensable foundations of labour discipline ". Every trade union must establish a commission " to fix norms of productivity for every trade and every category of workers ". The use of piece-rates " to raise the productivity of labour " was somewhat grudgingly conceded ; and " bonuses for increased productivity above the established norm of work may within certain limits be a useful measure for raising productivity without exhausting the worker ". Finally, if " individual groups of workers " refuse to submit to union discipline, they may in the last resort be expelled from the union " with all the consequences that flow therefrom ".[2]

These regulations soon provoked criticism. The Left opposition, in its theses read at the party gathering of April 4, 1918, and published a fortnight later in *Kommunist*,[3] referred indignantly to " a labour policy designed to implant discipline among the workers under the flag of ' self-discipline ', the introduction of labour service for workers, . . . of piece-rates, of the lengthening of the working-day, etc.", and argued that " the introduction of labour

---

[1] V. P. Milyutin, *Istoriya Ekonomicheskogo Razvitiya SSSR* (2nd ed., 1929), pp. 137-138 ; the published records of this session of Vesenkha have not been available. According to Lenin, *Sochineniya*, xxii, 622, note 186, Lenin was present at two meetings of the presidium of Vesenkha at which these proposals were discussed. It was undecided at this time whether or not to entrust the question to the trade unions ; among the projects canvassed was that of " workbooks ". " Capitalists, engineers and technicians " were also to be asked for their views on labour discipline.

[2] *Narodnoe Khozyaistvo*, No. 2, 1918, p. 38.

[3] For the theses and the journal of the Left opposition, see pp. 89-90 above.

discipline coupled with the restoration of the leadership of the capitalists in production . . . threatens the enslavement of the working class and excites the discontent not only of backward strata, but of the vanguard of the proletariat ".[1] The Menshevik journal declared that the Bolsheviks " under the flag of a restoration of the productive forces of the country are attempting to abolish the eight-hour day and introduce piece-rates and Taylorism "[2] — Taylorism being a once famous American system for increasing the efficiency of labour which Lenin had long ago described as " the enslavement of man by the machine ".[3] In VTsIK Lenin took up the challenge. It was only " the declassed petty bourgeois intelligentsia " which " does not understand that the chief difficulty for socialism consists in guaranteeing the discipline of labour " ; and " our dictatorship of the proletariat is the guarantee of the order, discipline, and productivity of labour ".[4] In the first draft of his pamphlet on *Current Tasks of the Soviet Power*, conceived as a considered reply to the Left opposition, he wrote of " the task of guaranteeing the strictest application of discipline and self-discipline of the workers " and added :

> We should be ridiculous utopians if we imagined that such a task could be carried out on the day after the fall of the power of the bourgeoisie, i.e. in the first stage of the transition from capitalism to socialism, or — without compulsion.[5]

In the published text discretion made him somewhat less explicit :

> A condition of economic revival is an improvement in the discipline of the workers, in knowing how to work, in speed and intensity of work, in its better organization. . . .
> The most conscious vanguard of the Russian proletariat has already assumed the task of improving labour discipline. . . . This work must be supported and pressed forward with all our might. Piece-rates must be put on the agenda, applied in practice and tried out ; we must apply much that is scientific and progressive in the Taylor system, wages must be brought into line with general totals of output or of results in terms of exploitation of railway and water transport, etc.[6]

[1] Quoted in Lenin, *Sochineniya*, xxii, 569.
[2] Quoted *ibid.* xxii, 625, note 201.   [3] *Ibid.* xvii, 247-248.
[4] *Ibid.* xxii, 486.   [5] *Ibid.* xxii, 424.
[6] *Ibid.* xxii, 454. A work on *The System of Taylor* was published in Moscow in 1918 ; its second edition was noticed by Lenin in 1922 (*Sochineniya*, xxvii, 302).

It is noteworthy that the strongest feelings were aroused at this time not by projects for compulsory labour service, but by the introduction of piece-rates and other forms of discriminatory rewards as incentives to higher production. What was at stake here was not so much the question of labour discipline, but the issue of equality. It was the division of labour under capitalism which, in the words of the *Communist Manifesto*, had made the worker " an appendage of the machine ". It was the accepted goal of socialists to do away with the differences between industrial and agricultural labour, between intellectual and manual work as the prelude to the establishment of an egalitarian society.[1] It must therefore be socialist policy to pay equal wages to all. Engels had praised the Paris commune for having " paid to all officials from the highest to the lowest only the same wages paid to other workers " ; and he argued that, since under socialism the education and training of the worker would be paid for by society, the more highly skilled worker could have no claim against the state for higher rewards than the less skilled.[2] These arguments, however, seemed to blur the dividing-line between immediate possibilities and ultimate goal. When Marx in his *Critique of the Gotha Programme* differentiated between the lower and higher phases of " communist society ", he made it plain that at the lower stage distribution would still be carried out not according to needs, but according to work done. Until production flowed abundantly enough to permit the full realization of communism with its principle " to each according to his needs ", equal rewards for equal work, though essentially a principle of inequality (since individual capacities are always unequal), was the only form of equality conceivable.[3] None the less Lenin in *State and Revolution*, written on the eve of the October revolution, treated it as " an immediate object " so to organize the national economy that " technicians, managers and bookkeepers, as well as *all* officials, shall receive salaries no higher than ' a worker's wages ' " ;[4] and in his less theoretical and more practical pamphlet of the same

---

[1] Marx i Engels, *Sochineniya*, iv, 58 ; Lenin in *State and Revolution* (*Sochineniya*, xxi, 436) described differences of wages as a main source of " contemporary *social* inequality " and their removal as a condition of the dying away of the state.

[2] Marx i Engels, *Sochineniya*, xvi, ii, 93 ; xiv, 204.

[3] *Ibid.* xv, 274-276.   [4] Lenin, *Sochineniya*, xxi, 404.

period, *Will the Bolsheviks Retain State Power?*, he apparently contemplated a temporary exception from a policy of equal wages
only for the benefit of " specialists ".[1]

The result of this teaching was to create an extremely powerful
sentiment among the Bolshevik leaders and, still more, the
Bolshevik rank and file against discrimination between different
forms of labour or different workers; and, though it provided no
formal warrant for any equalization of wages at the present early
stage of the revolution, it undoubtedly held up equality as an ideal.
An early decree limited the salary of a People's Commissar to 500
rubles a month with an additional 100 rubles for each non-working
dependent — a figure comparable with the wages of a skilled
factory worker;[2] and a party rule was in force for many years
requiring party members in receipt of salaries above a minimum
fixed from time to time to hand over the surplus to the party
chest.[3] From the party point of view the Mensheviks, whose
following was among the most highly skilled workers, were the
natural advocates of wage differentiation, the Bolsheviks of
equalization. Shlyapnikov, the first People's Commissar for
Labour, declared that the " general principle " accepted by Narkomtrud and by the central council of the trade unions was that
" among paid workers there can be no privileged groups ", and
that the policy in fixing wages and conditions of employment was to
" eliminate any difference between workers in collars and workers
in blouses ".[4] But no specific commitment was undertaken to
equalize wages; nor was any serious attempt made to enforce
equality in practice. A decree of January 19/February 1, 1918,

[1] *Ibid.* xxi, 263; this was also the attitude adopted in the party programme
of March 1919 (*VKP(B) v Rezolyutsiyakh* (1941) i, 291).

[2] *Sobranie Uzakonenii, 1917-1918*, No. 3, art. 46; a decree of July 2, 1918,
fixed the salary of a People's Commissar at 800 rubles a month with salaries of
other Soviet officials ranging down to 350 rubles, but permitted salaries up to
1200 rubles to be paid to " specialists " with the approval of Sovnarkom (*ibid.*
No. 48, art. 567).

[3] The original rule never appears to have been published, but is frequently
referred to in later party resolutions (e.g. *VKP(B) v Rezolyutsiyakh* (1941), i,
434, 470).

[4] *Protokoly II Vserossiiskogo S"ezda Komissarov Truda i Predstavitelei Birzh
Truda i Strakhovykh Kass* (1918), p. 11. Mention was made at the first All-
Russian Congress of Trade Unions in January 1918 of a project of Larin " to
limit earnings . . . by way of taxation to not more than 600 rubles a month "
(*Pervyi Vserossiiskii S"ezd Professional'nykh Soyuzov* (1918), p. 82); but nothing
more was heard of this.

which laid down a scale of wages for the Petrograd metallurgical industries, prescribed in a surprisingly pragmatic way the criteria to be applied in wage-fixing : these included the necessary sub-sistence minimum, the degree of professional skill required by the job, specially hard or dangerous conditions of work, and the relative importance of the industry in the national economy. Wage-rates fixed on this basis varied from highest to lowest in the ratio of three to two, and provisions were made for piece-rates in exceptional cases, for deductions from wages in case of non-fulfilment of the norm of production, and for transfer to a lower grade in case of proved incompetence.[1] A few days later a decree on wages in the postal and telegraphic services laid down scales for skilled workers varying from 215 to 600 rubles a month with a salary of 800 rubles for a " director ".[2] There was nothing unusual about these rates except the accident that they were fixed by official decree. Whatever arguments a few party theorists might propound, the new régime had never seriously challenged the practice of differential wages. What now evoked criticism was the proposal to use and intensify such differentiations consciously and deliberately as an incentive to increased production.

In this as in other aspects of economic policy, the first All-Russian Congress of Councils of National Economy in May 1918 provided a conspectus of the urgent problems and controversies of the first period of the revolution. Tomsky, appearing as delegate of the All-Russian Central Council of Trade Unions declared that " all the tasks of the trade unions at the present time are closely interwoven with the tasks of restoring production destroyed by the war ", and reached the conclusion that " the Supreme Council of National Economy and the trade unions are organizations so completely akin, so closely interwoven with each other, that independent tactics on the part of these two organiza-tions are impossible ".[3] Obolensky, the first president of Vesenkha and now a member of the Left opposition, led an attack on piece-rates and " Taylorism ".[4] Lozovsky denounced Taylorism as " a theory of building everything on élite workers, of strengthening the labour aristocracy " ; another delegate, far from thinking this

[1] Sobranie Uzakonenii, 1917-1918, No. 16, art. 242.

[2] Ibid. No. 18, art. 262.

[3] Trudy I Vserossiiskogo S"ezda Sovetov Narodnogo Khozyaistva (1918), p. 10.   [4] Ibid. p. 66.

a disadvantage, maintained that, " if we take the best Bolshevik and give him piece-rates, he will produce a tremendous output in excess of the norm ".[1]   The conclusions of the congress were non-committal.   It passed a resolution " On the Administration of Nationalized Industries " providing that one-third of the members of the administration should be appointed by trade union workers ; and it formally endorsed a resolution of the trade union central council " On Raising the Productivity of Labour ", which asserted the principle that " a definite fixed rate of productivity must be guaranteed in return for a definite guaranteed wage " and cautiously admitted the principle of piece-rates and " bonuses for productivity in excess of the norm ".   The trade unions also accepted responsibility for working out " rules of internal order ", and placed on factory committees the task of " watching in the strictest manner the inflexible execution of these rules ".[2]   A climate of opinion rather than a settled policy was in course of formation. But in the summer of 1918 the gradual process was sharply interrupted, and the civil war and the resulting régime of war communism gave rapid shape and substance to these slowly maturing tendencies.

(d) Trade and Distribution

In civilized society the cardinal issue of distribution is always the relation between town and country.   In war-time Russia it had already presented itself in the stark form of a food crisis. Bread cards had been introduced in Petrograd and Moscow as early as the summer of 1916, and food queues in Petrograd had been an important contributory factor in the February revolution. The Provisional Government quickly set up a supply committee, decreed a state monopoly of grain, which was to be delivered to the state at fixed prices, and, in May 1917, when a coalition government was formed with the SRs and the Mensheviks, replaced the supply committee by a full Ministry of Supply.[3]   These measures seem to have encouraged a black market and to have incited the

---

[1] *Ibid.* pp. 78, 393.   [2] *Ibid.* pp. 477-478, 481-482.
[3] *Sobranie Uzakonenii i Rasporyazhenii Vremennogo Pravitel'stva, 1917,* No. 60, art. 358 ; No. 85, art. 478 ; No. 103, art. 574.   This ministry and the commissariat which succeeded it (Narkomprod), are often referred to as the Ministry (or Commissariat) of Food ; but the Russian word *prodovol'stvie* has the same wider connotation as the French *ravitaillement*.

peasants to withhold grain for higher prices. The functions of
the Ministry of Supply included not only the administration of the
grain monopoly and the fixing of prices for grain, but the supply
to the peasants at suitable prices of such articles as they required
in exchange for their products. Thus an order was issued in
September 1917 to take over 60 per cent of surplus textile production after the needs of the army had been met in order to set up
a process of exchange with the peasants.[1] This also failed to prove
effective ; and two increases in the official price for grain in response
to agrarian pressure served to discredit the Provisional Government
during the last period of its existence in the eyes of the hungry
town populations.

Between February and October the Bolsheviks naturally
exploited every failure of the Provisional Government to establish
an equitable system of distribution. Lenin's April theses of 1917
had called for Soviet control over distribution as well as production ; and the " most powerful capitalist syndicates " over which
" state control " was demanded by the resolution of the April
conference included both manufacturing and trading syndicates.[2]
From this time distribution was commonly coupled with production as activities requiring public, or workers', control, and was
included in that " state apparatus " which, in Lenin's words, " is
not fully ' state ' under capitalism, but will be fully ' state ' with
us, under socialism ".[3] On the morrow of the October revolution,
the Petrograd Soviet demanded " workers' control over the production and distribution of goods ".[4] The decree of November 14/27,
1917, on workers' control nominally applied to enterprises engaged
in distribution as well as production. But the whole decree, like
the party utterances of the pre-revolutionary period, was clearly
directed in the minds of its authors to workers in factories ; the
employees of shops and other distributive concerns were not
workers in the narrower sense of the word and were not organized
as such ; nor had the Bolsheviks any large following among them.
The staff of the old Ministry of Supply purported to continue to
take its orders from a council of supply set up by the Provisional

[1] P. I. Lyashchenko, *Istoriya Narodnogo Khozyaistva SSSR*, ii (1948), 676.
[2] *VKP(B) v Rezolyutsiyakh* (1941), i, 237.
[3] Lenin, *Sochineniya*, xxi, 260.
[4] *Ibid.*, xxii, 6.

Government, and refused for several weeks to recognize the newly appointed People's Commissar for Supply.[1] The new régime was faced with an almost complete breakdown of the existing machinery of distribution, both commercial and official, in a situation where it still had no resources to create its own.

The straightforward simplicity of the problem did not make it any easier to solve. The decree issued three days after the October revolution making the municipal authorities responsible for the distribution of food, as well as other " goods of prime necessity " and for the control of food shops, restaurants, inns and flour mills in all towns of 10,000 inhabitants or over [2] was no more than a gesture ; for, according to all the evidence, shortages were chiefly due not to inadequacies in distribution within the towns, but to failure of supplies to reach the towns from the country. A proclamation to the army revealed the anxieties caused in Sovnarkom by breakdowns of the commissariat at the front :

> There is no shortage of food in the country. The land-owners, *kulaks* and merchants have hidden away large quantities of food. High state officials and employees of the railways and banks are helping the bourgeoisie against the soldiers, workers and peasants. . . . The directors of the banks refuse to grant the Soviet Government money with which to secure food.[3]

The proclamation promised " very energetic measures " against " speculators, robbers, grafters and counter - revolutionary officials " ; and a decree threatened all such persons with " *arrest and detention in the Kronstadt prisons* " by the military-revolutionary committee.[4] But the tone of these pronouncements suggested that it was much easier to find scapegoats than to find remedies. Speculation is endemic in all periods of political and economic disintegration ; the first economic decree of the French revolution had been directed against speculators who hoarded supplies. Before the end of 1917 newspapers were beginning to give attention to the new phenomenon of " bagging ", and to describe the

---

[1] *Sobranie Uzakonenii, 1917–1918*, No. 5, art. 88.

[2] *Ibid.* No. 1 (2nd ed.), art. 9 ; see also *Protokoly Zasedanii VTsIK 2 Sozyva* (1918), pp. 5-6.

[3] *Sobranie Uzakonenii, 1917–1918*, No. 3, art. 29.

[4] *Ibid.* No. 3, art. 33 ; the military-revolutionary committee was shortly to give birth to the first Cheka (see Vol. 1, p. 158).

doings of "bagmen", who scoured the countryside buying up
food from the peasants which they carried in sacks to the towns
and disposed of at exorbitant prices.[1] On December 24, 1917/
January 6, 1918, a decree of VTsIK cited the resolution of the
second All-Russian Congress of Soviets and provided for an
all-Russian supply committee to be attached to Sovnarkom, with
local supply committees attached to local Soviets and responsible
to it.[2] But this was one more example of the attempt to meet a
crisis by creating on paper machinery which never became
effective.

The break-down of distribution was as disconcerting as the
decline in production and still more difficult to check. After three
and a half years of war the Russian peasant was hungry for
textiles, implements, utensils and consumer goods of almost every
kind. Nor at this time was shortage of goods the primary obstacle.
Many factories were still reporting accumulations of unsold
stocks.[3] What had happened was clear enough. The revolution
had been followed by a general disruption of regular commercial
relations ; and the hasty attempts of the new régime to improvise
an official machinery of distribution were wholly ineffective.
Between December 1917 and March 1918 a series of decrees gave
official organs a monopoly of the purchase and sale of textiles, of
food supplies in general, and of matches, candles, rice, coffee and
pepper.[4] A further decree made all grain repositories the property
of the state.[5] The government attempted to keep pace with the
currency inflation by adopting the course of action which its
leaders had so bitterly condemned in the Provisional Government :
two further increases in the fixed prices of grain were conceded

[1] Quoted in Bunyan and Fisher, *The Bolshevik Revolution, 1917–1918* (Stanford, 1934), pp. 330-331 ; according to L. Kritsman, *Geroicheskii Period Velikoi
Russkoi Revolyutsii* (n.d. [? 1924]), p. 135, the practice had started after the
institution of the grain monopoly by the Provisional Government.

[2] *Sobranie Uzakonenii, 1917–1918*, No. 12, art. 181.

[3] For an example from the textile industry, see p. 72 above ; in March 1918
stocks of metal goods were still piling up " in spite of an obvious excess of
demand over supply ", and 60 per cent of sales were being effected on the black
market (*Byulleteni Vysshego Soveta Narodnogo Khozyaistva*, No. 1, April 1918,
pp. 44-45). See also *Trudy I Vserossiiskogo S"ezda Sovetov Narodnogo Khozyaistva* (1918), p. 413.

[4] *Sobranie Uzakonenii, 1917–1918*, No. 9, art. 134 ; No. 12, art. 181 ; No.
29, art. 385.

[5] *Ibid*. No. 25, art. 344.

in the first six months.[1] On February 16, 1918, " a most resolute
struggle against bagging " was announced, and instructions to
local Soviets and all railway organizations to arrest bagmen and,
in case of armed resistance, to shoot them on the spot.[2] A fortnight later Lenin angrily demanded that " the railways should be
cleared of bagmen and hooligans ", and denounced the bagman
as " the speculator, the freebooter of trade, the breaker of the
grain monopoly " and " our chief ' internal ' enemy ".[3] But this
official indignation was of little avail. The government had no
stocks of the commodities which it purported to control and distribute ; food rations in the cities fell to starvation level ; only the
black market made life possible by keeping supplies moving in
small quantities and at exorbitant prices. Official efforts were,
however, not relaxed. On March 25, 1918, Sovnarkom assigned
more than a milliard rubles to a fund for the purchase of goods to be
sold to the peasant in exchange for grain.[4] Finally a decree of
April 2, 1918 — the first systematic attempt by the new régime to
tackle the problem of distribution as a whole — authorized Narkomprod to acquire stocks of consumer goods of all kinds from
articles of clothing to nails and horseshoes to exchange with the
peasant against grain and other foodstuffs. Distribution was to be
in the hands of local organs of Narkomprod or of organizations
authorized by it, but the poor peasants were to be drawn into the
work of distribution, so as to ensure that the " needy population "
got its share : thus the enactment had its class basis which might
easily conflict with its economic purpose.[5] It is doubtful whether

[1] A speaker at the first All-Russian Congress of Councils of National
Economy gave particulars of increases in the price of rye bread, the staple
foodstuff of the cities : between the beginning of 1916 and the February
revolution it had risen by 170 per cent, between the February and October
revolutions by 258 per cent, and between the October revolution and May
1918 by 181 per cent, making a total increase of 800 per cent since January 1916
(*Trudy I Vserossiiskogo S"ezda Sovetov Narodnogo Khozyaistva* (1918), p. 384).

[2] Quoted in L. Kritsman, *Geroicheskii Period Velikoi Russkoi Revolyutsii*
(n.d. [? 1924]), p. 136.

[3] Lenin, *Sochineniya*, xxii, 305, 514 ; much later Lenin described the bagman
as " a creature who instructs us extremely well in economics, quite independently of economic or political theory " (*ibid.* xxvii, 41).

[4] *Ibid.* xxiv, 744, note 31.

[5] *Sobranie Uzakonenii, 1917–1918*, No. 30, art. 398. Vesenkha had proposed
that distribution should be in the hands of the local Sovnarkhozy and local
branches of the *glavki* and centres ; Sovnarkom ruled in favour of Narkomprod
as the department concerned with collecting the grain (*Trudy II Vserossiiskogo*

these decrees were more effective than their predecessors. The writ of the Soviet authorities still scarcely ran outside the large towns. Supply committees or other state organs capable of handling trade on any significant scale scarcely yet existed.

Meanwhile another and ultimately more promising approach was being made to the question. The cooperative movement had developed widely in Russia, where it had taken three forms — producers' cooperatives, comprising both agriculture and rural handicrafts, credit cooperatives and consumers' cooperatives. All were ostensibly non-political; but the producers' and credit cooperatives, which were almost exclusively rural, were associated with the SRs, and the consumers' cooperatives, which were predominantly urban, with the Mensheviks. In an early work Lenin had expressed his contempt for peasant banks and " cheap credit ", which were planks in the *narodnik* platform, as calculated " only to strengthen and develop the bourgeoisie " ;[1] and socialists had in the past traditionally looked askance on producers' cooperatives as tending to degenerate into thinly discussed capitalist enterprises. In 1910 Lenin had drafted a resolution for the Copenhagen congress of the Second International, which pronounced on producers' cooperatives as " significant for the struggle of the working class only if they form component parts of the consumers' cooperatives ", but gave a guarded approval to consumers' cooperatives.[2] It was to the Russian consumers' cooperatives that the Bolsheviks now turned. They were divided into two types — workers' cooperatives centred round the factories, and general cooperatives patronized mainly by the petty bourgeoisie. The growth of the workers' cooperatives had been stimulated by the revolution. A united factory workers' cooperative in Moscow was said to have 200,000 members, the workers' cooperative in the Putilov factory in Petrograd 35,000. A congress in Petrograd in August 1917 passed a resolution to set up a special central organ for workers'

S"ezda Sovetov Narodnogo Khozyaistva (n.d.), p. 47). The decree of April 2, 1918, thus marked the emergence of Narkomprod as the department in charge of internal trade and distribution. The fixing of prices remained a joint responsibility of Vesenkha and Narkomprod (*ibid.*).

[1] Lenin, *Sochineniya*, i, 143.
[2] For the draft resolution see *ibid.* xiv, 434-435 ; for Lenin's comments see *ibid.* xiv, 357-363.

cooperatives.[1] This, however, seems to have remained a dead letter.   At the time of the October revolution there were from 20 to 25 thousand consumers' cooperative societies of all kinds with seven or eight million members,[2] grouped around a powerful central organ known as Tsentrosoyuz.

The first move was made when Lenin, during his Christmas retreat in Finland in the last days of 1917, drafted a somewhat naïve plan for the grouping of the whole population into local consumers' societies.   Each society would have a purchasing committee attached to it, and these societies and their committees would have a monopoly of trade in consumer goods.   But the project turned on the intention to create this machinery by the simple process of taking over the existing cooperatives : " All existing consumers societies are nationalized and are under an obligation to include in their membership the whole population of a given locality individually ".[3]   In January 1918 the project was published by Narkomprod in the form of a draft decree, this tentative approach showing that opposition was anticipated and that the Soviet Government did not feel strong enough to enforce its policy at a single stroke.   Negotiations with the cooperatives continued for nearly three months.   In the view of the Bolsheviks the position of the cooperatives and the correct attitude towards them had " radically changed since the conquest of state power by the proletariat ".   But it was not till after the Brest-Litovsk crisis had been overcome that what Lenin described as " a compromise with the bourgeois cooperatives and the workers' cooperatives which stick to a bourgeois point of view " was achieved.[4]   On April 11, 1918, the agreement was discussed and approved by VTsIK ; there too it was referred to as " a compromise decision suffering from substantial defects ".[5]   These apologetic utterances were a tribute to the strength of an organization which was able to fight an independent rear-guard action against a government still uncertain of its powers.   Under the decree now issued the consumers' cooperatives were to be open to all, to " serve the whole

[1] E. Fuckner, *Die Russische Genossenschaftsbewegung, 1865–1921* (1922), pp. 114-115.

[2] Lenin, *Socnineniya*, xxii, 451, puts the membership at " over 10 million ".

[3] *Ibid.* xxii, 172-173.

[4] *Ibid.* xxii, 423, 452.

[5] *Protokoly Zasedanii VTsIK 4⁹⁰ Sozyva* (1920), p. 104.

population "; on the other hand membership was not to be automatic and gratuitous, though poor persons were to be admitted on payment of a nominal fee of fifty kopeks. Nor did the cooperatives enjoy, as Lenin's draft had contemplated, a monopoly of trade in consumer goods. Private trading concerns were also recognized, though — by way of " a stimulus to others to join the cooperatives " [1] — a general sales tax of 5 per cent was imposed, which cooperative members were entitled to recover from their cooperatives at the end of the year.[2] In any area two, though not more than two, cooperatives could function — a " general citizens' cooperative " and a " workers' class cooperative " : this distinction corresponded to existing practice. Finally, the cooperatives as well as private trading concerns were subject to regulation, inspection and control by Vesenkha.[3] In order to deal with them Vesenkha set up a special section consisting of three members of its own praesidium, a representative of Narkomprod, and three representatives of the cooperatives.[4] This decree effectively brought the cooperatives within the orbit of the Soviet power. While appearing to strengthen them by swelling their membership and by favouring them at the expense of the private trader, it made them responsible to an organ of the Soviet Government and dependent on it; and Vesenkha, in process of administering the decree, was likely to make this dependence real.

In the chaotic conditions of the spring of 1918 the decree on the cooperatives did little to solve the problem of trade and distribution between Russian factories and Russian farms. But it introduced a fresh element of confusion into the rivalry between Vesenkha and Narkomprod. The decree made the cooperatives responsible not to the commissariat, but to Vesenkha. Yet the general drift at this time was towards a division of functions which would have given the control of production to Vesenkha and the

---

[1] *Trudy I Vserossiiskogo S"ezda Sovetov Narodnogo Khozyaistva* (1918), p. 437.

[2] According to a former official of the cooperatives, the cooperatives were obliged not only to refund the 5 per cent sales tax to their members but themselves to pay the tax to the state, so that the tax was in fact paid twice over (E. Fuckner. *Die Russische Genossenschaftsbewegung, 1865-1921* (1922), pp. 106-107).

[3] *Sobranie Uzakonenii, 1917-1918*, No. 32, art. 418.

[4] *Trudy I Vserossiiskogo S"ezda Sovetov Narodnogo Khozyaistva* (1918), p. 436.

control of distribution to Narkomprod. The so-called " food
dictatorship " decree of May 9, 1918, recognized Narkomprod as
the " single institution " in which all " dispositions of a supply
character " should be centralized, and placed all local supply
organizations under its authority.[1] This decree made no mention
either of Vesenkha or of the cooperatives. A further decree of
May 27, 1918, " On the Reorganization of the People's Commissariat of Supply and the Local Supply Organs ", the declared
purpose of which was " to unite in one organ the provisioning of
the population with all articles of prime necessity and supply, to
organize the distribution of these goods on a state scale, and to
prepare the transition to the nationalization of trade in articles of
prime necessity ", attempted to repair this omission. It contained
clauses providing that prices for articles of prime necessity should
be fixed by Vesenkha " together with " Narkomprod, and that
" distribution among the population is carried out by local supply
organizations with the participation of the cooperatives ". A
supply council attached to Narkomprod was to contain representatives both of Vesenkha and of Tsentrosoyuz. Nevertheless, the
major part of the decree was occupied by definitions of the
constitution and prerogatives of the local supply committees of
Narkomprod without regard to any other organizations working
in this field ; and the intention to concentrate authority over all
forms of distribution in the hands of Narkomprod was scarcely
disguised.[2]

The first major debate on the cardinal issue of trade and
exchange between town and country took place at the first All-
Russian Congress of Councils of National Economy at the end of
May 1918.[3] It raised many puzzling questions. It was notorious
that trade had almost ceased to flow in official channels at official
prices, and that distribution was being drawn into the hands of
" bagmen " and other illicit traders who conducted their transactions by barter or at prices which had no relation to official rates.
But two different explanations were offered by those who tried to

[1] See pp. 51-52 above.
[2] Sobranie Uzakonenii, 1917-1918, No. 38, art. 498.
[3] Trudy I Vserossiiskogo S"ezda Sovetov Narodnogo Khozyaistva (1918),
pp. 291-296, 395-436 ; the decree of May 27, 1918, was issued while the congress
was in session, but does not seem to have been referred to throughout the
proceedings.

diagnose the disease. According to some the hitch was due simply to a break-down of the apparatus of distribution, due to the disappearance of the firms or individuals who had managed this apparatus under the former capitalist system. According to others the trouble was primarily monetary. The official prices fixed by the government both for grain and for other articles of prime necessity had been put out of focus by the currency inflation due to progressive increases in the note issue. Those, however, who agreed on this second explanation differed about the remedy. Some argued that prices should be raised to take account of the depreciated value of the currency; others wanted a deflationary policy of holding down prices and reducing the note issue in order to restore its value.[1] The second explanation, which attributed the break-down to monetary causes, carried a good deal of conviction. But, since those who propounded it were divided against themselves, and since neither a progressive increase in prices nor a curtailment of the note issue was politically practicable in the first months of 1918, it was the first hypothesis of a defect remediable by better organization which won official acceptance and influenced policy at this time. The resolution of the congress revealed its jealousy of the encroachments of Narkomprod in the field of distribution, but had little that was constructive to propose. Its most novel suggestion was that, since " private trading organizations are destroyed or paralysed or engaged in highly developed speculation ", and in view of " the almost complete stoppages of the process of exchange which threaten the country with ruin ", an attempt should be made to utilize private trading concerns " under the direction and control of state organs and preferably on a commission basis ".[2]

The congress at the same time took care to make good the authority of Vesenkha over the cooperatives. It passed a resolution affirming that " the activity of the cooperatives must be coordinated and brought into close connexion with the activity of Soviet organizations "; that this process should extend to agricultural and credit cooperatives as well as to consumers' cooperatives; that the transformation of the cooperatives into

[1] *Trudy I Vserossiiskogo S"ezda Sovetov Narodnogo Khozyaistva* (1918), pp. 291-296, 395-420.

[2] *Ibid.* pp. 483-484.

general organizations embracing the whole population was essential to assure " the social distribution of products and articles of mass consumption "; and that regional and local Sovnarkhozy under the authority of Vesenkha should exercise general supervision over the cooperative movement.[1]   The general intention to turn the cooperatives into instruments of Soviet policy was plain enough. But the power to devise any coherent system of distribution was still lacking.   Relations between local Sovnarkhozy and local supply committees of Narkomprod remained as ill-defined as the relations of either to local Soviets.   The sense of departmental rivalry in Moscow was certainly acute ; and in the localities friction was frequent between the supply committees and cooperatives [2] which enjoyed the patronage of Vesenkha.   A serious clash of competence could hardly have been avoided if either Vesenkha or Narkomprod had in fact been able to exercise effective control of distribution, or if local Sovnarkhozy and supply committees had had time to strike any roots in the economy of the countryside.   But these new institutions were still embryonic ; many of them existed only on paper, if at all.   When civil war engulfed the country, the machinery of exchange and distribution established by recent decrees was quickly pushed aside ;   and for some time the most effective instruments in extracting grain from the peasant were the " iron detachments " of workers from towns and factories reinforced by the local committees of poor peasants.   The only supply organs whose long established foundations enabled them to some extent to resist the flood and ultimately to survive it were the cooperatives.   In the next period it was the cooperatives which, firmly and forcibly wedded to the Soviet power, became the principal instruments of Soviet distribution policy.

While Soviet control of internal trade advanced thus haltingly, and through many compromises and set-backs, foreign trade was the one field of economic activity in which the ultimate form of regulation — a full state monopoly — was reached within six months of the October revolution with virtually no intermediate stages. This rapid development was due not to doctrinal preconceptions — it would be difficult to find any Bolshevik pronouncements

[1] *Ibid.* pp. 484-485.   [2] *Ibid.* p. 429.

before the revolution on the subject of foreign trade — but to certain specific conditions. Russian foreign trade before 1914 showed a substantial excess of exports over imports, since Russia was engaged in paying for the services rendered by western capitalists. During the war, trade with Germany, Russia's largest trading partner, ceased entirely ; trade with the rest of the world was limited both by those general shortages which limited trade everywhere and by the peculiar difficulties of access to Russia ; and Russia's much reduced production, whether of food, raw materials or manufactured goods, was absorbed in its entirety by the war effort, leaving nothing available for export. In these conditions, Russian foreign trade by 1916 had dwindled to limited proportions, and was largely made up of supplies sent to Russia by her allies, so that the balance of what trade remained became acutely passive. When the allies stopped the flow of supplies to Russia after the October revolution — a regular blockade was established after the Brest-Litovsk treaty — trade with the outside world almost ceased. The cutting off of foreign trade was for the Bolsheviks a symptom and a symbol of their isolation in a hostile world. Other special factors made it easier in this than in other fields for the Soviet Government to pursue a radical policy. Before 1914 a large proportion of Russia's foreign trade had been conducted by foreign firms having branches in Petrograd and Moscow ; very many of these were German, or employed German agents, who disappeared on the outbreak of war. During the war more and more of Russia's dwindling foreign trade came directly or indirectly under government control. When the October revolution occurred, private interests in this field had already been displaced or weakened by the war and were particularly vulnerable.

Soviet foreign trade policy, like Soviet industrial policy, developed under many of the same impulses which affected the policies of all belligerent countries during the war. Before 1914 governments, anxious to promote the profits of their manufacturers and traders, were primarily concerned to encourage exports and to limit imports which might compete with national products. The war revealed everywhere a broader national interest conflicting with the individual interests which had hitherto been the regulators of international trade. The policy of governments was now to import maximum quantities of commodities indispensable in one way or another for the prosecution of the war and to reduce exports to the minimum amount necessary to finance these indispensable imports.   Imports and exports were both subject to a process of selection dictated not by the prospective profits of individuals, but by general considerations of national interest. These aims were achieved by a system of government control which was the corollary and concomitant of the prevailing system of " state capitalism " in industry.   If Soviet Russia carried the new policy of controlled foreign trade to its logical conclusion, while the capitalist Powers half-heartedly abandoned it when the immediate crisis was past, this was due partly to the confirmation which it received from socialist theory, but mainly to the greater weakness of the Soviet economy which made these supports indispensable.

Soviet foreign trade policy was first conceived as a defensive action.   A few days after the October revolution the American military attaché in Petrograd informed the Russian general staff that, " if the Bolsheviks will remain in power and will put through their programme of making peace with Germany, the present embargo on exports to Russia will remain in force "; [1]   and Izvestiya angrily retorted that " the North American plutocrats are ready to trade locomotives for the heads of Russian soldiers ".[2] In the régime of acute stringency which the embargo imposed on Russia, it was urgently necessary to seek protection against those enemies of the régime at home who might have an interest, on the one hand, in depleting Russia's meagre reserves for the benefit of their foreign customers, or, on the other hand, in importing such articles as could still be obtained at profitable prices from abroad rather than those of which the community stood in urgent need. The first decree of Vesenkha, issued on December 5/18, 1917, was an attempt to lay down the principles of export and import controls. Foodstuffs, " including even consignments of tea and other products already at Archangel ", were not to be exported ; " furs, Persian carpets and other articles of luxury " might be exported

---

[1] Foreign Relations of the United States, 1918 : Russia, i (1931), 266-267 ; no formal notification of the stoppage of supplies to Russia from allied sources seems ever to have been given.

[2] Izvestiya, November 14/27, 1917.

to " Sweden and other countries " which were prepared to grant permits for the export to Russia of " machines, spare parts and other objects required for Russian factories " ; raw materials were to be exported only if it had been ascertained that adequate supplies already existed for Russian industry ; only objects " absolutely necessary for the Russian economy " were to be imported. A division of Vesenkha was made responsible for the issue of import and export licences.[1] At the end of December Sovnarkom issued a decree formally prohibiting all imports and exports except under licence.[2] Difficulties of shipment in the winter of 1917–1918 were probably a more effective obstacle to foreign trade than governmental restrictions. On January 26/ February 8, 1918, another form of control was established through the nationalization of the mercantile marine.[3]

The signature of the Brest-Litovsk treaty on March 3, 1918, ended any chance of a reopening of trade with western Europe, but at once raised the question of Soviet-German trade. Nor would this be trade on equal terms. In its initial declaration, the Soviet delegation had proposed that the negotiations should condemn, among other things, " the attempts of strong nations to oppress weaker nations by such indirect methods as economic boycotts, economic subjection by imposing commercial treaties and separate tariff agreements ".[4] But these aspirations were brushed rudely aside. Apart from urgent German designs on the granaries of the Ukraine, Germany had every incentive to obtain from a prostrate Russia all supplies which might help her to elude the stranglehold of the allied blockade : the supplementary economic agreement attached to the Brest-Litovsk treaty obliged Soviet Russia not to raise its tariffs against the central Powers above the limits of the Russian tariff of 1903, and not to impose prohibitions or duties on the export of timber or ores.[5] It is difficult to measure the relative strength of the different forces driving the new régime to strengthen its controls over the trade

[1] *Sobranie Uzakonenii, 1917–1918*, No. 10, art. 159.
[2] *Ibid.* No. 14, art. 197 ; Larin claims to have been one of the authors of this decree (*Narodnoe Khozyaistvo*, No. 11, 1918, p. 19).
[3] *Ibid.* No. 19, art. 290.
[4] *Mirnye Perogovory v Brest-Litovske* (1920), pp. 9-11.
[5] *Mirnyi Dogovor* (1918), pp. 12-13 ; *Texts of the Russian " Peace "* (Washington, 1918), pp. 26-28.

of the country, both internal and foreign. But the directors of Soviet policy must quickly have discovered that, if the Soviet Government appeared, not merely as a regulating authority, but as a principal, in commercial transactions with Germany, it could, by the ordinary processes of commercial bargaining, place any limits or conditions it chose on the export of essential raw materials without formally infringing the Brest-Litovsk stipulations. A state monopoly of foreign trade enabled the government not only to override private interests which might conflict with public policy, but to nullify the conventional restrictions imposed in current international commercial agreements, down to and including the treaty of Brest-Litovsk.

All these considerations help to explain the promptness with which foreign trade was nationalized, well in advance of the main structure of industry and internal trade. By a decree of April 22, 1918, all foreign trade was declared nationalized, and all commercial transactions with foreign states or trading concerns abroad were to be conducted exclusively " in the name of the Russian republic by organs specially authorized for the purpose ". The execution of the decree was entrusted to the People's Commissariat of Trade and Industry, which was to set up a Council of Foreign Trade for the purpose — the council to contain representatives of Vesenkha and of its *glavki* and centres, of the cooperatives and the trade unions, and even of private trading organizations.[1] Foreign trade was thoroughly and unconditionally nationalized ; but, so long as so much of production and distribution remained outside public control, the foreign trade monopoly had still to rely on cooperative and private enterprises, working on a commission basis,[2] as well as on the *glavki* and centres, as its suppliers at home. This anomaly was inherent in the situation. What was much more serious was the lack of goods and the lack of personnel. Milyutin afterwards admitted that in practice almost everything remained to be done :

The chief difficulty in carrying the decree into effect consists, of course, in the creation of a broad decentralized apparatus for

[1] *Sobranie Uzakonenii, 1917-1918*, No. 33, art. 432.

[2] Bronsky seems to have had some difficulty at the first All-Russian Congress of Councils of National Economy in defending this practice against the criticisms of " Left " purists (*Trudy I Vserossiiskogo S"ezda Sovetov Narodnogo Khozyaistva* (1918), p. 160).

effecting purchases and concentrating goods in the hands of the state. This apparatus will have to be created, for hitherto it has not existed. . . . Only with the lapse of time and after much preliminary work will there be a possibility of putting the business of nationalized foreign trade on a firm footing.[1]

It is fair to add that these shortcomings were no more conspicuous in the organization of foreign trade than in any other branch of the Soviet economy; that the obstacles were, on the whole, less serious; and that in Krasin, who was appointed president of the Council of Foreign Trade in the autumn of 1918, the Bolsheviks had one of their few experienced business administrators. It was thus due partly to the comparatively minor rôle of foreign trade in the Russian economy, partly to the urgent necessities of defence against economic exploitation by the capitalist world, and partly to a series of accidents, that the monopoly of foreign trade was so early, and so firmly, established as a vital part of the Soviet system.

It was easier in the spring of 1918 to create a foreign trade organization — at any rate, on paper — than to frame a policy. But this task also was attempted. Radek read to the first All-Russian Congress of Councils of National Economy a statement of policy drawn up for the guidance of the Soviet negotiators in the Soviet-German economic negotiations. Since a passive balance in Soviet foreign trade was inevitable for some years to come, Soviet Russia could obtain " foreign goods indispensable for Russian production " only through foreign loans and credits. This in turn could be achieved only by granting concessions " for the creation of new enterprises necessary for the systematic development of the still unutilized productive resources of Russia according to a general plan ". Such concessions were not to be allowed to constitute " spheres of influence in Russia for foreign governments "; the Urals, the Donetz and Kuznetsk basins and the Baku region were to be excluded from the scheme; concessionaires were to be subject to Soviet legislation; the Soviet Government was to receive a proportion of the products at market price, and a share of the profits if these exceeded 5 per cent. Other conditions were that Germany should evacuate the Don region,

[1] V. P. Milyutin, *Istoriya Ekonomicheskogo Razvitiya SSSR* (2nd ed., 1929), pp. 109-110.

and undertake not to interfere in any commercial agreements concluded by Soviet Russia with the Ukraine, Poland or Baltic or Caucasian countries. The statement was drafted throughout with explicit or implicit reference to Germany alone, but contained this significant general clause :

> For Russia, as a neutral country, it is an indispensable condition of restoration of her national economy to establish economic relations with the central powers as well as to maintain and broaden relations with the Entente countries.[1]

Larin relates that during the winter of 1917–1918 he put forward a scheme for a commercial agreement with the United States offering a concession over Kamchatka in return for goods or a loan, but that only Radek took the idea seriously.[2] Nevertheless, when the American Colonel Robins returned from Moscow to the United States in May 1918, he carried with him a general offer of concessions on the lines of the Radek statement ;[3] and Bronsky at the first All-Russian Congress of Councils of National Economy described America as " the only country which could send us something to restore our national economy ".[4] Such schemes were at this time utopian. But the apparently more practicable project of a deal with Germany proved equally premature and unrealizable. A long and painful process of building up the structure of Soviet foreign trade stone by stone occupied the next three years. But it is interesting to note that the outlines of the future concessions policy of the Soviet Government were already sketched out in some detail at this early date.

(e) Finance

The financial policy of the Bolsheviks before the October revolution had been summed up in two demands repeatedly and

---

[1] *Trudy I Vserossiiskogo S"ezda Sovetov Narodnogo Khozyaistva* (1918) p. 21 : the statement was included in Chicherin's report to the fifth All-Russian Congress of Soviets a few weeks later.

[2] *Narodnoe Khozyaistvo*, No. 11, November 1918, p. 20. Hopes of American aid were widely entertained ; a speaker at the first trade union congress in January 1918 expressed the conviction that the United States with its " excessive gold reserve " could not " afford not to export its finance capital to such a country as Russia and, in particular, Siberia " (*Pervyi Vserossiiskii S"ezd Professional'nykh Soyuzov* (1918), p. 167).

[3] This offer will be discussed in Part V.

[4] *Trudy I Vserossiiskogo S"ezda Sovetov Narodnogo Khozyaistva* (1918), p. 163.

emphatically expressed : the nationalization of the banks and the annulment of the financial obligations of previous Russian governments.   In addition to these, the sixth party congress of August 1917 — the first to give any consideration to financial questions — called for the " immediate cessation of the further issue of paper money " and for various fiscal reforms, including a property tax, " high indirect taxes on articles of luxury ", and a reform of the income tax.[1]   These last aspirations were to be regarded as moves to discredit the inactivity of the Provisional Government rather than as items in a positive programme, and no thought was given to ways and means of carrying them out. After the October revolution, the first step was to give effect to the major demands for the nationalization of banks and annulment of debts.   This occupied the period down to Brest-Litovsk.   It was only after the Brest-Litovsk crisis was over that wider issues of financial and fiscal policy were seriously faced for the first time.

The nationalization of the banks was the simplest and most concrete item in the Bolshevik financial programme.   The conception of the banks as the controlling lever in a planned and organized economy goes back to Saint-Simon,[2] and had an honoured place in nineteenth-century socialist tradition.   At the end of the century the commanding rôle assumed by the banks all over Europe, and especially in Germany, in the development of industry seemed to provide a brilliant practical confirmation of this hypothesis.   Hilferding's *Finanzkapital*, published in 1909, was regarded by Marxists everywhere as an outstanding contribution to Marxist theory and was one of Lenin's main sources of inspiration in *Imperialism as the Highest Stage of Capitalism* ;   in it Hilferding maintained that " to take possession of six great Berlin banks would mean today to take possession of the most important sectors of big industry ".[3]   Lenin had long ago surmised that the failure of the Paris commune to take over the banks was one of the

---

[1] *VKP(B) v Rezolyutsiyakh* (1941), i, 257.

[2] Lenin quoted the crucial passage from Saint-Simon at second-hand at the end of *Imperialism as the Highest Stage of Capitalism* (*Sochineniya*, xix, 174-175).

[3] R. Hilferding, *Das Finanzkapital* (1909), p. 506 ; Zinoviev quoted this passage, not quite accurately, at the Halle congress of the German Independent Social-Democratic Party in October 1920 (*USPD : Protokoll über die Verhandlungen des ausserordentlichen Parteitags in Halle* (n.d.), p. 149, cf. p. 182).

main causes of its downfall.[1]   He returned again and again in his
writings of 1917 to the vital importance of nationalizing the banks.[2]
" A group of bankers ", he wrote shortly after his return to Russia,
" is feathering its nest out of the war, and holds the whole world
in its hands " ; and a little later he described the banks as " the
chief nerve centres of the whole capitalist system of national
economy ".[3]   The party conference of April 1917 demanded " the
establishment of state control over all banks and their unification
into a single central bank " ;   the sixth party congress of July-
August 1917 called for " the nationalization and centralization of
banking ".[4]   Finally, Lenin, on the eve of the October revolution,
adhered unconditionally to the traditional view of the rôle of the
banks under socialism :

> *Without the big banks socialism would be unrealizable.*   The big
> banks *are* the " state apparatus " which is *necessary* to us for the
> realization of socialism and which we *take ready-made* from
> capitalism. . . . A single (the largest possible) state bank with a
> branch in every district, in every factory — that is already nine-
> tenths of a *socialist* apparatus.[5]

When the moment came, the new régime found its policies
dictated, in this matter as in others, as much by current necessities
as by the items of its programme.   The Russian banking system
fell into three strata.   At the head was the State Bank which was in
everything but name a department of the government :   under its
statutes it was " directly subordinated to the Ministry of Finance ".
It controlled currency and credit (having had a monopoly of the
note issue since 1897), acted as banker to the government and to
the other banking institutions of the country, and in general

---

[1] Lenin, *Sochineniya*, viii, 82 : this point was specifically made in the party
programme of 1919 (*VKP(B) v Rezolyutsiyakh* (1941), i, 302).

[2] Lenin, *Sochineniya*, xx, 377, xxi, 164-168.

[3] *Ibid.* xx, 156 ; xxi, 164.   The conception was not peculiar to the Bolsheviks ;
Otto Bauer believed that under socialism the national bank would become " the
supreme economic authority, the chief administrative organ of the whole
economy ", and that the nationalization of the banks would by itself give society
" the power to regulate its labour according to a plan and to distribute its
resources rationally among the various branches of production " (*Der Weg zum
Sozialismus* (1921), pp. 26-27).   A similar belief in financial regulation as a
main lever for controlling national economic policy survived still later in the
capitalist world.

[4] *VKP(B) v Rezolyutsiyakh* (1941), i, 237, 257.

[5] Lenin, *Sochineniya*, xxi, 260.

performed the recognized functions of a central bank, though it also received deposits from private individuals or firms and granted credits. The second place was occupied by nearly 50 large joint-stock banks engaged in general banking business and forming the nucleus of the system ; among these the " big seven " accounted for more than half the total deposits.[1] Thirdly came a host of specialized banking and credit institutions serving particular branches of production or commerce or particular groups of the population : these varied in size from the great Moscow Narodnyi Bank, the bank of the cooperatives, to insignificant local or municipal credit institutions.

The Soviet authorities were concerned at the outset with the first two of these strata.[2] The first retort of the banks to the Bolshevik seizure of power had been an attempt to paralyse the new authority by a financial boycott. They opened their doors only for a few hours a day or not at all ; withdrawals were limited ; and no credits and no cash were forthcoming either to meet the pressing needs of the administration or to pay wages in factories where the workers had taken control.[3] A decree of October 30/ November 12, 1917, ordered the banks to resume business and honour cheques drawn on them, threatening recalcitrant managers with imprisonment. But it was explained that the decree was issued solely in the interest of the depositors, and rumours of an intention to confiscate bank capital were denied.[4] It is not perhaps surprising that an order couched in these apologetic terms was treated as a symptom of weakness, and ignored. Before the revolution was a fortnight old, however, shortage of cash com-

[1] M. S. Atlas, *Natsionalizatsiya Bankov v SSSR* (1948), p. 6. Statistics quoted *ibid.* p. 10 show that the capital of the joint-stock banks had multiplied almost fourfold between 1900 and 1917 and that foreign participation, negligible in 1900, had risen to 34 per cent of the total capital in 1917 ; of the foreign capital 47 per cent was French and 35 per cent German.

[2] A full, though hostile, account of the nationalization of the banks, written by the vice-president of the central committee of Russian Banks at Petrograd, will be found in E. Epstein, *Les Banques de Commerce Russes* (1925), pp. 74-108.

[3] *Ibid.* pp. 75-76 ; according to a later Bolshevik statement there was an " agreement between the manufacturers and the banks that the banks should give no money to factories where workers' control was introduced " (*Trudy I Vserossiiskogo S"ezda Sovetov Narodnogo Khozyaistva* (1918), p. 174).

[4] *Denezhnoe Obrashchenie i Kreditnaya Sistema Soyuza SSR za 20 Let* (1939), p. 1.

pelled the government to act, though even then hesitatingly and half-heartedly. The State Bank, now nominally and legally an agency of the Soviet Government, was tackled first. On November 7/20, 1917, the deputy People's Commissar for Finance, Men- zhinsky, made a formal demand to the director of the bank in the name of the military-revolutionary committee for an advance of 10 million rubles to cover current needs of Sovnarkom. The demand having been refused, Menzhinsky returned the same afternoon with a detachment of troops, and read to the assembled staff of the bank a formal order from the Workers' and Peasants' Government to hand over 10 million rubles.[1] The troops remained in occupation. But neither their presence nor an appeal from VTsIK on the following day to " loyal " members of the staff[2] broke the boycott ; and six days later the bank ignored a further decree instructing it to make a short-term advance of 25 million rubles to Sovnarkom. On the same day the government nomi- nated Obolensky as " state commissar " for the bank ; and on November 17/30, 1917, it issued a further decree instructing Obolensky to advance the requisite 2 million rubles to Sovnarkom, and as a provisional measure, for the space of three days, to honour demands for currency advances from " official and social institu- tions " and from " commercial or industrial enterprises for the payment of wages to workers ".[3]

This last measure was clearly an attempt to turn the resistance of the joint-stock banks, which, throughout these crucial weeks, continued to be treated with considerable forbearance and regard for legality. When the deadlock at the State Bank paralysed their activity by depriving them of supplies of currency, Obolensky invited their directors to a conference which lasted for three days. The result was an agreement by which the Commissar for the State Bank guaranteed supplies of currency, and the private banks were to operate under the supervision of the State Bank and submit their accounts to it.[4] The compromise proved unworkable and was short-lived. On the morning of December 14/27, 1917,

[1] The order is printed from unpublished archives in M. S. Atlas, *Natsionali- zatsiya Bankov v SSSR* (1948), pp. 72-73.

[2] *Protokoly Zasedanii VTsIK 2 Sozyva* (1918), p. 44.

[3] *Sobranie Uzakonenii, 1917-1918*, No. 3, art. 42.

[4] The fullest account of these negotiations is in E. Epstein, *Les Banques de Commerce Russes* (1925), pp. 77-80.

troops occupied the principal private banks in the capital.[1] Later in the day, at a meeting of VTsIK, Lenin maintained that only the persistent obstruction of the banks had compelled the government to apply compulsion :

> In order to apply control we invited them, the men who run the banks, and together with them we worked out measures, to which they agreed, so that they could receive advances under conditions of full control and accountability. . . . We wished to proceed along the path of agreement with the bankers, we gave them advances to finance industries, but they started sabotage on an unprecedented scale, and experience compelled us to establish control by other methods.[2]

Sokolnikov, one of the party's financial experts and a future People's Commissar for Finance, explained to VTsIK that the banks were financing opposition and sabotage and eluded control by presenting faked accounts.[3] At the end of the meeting VTsIK approved two decrees which were issued forthwith. By the first, banking was declared to be a state monopoly and private banks were merged in the State Bank ;[4] the second provided for the forced opening of all private safes, the confiscation of gold and bullion, and the crediting of notes to accounts opened in favour of their owners at the State Bank.[5] Shortly afterwards the name of the State Bank was changed to National, or People's, Bank. The

---

[1] The Moscow banks were occupied on the following day (E. Epstein, *Les Banques de Commerce Russes* (1925), p. 80).

[2] Lenin, *Sochineniya*, xxii, 132. A month later, at the third All-Russian Congress of Soviets, Lenin spoke in a different tone : " We acted simply, without fearing the criticism of 'educated' people or, rather, of the 'uneducated' backers of the bourgeoisie who trade on the remnants of their knowledge. We said : We have armed workers and peasants, today let them occupy all the private banks ; and when they have done that, when the power is in our hands, only then will we discuss what steps to take. And in the morning the banks were occupied, and in the evening VTsIK issued its resolution " (*ibid.* xxii, 214).

[3] *Protokoly Zasedanii VTsIK 2 Sozyva* (1918), p. 149.

[4] *Sobranie Uzakonenii, 1917–1918*, No. 10, art. 150. When this decree was invoked many years later in the House of Lords, Lord Cave thought that it read " more like a declaration of policy than a positive enactment which is to take immediate effect " (*Law Reports (House of Lords)*, 1925, p. 124). In a still later case, a Russian lawyer commented on this aphorism : " If I may say so, I cannot agree with that, and everybody in Russia felt in his own skin that it was not a declaration of policy " (*Law Reports (King's Bench Division)*, 1932, i, 629). Early Soviet decrees, being drafted by members of Sovnarkom and not by lawyers, often had informalities of phrase.

[5] *Sobranie Uzakonenii, 1917–1918*, No. 10, art. 151.

word " state " at this phase of the revolution still had an ugly, alien sound in Bolshevik ears.

Even now, however, the difficulty was not to pass decrees of nationalization, but to make them effective.

> There was not a single man in our group [said Lenin at the third All-Russian Congress of Soviets] who imagined that such a cunning, delicate apparatus as that of banking, developed in the course of centuries out of the capitalist system of production, could be broken or made over in a few days. That we never asserted. . . . We do not minimize the difficulty of our path, but the main thing we have already done.[1]

For some weeks after the nationalization decree had been promul gated a strike of bank clerks prolonged the resistance ; and it was not until the middle cf January 1918 that the banks began to work under their new management.[2]   In February the capital of the nationalized private banks was transferred to the State Bank ; all bank shares were formally annulled and transactions in them made illegal.[3]   In April negotiations were unexpectedly reopened with the representatives of the banks, and an agreement was actually drafted by which the private banks would have been re-established in the guise of nationalized enterprises, but under the autonomous management of the former directors [4] — the financial counterpart of the negotiations with Meshchersky and the industrialists.[5]   But these projects, though they fitted in with the doctrine of " state

---

[1] Lenin, *Sochineniya*, xxii, 214-215.

[2] M. Philips Price, *My Reminiscences of the Russian Revolution* (1921), p. 211 ; Lenin reported the capitulation of 50,000 bank employees on January 12/25, 1918 (*Sochineniya*, xxii, 241).   It is interesting to note the different procedures followed in the nationalization of the banks and of industry and the different obstacles encountered : in the case of the banks the proletarian element was absent and the stage of workers' control omitted.

[3] *Sobranie Uzakonenii, 1917-1918*, No. 19, art. 295.

[4] Particulars of the negotiations are recorded in E. Epstein, *Les Banques de Commerce Russes* (1925), pp. 96-106, which notes the " great astonishment of the representatives of the banks " at the willingness of the Soviet negotiators to conclude such an agreement.   Sadoul, writing on April 14, 1918, reported that Gukovsky had secured the support of " the principal People's Commissars ", including Lenin and Trotsky, for the denationalization of the banks and the retractation of the annulment of foreign dates (J. Sadoul, *Notes sur la Révolution Bolchevique* (1919), pp. 309-310) ; rumours that Gukovsky was in favour of the denationalization of the banks continued to circulate and were denied by him at the first All-Russian Congress of Councils of National Economy in May 1919 (*Trudy I Vserossiiskogo S"ezda Sovetov Narodnogo Khozyaistva* (1918), p. 133).

[5] See pp. 88-91 above.

capitalism " preached by Lenin at the time, encountered strong opposition from the Left ; and the plan for a revival of the private banks fell to the ground with the rest. The remaining category of specialized or localized banks and credit institutions (except for the two agricultural mortgage banks which, being owned by the state, were declared liquidated and merged in the State Bank [1]) retained an independence existence for some months longer. Most of them were wound up during the year 1918. Among the last to survive was the Moscow Narodnyi Bank, the central bank of the cooperatives. A decree of December 2, 1918, terminated its independent status and turned its branches into cooperative branches of the National Bank.[2] On the same day an outstanding anomaly was removed by a decree formally pronouncing the sentence of liquidation on " all foreign banks operating in the territory of the RSFSR ".[3]

The second and other main item in the Bolshevik financial programme was the annulment of state loans and obligations. This, as Lenin remarked at the third All-Russian Congress of Soviets, was easier than the nationalization of the banks.[4] The principle of non-recognition by the revolutionary régime of the debts of the Tsarist government had first been proclaimed in the famous " Viborg manifesto " issued by the Petrograd Soviet in December 1905 to discredit the government's attempts to raise a fresh loan abroad. The manifesto applied specifically to foreign obligations ; the less important Russian Government loans raised

---

[1] *Sobranie Uzakonenii, 1917–1918*, No. 4, art. 56 ; that this decree, like others of the period, was easier to issue than to carry out is shown by an order of the People's Commissar for Finance more than a year later containing detailed instructions for the liquidation of the two banks (*Sbornik Dekretov i Rasporya-zhenii po Finansam, 1917–1919* (1919), pp. 54-55).

[2] *Sobranie Uzakonenii, 1917–1918*, No. 90, art. 912. Krestinsky afterwards frankly stated the reason for the delay in taking over the Moscow Narodnyi Bank : " The October revolution was carried out by us in alliance with all the peasantry, which fought together with us for power and for the land. If at that time we had attacked the Moscow Narodnyi Bank, this would undoubtedly have alienated a part of the peasantry that was on our side and weakened our blows against the common enemy. But, when we saw that the process of splitting had begun in the country, we decided to seize the Moscow bank, knowing that we should be supported in this by the strata in the country which sympathized with us — the poor and middle peasants " (*Trudy Vserossiiskogo S"ezda Zaveduyush-chikh Finotdelami* (1919), p. 76).

[3] *Sobranie Uzakonenii, 1917–1918*, No. 90, art. 907.

[4] Lenin, *Sochineniya*, xxii, 215.

on the home market were not included. The first move of the
Soviet Government was a decree of December 29, 1917/January
11, 1918 stopping all payment of interest or dividends on bonds
and shares and prohibiting transactions in them.[1] Then, on
January 28/February 10, 1918, a detailed decree was issued covering both foreign and domestic loans of " governments of the
Russian landowners and bourgeoisie ". Foreign loans were unconditionally annulled. Small holders of internal loans up to a value
of 10,000 rubles would have their holdings transferred into a new
loan of the RSFSR : short term notes and Treasury bonds would
cease to draw interest, but would continue to circulate as currency.[2]
The decree excited no particular interest in Russia, where the
inability as well as the unwillingness of the Soviet Government to
discharge the financial obligations of its predecessors was taken for
granted.[3] But it provoked violent official and unofficial protests in
allied countries, a note signed by the principal foreign representatives in Petrograd declaring it " without value so far as their
nationals are concerned " ;[4] and it continued for many years to
serve as a theme for acrimonious debate.

Beyond these two demands for the nationalization of the banks
and the annulment of debts the financial conceptions of the
Bolshevik leaders were fluid and unformed, and current problems
were approached at the outset from the standpoint of strict
financial orthodoxy. Nobody in the first weeks of the revolution
disputed such established principles of bourgeois public finance
as that the budget must be balanced, that the unlimited issue of
notes to meet public expenditure was an evil to be ended as soon

---

[1] *Sobranie Uzakonenii, 1917–1918*, No. 13, art. 185.

[2] *Ibid.* No. 27, art. 353. According to a report in *Foreign Relations of the
United States, 1918 : Russia*, iii (1932), 31-32, the decree had been approved by
Sovnarkom on January 1/14, 1918, and by VTsIK on January 21/February 3,
1918 ; the postponement of its promulgation " for international reasons " is
confirmed in *Narodnoe Khozyaistvo*, No. 11, 1918, p. 19.

[3] The provision for the exchange of holdings up to 10,000 rubles into a
corresponding loan of the RSFSR was not carried out, since no such loan could
be floated ; in October 1918 a decree was issued providing for the value of these
holdings to be credited to their owners at the State Bank (*Sobranie Uzakonenii,
1917–1918*, No. 79, art. 834).

[4] *Foreign Relations of the United States, 1918 : Russia*, iii (1932), 33.

as possible, and that the direct taxation of incomes and the indirect taxation of luxuries were the proper means of raising revenue. In Soviet Russia in the winter of 1917 to 1918 not one of these principles could in fact be honoured. But this failure was still thought of as purely temporary and compared with the similar failure of all the great European belligerents and many of the neutrals. When the Soviet Government came into power in Russia almost every European country was obtaining some of its public revenue by the inflationary use of the printing press. Russia was exceptional only in the high proportion in which her financial needs were being met from this source, and this had nothing to do with Bolshevism. The deficit in the Russian state budget had already amounted in 1914 to 39 per cent of the total expenditure; in the three succeeding years it had risen to 74, 76 and 81 per cent respectively.[1]

These deficits were reflected in a progressive currency inflation. After Witte's monetary reform of 1897 the Russian ruble had maintained a stable value down to 1914, at which date a note issue of 1·6 milliards of rubles was almost fully covered by the gold reserves of the State Bank. Between the outbreak of war and February 1917, while the gold reserve had substantially declined, the note circulation had risen to nearly 10 milliards of rubles. Between the February and October revolutions a further 9 milliards was added to the note issue. On five occasions the Provisional Government raised the legal limit of the note circulation — in each case retrospectively; the last occasion was on October 6, 1917, when the legal limit was raised to 16·5 milliards — a figure which at that moment had already been exceeded.[2] But the currency question was not at first regarded by the Bolshevik leaders as a matter of major importance, and the government continued to print notes without restraint to meet its requirements. The modern world had had no experience of the depreciation of money on the catastrophic scale now impending both in Russia and in Germany, and scarcely took it into account as a serious possibility. An attempt by the Provisional Government to raise a so-called " liberty loan " on the domestic market had ended in failure.

[1] *Na Novykh Putyakh* (1923), ii, 2.
[2] Statistical information on the period 1914–1917 is conveniently collected in A. Z. Arnold, *Banks, Credit and Money in Soviet Russia* (N.Y., 1937), pp. 27-52; there was also a rapid expansion of bank credit, particulars of which are given in M. S. Atlas, *Natsionalizatsiya Bankov v SSSR* (1948), pp. 28, 36-37.

The Soviet decree annulling the obligations of preceding Russian Governments closed the door for some time to come on domestic as well as on foreign borrowing, and with a depreciating currency and an administration in chaos taxation was a diminishing resource. Thus the printing press was the only major source of revenue available to the Soviet Government. During the first few months the process continued automatically and almost without comment, though Lenin voiced the general opinion when he declared in May 1918 that " housekeeping with the aid of the printing press such as has been practised up to the present can be justified only as a temporary measure ".[1] No formal action was taken to raise the long-exceeded legal limit set by the Provisional Government in October 1917. But throughout this period the note circulation rose at about the same rate as under the Provisional Government. This increase was supplemented by a series of decrees converting into legal tender, first, bonds of denominations not exceeding 100 rubles in the Provisional Government's liberty loan, then, unpaid coupons of all government loans maturing before the annulment decree, and finally, all treasury bonds and short-term treasury obligations.[2] These measures, designed partly to mitigate the hardships of small investors and partly to relieve the treasury from obligations which it could not have met directly, had the effect of further increasing currency circulation without formal resort to the overburdened printing press.

The levying of taxes during the initial period of the régime was at best haphazard and intermittent. There was still no question of departure from orthodox principles of taxation. The original party programme of 1903 had demanded " as a fundamental condition of the democratization of our state " (that is to say, as part of the minimum programme of a bourgeois-democratic revolution) the " abolition of all indirect taxation and the establishment of a progressive tax on incomes and inheritance " ; [3] and Lenin repeated, in the speech of May 1918 already quoted, that " all socialists are against indirect taxes, since the only tax which is correct from the socialist standpoint is a progressive income tax and property tax ".[4] But it soon became clear that all

[1] Lenin, *Sochineniya*, xxiii, 19.
[2] *Sobranie Uzakonenii, 1917–1918*, No. 24, art. 331 ; No. 39, art. 509.
[3] *VKP(B) v Rezolyutsiyakh* (1941), i, 21.   [4] Lenin, *Sochineniya*, xxiii, 19.

this was, in prevailing conditions, a vain aspiration, a substitute for any serious fiscal policy. So long as the whole economy was in a state of disintegration, and economic policy was directed to eliminate large private incomes, neither an increased yield from income-tax nor a reorganization of the fiscal system could be seriously thought of. The new régime could for the moment indulge no ambition except to live from hand to mouth on such resources as had been left to it by its predecessors. Its first fiscal enactment was a decree of November 24/December 7, 1917, advancing the final date for the payment of income-tax at the rates laid down by the Provisional Government and increasing the penalties for non-payment; and another decree of the same date made minor amendments in the levying of the tobacco duty.[1] These were probably the two first Soviet decrees concerned with the application and enforcement of legislative acts of a previous Russian Government. In January 1918 a further decree noted that the amusements tax inherited from the Provisional Government was being generally ignored and demanded that it should be strictly levied in future.[2]

The first revolutionary initiative in taxation was taken by local Soviets which, deprived of any other sources of revenue, began to levy " contributions " from well-to-do citizens on arbitrary assessments. But, as the central authority gradually began to assert itself, this procedure, notwithstanding its revolutionary credentials, encountered strong opposition from the People's Commissariat of Finance (Narkomfin), partly, perhaps, as an offence to financial purists, partly as an encroachment on the taxing prerogatives of the central government.[3] At the end of March 1918 the commissariat issued a circular to local authorities prohibiting this practice.[4] The local Soviets, supported by the People's Commissariat of Internal Affairs, protested against this interference with their autonomous rights. VTsIK, by ruling in

[1] *Sobranie Uzakonenii, 1917-1918*, No. 5, art. 71 ; No. 12, art. 169.
[2] *Ibid.* No. 14, art. 205.
[3] Abuses naturally occurred in the assessment and levying of these contributions : Gukovsky, the People's Commissar for Finance, instanced a case where 2 million rubles had been demanded from a small town of 5000 inhabitants in the province of Perm (*Trudy I Vserossiiskogo S"ezda Sovetov Narodnogo Khozyaistva* (1918), p. 142).
[4] *Sobranie Uzakonenii, 1917-1918*, No. 31, art. 408.

their favour, gave its implicit support to the system of " contributions " ; [1] and the right of local Soviets to cover their requirements by raising taxes was recognized in the constitution of the RSFSR. This was the starting-point for a controversy between central and local authorities.[2] At a conference of representatives of the financial sections of local Soviets held in Moscow in May 1918 under the auspices of the People's Commissariat of Internal Affairs, the *rapporteur* advocated the complete separation of local finances from central control. This drew a rebuke from Lenin, who argued that " democratic centralism " was a condition of the financial reforms demanded by the new régime.[3] But relations between central and local finance remained chaotic throughout 1918.

This was, however, only a minor element in the vast problem of public finance which confronted the Soviet Government. In the general reorientation of policy which followed the Brest-Litovsk treaty, these issues came up for serious discussion for the first time. The chapter on the budget in the constitution of the RSFSR, which was being drafted at this moment, opened with the announcement that the financial policy of the republic sought to promote " the fundamental aim of the expropriation of the bourgeoisie and the preparation of conditions for the universal equality of citizens of the republic in the sphere of the production and distribution of wealth ", and that it would not shrink from " incursions on the right of private property ". But the ensuing provisions, which presumably emanated from Narkomfin, were unoriginal and wholly orthodox. On April 15, 1918, Gukovsky, the People's Commissar for Finance, presented to VTsIK what should have been a budget statement, but was in fact an admission of his inability to draw up a budget ; in the middle of May the conference already mentioned

---

[1] *Trudy Vserossiiskogo S"ezda Zaveduyushchikh Finotdelami* (1919), p. 34. VTsIK was merely endorsing what it could not prevent ; " if we tried to put into effect any tax assessment ", said Lenin in the course of the debate, " we should straightway come up against the fact that separate regions are at present imposing their own taxes, each as it pleases, each as it comes into its head, and as local conditions permit " (*Sochineniya*, xxii, 428).

[2] See Vol. 1, pp. 133-134.

[3] Lenin, *Sochineniya*, xxiii, 18-19 ; the complaint was afterwards made that this conference had taken place in complete detachment from Narkomfin and " in an atmosphere of local interests, local needs, local taxes, local budgets " (*Trudy Vserossiiskogo S"ezda Zaveduyushchikh Finotdelami* (1919), p. 4).

was held in Moscow of representatives of the financial sections of local Soviets; at the end of May the first full critical discussion of the principles of Soviet financial policy took place at the first All-Russian Congress of Councils of National Economy. From these debates (full records exist only of the third) a fairly clear picture can be extracted of the conflicting trends which were beginning to emerge in the light of hard experience.

The official view represented by Gukovsky was broadly speaking that of the Right, and adhered closely to orthodox principles. Gukovsky claimed that, " so long as we have money in circulation " (the proviso was a ritual obeisance to the doctrine of its eventual dying away), a gold backing for the note issue was essential. He believed that the function of Narkomfin was to cut down as low as possible the estimates submitted to it by the spending departments and then square expenditure with revenue. Gukovsky had the traditional preference of ministers of finance for indirect taxation ; this he justified by the argument that, while direct taxation had been quite properly advocated by socialists under a capitalist régime, its yield and its ability fell off progressively as the capitalists were destroyed. He vigorously attacked the levying of " contributions " by local Soviets both as unsound in itself and as constituting an encroachment on the taxing authority of the central power.[1] Lenin, whose most detailed utterance on the subject at this time was his speech to the Moscow conference in May, differed from Gukovsky only in upholding the old party preference for direct taxation ; he suggested that income-tax should be made universal and levied in monthly instalments — a proposal that was certainly quite impracticable. He was less hostile in principle to " contributions " than Gukovsky, but admitted that they belonged to the period of " transitional power ", and that the time would come to centralize tax collection.[2] The weakness of the official case was the impossibility of drawing up any coherent budget on these — or indeed for the present on any other — lines. At VTsIK in April 1918 Gukovsky estimated the expenditure for the first half-year of the régime at 40–50 milliards of rubles and gave no estimate at all of revenue. At

[1] Gukovsky's arguments can be studied in his long speech to the first All-Russian Congress of Councils of National Economy (*Trudy I Vserossiiskogo S"ezda Sovetov Narodnogo Khozyaistva* (1918), pp. 129-143).
[2] Lenin, *Sochineniya*, xxiii, 19-20.

the first All-Russian Congress of Councils of National Economy six weeks later he estimated the expenditure for the first half-year at 20–25 milliards and the revenue at 5 milliards.[1] But it was difficult to regard any of these figures as anything but guesses.

The Left opposition, whose spokesman at the congress was Smirnov, saw nothing surprising in the failure to draw up a budget (bourgeois budgets were, after all, a product of years of experience) and nothing alarming in a budget deficit, provided the expenditure promoted desirable ends. Similarly the depreciation of the ruble through the lavish use of the printing press gave no cause for regret, since, " when the full triumph of socialism occurs, the ruble will be worth nothing and we shall have moneyless exchange ". Neither direct nor indirect taxation could be expected to yield much in present conditions ; but the system of contributions was to be encouraged.[2] No attempt was made at the congress to answer Smirnov : this radical doctrine was either not understood or treated as too fantastic to deserve serious consideration. Sokolnikov, who made the main report on financial policy, occupied what was in some respects an intermediate position. He insisted on the importance of gold in foreign transactions, but thought the limitation of the note issue at home by the requirement of a gold backing was neither necessary nor practicable. The dangers of an excessive currency circulation could be removed by maintaining fixed prices : " We need not aim at lowering the prices of goods, but we must aim at keeping these prices everywhere stable ". Sokolnikov did not, however, reject taxation ; on the contrary, he argued that without direct taxation of the peasants " Russia cannot exist " and " the Soviet power cannot conduct the economy ". As regards the absence of a budget, he observed consolingly that France still had no budget for 1918.[3] The congress itself refrained from any pronouncement on these apparently

---

[1] *Trudy I Vserossiiskogo S"ezda Sovetov Narodnogo Khozyaistva* (1918), p. 140 ; elsewhere (*ibid.* p. 133) Gukovsky stated that demands from departments had amounted to 24 milliards and had been cut down to 14 milliards, but these figures were evidently incomplete. A budget for the first half of 1918 was approved by Sovnarkom on July 11, 1918 (*Sobranie Uzakonenii, 1917–1918*, No. 50, art. 579) ; according to the official figures, expenditure in this period amounted to 17·6 milliards of rubles, revenue to 2·8 milliards (G. Y. Sokolnikov, etc., *Soviet Policy in Public Finance* (Stanford, 1931), p. 126.
[2] *Trudy I Vserossiiskogo S"ezda Sovetov Narodnogo Khozyaistva* (1918), pp. 147-149.   [3] *Ibid.* pp. 116-128, 173.

insoluble problems. Its sole contribution, which occurred incidentally in the course of its resolution on trade and exchange,
showed how little financial realism had yet penetrated the counsels
of the directors of Soviet economic policy : it demanded " increased
taxation, direct and indirect, increased use of cheques, and a most
decisive curtailment of the policy of currency emissions ".[1] The
civil war broke with the financial and fiscal policies of the Soviet
Government still in the main indeterminate and unformulated.

[1] *Trudy I Vserossiiskogo S"ezda Sovetov Narodnogo Khozyaistva* (1918),
p. 483.

CHAPTER 17

WAR COMMUNISM

(a) Agriculture

THE inauguration of " war communism " in agriculture coincided with the final political break with the Left SRs, who had remained in VTsIK and in the Soviets after the resignation of the Left SR members of the government in March 1918. The last occasion on which Bolsheviks and Left SRs sat side by side on terms of formal partnership was the second sitting of the fifth All-Russian Congress of Soviets on July 5, 1918 (the eve of the assassination of Mirbach) ; and the sitting was appropriately occupied by an acrimonious debate on agricultural policy, in the course of which Spiridonova declared herself " the bitter opponent of the Bolshevik party ".[1] The policy of the Soviet Government was open to attack from the Left SRs on three counts. The Bolshevik workers' detachments, as a Left SR speaker declared, were conducting " little short of war declared by the town on the country " ;[2] and SRs had always been the traditional defenders of the country against the town. The committees of poor peasants were an attempt by the Bolsheviks to supplant the authority of the land committees, in most of which SRs still had a predominant voice, the distinction reflecting the fact that most well-to-do peasants had retained their allegiance to the SRs, whether Right or Left, whereas the poor and less politically conscious peasants, if not already won over by the Bolsheviks, were at least amenable to Bolshevik wooing. Finally, the encouragement given by the government — however ineffective at this time — to the creation of large-scale farms on confiscated estates ran directly counter both to the SR policy of distribution to the peasants and to the SR ban on the employment of wage labour on

---

[1] *Pyatyi Vserossiiskii S''ezd Sovetov* (1918), p. 55.   [2] *Ibid.* p. 75.

the land; complaints were heard at the congress that estates were being kept undivided in regions where the peasants were hungry for land, and that workers were being hired to cultivate them in defiance of true socialist principles.[1] A recent decree nationalizing the forests and placing them under the management of a central forest administration — the first attempt at direct state administration of natural resources — came in for a similar attack.[2]

The outlawing of the Left SRs as the result of Mirbach's murder removed all opposition at the centre to a purely Bolshevik policy for agriculture. The rapidly spreading emergency of the civil war made the collection of grain from the peasants for the towns and for the army a matter of life and death; on the other hand it made the provision of clothing and other consumer goods to the peasant still more difficult, since the army now claimed all available supplies. Thus there was no alternative but to intensify the method of requisition through the machinery of workers' detachments and committees of the poor. No less than three decrees of the first week in August 1918 dealt with the work of these detachments. The first authorized trade unions, factory committees and town and county Soviets to organize food detachments of " workers and poorest peasants " to visit grain-producing provinces " to obtain grain at fixed prices or requisition it from *kulaks* ". Half the grain obtained was assigned to the organization or organizations which sent out the detachment; the other half was to be handed over to Narkomprod for general distribution. The second decree instructed provincial and county Soviets, committees of poor peasants and trade unions to organize similar detachments where necessary to get in the harvest. A third decree dealt in detail with the organization and composition of these detachments which were to consist of " not less than 25 workers and poor peasants of unimpeachable honesty and devoted to the revolution ".[3] So that no stone might be left unturned, the

[1] *Pyatyi Vserossiiskii S"ezd Sovetov* (1918), pp. 56-57 ; quotations from SR journals of the period are in *Izvestiya Akademii Nauk SSR : Seriya Istorii i Filosofii*, vi (1949), No. 3, pp. 235-236. Opposition to hired labour had always been a plank in the SR platform ; Lenin had long ago argued that " the chief sign and indicator of capitalism in agriculture is hired labour " (*Sochineniya*, xvii, 644).

[2] *Sobranie Uzakonenii, 1917-1918*, No. 42, art. 522 ; *Pyatyi Vserossiiskii S"ezd Sovetov* (1918), p. 56.

[3] *Sobranie Uzakonenii, 1917-1918*, No. 57, arts. 633, 635 ; No. 62, art. 677.

same week produced yet another decree on the " obligatory exchange of goods ". This provided that in the grain-producing
provinces cooperatives and other organizations concerned with
the distribution of goods should not be allowed, under strict
penalties, to release goods to any district or village except on
payment of at least 85 per cent of the value in agricultural produce.[1]

The realities that lay behind these decrees are difficult to
assess. Tsyurupa, the People's Commissar for Agriculture,
speaking at the fifth All-Russian Congress of Soviets, declared that
all ordinary means of obtaining the grain were tried and that,
" only when nothing is got, only then are the detachments sent
in ". As regards rumours that, " as soon as the detachments reach
the country, they begin to break out and get drunk ", such things
occurred, but every precaution, including the most careful recruit-
ment, was taken to prevent them.

> We do not regard these detachments [continued Tsyurupa]
> merely as a military force ; we see in these detachments people
> who go into the country armed, it is true, but at the same time
> as agitators who will conduct propaganda in the country, who
> will carry our ideas into the country.[2]

The peasants, when they dared, resisted the seizure of their grain.
Sometimes resistance was serious, and it came to real fighting ;
and such cases, though exceptional, were probably not very rare.[3]
Nor is it easy to estimate the number of detachments or the extent
of their activities. According to a speaker at the second All-
Russian Congress of Trade Unions in January 1919 the Petrograd
Soviet had up to that time sent out 189 detachments amounting
to 7200 men, and the Moscow Soviet about the same number.[4]
By this time the collection had been extended from grain and
fodder, sugar and potatoes, to meat, fish and all forms of animal
and vegetable fats, including hemp-seed, sunflower-seed and

---

[1] *Ibid.* No. 58, art. 638.

[2] *Pyatyi Vserossiiskii S"ezd Sovetov* (1918), pp. 143-144.

[3] A British observer visiting a group of villages in the Volga region two years
later was told of " one village in the neighbourhood where a disturbance had
occurred and many peasants lost their lives " at this time (*British Labour
Delegation to Russia 1920 : Report* (1920), p. 132).

[4] *Vtoroi Vserossiiskii S"ezd Professional'nykh Soyuzov* (1921), i (Plenumy),
170 ; another delegate gave a figure of 30,000 for all detachments sent out by
workers' organizations (*ibid.* i, 174).

linseed oil.[1] Lenin offered the only possible excuse for such measures at the moment when they were finally abandoned :

> The peculiarity of war communism consisted in the fact that we really took from the peasants all their surpluses, and sometimes even what was not surplus, but part of what was necessary to feed the peasant, took it to cover the costs of the army and to maintain the workers. We took it for the most part on credit, for paper money. Otherwise we could not beat the landowners and capitalists in a ravaged small-peasant country.[2]

These were desperate expedients. From the point of view of socialist theory the criterion of need may have seemed natural and proper : the peasant was required to deliver everything in excess of his own and his family's needs. From the point of view of practice it was fatal. Naked requisition from so-called *kulaks* of arbitrarily determined surpluses provoked the two traditional replies of the peasant : the short-term reply of concealment of stocks and the long-term reply of refusal to sow more land than was necessary to feed his own family.

The Soviet leaders were well alive to these dangers. On October 30, 1918, the new experiment of a tax in kind was introduced for the first time. It was apparently not a substitute for the collections, but a supplement to them, though anyone who had delivered all his grain surpluses before the tax was announced was declared exempt. The tax was to be assessed by a complicated calculation in which the amount of land and live-stock owned by the taxpayer was taken into account as well as the number of persons supported by him.[3] What was proposed was no longer a simple taking of surpluses, but the taking of fixed amounts, assessed on supposed capacity to pay. But this was one of the many decrees of the period which were never carried into effect.[4] In January 1919 another new principle was brought into action. A decree of Sovnarkom, supplemented by a detailed instruction of Narkomprod, fixed the total grain and fodder requirements of the central government and " apportioned " them for requisition between the producing provinces : the provinces were to apportion

---

[1] *Sobranie Uzakonenii, 1919*, No. 1, art. 13.
[2] Lenin, *Sochineniya*, xxvi, 332.
[3] *Sobranie Uzakonenii, 1917–1918*, No. 82, art. 864 ; No. 91-92, art. 928.
[4] See p. 249 below.

between counties, the counties between rural districts, and the districts divided their quota among villages or individual peasants.[1] The advantage of this system was to relieve the central authorities of the onerous task of tax-gathering; and it restored the principle of collective responsibility which had applied to the agrarian taxation of the Tsarist government. But these constantly changing expedients merely illustrate the insuperable nature of the difficulty which confronted the Soviet Government. The needs of the Red Army and the urban population could not be met in a devastated, mutilated and disorganized country by anything short of the total surplus of agricultural production. Yet industry was incapable of producing the equivalent in manufactured goods to set the ordinary processes of exchange in motion; and, if the attempt were persisted in to seize the surpluses by force, stocks would be concealed and sowings shrink to the dimensions of the peasants' own requirements. The crisis was somehow surmounted; the army was supplied and the towns saved from starvation, though not from hunger. As the machinery of collection gradually improved and the areas where civil war had raged were brought back under the control of Moscow, collections of grain increased.[2] But during the period of war communism, it may fairly be said that the peasants' grain either found its surreptitious way on to the free market or was forcibly seized by the agents of the government. Even those peasants who had fought on the side of the Soviet Government against the worse evil of a " white " restoration continued to wage the battle of the grain.

The turn towards the poor peasants in the summer of 1918 had been linked in Soviet policy with that other fundamental aim, the development of large-scale agriculture. It had involved a final

---

[1] *Sobranie Uzakonenii*, 1919, No. 1, arts. 10, 11.

[2] Official figures of Narkomprod gave the total collections for these years (in millions of puds) as follows: 1917–1918 — 47·5; 1918–1919 — 107·9; 1919–1920 — 212·5; 1920–1921 — 283·0 (*Pyat' Let Vlasti Sovetov* (1922), p. 377). These figures are not of great value, partly because accurate statistics were hardly kept in these early years, partly because the area concerned is not constant: in 1918–1919 the Volga basin was included for the first time, in 1919–1920 the Ukraine, Transcaucasia and central Asia. The same figures are repeated with slight variations in G. Y. Sokolnikov, etc., *Soviet Policy in Public Finance* (Stanford, 1931), p. 93.

break with the Left SRs, irreconcilable opponents of this aim; and the poor peasants were the only peasant group who could be regarded as indifferent to peasant ownership and potentially favourable to collective cultivation.[1]   These collective establishments were of several types.   The original Soviet farms (Sovkhozy) — the model farms of Lenin's April theses and several later pronouncements — were for the most part formed from estates growing special crops for which technical skill or special organization were required, such as sugar-beet or flax.[2]   There were agricultural communes in which peasants united to cultivate undistributed land, sharing the labour and the proceeds in common; these seem to have represented the strain of primitive communism in the Russian peasantry.[3]   Finally there were agricultural artels, in which the communal element was confined to marketing and did not extend to production.   Lenin probably took all these forms of collective agriculture into account when he admitted in the autumn of 1918 that there were still only " some hundreds of state-supported agricultural communes and Soviet farms ".[4]   By this time the rough-and-ready distribution of agricultural land in the areas under Soviet control was virtually complete.   The best land, other than the limited areas devoted to

[1] In the following year, when official policy had begun to favour the middle peasants, it was claimed that they were more inclined to favour collectives than the poor peasants who " will not abandon petty agriculture " (Bukharin i Preobrazhensky, *Azbuka Kommunizma* (1919), ch. xiii, § 114); in fact, poor and middle peasants clung with the same tenacity to the old forms of land tenure.

[2] In May 1918 all land, other than peasant holdings, which had been sown with beet in any year since 1914, was assigned to an " inalienable land fund of the nationalized sugar factories " (*Sobranie Uzakonenii, 1917-1918*, No. 34, art. 457); by decree of July 13, 1918, the administration of this land was entrusted to the Chief Sugar Committee (Glavsakhar) of Vesenkha (*Proizvodstvo, Uchet i Raspredelenie Produktov Narodnogo Khozyaistva* (n.d.), p. 16). In October 1918 Narkomzem was authorized to take over model farms, " technical " farms, and " former large estates with specialized economies " (*Sobranie Uzakonenii, 1917-1918*, No. 72, art. 787).

[3] In February 1919 Narkomzem issued a " model statute " for agricultural communes which breathed the pure spirit of primitive communism : " He who wishes to enter a commune renounces in its favour all personal ownership of money, the means of production, cattle and, in general, of all property required for the conduct of a communist economy. . . . Every member of the commune must give all his strength and all his capacities to the service of the commune. . . . The commune takes from every member according to his strength and capacities, and gives to him according to his real needs " (*Normal'nyi Ustav Sel'skokhozyaistvennykh Proizvoditel'nykh Kommun* (1919), pp. 4-5).

[4] Lenin, *Sochineniya*, xxiii, 403.

beet, flax and other special forms of cultivation, had found its way
into peasant ownership ; what was left over for collectivist experiments was likely to be the worst and most difficult to work. As a
Bolshevik commentator afterwards wrote :

> The vast majority of landowners' land had been subjected
> to partition, and there was reason to fear the disappearance of
> large-scale production in agriculture. Apart from this the
> danger existed of a great strengthening of the ideals of petty
> ownership.[1]

Heroic measures were required. On July 4, 1918, Sovnarkom
voted 10 million rubles for the encouragement of agricultural
communes.[2] On November 2, 1918, a fund of a milliard rubles
was set aside for advances to agricultural communes and workers'
associations, village communities or groups, on the condition of a
" transition from individual to common cultivation and harvesting
of the soil ".[3] In the following month Lenin made a long and
important speech to what was described as " the first all-Russian
congress of land sections, committees of poor peasants and
agricultural communes ". His theme was the coming of socialism
to the countryside, and it was his first major pronouncement on
the socialization of agriculture. He drew on one of his broad
historical perspectives. By the united effort of the peasantry as a
whole, " the power of the landowners has been really swept away
and finally annihilated ". But if the revolution in the Russian
countryside stopped there, it would stop where the revolutions of
1789 and 1848 had stopped in the west :

> It has not yet touched the stronger, the more modern
> enemy of all toilers — capital. It therefore threatens to end as
> abruptly as the majority of revolutions in western Europe, where
> a temporary alliance of town workers and the whole peasantry
> was successful in sweeping away the monarchy, in sweeping
> away the remnants of mediaevalism, in sweeping the land more
> or less clean of landowners' property and landowners' power,
> but never succeeded in uprooting the very foundations of the
> power of capital.

[1] V. P. Milyutin, *Istoriya Ekonomicheskogo Razvitiya SSSR* (2nd ed., 1929),
pp. 171-172.
[2] This decision is recorded in a note to Lenin, *Selected Works* (n.d.), viii,
409 ; the original source has not been traced.
[3] *Sobranie Uzakonenii, 1917-1918*, No. 81, art. 856.

The committees of poor peasants had performed the function of splitting the peasantry : " the country has ceased to be united ". This achievement had " transferred our revolution on to those socialist rails on which the working class of the towns wanted to place it firmly and decisively in October ". What was now needed — Lenin reiterated it over and over again — was " the transition from small individual peasant farms to the socialized working of the land ". He made no attempt to disguise the magnitude of the task :

> We know well that such great revolutions in the life of tens of millions of people, affecting the deepest foundations of living and being, as a transition from small individual peasant cultivation to the common working of the land, can be brought about only by prolonged work, can be realized only when necessity compels people to reshape their life.

The war had created this necessity by the devastation it had left behind it. At the same time it had brought into existence, and into the consciousness of the people, those " wonders of technique " which could transform agricultural production. The congress passed a resolution declaring that the chief aim of agrarian policy must be " the consistent and unswerving pursuit of the organization of agricultural communes, Soviet communist farms and the socialized working of the land ".[1]

For some weeks the campaign was in full swing. It was ventilated at the second All-Russian Congress of Trade Unions in January 1919, where an official spokesman voiced the view that " the question of feeding the towns can be solved only by the creation of large units of production in the country ".[2] It culminated in a long decree issued by VTsIK on February 14, 1919, the first major piece of legislation on agrarian policy since the " socialization " decree issued in conjunction with the Left SRs just over a year earlier. The new decree boldly proclaimed " the transition from individual to collective forms of the utilization of land ", declared that " all forms of individual utilization of land could be regarded as transitory and obsolete ", and described as its fundamental purpose " the creation of a single productive economy to furnish the Soviet republic with the largest quantity of economic

---

[1] Lenin, *Sochineniya*, xxiii, 420-429, 588, note 135.
[2] N . . . sky, *Vtoroi Vserossiiskii S"ezd Profsoyuzov* (1919), p. 85.

goods with the lowest expenditure of the people's labour ". Its 138 clauses included elaborate provisions for the constitution, prerogatives and obligations of Soviet farms and agricultural communes. The Soviet farms, which might be managed by a single administrator or by a working committee, were directly responsible to the provincial or local Soviet and through it to the appropriate department of Narkomzem : the organization was closely analogous to that of nationalized factories under Vesenkha. Agricultural communes, being " voluntary unions of workers ", enjoyed a wider autonomy, though they remained ultimately responsible to the local land section and to Narkomzem.[1]

Another experiment in this field arose from an attempt at organized self-help on the part of the urban workers. By the end of 1918 food conditions in the cities created a danger of the complete disintegration of the proletariat through the return of the workers to the villages from which most of them had originally come. A decree of December 1918 had recognized the right of trade unions and workers' organizations to store and transport for the use of their members all foodstuffs other than grain and flour — exceptions which were soon to be disregarded.[2] From the collective acquisition of foodstuffs it was only a short step to collective cultivation ; and in the winter of 1918–1919 this step was taken, apparently through the ingenuity and enterprise of Vesenkha. On February 15, 1919, immediately after the decree on Soviet farms, a decree was issued authorizing industrial enterprises, or groups of industrial enterprises, city Soviets, trade unions and cooperatives to acquire land and organize Soviet farms for the supply of their needs.[3] More than 30 *glavki* and centres were reported to have acquired in all some 80,000 desyatins of land on behalf of factories controlled by them.[4] It was evidently contemplated that local labour on these industrial Sovkhozy should be supplemented from time to time by teams of workers from the

[1] *Sobranie Uzakonenii*, *1919*, No. 4, art. 44.
[2] *Sobranie Uzakonenii*, *1917–1918*, No. 91-92, art. 927.
[3] *Sobranie Uzakonenii*, *1919*, No. 9, art. 87 : a later decree attempted to restrict the scheme to large organizations controlling groups of Soviet farms, though " temporarily, as an exception " individual farms could still be " assigned " to individual factories (*ibid.* No. 24, art. 277).
[4] *Dva Goda Diktatury Proletariata* (n.d. [? 1919]), pp. 47-50 : the enthusiastic writer even describes a project for building sanatoria for workers on the farms thus acquired.

factories themselves : the return of the factory worker to his village for the harvest had been a common phenomenon in Russian industry. The scheme was an evasion of the principles of rationing and orderly distribution (though the decree provided that amounts of food in excess of the ration should not be distributed, but should be handed over to Narkomprod). But it met a pressing need, and provided a minor illustration of the cardinal fact that the adequate feeding of the towns was ultimately incompatible with a system of small-scale peasant agriculture.

The place occupied by collective farms in the official propaganda of the time seems to have been quite out of proportion to the results achieved. The most detailed available statistics for European Russia, not including the Ukraine, show 3100 Soviet farms in 1918, 3500 in 1919 and 4400 in 1920. But this modest increase was more than accounted for by a rapid rise in the number of farms " assigned " to factories, which in 1920 accounted for nearly half the total of Soviet farms, so that the number of farms directly cultivated by public authority may actually have declined. Most of the Soviet farms of this period were quite small and present no analogy to the giant Sovkhozy of a later decade : in 1920 it was estimated that more than 80 per cent of them had an area of less than 200 desyatins. The general quality of the land was not high and less than half of it was under the plough. It was reported that in February 1919 only 35 Sovkhozy with a total area of 12,000 desyatins (these would have been among the larger farms) were under the direct administration of Narkomzem ; the rest were under local Soviets and " dragged out a miserable existence ". In the middle of 1919 there was 2100 agricultural communes ; thereafter the number gradually declined with a waning of the enthusiasm which had favoured this form of communal enterprise. Agricultural artels, on the other hand, rose from 1900 in 1919 to 3800 in 1920, and thereafter increased still more rapidly ; but this form of agricultural cooperation did not provide for collective cultivation.[1]

These figures plainly reveal the lack of any spontaneous support among the peasants for the large unit of production in

[1] The statistics in the above paragraph are taken from O Zemle, i (1921), 30-40, a publication of Narkomzem ; Otchet Narodnogo Komissariata Zemledeliya IX Vserossiiskomu S"ezdu Sovetov (1921), pp. 106-107, and V. P. Milyutin, Istoriya Ekonomicheskogo Razvitiya SSSR (2nd ed., 1929), p. 171, give even lower figures for Sovkhozy in 1918 and 1919.

agriculture, and represent a total defeat for Bolshevik policy. The drive for large-scale agriculture came exclusively from the towns and from official quarters. The arguments in its favour, whether from the standpoint of theoretical socialism or of practical efficiency, were irrefutable. The decrees carefully provided that the land available for the creation of these units should be confined to undistributed large estates and other waste or occupied land. But such intrusions could scarcely fail to excite the jealousies of a traditionally land-hungry peasantry. Nor is it difficult to imagine the feelings of some of those called on to sacrifice their dreams of becoming small peasant proprietors and to work as " rural proletarians " on Soviet or other collective farms, particularly at a time when material conditions could bring little or no mitigation of past hardships. " The peasant thinks : If this is a big estate, then I am once more a hired labourer." [1] When Lenin in March 1919 addressed a congress, which had been summoned to found a trade union of agricultural workers of the Petrograd province, on the advantages of collective cultivation, he was heckled on an article in the decree of February 14, which forbade workers on Soviet farms to keep their own animals, birds or vegetable plots ; Lenin a little reluctantly admitted that it was sometimes necessary to make exceptions, and that it might be possible, after discussion, to grant the Petrograd province an exemption from this provision " for some short period ".[2] The peasant was, as always, inarticulate. But the civil war dwarfed every other issue, and peasant opposition and obstruction effectively blocked any extension of Soviet and other collective farms. The Soviet Government could not entertain any policy which, however desirable on a long view, threatened a further immediate reduction in the forthcoming harvest.

But by this time another radical change had occurred in Soviet agrarian policy. The creation of the committees of poor peasants in June 1918 had been mainly a political gesture designed to split the peasantry. They had fulfilled one practical function — that of providing informers. Before they were brought into existence, officials or workers strange to the district had no means of locating hidden supplies of grain or of estimating what store a particular *kulak* might be expected to possess, so that many " mistakes " of

[1] Lenin, *Sochineniya*, xxiv, 167-168.   [2] *Ibid.* xxiv, 42-44.

assessment were made.[1] The poor peasants of the locality could be relied on to denounce *kulak* irregularities or evasions, and the resulting resentments and animosities would fan the flame of class warfare in the countryside. None the less, the institution failed to work. Now that the land had been distributed, the " poor peasants " — in the sense of peasants who had nothing to lose — proved less numerous than the Bolsheviks had supposed. The committees, where they were effective, seem to have been led by ardent Bolsheviks who were not always experienced in rural work and quickly clashed with the local Soviets, still at this time often of predominantly non-party composition. A struggle for power ensued in which it became clear that there was no room, in the local administration of rural affairs, both for the committees and for the Soviets.[2] A congress of committees of poor peasants of the Petrograd region held in Petrograd at the beginning of November 1918 was prepared to draw the logical conclusion : most of the delegates came to demand the transfer of all political power from the Soviets to the committees. This was, however, too much for the authorities. VTsIK intervened ; and the congress was induced to adopt unanimously a resolution of very different content. The resolution carefully mingled praise with implied censure. The committees had fought their fight against the *kulaks*, but in carrying out this task " were inevitably obliged to go beyond the limits of the decree of June 11 " : thus " a dual power was created in the countryside leading to fruitless dispersal of energy and confusion in relations ". The " dictatorship of the workers and the poorest peasants " could be embodied only in " the supreme organs of Soviet power from highest to lowest " ; and the function of the committees must be to " take the most active part in the transformation of rural district and village Soviets, converting them on the model of town Soviets into genuine organs of Soviet power and communist construction ". A week later this resolution was submitted by Zinoviev, who had directed the Petrograd congress, to the sixth All-Russian Congress of Soviets in a rambling and rather awkward speech, and approved unani-

[1] *Pyatyi Vserossiiskii S"ezd Sovetov* (1918), p. 143.

[2] The clash was not wholly unpremeditated on either side ; an SR spokesman in VTsIK had described the institution of the committees as a plan " to wage a war of extermination on the Soviets of Peasants' Deputies " (*Protokoly Zasedanii VTsIK 4go Sozyva* (1920), p. 403).

mously without discussion.[1] In effect the committees of poor
peasants lost their independent status, and were relegated to the
rôle of ginger groups within the local Soviets. A decree issued
by VTsIK on December 2, 1918, in pursuance of the congress
decision, declared that, in view of the conditions of " dual power "
which had grown up in the countryside, re-elections to village
Soviets had become urgently necessary ; that the committees of
poor peasants should play an active part in organizing these
elections ; but that the re-elected Soviets should then remain
" the only organs of power ", and the committees be disbanded.[2]
Lenin's subsequent account of the matter at the next party congress
was that the committees had " so well established themselves that
we found it possible to replace them by the properly elected
Soviets, i.e. to reorganize the local Soviets in such a way as to
become organs of class rule, organs of the proletarian power in the
countryside ".[3] This was an idealized picture. The abolition of
the committees was a timely recognition of failure — a retreat from
an untenable position. But the decision was not one of principle,
and did not prevent a repetition of the same experiment elsewhere.
Early in 1919, when Soviet power was re-established in the
Ukraine after the German collapse, committees of poor peasants
were set up there at the very moment when they were going out
of existence in the territory of the RSFSR.[4]

The decision to disband the committees of poor peasants was
closely bound up with the desire to win over the " middle peasant "

[1] For the Petrograd congress see Zinoviev's account in *Shestoi Vserossiiskii
Chrezvychainyi S"ezd Sovetov* (1918), p. 89, and Lenin, *Sochineniya*, xxiii, 254,
567-568, note 66 ; for the proceedings of the sixth All-Russian Congress
Shestoi Vserossiiskii Chrezvychainyi S"ezd Sovetov (1918), pp. 86-93 ; the resolution is also in *S"ezdy Sovetov RSFSR v Postanovleniyakh* (1939), pp. 120-121.
The day before the submission of the Petrograd resolution to the All-Russian
Congress of Soviets, Lenin addressed a congress of committees of poor peasants
of the Moscow region to which he described the effect of the proposals as
follows : " We shall fuse the committees of poor peasants with the Soviets, we
shall arrange it so that the committees become Soviets " (Lenin, *Sochineniya*,
xxiii, 283) ; the Moscow congress seems to have given less trouble than its
Petrograd counterpart.
[2] *Sobranie Uzakonenii, 1917-1918*, No. 86, art. 901.
[3] Lenin, *Sochineniya*, xxiv, 162.
[4] Differentiation between prosperous *kulaks* and hungry landless peasants
was more extreme in the Ukraine, especially since the Stolypin reform, than in

to support the Soviet power. It had become customary in Russia some time before the revolution to distinguish between not two, but three, grades of peasants — the well-to-do peasants, who grew for the market as well as for their own use, employing hired labour and selling their surplus production (*kulaks*), the poor peasants, landless or possessing too little land to maintain themselves and their families and compelled to hire out their labour to others in order to live (" poor peasants " or *batraks*), and an intermediate category of peasants who could maintain themselves and their families, but did not habitually employ hired labour or have surpluses to sell (the " middle peasants "). Such a classification was necessarily vague, and statistics relating to it uncertain. But it was commonly assumed that the *kulaks* formed less than 10 per cent of the peasantry, that the " poor peasants " accounted for some 40 per cent and that the remaining 50 per cent were " middle peasants ".[1] The middle peasants corresponded to what were generally known as small peasants in western Europe. The Russian " poor peasants " were in western terminology primarily agricultural labourers ; but some of them owned small plots of land which, though inadequate for the support of their families,

Great Russia. Lenin told a British observer at this time that the civil war was " likely to be more bitter in the Ukraine than elsewhere, because there the instinct of property has been further developed in the peasantry and the minority and majority will be more equal " (A. Ransome, *Six Weeks in Russia in 1919* (1919), p. 151) ; he made the same point again two years later (Lenin, *Sochineniya*, xxvi, 305). The device of the committees of poor peasants seemed therefore particularly fitted to the Ukraine. This did not, however, prevent errors in agrarian policy. According to the official party historian, the mistakes made in the RSFSR were repeated in the Ukraine in the spring of 1919. Here too there was the same attempt at a " mechanical planting of Sovkhozy and communes, with industry in ruins, without the slightest technical prerequisites (not to speak of political preparation), and without taking into account the needs of the middle peasant " ; the third party congress in Kharkov in March 1919 obstinately continued to demand " a transition from one-man economy to collective economy " (N. N. Popov, *Ocherk Istorii Kommunisticheskoi Partii (Bol'shevikov) Ukrainy* (5th ed., 1933), pp. 181, 185-186). Lenin at the same moment, at the eighth party congress in Moscow, noted cautiously that in the " borderlands of Russia ", including the Ukraine, it might be necessary, as it had been in the RSFSR, to change this policy, and that it was a mistake to copy out Russian decrees " uncritically and wholesale . . . for all parts of Russia " (*Sochineniya*, xxiv, 125-126). Nevertheless, the Ukrainian committees of poor peasants (Komnezamozhi) survived till the introduction of NEP : their activities were defended by a delegate at the eighth All-Russian Congress of Soviets in December 1920 (*Vos'moi Vserossiiskii S"ezd Sovetov* (1921), p. 202).

    [1] V. P. Milyutin, *Agrarnaya Politika SSSR* (2nd ed., 1927), pp. 161-162.

technically excluded them from the category of " landless " peasants.

Lenin had recognized this tripartite classification of the Russian peasantry at the time of the October revolution, when he declared that the policy of the Soviet régime must be " to help the toiling peasant, not to injure the middle peasant, and to constrain the rich peasant ".[1] But this policy remained for the moment in abeyance. The revolution in the countryside was still at its bourgeois stage ; the alliance between Bolsheviks and Left SRs was in force ; and the main purpose of the winter of 1917-1918 was to carry out the expropriation of the great landowners for the benefit of the peasantry as a whole. Then, in the summer of 1918, came the split with the Left SRs and the creation of the committees of poor peasants to initiate the socialist revolution against the *kulaks*. In the enthusiasm of the new move not much account was taken of the " middle peasants ". At the time the measure was introduced Lenin spoke specifically of the need of " agreement " and " alliance " with the middle peasants and of " concessions " to them ;[2] and in August 1918 a circular over the signature of Lenin and Tsyurupa was sent out to all local authorities, instructing them that the Soviet Government was in no way opposed to " peasants of the middle rank, not exploiting workers ", and that the benefits of the decree of June 11, 1918, should be extended to middle as well as to poor peasants.[3] But, so long as the committees of poor peasants were active and powerful, the tendency to concentrate on the interests of the poorest peasants and to assimilate middle peasants to *kulaks* was irresistible.

It would be misleading to diagnose the change in Soviet agrarian policies which followed the disbanding of the committees of the poor peasants in the winter of 1918-1919 either as a move towards the Right or as an anticipation of the New Economic Policy of 1921. But it meant a certain watering down of the extremer applications of war communism, and a return to a policy of compromise with what had hitherto been regarded as petty bourgeois elements in the countryside. It was the crucial moment of the civil war when the Soviet leaders felt the need to

---

[1] Lenin, *Sochineniya*, xxii, 50.

[2] *Ibid.* xxiii, 128, 173.

[3] *Izvestiya*, August 18, 1918, quoted in Lenin, *Sochineniya*, xxiv, 767-768, note 61.

rally all possible allies to their side in the desperate struggle. The concession to the middle peasant coincided in time with the abortive attempt to clip the wings of the Cheka and with the movement of qualified toleration of Mensheviks and SRs which began in November 1918 and went on through the winter,[1] as well as with a more general appeal to bourgeois intellectuals and " specialists " of all kinds to enter the service of the new régime. Lenin specifically wrote of " agreement with the middle peasant, with yesterday's Menshevism among the workers and with yesterday's sabotage among officials or among the intelligentsia " as parts of a single policy.[2] These were all treated as doubtful elements of petty bourgeois complexion, always wavering between the bourgeois and the proletarian cause and prone to change from side to side.[3] The civil war could not have been won if there had not been at this time some consolidation of these elements behind the Soviet power. But the change also constituted a recognition by the Bolshevik leaders that they had under-estimated the increase in the numbers and influence of the middle peasantry resulting from the agrarian reform. Bolshevik theorists had always argued that the distribution of land in small peasant holdings must strengthen the forces of petty bourgeois capitalism in the countryside. Theory had now been verified by practice. The " poor " peasants, as Lenin afterwards wrote, " turned into middle peasants ".[4] The attempt to implant socialism by shock tactics through the committees of poor peasants had failed, and compromise was the order of the day. To this extent the change of front was a foretaste of the far wider operation undertaken in March 1921.

The appeasement of the middle peasant was an essential and important feature of Soviet policy throughout 1919. It was in full swing at the time of the eighth party congress in March 1919. Lenin returned to it at the congress no less than three times — in his opening speech, in his general report on the work of the central committee and in a separate report " on work in the country ". It was no longer sufficient to " neutralize " the middle

[1] See Vol. 1, pp. 171-172.   [2] Lenin, *Sochineniya*, xxiii, 295.
[3] Lenin admitted that the middle peasantry " will of course vacillate and consent to come over to socialism only when it sees a solid and practically convincing example of the inevitability of making the transition " (*ibid.* xxiii, 426) ; he afterwards described it as " the kind of class which wavers " being " part proprietor, part worker " (*ibid.* xxiv, 164).   [4] *Ibid.* xxvi, 330.

peasants ; at the stage of socialist construction which had been reached it was necessary to put relations " on the basis of a firm alliance ". Lenin twice quoted the conciliatory recommendations made by Engels in his last pamphlet *On the Peasant Question in France and Germany* against the application of compulsion to the small peasant.[1] There could, of course, be no question of conciliating *kulaks :* " we stood, stand, and shall stand, in a posture of direct civil war with the *kulaks* ". But it was a serious mistake when, " through the inexperience of Soviet workers ", blows intended for the *kulaks* fell on the middle peasants.[2] The agrarian section of the new party programme approved by the congress, after registering the principle of support for Soviet and other collective farms and for agricultural cooperatives, passed on to the individual peasant. Since " small peasant economy will continue to exist for a long time ", the party must concern itself with measures " directed to raise the productivity of peasant economy ". Thus all practical assistance must be given to the peasant to improve his crops and his land ; more and more industrial workers must be drawn into the work of " socialist construction " in the countryside ; the opposition of " the *kulaks*, the rural bourgeoisie ", must be resolutely crushed ; and a final paragraph defined the attitude to the middle peasantry :

> The party makes it its task to separate the middle peasantry from the *kulaks*, to win it over to the side of the working class by attentive consideration for its needs, struggling against its backwardness by measures of ideological persuasion, and not at all by measures of repression, striving in all cases where its vital interests are affected for practical agreements with it, and making concessions to it in the choice of means of carrying out socialist transformations.

By way of reinforcing this conclusion the congress adopted a special resolution on the middle peasantry. In virtue of its " comparatively strong economic roots " and the backwardness of technical development in the Russian countryside, the middle peasantry was likely to " hold its ground for a fairly long time after the beginning of the proletarian revolution " ; Soviet workers

---

[1] See pp. 392-393 below ; Lenin had already quoted this passage in a discussion of agrarian policy in November 1918 (*Sochineniya*, xxiii, 307-309).

[2] *Ibid.* xxiv, 114, 126-127, 158-171.

must recognize that " it does not belong to the exploiters, since it does not draw profits from the labour of others ". While therefore middle peasants were to be encouraged to enter agricultural communes and associations of all kinds, " not the smallest compulsion " was to be applied for this purpose. All " arbitrary requisitions " were to be rigorously condemned; the weight of taxation should be made to fall " wholly on the *kulaks* "; the middle peasantry should be taxed " with extreme moderation only to a degree fully within its powers and not oppressive to it ".[1]

No occasion was missed of applying these somewhat difficult directions. Sverdlov, who occupied the honourable and representative office of president of VTsIK, had died on the eve of the party congress. The succession went to Kalinin, a Petrograd worker who was a former peasant — a middle peasant — from the province of Tver and, as Lenin explained, " still keeps up his connexion with the country . . . and visits it every year ". The symbolism of the appointment was frankly stated : " We know that our chief task in a country of small peasant agriculture is to assure the indestructible alliance of the workers and the middle peasantry ".[2] But the course thus confidently advocated throughout 1919 proved also to have its drawbacks. The middle peasant showed much of the traditional outlook of the *kulak*; and, if support for the poor peasant had failed to stimulate production, support for the middle peasant drove more and more of what was produced on to the black market. Lenin sounded the first note of alarm at a conference of party workers in November 1919 :

> The middle peasant produces more food than he needs, and thus, having surpluses of grain, becomes an exploiter of the hungry worker. This is our fundamental task and the fundamental contradiction. The peasant as a toiler, as a man who lives by his own toil, who has borne the oppression of capitalism, such a peasant is on the side of the worker. But the peasant as a proprietor, who has his surpluses of grain, is accustomed to look on them as his property which he can freely sell.

And again :

> By no means all the peasants understand that free trade in grain is a state crime. " I produced the grain, it is my handi-

---

[1] *VKP(B) v Rezolyutsiyakh* (1941), i, 292, 307-309.
[2] Lenin, *Sochineniya*, xxiv, 189, 215.

work, I have the right to trade it " — that is how the peasant reasons, by habit, in the old way. And we say that this is a state crime.[1]

The middle peasant took the traditional peasant view of governmental regulation as an attack by the town on the sacred prerogatives of the countryside. The transfer of support from the poor to the middle peasant had once again opened the door to the forces of petty bourgeois peasant capitalism. But for the present there was nothing to be done. The seventh All-Russian Congress of Soviets in December 1919 passed a stern resolution commending the policy of requisitions, and demanding that it should be extended from grain and meat to " potatoes and, as required, other agricultural products ".[2]

Nor did the turn from the poor to the middle peasant do anything to help the Soviet farms or other forms of large-scale cultivation. At the ninth party congress of March 1919 which proclaimed the policy of conciliating the middle peasant Lenin touched on one of the sore points of collective agriculture. The middle peasant would be won over to the communist society " only . . . when we ease and improve the economic conditions of his life ". But here was the rub :

> If we could tomorrow give 100,000 first-class tractors, supply them with benzine, supply them with mechanics (you know well that for the present this is a fantasy), the middle peasant would say : " I am for the commune (i.e. for communism) ". But in order to do this, it is first necessary to conquer the international bourgeoisie, to compel it to give us these tractors.[3]

Lenin did not pursue the syllogism. To build socialism in Russia was impossible without socialized agriculture ; to socialize agriculture was impossible without tractors ; to obtain tractors was impossible without an international proletarian revolution. Meanwhile, the slogan of the peasants was : " For Soviet power, for the Bolsheviks, down with the commune ".[4] Complaints began to

---

[1] *Ibid.* xxiv, 538, 540-541.

[2] *S"ezdy Sovetov RSFSR v Postanovleniyakh* (1939), pp. 142-144.

[3] Lenin, *Sochineniya*, xxiv, 170.

[4] *Ibid.* xxiv, 241 ; Lenin reverted to this slogan two years later, when he reported it in the form : " We are Bolsheviks, but not communists. We are for the Bolsheviks because they drove out the landowners, but we are not for the communists because they are against individual holdings " (*ibid.* xxvi, 456).

be heard that the Sovkhozy were nothing more or less than " a restoration of the great estates under the Soviet flag ".[1] At a party conference in November 1919 on party work in the country Lenin admitted the " mistrust and anger " of the peasants against the Sovkhozy, especially when " old exploiters " were engaged as managers and technicians, but vigorously defended the practice :

> No, if you yourselves do not know how to organize agriculture in the new way, we must take the old specialists into our service ; without this we shall never escape from beggary.[2]

Nevertheless, the seventh All-Russian Congress of Soviets in December 1919 was the occasion of a thorough-going attack on the Sovkhozy. They were accused of keeping aloof from the local Soviets, of attracting specialists by the offer of high salaries and of interfering in the distribution of land. The directors lived luxuriously in the former landowners' houses ; in some cases evicted landowners had actually been reinstated in the guise of directors of Sovkhozy : " Soviet farms have been turned into instruments of counter-revolutionary agitation against the Soviet power ".[3] Lenin in his reply admitted that abuses of this kind might have occurred, and could only argue that the remedy was for Sovkhozy to establish " close links both with the peasant population and with communist groups ".[4] The middle peasant remained an impenitent individualist. When a German delegate at the second congress of Comintern in the summer of 1920 reproached the Soviet Government, through its support of small-holders as against large-scale agriculture, with a " direct relapse into long outworn petty bourgeois ways of thought " and " a sacrifice of the interests of the proletariat in favour of the peasantry ", Lenin tartly replied that " otherwise the small peasant will not notice the difference between the former government and the dictatorship of the Soviets ", and that " if the proletarian state power does not act in this way, it will not be able to maintain itself ".[5] Yet this view, so long as it prevailed, was an effective

[1] *Narodnoe Khozyaistvo*, No. 6, 1919, p. 18.
[2] Lenin, *Sochineniya*, xxiv, 539-540.
[3] 7[i] *Vserossiiskii S"ezd Sovetov* (1920), pp. 199, 219.
[4] Lenin, *Sochineniya*, xxiv, 622-623.
[5] *Der Zweite Kongress der Kommunistischen Internationale* (Hamburg, 1921), p. 318 ; Lenin, *Sochineniya*, xxv, 359. For " advanced capitalist countries " the congress resolution on the agrarian question recommended " the mainten-

bar to what Lenin and all Marxists regarded — and, in Russian conditions, rightly — as the only way to a more efficient agriculture.

When, therefore, the civil war at long last petered out in the autumn of 1920, and the former territories of the Russian Empire, now consolidated under Soviet power, were left to themselves to face the uphill task of reconstruction, it was abundantly clear that the revolution, in changing the face of the Russian countryside, had solved none of its fundamental problems. Important food-producing areas had been brought back into the Soviet economy in time for the harvest of 1920.[1] In Siberia, now opened up by the defeat of Kolchak, large stocks were believed to exist from previous harvests; and every kind of compulsory measure was decreed in order to extract these from their holders.[2] But such windfalls, while they may have brought some temporary alleviation of the now chronic food shortages in the cities, did not affect the progressive decline in production which was threatening to bring the whole economy to a standstill. Agricultural statistics of the period of war communism are in the nature of things unreliable. It was impossible with the best will in the world to obtain even approximately accurate figures from the countryside; the peasant had every motive for concealing his production and his stocks;[3] and the collation and analysis of such reports as were received left much to be desired. Different figures were issued by different authorities, and it was not always clear to what areas they purported to relate. But, with all these reservations, the picture of Russian agriculture on the eve of NEP can be drawn in broad statistical outlines.

The agrarian redistribution initiated by the October revolution was virtually completed by the end of 1918 in areas then under Soviet control and extended by the summer of 1920 over the

ance of large-scale agricultural enterprises and the conduct of them on the lines of Soviet farms ", while admitting that in economically backward Russia Soviet farms were still " a comparatively rare exception " (*Kommunisticheskii Internatsional v Dokumentakh* (1933), p. 136).

[1] The harvest in the Ukraine must have suffered heavily from the Polish invasion in May and June : how far the poor results were attributable to this cause, how far to the drought, and how far to previous devastations, cannot be estimated.

[2] *Sobranie Uzakonenii, 1920*, No. 66, art. 298.

[3] According to an estimate in L. Kritsman, *Geroicheskii Period Velikoi Russkoi Revolyutsii* (n.d. [? 1924]), pp. 131-133, about one-third of the crucial 1920 harvest was concealed by the peasants.

whole territory of the Soviet republics. It led to a striking equalization of the size of the unit of production. A table circulated at this time classified in percentages the holdings of different sizes in 1917, 1919 and 1920 respectively :

	1917 %	1919 %	1920 %
No arable land	11·3	6·6	5·8
Arable land up to 4 desyatins	58·0	72·1	86·0
Arable land from 4 to 8 desyatins	21·7	17·5	6·5
Arable land above 8 desyatins	9·0	3·8	1·7 [1]

The smallholding worked by the labour of the peasant and his family, commonly owning one horse, already typical in 1917, had become by 1920 the predominant unit in Russian agriculture. The large landowner's estate had disappeared. The attempt to recreate the large unit in the form of the Soviet farm or the agricultural commune had everywhere encountered stubborn opposition and met with trivial success. Among the ample causes for a decline in production in the three years after the October revolution — the devastation of the countryside, the loss of man-power, the destruction of livestock, the shortage of implements and fertilizers — it would be unfair to assign more than a minor place to the lowered efficiency of the small as against the large unit. But this was a permanent handicap which was destined to outlast the adverse factors arising directly out of the war and the civil war, and constituted the basic dilemma of the Soviet economy.

The growth of small peasant agriculture at the expense of large-scale working had certain specific consequences. In the first place, it encouraged a switch-over from the more valuable specialized crops to bare subsistence farming. The third All-Russian Congress of Councils of National Economy in January 1920 took note of " a dangerous transition from technical and specialized crops to food crops (reduced sowing of flax, timber, oil-seed plants, cotton, etc.), as well as a diminution of livestock

[1] L. Kritsman, *Geroicheskii Period Velikoi Russkoi Revolyutsii* (n.d. [? 1924]), p. 68 ; another table (*ibid.* p. 67) shows that, of holdings up to 4 desyatins, more than half were of less than 2 desyatins. Similar results are obtained from a table (*ibid.* p. 67)· showing the number of horses per holding. The percentage of holdings without a horse fell from 29 in 1917 to 7·6 in 1920, the percentage with one horse rose from 49·2 to 63·6, the percentage with more than two horses fell from 4·8 to o·9.

farming ".[1] According to the *rapporteur* on agricultural questions at the eighth All-Russian Congress of Soviets in December 1920 the area under cultivation in the Soviet republics had declined between 1917 and 1919 by 16 per cent : the decline had, however, been least in the area under rye (6·7 per cent) and highest in the area under specialized crops (27 per cent for hemp, 32 per cent for flax, 40 per cent for fodder).[2] Secondly, the small peasant holding not only produced less, but consumed a higher proportion of what it produced, so that the balance that found its way to the towns was doubly curtailed ; and, where surpluses existed, the processes of collection were rendered infinitely more difficult and hazardous, since it was impossible, both materially and morally, to apply to a mass of small and " middle " peasants the measures of coercion which could be used against a few wealthy large-scale cultivators, or against collective units sponsored by the state or by the urban proletariat. As Lenin had always foreseen, the distribution of land to the peasants, by reducing the average size of the unit of production, proved a fatal obstacle to that increased flow of food and raw materials to the towns which was required to seal the victory of the proletarian revolution. The difficulty of building a socialist order in a country whose economy depended on a backward peasant agriculture was once more plainly shown up.

But, quite apart from all handicaps arising out of the agrarian system, the main difficulty in securing supplies of food for the towns was the fact that no adequate return could be offered to the peasants and that requisition in one form or another was virtually the sole legal method of obtaining grain. The Soviet leaders, having no practicable alternative to propose, were obstinately slow to recognize the hard fact.[3] But by the autumn of 1920 peasant discontent was too widespread to be concealed. From September

---

[1] *Rezolyutsii Tret'ego Vserossiiskogo S"ezda Sovetov Narodnogo Khozyaistva* (1920), p. 22.

[2] *Vos'moi Vserossiiskii S"ezd Sovetov* (1921), p. 123.

[3] In the summer of 1920, when Lenin read a remark by Varga, inspired by the experience of the Hungarian revolution, that " requisitions do not lead to the goal since they bring in their train a decrease of production ", he annotated it with two marks of interrogation (*Leninskii Sbornik*, vii (1928), 363) ; a few months later a statement in Bukharin's *Ekonomika Perekhodnogo Perioda* that coercion of the peasantry was not to be regarded as " pure constraint ", since it " lies on the path of general economic development ", was annotated by Lenin with a " very good " (*ibid.* xxxv (1945), 175).

onwards the demobilization of the armies had led to " banditry " —
the traditional form of peasant upheaval — throughout the central
and south-eastern regions ; the province of Tambov seems to
have been the centre of these disturbances.[1] The hostility of the
peasants was frankly expressed at a meeting of presidents of the
executive committees of the rural Soviets of Moscow province
which was addressed by Lenin : Lenin admitted in his concluding
remarks that " the majority of the peasants feel only too bitterly
the cold and hunger and intolerable imposts " and that " the
majority of those who have spoken openly or indirectly abused the
central power ".[2]

The last serious examination of the agricultural problem in the
period of war communism took place at the eighth All-Russian
Congress of Soviets in December 1920. The defeat of Wrangel
had finally ended the civil war, and the congress occupied itself
almost exclusively with economic reconstruction. Lenin in his
introductory speech still clung to the view that " in a country of
small peasants it is our chief and fundamental task to discover how
to achieve state compulsion in order to raise peasant production ".[3]
Dan, the Menshevik, summed up the indictment of Soviet action.
The " supply policy based on force " was bankrupt. It had been
successful in extracting 30 million puds from the peasant, but
" this has been purchased at the cost of a universal diminution in
the sown area to the extent of almost a quarter of the former total,
a reduction of livestock, a falling off in the sowing of technical
crops and a grave decline in agriculture ".[4] A resolution put
forward by the Left SR delegate proposed that " in order to
provide an incentive for the development of agriculture ", requisitioning should be limited to a part of what the peasant produced
and the remainder should be left to him " either for his own
consumption or for exchange through the system of consumer
cooperatives against articles necessary for the working peasant
household ".[5] A Menshevik resolution went further still, recognizing that the Russian peasants formed " a class of producers who

---

[1] *Desyatyi S"ezd Rossiiskoi Kommunisticheskoi Partii* (1921), pp. 37-38 ;
during the winter Narkomprod was compelled to suspend the collection of
grain altogether in thirteen provinces (*ibid.* p. 231).

[2] Lenin, *Sochineniya*, xxv, 426.   [3] *Ibid.* xxvi, 38.

[4] *Vos'moi Vserossiiskii S"ezd Sovetov* (1921), p. 42.

[5] *Ibid.* p. 122.

develop or contract their economic activity in accordance with the principles of a market economy " — i.e. a class of small capitalists — and proposing that " the peasantry should have the possibility to dispose of all surpluses remaining after the fulfilment of its state obligations, strictly defined, on the basis of a voluntary exchange of goods or of prices fixed in agreement with it ".[1] The Menshevik proposal was ill received, a Bolshevik delegate comparing it to " what we have heard over and over again from all the *kulaks* and bandits, especially in the Ukraine ".[2] But the debate as a whole was both gloomy and barren. Teodorovich, the *rapporteur*, diagnosed the three main features of the situation : a " general impoverishment of the countryside ", a curtailment of agricultural production, coupled with a transition from specialized to " natural " crops, and a " levelling of peasant holdings ". These conditions produced two " fundamental defects " : a decline in the area under cultivation and a low productivity (" three or four times less than in several countries of western Europe "). Teodorovich once more expounded the eternal dilemma — the " vicious circle " — of town and country and their respective demands :

> In order to revive the country it is necessary to supply it with goods from the town in normal quantity ; but, in order in its turn to produce these, the town must be supplied with a definite quantity of raw material and food.[3]

But conceptions of how to break out of this vicious circle and obtain the " definite quantity " of supplies required by the town were still naïve and still dictated by a predominantly urban outlook. In 1919 the executive committee of the Tula provincial Soviet had had the idea of setting up a " sowing committee " to conduct a campaign among the peasants for greater production.[4] The idea had been taken up elsewhere, and seemed suitable for general use.[5] It was decided to establish provincial, county and rural district " sowing committees ". An " all-state plan of obligatory sowing " was to be prepared by Narkomzem. The provincial committees

---

[1] *Ibid.* p. 201.   [2] *Ibid.* p. 202.
[3] *Ibid*, pp. 123-125.   [4] *Ibid.* p. 148.
[5] The project had been elaborated by Osinsky (Obolensky) in a pamphlet *Gosudarstvennoe Regulirovanie Krest'yanskogo Khozyaistva* (1920): Osinsky condemned any proposal " to replace the monopoly of food supplies by a tax in kind " as leading to free trade and implying a " pro-*kulak* " policy (*ibid.* p. 16).

were " to work out a plan of obligatory sowing and fix areas of sowing . . . for the whole province and for each county individually " ; the subordinate committees would see to the execution of the plan. It was declared to be a " state service " to sow " the area of land laid down in the state sowing plan ".[1]

The debate at the eighth All-Russian Congress of Soviets marked a certain advance. Throughout the first three years of the Bolshevik régime, the food shortage had been treated as a problem of collection and distribution, not of production. This assumption, natural in what had so lately been a grain-exporting country, was now at length revealed as a tragic fallacy. The civil war, the agrarian reform and the producers' strike due to requisitioning had combined to bring about a steady reduction of acreage under cultivation and of crops harvested. When the civil war ended, it was patent that the basic task of Soviet agricultural policy was no longer to extract from the peasant his non-existent surplus, but to stimulate agricultural production. So much was recognized by the congress. Yet, in defiance of all experience, it was once again assumed that the peasant could be compelled or inveigled into complying with these requirements. This time the illusion was short-lived. When three months later Lenin announced the New Economic Policy, it followed lines not far removed from those adumbrated by Left SRs and Mensheviks at the eighth All-Russian Congress of Soviets.

(b) Industry

The impact of the civil war on industry was more direct and, on the short view, more disruptive than on agriculture. In agriculture it intensified every demand, and increased every difficulty of production and supply, thus forcing issues which would otherwise have matured at a more leisurely and manageable pace. In industry it did all these things, and much more. It once more distorted the shape of production at the moment when

[1] The resolution (*S"ezdy Sovetov RSFSR v Postanovleniyakh* (1939) pp. 170-175) was published with the other resolutions of the congress in *Sobranie Uzakonenii, 1921*, No. 1, art. 9 ; early in January a decree was issued formally establishing the sowing committees (*ibid.* No. 2, art. 14), and at the end of the month a further decree defining their functions (*ibid.* No. 7, art. 52) — the last still-born product of the agricultural policies of war communism.

reconversion to the purposes of peace had been the order of the day; it transformed all major industry into a supply organization for the Red Army, and made industrial policy an item of military strategy; and every decision was dictated by emergency and taken without regard to long-term prospects and principles. In so far as continuity was maintained in Soviet industrial policy before and after the civil war, it merely illustrated the principle that wars and convulsions serve as a forcing house for revolutionary changes due to previous and profounder causes. State control of the industrial machine, already stimulated by the first world war before the Bolshevik advent to power, now received a fresh and overwhelming stimulus from the civil war; and its place in Bolshevik doctrine was confirmed anew by hard practical experience. The main lessons which the civil war drove home in industry were the necessity for centralized control, direction and planning. It also inculcated two conclusions less obviously compatible with socialist principles, but patently demanded by considerations of efficiency — the need for technical specialists and the need for one-man responsibility in management.

The legal relations between state and industry were defined by progressive nationalization of all industrial concerns. The period of war communism in industry began with the decree of June 28, 1918, which nationalized all major branches of industry.[1] During the latter part of 1918 a number of decrees of nationalization filled the gaps left by the enactment of June 28; and a decree of October 1918 reiterating the rule that no body other than Vesenkha, " in its quality as the central organ regulating and organizing the whole production of the republic ", had the right to sequester industrial enterprises [2] suggests that local Soviets and Sovnarkhozy were still indulging in nationalizations on their own account. But, except for quite small industrial concerns, formal nationalization was a closed issue by the end of 1918, irrespective of whether any actual process of taking over had occurred or not. Early in 1919 attention was turned to small rural handicraft industries, scattered and unorganized, dependent in large part on the part-time or home labour of the poorer peasants and their

---

[1] *Sobranie Uzakonenii, 1917–1918*, No. 47, art. 559; for this decree see pp. 99-100 above.

[2] *Sbornik Dekretov i Postanovlenii po Narodnomu Khozyaistvu*, ii (1920), 83.

families. Such enterprises played an immense part in the Russian economy ; it was they, quite as much as the large-scale mechanized industry of the factories, which supplied the simple needs of the peasant — his tools and utensils, his clothing, the primitive furniture and equipment of his house.[1] The party programme of March 1919, interested at all costs in increased production, advocated support for small rural industries by giving them state orders and financial credits, and wished to combine " individual rural workers, artels of rural workers and producers' cooperatives and small enterprises into larger productive and industrial units ".[2] The establishment of special sections for the organization of rural industries in Vesenkha and in the local Sovnarkhozy had been decided on in December 1918 ;[3] the third All-Russian Congress of Councils of National Economy in January 1920 proposed to group them under the leadership of the cooperatives.[4] How much was actually done in this field remains problematical. All doubt about the legal situation was finally removed by a decree promulgated at the end of November 1920, which nationalized all enterprises employing more than five workers with mechanical power, or ten workers without mechanical power. But, like the decree of June 28, 1918, this decree affected only the legal title : owners remained in effective possession till such time as Vesenkha or the local Sovnarkhozy took action.[5]

The final balance-sheet of the nationalization of industry under war communism was never drawn. A census of industry taken in 1920 throughout the territories then under Soviet rule (comprising virtually all the territories that were later to form the USSR except

[1] The *narodniks* had glorified these rural handicraft industries as a healthy alternative to the capitalist industry of the towns ; Russian Marxists, on the other hand, took the adjective which defined them (*kustarnyi*) and applied it in a metaphorical sense to anything petty, unorganized and backward. Before the revolution, these rural industries were already in process of infiltration by small-scale entrepreneurs who organized and " sweated " the labour of peasant households.

[2] *VKP(B) v Rezolyutsiyakh* (1941), i, 290.

[3] *Trudy II Vserossiiskogo S"ezda Sovetov Narodnogo Khozyaistva* (n.d.), p. 396.

[4] *Rezolyutsii Tret'ego Vserossiiskogo S"ezda Sovetov Narodnogo Khozyaistva* (1920), pp. 30-32. Another resolution of this congress, proposed by Tomsky, revealed trade union jealousy of rural industries, only " absolutely indispensable branches " of which were to be supported ; the general policy was " to replace rural industry by the factory " (*ibid.* p. 28).

[5] *Sobranie Uzakonenii, 1920*, No. 93, art. 512.

eastern Siberia) revealed a total of 404,000 " industrial establishments " of which 350,000 were being operated. Of these 350,000 nearly three-quarters were one-man or family concerns ; only 26 per cent employed any hired labour. The total of hired workers in industry was 2,200,000 or 89 per cent of all workers engaged in industry ; and of this number 1,410,000 worked in so-called large concerns employing over 30 workers each. The total number of industrial establishments nationalized under the decree of November 1920 was 37,000 employing 1,615,000 workers ; in addition, 230,000 workers were employed in industrial cooperative enterprises.[1] But the figures compiled by Vesenkha before this wholesale act of nationalization are more significant of the real situation. According to these, a total of 6908 industrial enterprises accounted to Vesenkha, and of these Vesenkha regarded 4547 as effectively nationalized in the sense of having been brought under state control. At the same time the Central Statistical Administration put the number of nationalized enterprises as low as 3833.[2] All authorities agree that nationalization was most nearly complete in the transport, engineering, electrical, chemical, textile and paper industries.

The real issue in the period of war communism was not the nationalization of industry — this was not in itself, as Lenin had often pointed out, a socialist measure, and was at this moment occurring in some degree even in countries where the structure of bourgeois capitalism was still intact [3] — but the attempt of the state to administer industry on socialist lines. The most numerous

---

[1] The results of the census are fully summarized in *Na Novykh Putyakh* (1923), iii, 165-178.

[2] These figures are collected in L. Kritsman, *Geroicheskii Period Velikoi Russkoi Revolyutsii* (n.d. [? 1924]), pp. 127-128, without any attempt to reconcile the discrepancies ; V. P. Milyutin, *Istoriya Ekonomicheskogo Razvitiya SSSR* (2nd ed., 1929), gives a figure for February 1920 of just under 6500 nationalized enterprises, of which almost 3000 were " trustified and especially important enterprises ", and the remaining 3500 were administered by local Sovnarkhozy.

[3] A manifesto of the first congress of Comintern in March 1919, apparently drafted by Trotsky, stressed this point : " The nationalization of economic life against which capitalist liberalism protested so much has become an accomplished fact. There can be no going back from this fact — either to free competition or even to the dominion of trusts, syndicates and other economic combines. The only question is who hereafter will be the bearer of nationalized production : the imperialist state or the state of the victorious proletariat " (*Kommunisticheskii Internatsional v Dokumentakh* (1933), pp. 57-58 ; Trotsky, *Sochineniya*, xxii, 41).

and important industrial decrees of the period from July 1918 to the end of 1919 provided for " the transfer to the management of the republic " (this was the routine formula) of industrial undertakings; sometimes the decree named the section of Vesenkha which would assume responsibility for administering, sometimes this was left vaguely to Vesenkha or its presidium. The decrees related to specified enterprises. Not all the firms or factories in a single industry were taken over at once: more than a dozen decrees were required to take over the extensive and varied textile industry. But the policy was to complete the enforced " trustification " of industry which Lenin had proclaimed since the autumn of 1917 as the final step in capitalist organization and therefore a necessary condition of the organization of socialism.[1] Every industry was to be grouped in a single " trust " under its *glavk* or centre, responsible to Vesenkha as the supreme arbiter of policy. By the end of 1919 some 90 of these " state trusts " had been organized.[2]

It is not always easy to discover any precise or consistent policy at work in the multifarious enactments of the period in the sphere of industrial policy. Vesenkha, as its president, Rykov, said at this time, had been diverted from " the regular organization of the economy ", and " compelled to resort to extreme measures to guard against attack from the rear ".[3] Beyond doubt the civil war, dominating every other factor, provided the main impulse to the taking over of industrial enterprises directly or indirectly supplying its needs. The establishment of state control over the metallurgical industry was virtually complete when the nationalization decree of June 28, 1918, was promulgated. War requirements dictated the speed with which enterprises in such capital industries as leather, textiles and the chemical and electrical industries were taken over in the autumn of 1918; and no explanation is needed of the creation in December 1918 of a chief fuel committee (Glavtop) with dictatorial powers over the production and distribution of all forms of fuel. More general considerations may account for the

---

[1] See pp. 64-65 above.

[2] V. P. Milyutin, *Istoriya Ekonomicheskogo Razvitiya SSSR* (2nd ed., 1929), p. 170: the textile industry, which was too big and too dispersed for complete trustification, had at this time been organized in 40 " unions " under a single central administration (*ibid.* p. 171).

[3] *Narodnoe Khozyaistvo*, No. 10, 1918, p. 31.

early taking over of factories producing paper, tobacco and cigarettes, and fire-resisting pottery, or of the wine and spirit industry,
which, unaccountably overlooked in the June decree, was nationalized in November 1918 and taken over in the following month.
But it is more difficult to guess why steps should have been taken
in December 1918 to nationalize and take over the music-publish-
ing and music-printing industry, or the confectionery industry
in Moscow and Petrograd.[1] The machine of " nationalization ",
set in motion for good and sufficient reasons, had acquired a
momentum of its own, or was being driven forward by that
confused and partly accidental mixture of different motives and
impulses characteristic of any large-scale administrative process.

The sequel of these measures was to divert Vesenkha from the
rôle originally contemplated for it of supreme director and arbiter
of the whole Soviet economy and to establish its position as the
department responsible for the management of Soviet nationalized
industry. Of the two functions assigned to it in a long decree of
August 1918 to " regulate and organize all production and distribution " and to " administer all enterprises of the republics ",
its effective rôle was henceforth confined to the second. The same
decree laid down a detailed constitution for Vesenkha. Of its 69
members, 10 were appointed by VTsIK, 20 by regional Sovnarkhozy and 30 by the central council of trade unions ; it was to
meet not less than once a month. Its current business was
entrusted to a presidium of 9, of whom the president and his
deputy were appointed by Sovnarkom, the other members by
VTsIK. The presidium quickly became the directing and
policy-making body. After the autumn of 1918 Vesenkha ceased
altogether to meet as a council : it became a department of state
bearing, like the British Board of Trade, the title of a defunct
organ.[2]

The machinery through which Vesenkha attempted to rule its
new industrial kingdom was developed from the system of central

[1] These and other similar decrees of these months are collected in *Sbornik
Dekretov i Postanovlenii po Narodnomu Khozyaistvu*, ii (1920), 9-10, 112-134 ;
the numerous decrees of the same period taking over individual concerns are
collected *ibid.* ii, 137-167.

[2] *Sobranie Uzakonenii, 1917-1918*, No. 58, art. 644 ; V. P. Milyutin,
Istoriya Ekonomicheskogo Razvitiya SSSR (2nd ed., 1929), p. 168. A detailed
description of the organization of Vesenkha at this time is in L. Kritsman,
Geroicheskii Period Velikoi Russkoi Revolyutsii (n.d. [? 1924]), pp. 99-105.

bodies — the *glavki* and centres — the first of them set up before nationalization began. Some of the less important industries contracted out of this system by being subordinated directly to departments of Vesenkha. But this was a distinction without any substantial difference, since the centres and *glavki* gradually lost their quasi-independent status and became assimilated to sections of Vesenkha. This direct subordination of the centres and *glavki* became inevitable when all credits to nationalized industries were channelled through Vesenkha — a situation formally confirmed by a resolution of the second All-Russian Congress of Councils of National Economy in December 1918.[1] What was more uncertain and fluctuating at first was the relation of the centres and *glavki* to the industries under their control. The functions of the chief oil committee (Glavneft), one of the early *glavki* established in advance of the nationalization of the industry, were defined as being to " organize and conduct oil business for the account of the state ", to " control and regulate the private oil-extracting and oil-refining industry ", and to " close, open or amalgamate " different enterprises within the industry.[2] The chief tobacco committee (Glavtabak), also an early creation, was instructed to organize the " planned provision of raw materials " and the " planned distribution of products ".[3] Direct administration of enterprises by Vesenkha or by the *glavki* was not contemplated either before or after nationalization. In the textile industry, as more and more businesses were taken over, a new organ called Natsional'tkan' was established in December 1918 to administer state textile factories under the authority of Tsentrotekstil.[4] On the other hand the chief leather committee (Glavkozh) was instructed to " organize the administration " of nationalized concerns; the chief paint and varnish committee (Glavlak) was entrusted with the " general administration " of such concerns; and the chief paper committee (Glavbum) was " transformed into

---

[1] *Trudy II Verossiiskogo S"ezda Sovetov Narodnogo Khozyaistva* (n.d.), pp. 396-400; for this resolution see pp. 253-254 below. The same congress adopted detailed resolutions on the administration of industry (*ibid.* pp. 402-403).
[2] *Byulleteni Vysshego Soveta Narodnogo Khozyaistva*, No. 6-8, 1918, pp. 34-38.
[3] *Glavtabak*, No. 1, August 1918, p. 50.
[4] *Sbornik Dekretov i Postanovlenii po Narodnomu Khozyaistvu*, ii (1920), 66; for Tsentrotekstil see pp. 79-80 above.

the chief administration of state enterprises in the paper industry ".[1] These variations of terminology no doubt corresponded to variations of practice. The feverish atmosphere of the civil war was particularly unfavourable to the growth of any orderly and uniform system.

It may well be that the most serious shortcomings of the centres and *glavki*, of which there were 42 in 1920,[2] was their inadequacy to perform a function for which they had not been originally designed and were not equipped : they interfered rather than administered. Among later writers they became a byword for every kind of inefficiency, and were treated as the embodiment of the excessive centralization which was one of the errors of war communism. In the conditions of the time, however, the case for centralization was overwhelming. The reaction against the administrative chaos of the first winter of the revolution was as healthy as it was inevitable.

Chaos [said Lenin in January 1919] can be abolished only by centralization together with renunciation of purely local interests, which have evidently provoked the opposition to that centralism which is, however, the only way out of our position. . . . Our position is bad . . . because we have no strict centralization.[3]

Centralization was stimulated by the impact of the civil war, which, like every other war, demanded a concentration of important decisions — and sometimes a concentration of production — at a single point. As early as October 1918 the shortage of raw materials made it imperative to close the less efficient factories in many branches of industry and concentrate production in the most efficient ;[4] such decisions could only be taken by a strong central authority. When the territory of the RSFSR shrank in the summer of 1919 to the dimensions of ancient Muscovy, the centralized control of industry was a far more practicable proposition that it could have appeared earlier or later. Every

[1] *Ibid.* ii, 37, 39, 72.
[2] A list is in L. Kritsman, *Geroicheskii Period Velikoi Russkoi Revolyutsii* (n.d. [? 1924]), pp. 100-101 ; a later list records a total of 74 *glavki*, centres and sections of Vesenkha in November 1920 (*Narodnoe Khozyaistvo*, No. 4, 1921, p. 48).
[3] Lenin, *Sochineniya*, xxiii, 472.
[4] *Narodnoe Khozyaistvo*, No. 12, 1918, pp. 30-31.

circumstance conspired to promote a degree of centralization which could not ultimately be maintained and exacted a high price in bureaucratic inefficiency.

The policy of centralization soon encountered jealous resistance from the provincial Sovnarkhozy. By the time the second All-Russian Congress of Councils of National Economy met in December 1918, the cumbrous fiction of a system of economic Soviets parallel to the political Soviets had been abandoned. A new decree abolished the regional Sovnarkhozy, recognized the provincial Sovnarkhozy as " executive organs " of Vesenkha, and turned local Sovnarkhozy — it is doubtful how many of these had ever been formed — into " economic sections " of the executive committees of the corresponding local Soviets. But, while the decree purported to accord fairly wide autonomous powers to provincial Sovnarkhozy, it further clipped their wings by allowing the *glavki* and centres to have their own subordinate organs at provincial headquarters ; and, though these organs were in some vague way attached to the provincial Sovnarkhozy, this measure clearly represented a further step towards the centralized control of every branch of industry all over the country by its *glavk* or centre in Moscow under the supreme authority of Vesenkha. The provincial Sovnarkhozy were left with little to administer but a rapidly diminishing category of industries of " local significance ".[1] This development at the administrative level went hand in hand with the increasing predominance of the centralized trade union organization over local factory committees and other trade union organs,[2] and was even attributed to the strength of trade union influence in the *glavki*.[3] A special conference between representatives of the *glavki* and the Sovnarkhozy in April 1919 failed to reach any compromise or to check the aggrandisement of the central organs.[4] Yet there was no field in which extreme central-

---

[1] *Trudy II Vserossiiskogo S"ezda Sovetov Narodnogo Khozyaistva* (n.d.), pp. 406-408. It was emphasized at the second All-Russian Congress of Councils of National Economy that " all production of local significance and its organization . . . remains in the hands of the local (i.e. provincial) Sovnarkhozy ", and that the " *glavki* and centres, which regulate industry on an all-Russian scale, must keep in direct contact with the presidium of the local Sovnarkhozy " (*ibid.* p. 208) ; but it is doubtful whether these consoling assurances amounted to much in practice.   [2] See pp. 204-205 below.

[3] *Narodnoe Khozyaistvo*, No. 4, 1919, pp. 16-19.

[4] *Ibid.* No. 5, 1919, pp. 40-45.

ization was more obviously impracticable, or some form of devolution more urgently needed, than in the day-to-day conduct of
industry.

What therefore began as a straight fight between centralization
and local autonomy in economic administration soon turned into a
struggle between functional and geographical devolution. The
glavki represented a " vertical " system of organization under
which every industry would function as a single entity ultimately
responsible to a single authority for that industry. The provincial
Sovnarkhozy contested this system in the name of a " horizontal "
arrangement under which the industrial enterprises of a given
province would be coordinated and controlled by a high provincial
authority. The issue was merged in the general debate of the
seventh All-Russian Congress of Soviets in December 1919 on
the responsibility of local organs of the People's Commissariats to
the local Soviets and their executive committees. Sapronov, who
at the eighth party congress had attacked the Sovnarkhozy for
encroaching on the local Soviet power,[1] now transferred his attack
to the unpopular *glavki*, arguing that they represented an attempt
to substitute " organization by departments " for " organization
by Soviets " — the bureaucratic for the democratic system.
Another speaker declared that, if people were asked " what should
be destroyed on the day after the destruction of Denikin and
Kolchak ", 90 per cent would reply : " the *glavki* and the centres ".
Kalinin came to the rescue by retorting that " the most centralized
of all the *glavki* and the most oppressive to the population " was —
the Red Army.[2] The debate led to no result and was resumed at
the third All-Russian Congress of Councils of National Economy
in January 1920, where the presidium of Vesenkha, ranged in
alliance with the trade unions in support of the *glavki*, was once
more challenged by representatives of the provincial Sovnarkhozy.
A two-thirds majority was obtained for a resolution on the administration of industry which divided enterprises into three categories :
" trustified " enterprises or enterprises of state importance, administered directly by the central organs of Vesenkha, enterprises
administered by the provincial Sovnarkhozy " under the immediate direction of the central organs of Vesenkha ", and enterprises

---

[1] See Vol. 1, p. 217.
[2] 7[i] *Vserossiiskii S"ezd Sovetov* (1920), pp. 197, 218, 222.

of local significance administered and controlled solely by the provincial Sovnarkhozy.[1]   The ninth party congress in March 1920 took a hand and passed a resolution which declared that " the organizational task " was, " while retaining and developing vertical centralization along the line of the *glavki*, to combine it with a horizontal co-subordination of enterprises along the line of economic regions ".[2]   But fine words settled nothing.   The forces making for centralization derived their strength from the civil war and could scarcely be curbed so long as that continued.   The reaction set in only with the introduction of NEP and as part of a general policy.

Another bitter controversy was involved, sometimes explicitly, more often implicitly, in the attacks on the centralized organization of Vesenkha — the controversy about the use of specialists.   Here too the claims of business efficiency were widely felt to conflict with those of socialist, or even democratic, self-government.   But the argument about the specialists touched also deeper levels of party doctrine and party prejudice.   It revived the apparent discrepancy between the belief in the smashing of the old administrative apparatus and the dying away of the state, which Lenin had reiterated so eloquently in the autumn of 1917 in *State and Revolution*, and the practical need, which he had propounded almost at the same moment with no less vigour in *Will the Bolsheviks Retain State Power?*, to take over and utilize the technical apparatus of economic and financial control created and left behind by capitalism.[3]   In the initial period of the revolution the anarchy of workers' control was succeeded by attempts to apply the doctrine, which derived encouragement from certain passages in Lenin's *State and Revolution*, that the administration of industry was a simple affair well within the competence of any moderately intelligent citizen.   In March 1918 an official of Vesenkha could still write that it was " treason to the workers " to leave any bourgeois engineer in a factory.[4]   But before long a radical change

---

[1] *Rezolyutsii Tret'ego Vserossiiskogo S"ezda Sovetov Narodnogo Khozyaistva* 1920), pp. 6-7, 15-16.
[2] *VKP(B) v Rezolyutsiyakh* (1941), i, 331.
[3] See p. 66 above.
[4] *Narodnoe Khozyaistvo*, No. 1, 1918, p. 19.

set in. In *Will the Bolsheviks Retain State Power?* Lenin had
cautiously foreseen that the new régime would need a greater
number than ever before of " engineers, agronomists, technicians,
scientifically trained specialists of every kind ", who would have
" for the period of transition " to be paid a higher wage than other
workers.[1] After Brest-Litovsk, when Trotsky had already begun
to draw on the old officer class to build up the Red Army, Lenin
bluntly declared that " without the leadership of specialists in
different branches of knowledge, technique and experience the
transition to socialism is impossible ", and regretted that " we
have *not yet* created the conditions which would put bourgeois
specialists at our disposal ".[2] When the Left opposition spoke of
this as a " revival of the leadership of the capitalists ", he retorted
that this " leadership " was being offered to the capitalists, " not
as capitalists, but as specialist-technicians or as organizers ".[3] At
the first All-Russian Congress of Councils of National Economy
in May 1918 he spoke frankly of " the task of utilizing bourgeois
specialists ", and of the need, if socialism was to be achieved, to
build up " an immense cadre of scientifically trained specialists ",
relying for this even on " hostile elements ". And he repeated :
" We know that without this socialism is impossible." [4] From
some 300 in March 1918, the number of officials in Vesenkha rose
in the next six months to 2500, or, including the staff of the *glavki*
and centres, to 6000.[5] The number seems modest in face of the
immense task imposed on Vesenkha of reorganizing Russian
industry in the face of civil war. But it provoked the usual complaints of inflated bureaucracy, intensified by knowledge of the
sources from which, following Lenin's injunctions, many of the
new officials had been drawn.

The issue of the " specialists " was a constant bone of contention in the next two years. At the second All-Russian Congress of
Councils of National Economy in December 1918, Molotov
analysed the membership of the 20 most important *glavki* and
centres. Of the 400 persons concerned, over 10 per cent were
former employers or employers' representatives, 9 per cent
technicians, 38 per cent officials from various departments includ-

---

[1] Lenin, *Sochineniya*, xxi, 263.   [2] *Ibid.* xxii, 446.
[3] *Ibid.* xxii, 524.   [4] *Ibid.* xxii, 40-41.
[5] *Narodnoe Khozyaistvo*, No. 10, 1918, p. 31.

ing Vesenkha, and the remaining 43 per cent workers or representatives of workers' organizations, including trade unions. Thus a majority was composed of persons " having no relation to the proletarian elements in industry ", and the *glavk* had to be regarded as " an organ far from corresponding to the proletarian dictatorship "; those who directed policy were " such forces as employers' representatives, technicians and specialists ".[1] The Menshevik delegate Dalin, boldly asserting that in the " great European trusts " there was " very little bureaucracy ", and repeating the Menshevik argument against the premature attempt to introduce socialism " on unprepared ground with an unprepared mechanism ", launched a general attack :

> There is no proletariat, there remains only the dictatorship, not of the proletariat, but of a vast bureaucratic machine holding in its grip dead factories and work-shops. . . . Thus we are creating a new bourgeoisie which will have no prejudices of culture and education, and will be like the old bourgeoisie only in its oppression of the working class. You are creating a bourgeoisie which knows no limits to persecution and exploitation.

This growth of what the speaker called " an American bourgeoisie " was responsible for the decline in production and the apathy of the workers, and was linked with the policy of appeasing the petty bourgeoisie, typified by the new attitude to the middle peasant.[2]

Such attacks did little to arrest the progressive incorporation of bourgeois " specialists " into the Soviet machine ; the civil war, which made their help all the more indispensable, at the same time made reconciliation easier on the basis of the defence of the fatherland against the foreign aggressor. " What, are we to throw them out ? " exclaimed Lenin of the former bourgeois employed

---

[1] *Trudy II Vserossiiskogo S"ezda Sovetov Narodnogo Khozyaistva* (n.d.), p. 213. According to figures given by Rykov two years later, the presidia of Vesenkha and the provincial Sovnarkhozy then contained 57 per cent of workers, the *glavki* and centres 51 per cent and factory managements 63 per cent ; in the whole economic administration under Vesenkha, 61 per cent of those employed were workers and 30 per cent specialists (*Vos'moi Vserossiiskii S"ezd Sovetov* (1921), p. 103). Many of the workers had, however, primarily a " representative " function.

[2] *Trudy II Vserossiiskogo S"ezda Sovetov Narodnogo Khozyaistva* (n.d.), pp. 25-26.

in Soviet military or economic work. "You cannot throw out hundreds of thousands ; and if we did throw them out, we should be cutting our own throats ".[1] The new party programme adopted in March 1919 had a friendly word for the bourgeois specialists working "hand in hand with the mass of rank-and-file workers under the leadership of conscious communists ".[2] In these anxious months no other criterion could be allowed to take precedence over administrative efficiency. A "white" professor who reached Omsk in the autumn of 1919 from Moscow reported that "at the head of many of the centres and *glavki* sit former employers and responsible officials and managers of businesses, and the unprepared visitor to these centres and *glavki* who is personally acquainted with the former commercial and industrial world would be surprised to see the former owners of big leather factories sitting in Glavkozh, big manufacturers in the central textile organization, etc.".[3] At the party conference of December 1919 when the civil war seemed almost won and it was possible to look forward again to the future, Lenin paid a handsome tribute to the "bourgeois specialists" :

> We recognize the necessity of putting these groups in a better position because the transition from capitalism to communism is impossible without the utilization of bourgeois specialists, and all our victories, all the victories of our Red Army, led by the proletariat which has won over to its side the half proletarian, half property-minded peasantry, have been won thanks in part to our skill in utilizing bourgeois specialists. This policy of ours, applied in military affairs, must become the policy of our domestic reconstruction.[4]

But at the ensuing seventh All-Russian Congress of Soviets he found himself once more on the defensive. It was impossible to construct a state machine "without the help of old specialists", inevitably drawn from "capitalist society". None the less, even where they had not proved traitors — "and this phenomenon ", added Lenin grimly, "has been not occasional, but constant " —

[1] Lenin, *Sochineniya*, xxiv, 67.
[2] *VKP(B) v Rezolyutsiyakh* (1941), i, 291.
[3] G. K. Gins, *Sibir', Soyuzniki, Kolchak* (Peking, 1921), ii, 429 ; the statement in L. Kritsman, *Geroicheskii Period Velikoi Russkoi Revolyutsii* (n.d. [? 1924], p. 200), that from the moment of nationalization representatives of the capitalists were thrown out of the *glavki* is contradicted by all other evidence.
[4] Lenin, *Sochineniya*, xxiv, 568.

they were incapable of understanding " new conditions, new tasks, new demands ". In the *glavki* and centres, and in Soviet farms, there had been " more counter-revolutionary elements, more bureaucracy " than in the army administration. This was because less workers and peasants had entered these fields, and there was consequently less control over the specialists. Constant watchfulness was the only remedy.[1] Throughout this time the impression prevails of an uphill but determined fight by Lenin and a few other leaders to maintain the privileged position of the bourgeois specialists against the inevitable jealousies and resentments of the party rank and file.[2] But the policy was not, and could not be, relaxed; and the ninth party congress in March 1920 passed an unequivocal resolution instructing party workers to " strive for the establishment of an atmosphere of comradely cooperation between workers and the specialist-technicians inherited by the proletarian régime from the bourgeois order ".[3] It is a curious reflection that the most far-reaching policies of war communism in industry were carried out in large measure through the agency, and with the active cooperation, of former bourgeois technicians and industrialists.

It would, however, be erroneous to suppose that Lenin ever

---

[1] Lenin, *Sochineniya*, xxiv, 621-623 ; Milyutin at this time also spoke of " the secret, if not open, sabotage " of the specialists, and looked to the " process of producing organizers from the ranks of the workers " as the remedy (V. P. Milyutin, *Istoriya Ekonomicheskogo Razvitiya SSSR* (2nd ed., 1929), p. 168).

[2] A curious and revealing document is a letter addressed to Lenin by a former professor of the Voronezh agricultural institute, now president of the administration of state leather factories under Glavkozh, and published together with Lenin's reply in *Pravda*, March 28, 1919 (Lenin, *Sochineniya*, xxiv, 184-187). The writer complained of the persecution by minor communist officials of bourgeois specialists and intellectuals working for the government, including " trivial denunciations and accusations, fruitless but highly humiliating searches, threats of shooting, requisitions and confiscations ". Lenin suggested that some of the complaints were exaggerated, and hinted that bourgeois specialists presumed too much on their privileged position, but admitted abuses and offered on behalf of the party a " comradely relation to the intellectuals ". One cause for indignation was the insistence of a communist official that the professor and his wife should share a bed ; Lenin pointed out that there were not enough beds for every Russian " on an average " to have one for himself. Nearly three years later Lenin was denouncing " cases of murder of engineers by workers in the socialized mines, not only of the Urals, but of Donbas ", and the suicide of the chief engineer of the Moscow waterworks as the result of petty persecution (*Sochineniya*, xxvii, 155).

[3] *VKP(B) v Rezolyutsiyakh* (1941), i, 334.

regarded the use of bourgeois specialists as anything more than a necessary (and by its nature temporary) evil, or abandoned his ultimate ideal of the administration of the state by the workers themselves. It was because the workers had proved unequal to the work of administration, or were not yet ripe for it in sufficient numbers, that this dependence on bourgeois specialists was unavoidable :

> One of the chief defects of this work [he said in 1920 of party work in the country] is that we do not know how to manage state business, that among the groups of our comrades, even those who are directing the work, the habit of the old under- ground, when we sat in little groups, here or abroad, and did not dare to reflect or think about how to manage state work, is still too strong. . . . We have an immense state apparatus which still works badly because we are not clever enough, we are not able to manage it properly.[1]

The reproach of bureaucracy became a constant theme. At the eighth All-Russian Congress of Soviets in December 1920 Zinoviev launched an attack on the " armies " of Soviet officials who " weigh down all our institutions ".[2] The introduction of NEP entailed a strong pressure for reduction of superfluous staffs, and Lenin during the last year of his life was much pre- occupied with the evil of bureaucracy. It is indisputable that the Soviet bureaucrat of these early years was as a rule a former member of the bourgeois intelligentsia or official class, and brought with him many of the traditions of the old Russian bureaucracy. But the same groups provided the modicum of knowledge and technical skill without which the régime could not have survived. Lenin's repeated testimony in 1918 and 1919 that socialism was impossible without invoking the aid of these " class enemies " was an expression of the fundamental dilemma of the revolution.

The controversies which ranged round centralization and the use of specialists were repeated on the issue of " one-man manage- ment ", and with the same forces confronting one another. The principle of what was called " collegiality " did not figure in any party programme and was not a formally prescribed item of party

[1] Lenin, *Sochineniya*, xxv, 301.
[2] *Vos'moi Vserossiiskii S"ezd Sovetov* (1921), p. 214.

doctrine. But it had a respectable ancestry in the practice of the French revolution; and it seemed to accord with the spirit of democratic socialism that decisions should rest not with an individual but with a collective group. Each People's Commissar was surrounded by a collegium of five colleagues whom he was supposed to consult on major issues and who had a right of appeal to Sovnarkom against his decisions. The first dramatic derogation from this principle occurred in March 1918 when Sovnarkom faced, not for the first time, the chronic problem of delays and disorganization on the railways. Lenin categorically demanded " the appointment in every local centre of individual responsible executive officials chosen by the railwaymen's organizations " and " unquestioning obedience to their orders ".[1] The resulting decree of Sovnarkom [2] was bitterly attacked by the Left SRs and by the Bolshevik Left opposition, both of whom coupled it with the evil of centralization. " With *centralization of administration* ", wrote Osinsky bitterly in the Left opposition journal *Kommunist*, " is coupled here its *autocratic* character "; and the word " autocratic " deliberately recalled the most offensive of the former Tsar's titles.[3] Lenin was wholly impenitent and quite prepared to generalize the principle :

> Any large-scale machine industry [he wrote in *Current Tasks of the Soviet Power*] — and this is precisely the material productive source and basis of socialism — calls for unconditional and strict unity of the will which directs the simultaneous work of hundreds and thousands and tens of thousands of people. . . . *Unqualified submission* to a single will is unconditionally necessary for the success of the process of labour organized on the pattern of large-scale machine industry.[4]

This was a theme which evidently aroused the most obstinate prejudices. It was only in December 1918, when the civil war was in full swing, that Lenin cautiously returned to it at the second All-Russian Congress of Councils of National Economy, and applied it specifically to the management of nationalized industry :

> The war situation places on us a special responsibility for heavy tasks. Collegial administration is indispensable with the participation of trade unions. Collegia are indispensable, but

[1] Lenin, *Sochineniya*, xxii, 622, note 187.
[2] For the decree see p. 396 below.
[3] Lenin, *Sochineniya*, xxii, 627, note 215.   [4] *Ibid.* xxii, 462.

collegial administration must not be turned into an obstacle to practical business. . . . Of all Sovnarkhozy, *glavki* and centres we shall unconditionally demand that the collegial system of administration should not issue in chatter, in the writing of resolutions, in the composition of plans, and in departmentalism.[1]

But the hint was not taken up in the discussion and left only the barest trace in a resolution demanding " personal responsibility of members of directing collegia for the business entrusted to them and for the work of the enterprises and organs at the head of which they stand ".[2] And almost a year later, at the seventh All-Russian Congress of Soviets Lenin was still making the same plea :

> Individual responsibility is essential for us ; as collegiality is essential for the discussion of basic questions, so individual responsibility and individual execution are essential in order to prevent red tape, in order that it should be impossible to evade responsibility. We need people who in any event have learned how to administer independently.[3]

At the third All-Russian Congress of Councils of National Economy Lenin made the issue the principal theme of his speech, coupling it with the question of " labour armies ". The argument was once more conciliatory and practical :

> Collegiality, as the fundamental type of organization of Soviet administration, represents something rudimentary, essential at the first stage when things have to be built anew. But, once more or less stable forms are established, the transition to practical work is bound up with one-man management as the system which more than anything else guarantees the best utilization of human capacities and a real, not merely verbal, check on work done.[4]

But the resolution of the congress once more reaffirmed the " collegial principle " as " the basis for the management of nationalized industry ", and conceded only that one-man management might be introduced " with the consent of the appropriate trade union in each particular case ".[5]

[1] *Ibid.* xxiii, 447.
[2] *Trudy II Vserossiiskogo S"ezda Sovetov Narodnogo Khozyaistva* (n.d.), p. 393. [3] Lenin, *Sochineniya*, xxiv, 623.
[4] *Ibid.* xxv, 17 ; stenographic records of this congress were not published, and the only report of Lenin's speech comes from the contemporary press. For " labour armies " see pp. 211-214 below.
[5] *Rezolyutsii Tret'ego Vserossiiskogo S"ezda Sovetov Narodnogo Khozyaistva* (1920), p. 13.

It had by this time become clear that resistance to the principle of one-man management was crystallizing round the trade unions. Twice Lenin spoke in favour of his project in the Bolshevik fraction of the All-Russian Council of Trade Unions, in January and in March 1920, and on both occasions met with a rebuff; on the second occasion the fraction adopted theses presented by Tomsky " On the Tasks of the Trade Unions " which rallied emphatically to the rule of collegiality :

> The fundamental principle in the construction of the organs regulating and administering industry, which alone can guarantee the participation of broad non-party masses through the trade unions, is the now existing principle of collegial administration in industry, from the presidium of Vesenkha down to factory administrations inclusive.[1]

Lenin now decided to carry the issue to the highest instance, and the one where his own prestige would tell most heavily, the ninth party congress held in the latter part of March 1920. It was responsible for the stormiest debates of the congress. A draft resolution prepared by Trotsky, cautiously commending the principle of one-man management, was confronted by counter-proposals from Osinsky and Sapronov, who headed what called itself a " democratic centralism " group,[2] and from Tomsky in the name of the trade unions. While the intermediate group were prepared to go half way by admitting the principle of one-man management in small industries and in " separate militarized enterprises " by agreement with the trade unions, Tomsky's theses uncompromisingly demanded the maintenance of " the existing principle of collegial management in industry ".[3] Rykov, soon to be ousted from the presidency of Vesenkha, strongly defended collegiality; Smirnov pertly enquired why one-man management was not applied in Sovnarkom ; and Tomsky, seeking to father the hated innovation on a less imposing sponsor, declared that " not Trotsky but Krasin " was the original champion of one-man management, and that Lenin had hesitated for two years

---

[1] An account of these discussions is given in Lenin, *Sochineniya*, xxv, 593, note 26.

[2] See Vol. I, p. 195.

[3] Trotsky's draft resolution and the two sets of counter-theses are in *Devyatyi S"ezd RKP(B)* (1934), pp. 513, 535, 537-539.

before supporting it.[1] As usual, Lenin's speeches [2] swung the congress. The congress resolution which ended the debate contained an unequivocal acceptance of the principle of one-man management, and, admitting that the management of industry was still in its experimental stage, suggested four possible variants that might be tried " on the way to full one-man management " — a director-manager drawn from the trade unions with an engineer as his technical assistant, an engineer-specialist as manager with a trade unionist commissar attached to him, a specialist as manager with one or two trade unionists as his assistants, or a small closely knit collegium where such already existed and worked efficiently, on the indispensable condition that the president assumed full responsibility for the administration. At the same time it was emphatically laid down that " no trade union organization interferes directly in the working of the enterprise ".[3] Party discipline was strong enough to end the controversy once the highest party organ had spoken. Lutovinov, in the name of the group which was just beginning to crystallize as the " workers' opposition ", declared that he and his colleagues would loyally work to carry out a decision which they did not like.[4] At the third All-Russian Congress of Trade Unions which met a few days later the decision was tacitly accepted by avoidance of the issue ; the speeches of Lenin and Trotsky shifted the emphasis to the new controversy on labour service and labour discipline.[5] In November 1920 it was stated that collegial management survived only in 12 per cent of nationalized enterprises.[6] The statement presumably related to large enterprises controlled by the central organs of Vesenkha ; of those about which particulars were available, 2051 in all, 1783 were said to be under one-man management by the end of 1920.[7]

Statistics of industrial production under war communism are no more abundant than those of agricultural production, and equally conjectural. Production fell even more steeply in industry

[1] *Devyatyi S''ezd RKP(B)* (1934), pp. 140, 168, 169.
[2] Lenin, *Sochineniya*, xxv, 102-108, 109-115.
[3] *VKP(B) v Rezolyutsiyakh* (1941), i, 332-333, 339.
[4] *Devyatyi S''ezd RKP(B)* (1934), p. 257.
[5] See pp. 214-216 below.
[6] *Narodnoe Khozyaistvo*, November 1920, p. 12.
[7] *Ibid.* No. 4, 1921, p. 56.

than in agriculture; the decline in the productivity of the individual worker was probably greater (since under-nourishment was added to the other causes),[1] and was accompanied by a sharp decline in the number of workers employed in industry which had no counterpart in agriculture. The decline was progressive and cumulative, since a stoppage of production in one industry frequently brought other industries dependent on it to a standstill. It was not till 1919 that the full effects of the industrial crisis began to make themselves felt. Stocks of material in hand at the time of the revolution were by now completely exhausted, and the civil war or the allied blockade had generally prevented their renewal. Turkestan, the exclusive source of supplies of raw cotton, was completely cut off till the autumn of 1919; the Baltic countries, one of the main sources for flax, were abandoned, and trade with them was not renewed till 1920. The oil supplies of the Baku region and of the Caucasus were wholly lost from the summer of 1918 till the end of 1919. It was not till 1920 that the major coal and iron resources of the Ukraine were once more available. The fuel crisis was a main factor in the industrial breakdown. According to an estimate made in May 1919, industry was receiving at that time only 10 per cent of its normal supplies of fuel.[2] In the winters of 1918–1919 and 1919–1920 cold was probably a greater cause of human misery and human inefficiency than hunger. Another major factor, which was at once a part and a contributory cause of the breakdown, was the crisis in railway transport. Of the 70,000 versts of railway in European Russia only 15,000 versts had remained undamaged in the war or the civil war. Rolling-stock had suffered proportionately; at the end of 1919, when the crisis had reached its most acute stage, more than 60 per cent of a total of 16,000 locomotives were out of order.[3] All these factors

[1] According to one calculation the productivity of the worker in large-scale industry in 1920 was 39 per cent of the 1913 figure, in small industry 57 per cent (L. Kritsman, *Geroicheskii Period Velikoi Russkoi Revolyutsii* (n.d. [? 1924]), p. 190); small industry was, in large part, rural, and conditions in it approximated to those in agriculture.

[2] *Trudy Vserossiiskogo S"ezda Zaveduyushchikh Finotdelami* (1919), p. 49.

[3] The fullest summary of the transport crisis is in Trotsky's report to the eighth All-Russian Congress of Soviets in December 1920 (*Vos'moi Vserossiiskii S"ezd Sovetov*) (1921), pp. 154-175; for the famous " Order No. 1042 " and Trotsky's successful attempts to improve the transport situation see pp. 373-374 below.

helped to create a situation in which, as the third All-Russian Congress of Councils of National Economy recorded in January 1920, " the productive forces of the country could not be fully utilized, and a considerable part of our factories and workshops were at a standstill ".[1]

Perhaps, however, the most striking symptom of the decay of industry was the dissipation of the industrial proletariat. In Russia, where the mass of industrial workers were converted peasants who had rarely severed all their ties with the countryside and in some cases returned to it regularly for the harvest, a crisis in the cities or factories — hunger, stoppage of work, unemployment — produced not a problem of proletarian unemployment in the western sense, but a mass flight of industrial workers from the towns and reversion to the status and occupation of peasants. The dislocation of industry in the first winter of the revolution had already started such a movement; Bukharin spoke at the seventh party congress in March 1918 of the disintegration of the proletariat.[2] The process was vastly accelerated when civil war once more swept hundreds of thousands of a depleted and exhausted population into the armed forces of both camps. Industry suffered most of all both from the mobilization and from the breakdown in the complicated mechanisms of supply and production. Krasin spoke at the end of 1918 of the " great blow " caused by the hasty evacuation of Petrograd " under the influence of panic fear " at the time of Brest-Litovsk, which had resulted in " the almost complete destruction of the industry of Petrograd ".[3] Such approximate figures as were compiled confirm that the fall in the number of industrial workers came first and most rapidly in the Petrograd region, where by the end of 1918 the number of workers was not much more than half the number employed two years earlier. The note of alarm was sounded by Rudzutak at the second All-Russian Congress of Trade Unions in January 1919 :

We observe in a large number of industrial centres that the workers, thanks to the contraction of production in the factories,

---

[1] *Rezolyutsii Tret'ego Vserossiiskogo S"ezda Sovetov Narodnogo Khozyaistva* (1920), p. 22.
[2] *Sed'moi S"ezd Rossiiskoi Kommunisticheskoi Partii* (1924), pp. 33, 45.
[3] *Trudy II Vserossiiskogo S"ezda Sovetov Narodnogo Khozyaistva* (n.d.), pp. 75.

are being absorbed in the peasant mass, and instead of a population of workers we are getting a half-peasant or sometimes a
purely peasant population.[1]

Calculations based on trade union statistics for the whole area
under Soviet control in 1919 indicated that the number of workers
in industrial enterprises had fallen to 76 per cent of the 1917 total,
in building to 66 per cent and on the railways to 63 per cent.[2]
A comprehensive table published some years later showed that
the numbers of hired workers in industry rose from 2,600,000 in
1913 to 3,000,000 in 1917 and then declined progressively to
2,500,000 in 1918, to 1,480,000 in 1920/1921, and to 1,240,000 in
1921/1922, by which time it was less than half the 1913 total.[3] In
the important Bryansk iron and steel works, according to a report
of May 1920, 78 per cent of workers on the books were present in
January 1919, 63 per cent in July 1919, 59 per cent in January
1920 and 58 per cent in April 1920; the wastage was heaviest
among the skilled workers. In the spring of 1920 Vesenkha called
for the creation of " shock groups " in the 60 most important
metal-working concerns; and absenteeism in the Kolomensky
factories was said to have fallen from 41 per cent in January 1920
to 27 per cent in May 1920. The general conclusion of the report
containing these figures was that " the metallurgical and metal-
working industry of Russia has got into a blind alley ".[4] Tomsky,
reviewing in January the whole depressing complex of conditions
made up of " the general curtailment of all production, the
extraordinarily low productivity of labour, and the very small
utilization of enterprises that are functioning ", sought the main
cause in " the flight of healthy elements with a capacity for work
(1) into the country, (2) into the army, (3) into workers' communes
and Soviet farms, (4) into rural industry and producers' coopera-

---

[1] *Vtoroi Vserossiiskii S"ezd Professional'nykh Soyuzov* (1921), i (Plenumy),
138.
[2] The figures are taken from a study by S. G. Strumilin in the publication
of Vesenkha *Dva Goda Diktatury Proletariata, 1917-1919* (n.d.), pp. 17-18,
which frankly admits the impossibility of any precise estimates; the trade union
figures for 1919 are likely to have over-stated the numbers employed at that time.
[3] Y. S. Rozenfeld, *Promyshlennaya Politika SSSR* (1926), p. 317.
[4] *Narodnoe Khozyaistvo*, No. 9-10, 1920, pp. 2-6; statistics of particular
factories or industries, where available, are at this period more likely to be
reliable than general statistics.

tives, and (5) into state service (food detachments, inspection, army, etc.)," and in the absence of any fresh recruits to industry from the country.[1] The British Labour delegation visiting Russia in the spring noted " the ragged and half-starved condition " of factory workers, and learned that the peasants employed men at higher wages than the factories " plus a plentiful supply of food which the town worker does not get ".[2] However difficult conditions under war communism might be in the countryside, they were at any rate better than in the towns and the factories. In the autumn of 1920 the population of 40 capitals of provinces had declined since 1917 by 33 per cent from 6,400,000 to 4,300,000, the population of 50 other large towns by 16 per cent from 1,517,000 to 1,271,000. The larger the city, the greater the decline; Petrograd had lost 57·5 per cent of its population in three years, Moscow 44·5 per cent.[3]

The figures seemed catastrophic enough. But since the productivity of labour declined even more steeply than its numerical strength, the fall in actual production was far greater than the decrease in the number of workers would by itself have warranted. Published statistics showed that production in all branches of industry declined continuously till 1920. The worst declines were in the production of iron ore and of cast iron which fell in 1920 to 1·6 and 2·4 per cent respectively of the figures for 1913. The best record was for oil, the production of which stood in 1920 at 41 per cent of the 1913 level. Textiles came next, and the figure for coal was 27 per cent, but percentages ranging from 10 to 20 were common.[4] A calculation of value in terms of prewar rubles showed that the production of fully manufactured goods reached only 12·9 per cent of the 1913 value in 1920 and the production of semi-finished goods 13·6 per cent.[5] The paradox arose that the establishment of the " dictatorship of the proletariat " was followed by a marked diminution both of the numbers and of the specific weight in the economy of the class in whose

[1] *Rezolyutsii Tret'ego S"ezda Sovetov Narodnogo Khozyaistva* (1920), p. 25.
[2] *British Labour Delegation to Russia, 1920 : Report* (1920), p. 18.
[3] *Ekonomicheskaya Zhizn'*, December 1, 1920.
[4] *Za Pyat' Let* (1922), pp. 406-408 ; detailed figures for the Donetz coal mines are in *Na Novykh Putyakh* (1923), iii, 47-49.
[5] *Ibid.* iii, 180-181.

name the dictatorship was exercised.[1] An incidental consequence
was a decline in the authority of Vesenkha, which after 1919
ranked as no more than an equal among several commissariats
concerned with different branches of the economy, yielding pride
of place to Narkomprod, which, being in charge of the grain
requisitions, was a key department under war communism; and
as a supervisory economic organ Vesenkha was altogether eclipsed
by the Council of Labour and Defence (STO).[2]

The end of the civil war, which, by releasing available resources,
should have stimulated an industrial revival, appeared at first to
have the opposite effect. The reasons for this were partly psychological. The removal of the special incentives provided by the
war led to a relaxation of tension and, with it, of exertion; a tired
population no longer had the will to economic recovery. But the
continued decline also had its practical causes : the processes of
industrial decay, the complete exhaustion of plant and of stocks,
had struck too deep to be easily reversed. The ninth party congress
of March 1920 was able for the first time to transfer the emphasis
from the civil war to what Lenin called " the bloodless front " of
economic reconstruction.[3] But the mood of 1920 remained on
the whole one of complacency, stimulated by the series of striking
victories over the Poles and over Wrangel. In December, at the
eighth All-Russian Congress of Soviets, Rykov excused the fall
in Soviet industrial production and in the productivity of the
Soviet worker by similar declines alleged to have occurred in
Germany, in Great Britain and in the United States, and diagnosed
" the beginning of a general economic revival ".[4] The book of

---

[1] This was a common taunt of Menshevik and other opponents of the régime :
Lenin replied in May 1921 that, " even when the proletariat has to live
through a period of being declassed, it can still carry out its task of conquering
and retaining power " (*Sochineniya*, xxvi, 394).

[2] L. Kritsman, who notes the decline of Vesenkha, enumerates several
functions lost by it during 1920 to Narkomprod and other commissariats
(*Geroicheskii Period Velikoi Russkoi Revolyutsii* (n.d. [? 1924], p. 208) ; Lenin in
1921 described Narkomprod as " one of the best of our departments " (*Sochineniya*, xxvi, 248). For STO see p. 371 below.

[3] Lenin, *Sochineniya*, xxv, 107.

[4] *Vos'moi Vserossiiskii S"ezd Sovetov* (1921), pp. 89-90. On the other
hand, Rykov warned the congress that " old stocks inherited from the bourgeoisie " were now exhausted and that " the workers and peasants will have to
show whether they are able merely to spend what they have inherited or to
produce what they want themselves " (*ibid.* p. 94).

the year in the field of economic thought was Bukharin's *Economics of the Transition Period*. Predicting the imminent collapse of capitalism (and thus paying tribute to the optimistic mood which dominated the second congress of Comintern in July 1920), Bukharin went on to argue that the proletarian revolution must break up not only the political, but the economic, apparatus of capitalist society. This naturally meant a transitional period of diminished production :

Anarchy in production, or, in Professor Grinevetsky's words, " the revolutionary disintegration of industry ", is an historically inevitable stage which no amount of lamentation will prevent. The communist revolution, like every other revolution, is accompanied by an impairment of productive forces.[1]

A later writer compared the economic destructiveness of the revolution to the act of a military commander who blows up a railway bridge or fells a forest in order to open a path for his artillery fire : " measures directly inefficient in the economic sense may be efficient from the revolutionary point of view ".[2] The manifestations of the economic chaos and the break-down of the industrial machine could be hailed as milestones on the road to socialism. These theories, like others bred of the period of war communism, were *ex post facto* justifications of something which had not been expected but which it had not been possible to prevent ; and the paraphernalia of industrial controls set up at this time afterwards increased the general discredit which overtook the procedures of war communism. Nevertheless, it is fair to record, first, that the causes of the industrial collapse were rooted in conditions far deeper than any defect of organization, so that the later tendency to attribute it to the bureaucratic shortcomings of the *glavki* or of Vesenkha could not be seriously justified, and, secondly, that the final bankruptcy of war communism was due

---

[1] N. Bukharin, *Ekonomika Perekhodnogo Perioda* (1920), p. 48 ; the work of Grinevetsky quoted, *Poslevoennye Perspektivi Russkoi Promyshlennosti*, was written in 1918. Trotsky had already consoled the third All-Russian Congress of Councils of National Economy in January 1920 with the reflection that " the transition from one economic order to another is always paid for by innumerable sacrifices, including economic sacrifices " (Trotsky, *Sochineniya*, xv, 55).

[2] L. Kritsman, *Geroicheskii Period Velikoi Russkoi Revolyutsii* (n.d. [? 1924]), p. 56.

not so much to the breakdown of industry, as to the failure to evolve any agricultural policy capable of obtaining from the peasants food surpluses adequate to feed the cities and factories. The turnover from war communism to NEP affected industry, as it affected every part of the Soviet economy; but its directly compelling motives lay outside the sphere of industrial policy.

(c) *Labour and the Trade Unions*

The impact of the civil war removed the hesitations and ambiguities which had complicated labour policy in the first months of the new régime. The existence of an overwhelming national purpose made it easy and imperative to press forward with policies for the direction and disciplining of labour. The question of the relation between the trade unions and the state was fallaciously simplified now that both the state and the unions depended for their survival on mobilizing every man and every machine in the interests of military victory over the " white " armies. Under war communism labour policy became a matter of recruiting workers for the war effort and of sending them where they were most urgently required; the trade unions were the instrument through which this policy could be most efficiently carried out. So long as the civil war lasted, every issue of principle seemed clear-cut, straightforward, uncontroversial.

The first inconspicuous step towards the erection of a new machinery of control was taken in a decree of July 2, 1918, which regulated the conditions for the conclusion of collective agreements between the trade unions acting on behalf of the workers, and employers or factory managements. The most significant article of the decree authorized Narkomtrud, in the event of the employer refusing the contract offered by the trade union, to impose its acceptance by an official order.[1] This article, while it purported merely to apply coercive action against unreasonable employers, in effect gave Narkomtrud in agreement with the trade unions an unfettered right to determine conditions of employment; and this was its sole lasting effect. The legal basis for the organization of labour under war communism was contained in the first labour code of the RSFSR adopted by VTsIK on October 10, 1918, and

[1] *Sobranie Uzakonenii, 1917-1918*, No. 48, art. 568.

promulgated six weeks later.[1] Clauses of the code reaffirmed existing legal provisions for the protection of labour, and provided that wage-scales should be worked out by the trade unions in consultation with managers or employers and confirmed by Narkomtrud, though since the personnel of Narkomtrud was virtually nominated by the trade unions this confirmation was little more than a formality; the collective contract was shelved altogether. This was a logical consequence of the doctrines and practices of war communism. In theory, after the decree of June 28, 1918, nationalizing all major industry, the state was the principal employer. Labour was a form of service to society : the capitalist conception of a contract for the sale and purchase of labour power was obsolete. In determining wage rates the arduousness or dangerousness of the work, and the degree of responsibility and the qualifications required were to be taken into account. Piece-rates, already sanctioned by the trade union order of April 1918,[2] were treated not merely as permissible, but as normal, and were never again subject to challenge as a regular part of Soviet wages policy.

The labour code of 1918 laid down the general obligation to work, balanced by the right of the worker to employment in work suited to his qualifications at the appropriate rate of pay, though this right was modified in a later article by an obligation to accept temporary work of other kinds if no suitable work was available. But the code evaded the general issue of enforcement and compulsion. Even earlier, in September 1918, a decree had forbidden an unemployed person to refuse work offered to him on pain of loss of unemployment benefit.[3] But no other penalty was imposed ; and, where the natural reaction of the unemployed worker was to migrate to the country, this sanction had little effect. Under a decree of October 29, 1918, the labour exchanges were transformed into local organs of Narkomtrud and became the sole and obligatory channel for the engagement of labour, both for worker and for employer, but without any fresh sanction for a refusal of work by the worker.[4] In the same month came a decree formally authorizing the conscription of members of the bourgeoisie of both

---

[1] *Ibid.* No. 87-88, art. 905.   [2] See p. 110 above.
[3] *Sobranie Uzakonenii, 1917-1918*, No. 64, art. 704.
[4] *Ibid.* No. 80, art. 838.

200 THE ECONOMIC ORDER PT. IV

sexes and all ages from 16 to 50 for socially necessary work. All members of the bourgeoisie between the ages of 14 and 55 were issued with " labour books "; these had to be produced in order to obtain ration cards or travelling permits and were valid for this purpose only if they contained evidence that the bearer was performing socially useful work.[1]

The shape of labour organization emerged clearly at the second All-Russian Congress of Trade Unions in January 1919. The civil war was in full swing; a month earlier the second All-Russian Congress of Councils of National Economy had made a strong move towards centralized industrial control; and Lenin had just spoken of " centralization " and " renunciation of purely local interests " as the only cure for chaos.[2] It was in these conditions that the trade union congress, which had 450 Bolshevik delegates out of a total of rather more than 600, once more faced the issue of the relation of the trade unions to the state. It was again hotly contested. A tiny anarchist group wanted all power vested in independent trade unions; 30 Mensheviks voted for a resolution which asserted the principle of trade union independence and denied the claim of the Soviet power to represent the workers; 37 " international social-democrats " led by Lozovsky more cautiously demanded a delimitation of the functions of the trade unions from those of state organs, and maintained that the absorption of the trade union organs into those of the state " at the present stage of the revolution " would be " senseless ".[3] The vast majority of the congress carried the Bolshevik resolution, which Lenin supported in a long speech, accepting the principle of

[1] *Sobranie Uzakonenii, 1917-1918*, No. 73, art. 792. The labour book had a symbolical significance for Lenin, who wrote as early as September 1917 : " Every worker has his labour book. This document does not degrade him, though *now* indisputably a document of capitalist hired slavery, a token that the working man belongs to this or that blockhead. The Soviets will introduce the labour book *for the rich* and then gradually for the whole population. . . . It will be transformed into a token that in the new society there are no more ' workers ', but on the other hand nobody who does not work " (*Sochineniya*, xxi, 263). Labour books for the workers — and then only for those of Moscow and Petrograd — were first introduced by a decree of June 1919 ; Red Army and Navy men also received labour books (*Sobranie Uzakonenii*, 1919, No. 28, art. 315).

[2] See p. 179 above.

[3] The three draft resolutions are in *Vtoroi Vserossiiskii S"ezd Professional'nykh Soyuzov* (1921), i (Plenumy), 72-78, 92-94, 94-96, the voting figures *ibid.* i, 97.

" statization",[1] though this was to come about, not by an act of fusion between trade union and state organs, but as a " completely inevitable result of their concurrent, intimate and coordinated work and of the preparation of the broad working masses by the trade unions for the task of administering the state apparatus and all economic organs of control ".[2] The resolution allowed a certain ambiguity to persist as to whether the state was gradually to absorb the unions or the unions to absorb the state. But the People's Commissar for Labour, Shmidt, having been secretary of the All-Russian Central Council of Trade Unions and owing his appointment as commissar to this body, tactfully upheld the principle of trade union initiative :

> The rôle of the commissariat . . . must be to give obligatory effect to recommendations and plans worked out by the trade unions. Moreover, not only must the commissariat not interfere with the rights of the unions, but even the organs of the commissariat . . . should as far as possible be formed by the unions themselves. Here at the centre we act consistently on this principle.

The All-Russian Central Council asserted without hesitation that the work of Narkomtrud was " one and the same " as that of the trade unions :

> The basis on which it works is what the trade unions proclaim in their daily work and what they lay down in the regular decisions and resolutions adopted at their congresses. These decisions are accepted by the Commissariat of Labour, which in its quality as the organ of state power carries them into effect.

Shmidt went on to explain that the People's Commissar himself was nominated by the central council of trade unions, and that the whole collegium of Narkomtrud was composed of representatives of the central council. All that was lacking was to establish

---

[1] Lenin, *Sochineniya*, xxiii, 490 ; this word (*ogosudarstvlenie*) became a regular catchword of the trade union controversy ; it was also occasionally applied to the nationalization of industry, though here the word *natsionalizatsiya* was commonly used.

[2] *Vtoroi Vserossiiskii S"ezd Professional'nykh Soyuzov* (1921), i (Plenumy), 96-97 ; Ryazanov, in supporting the Bolshevik resolution, claimed that " our ideal is not further statization, but the de-statization of our whole social life " (*ibid.* i, 69) — a by no means unique instance of the way in which the conception of the dying away of the state was invoked to cover an immediate accretion of state power.

similarly close coordination between local representatives of
Narkomtrud and of the trade unions.[1] A hint of the other side
of the tacit bargain was, however, conveyed in an *obiter dictum* of
Tomsky :

> At a time when the trade unions regulate wages and condi-
> tions of work, when the appointment of the Commissar for
> Labour also depends on our congress, no strikes can take place
> in Soviet Russia. Let us put the dot on this i.[2]

This clear enunciation of policy on a vital practical point was
more significant than the theoretical uncertainty which still
enveloped the relations of the trade unions to the state.

The second trade union congress also attempted for the first
time to lay down a comprehensive wages policy. A Menshevik
delegate pleaded for a return to the practice of collective contracts.[3]
But he was before or behind the times. The labour code had entrusted what was virtually the unilateral determination of wages
to the trade unions in consultation with the employers, subject
to the formal approval of Narkomtrud ; the major wage-fixing
decrees of the period of war communism were issued by VTsIK
and Sovnarkom. The resolution of the congress spoke of the
responsibility of the workers to the unions, and of the unions to
the proletariat as a whole, for increased productivity to bring about
the economic reconstruction of the country. Wages policy must
be based on emulation and incentives, i.e. on the principle of
piece-work and bonuses, or, where piece-work was inapplicable,
on strictly fixed norms of production. Wages tariffs were to be

---

[1] *Vtoroi Vserossiiskii S"ezd Professional'nykh Soyuzov* (1921), i (Plenumy),
98-99.

[2] H . . . sky, *Vtoroi Vserossiiskii S"ezd Professional'nykh Soyuzov* (1919),
p. 96 ; Zinoviev, who had offered the first trade union congress state subsidies
for strike funds (see p. 105 above), told the third congress in January 1920 that,
since the trade unions no longer needed strike funds, these could be used to form
an international fund for revolutionary trade unions in other countries (*Tretii
Vserossiiskii S"ezd Professional'nykh Soyuzov* (1920), p. 14). Unofficial strikes
continued to occur from time to time even at the height of the civil war : in
1919 Shlyapnikov at the central council of trade unions proposed a resolution
urging that the trade unions should seek to remove the grievances of the workers
and thus " fight with all our power against disorganizing strike tendencies by
explaining to them the disastrous nature of these methods " (quoted from
unpublished archives in *Desyatyi S"ezd RKP(B)* (1933), pp. 869-870).

[3] *Vtoroi Vserossiiskii S"ezd Professional'nykh Soyuzov* (1921), i (Plenumy),
156-157.

classified in groups, the two highest being reserved for the " highest technical, commercial and administrative personnel " and for " similar personnel of a medium grade ". All groups, whether of administrative personnel or of workers, were divided into twelve categories graded according to degrees of skill; and within each group the spread of wages between the categories was uniform, the variation between the first and the twelfth being in the ratio of 1 : 1·75.[1] While this was far from the hypothetical ideal of equal wages for all, it represented a narrowing of the spread between skilled and unskilled wages which had existed before 1914.[2] Shmidt, in making the report on the subject to the congress, claimed that " the core of the establishment is the worker of average skill " and that the important thing was that this core should be paid more justly; but one speaker argued that the scales bore unfairly on the " skilled class of the proletariat ".[3] The new tariffs were sanctioned for the city and environs of Moscow by a decree of VTsIK published on February 21, 1919, with retrospective effect to February 1. Under this decree the minimum wage for an adult worker was fixed at 600 rubles a month, the highest for the most qualified administrative personnel at 3000 rubles a month; higher rates could be paid only by special decisions of Sovnarkom in each individual case. Three weeks later a further decree fixed the percentages according to which, taking the Moscow standard as 100, the Moscow scales were to be applied to the rest of the country.[4] In April 1919 a decree on the salaries of " responsible political workers " fixed the salaries of People's Commissars, members of VTsIK and a few other officials of the highest category at 2000 rubles a month — or two-thirds of the rate for the highest category of technical and administrative

---

[1] *Ibid.* i (Plenumy), 153-154.

[2] This is shown in A. Bergson, *The Structure of Soviet Wages* (Harvard, 1944), p. 182.

[3] *Vtoroi Vserossiiskii S"ezd Professional'nykh Soyuzov*, i (Plenumy), 152, 157.

[4] *Sobranie Uzakonenii, 1919*, No. 5, art. 52 ; No. 15, art. 171. Rates for Petrograd were 120 per cent of the Moscow rates and for workers on the Murmansk railway north of Petrosavodsk went as high as 125 per cent (presumably on account of the particularly arduous conditions). All other towns (except Yaroslavl, which rated 100 per cent) had lower rates than Moscow, and country regions lower rates than the towns ; the lowest were 45 per cent for the northern Caucasus. It may be doubted how much of these elaborate regulations was applied in practice.

personnel.[1] In August 1919 rising prices led to an upward revision
of rates ; the lowest rate was raised from 600 to 1200 rubles, the
highest from 3000 to 4800,[2] the trend towards greater equality
being cautiously maintained. It is fair to say that, in the early
period of war communism, while no attempt was made to realize
the ideal of equal wages, the principle of equalizations acted as
an effective brake on tendencies dictated by other motives towards
greater wage differentiation. These tendencies were, however,
soon to assert themselves.

An important part of the work of the second trade union
congress was the progress made towards the tightening of trade
union organization. The first congress had laid down the general
principle that unions shall be formed " by industries ", not on a
craft basis, and that " narrowly professional " groups of workers
should be absorbed, so that all workers in an enterprise should
belong to one union.[3] Attempts were made to apply the ruling ;
one source describes how the small independent unions were
driven from the Treugolnik rubber factory in Petrograd in the
autumn of 1918, and the workers enrolled in the chemical workers'
union.[4] But progress was slow. The second congress, noting that
the fulfilment of this purpose had been delayed by " the political
and economic prejudices which separate the worker from office
and technical staff ", considered that " after a year of the dictatorship of the proletariat " it was time to enforce the rule. Unions
were to take responsibility " for the correct working of the undertaking or institution, for labour discipline among the workers and
for observance of rules laid down by the union for the fixing of
wages and of norms of productivity " ; they were to attempt to
make membership compulsory " by means of general meetings of
workers ". Decisions of the All-Russian Congress of Trade
Unions were binding on all unions and on their individual mem-

[1] *Sobranie Uzakonenii, 1919*, No. 18, art. 206 ; in October 1919 the salaries
of " responsible political workers " were once more raised to take account of
rising prices, the highest category receiving 4200 rubles a month (*ibid.* No. 50,
art. 489) ; in June 1920 there was a further rise, bringing this category to 7600
rubles (*Sobranie Uzakonenii, 1920*, No. 53, art. 231). Thereafter under war
communism salaries in money became meaningless, and after the introduction
of NEP figures of official salaries were no longer normally published.

[2] *Ibid.* No. 41, art. 396.

[3] *Pervyi Vserossiiskii S"ezd Professional'nykh Soyuzov* (1918), p. 375.

[4] *Professional'nye Soyuzy SSSR*, ed. Y. K. Milonov (1927), p. 164.

bers, and the All-Russian Central Council of Trade Unions was
authorized to act on behalf of the congress and to take binding
decisions in its name when it was not in session.[1] With organization improving, the membership of the trade unions increased
rapidly ; the figure claimed rose from 1,500,000 at the July conference of 1917 to 2,600,000 at the time of the first congress of
January 1918 and to 3,500,000 at the second congress of January
1919.[2]

When the second trade union congress met in January 1919,
the civil war was not yet at its height and the economy as a whole
had not yet been fully geared to meet war requirements.   In the
next two months a notable advance was made in these respects.
The eighth party congress assembled in March 1919 in an atmosphere of gathering storm.   The main formal business of the
congress was to adopt a new party programme to replace the long
obsolete programme of 1903.   Hitherto the party had had no
occasion since the revolution to define its attitude to the trade
unions.   Now it declared that " the organizational apparatus of
industry " must rest primarily on them, and added, in a formula
which was to give trouble later, that " the trade unions must
achieve a *de facto* concentration in their hands of the whole administration of the whole national economy considered as a single
economic unit ".   But the key to the main function of the trade
unions in the civil war emergency was to be found in another
paragraph of the economic section of the programme :

> The maximum utilization of the whole available labour force
> of the state, its correct distribution and redistribution, both
> between different territorial regions and between different
> branches of the national economy, which is indispensable for
> the purpose of the planned development of the national economy,
> must form the immediate task of the economic policy of the
> Soviet power, which can be realized by it only in close unity

[1] *Vtoroi Vserossiiskii S"ezd Professional'nykh Soyuzov* (1921), i (Plenumy),
191-193.
[2] These were the figures quoted by Zinoviev at the tenth party congress
(*Desyatyi S"ezd Rossiiskoi Kommunisticheskoi Partii* (1921), p. 188).   He
admitted that they were inflated figures, but claimed them as valid for purposes
of comparison ; this was probably true.   Slightly different figures are quoted by
other sources.

with the trade unions. The individual mobilization of the whole population fit for work by the Soviet power, with the participation of the trade unions, for the carrying out of definite social work, must be applied in an incomparably broader and more systematic way than hitherto.

And the programme, adding that " the socialist method of production can be made secure only on the basis of the comradely discipline of the workers ", assigned to the trade unions " the chief rôle in the work of creating this new socialist discipline ".[1] The party congress of March 1919 was followed by a decree of Sovnarkom in April 10 ordering a general mobilization ;[2] and on the following day Lenin presented to the central council of trade unions in the name of the central committee of the party a set of theses " In Connexion with the Position of the Eastern Front ", appealing to all party and trade union organizations throughout the country to cooperate in the work of mobilization. The example of Pokrovsk, where the trade unions had decided of their own accord to mobilize at once 50 per cent of their members was held up for emulation, and trade unions were exhorted to carry out a re-registration of their members " in order to despatch those who are not unconditionally necessary at home to the Volga or Ural front ".[3]

> When it was hard at the front [said Trotsky rhetorically a year later], we turned to the central committee of the communist party on the one hand and to the presidium of the trade union central council on the other ; and from those two sources outstanding proletarians were sent to the front and there created the Red Army in their own image and pattern.[4]

The decree and Lenin's exhortations were formally confined to the calling up for military service, and no decree instituting compulsory labour service was issued at this time. But the distinction

---

[1] *VKP(B) v Rezolyutsiyakh* (1941), i, 290-291 ; the disciplinary rôle of the trade unions is more strongly stressed in the final text than in Lenin's original draft, probably written in February 1919, which, however, already demanded " the greatest and strictest possible centralization of labour on an all-state scale " (*Sochineniya*, xxiv, 102) ; the gravity of the civil war had increased considerably in the interval.

[2] *Izvestiya*, April 11, 1919.

[3] Lenin, *Sochineniya*, xxiv, 224-226, 229-242.

[4] *Tretii Vserossiiskii S"ezd Professional'nykh Soyuzov* (1920), i (Plenumy), 87.

between military service and labour service soon became unreal. At the same moment as the mobilization decree, a decree was issued by STO forbidding coal-miners to leave their employment and declaring that all miners belonging to age-groups which had been called up were to be considered mobilized at their jobs.[1]

The adoption of the new party programme at the eighth congress, the decree of Sovnarkom on mobilization, and the appeal of the party central committee to the trade unions marked the beginning of a critical year in which the principles of war communism were fully and unflinchingly applied to the organization of labour. The essence of the labour policy of war communism was the abandonment of the labour market and of recognized capitalist procedures for the engagement and management of the workers; and this made it seem, like other policies of the period, not merely a concession to the needs of the civil war, but an authentic advance into the socialist order. It was difficult to contest the argument that the workers' state, whose right to mobilize its citizens for service at the front was disputed by nobody, was equally entitled to call up those who were required to man the factories; and this conception of labour as a service to be rendered rather than as a commodity to be sold was in theory the hall-mark of everything that distinguished the loftier ideals of socialism from the base mechanics of the capitalist wage-system. The progressive substitution of payment in kind for money wages, though mainly an enforced consequence of the depreciation of money and of the breakdown of the normal processes of exchange, also fitted easily into this conception. " Under the system of a proletarian dictatorship ", wrote Bukharin in the following year, " the worker receives a socially determined ration, and not wages ".[2] The state, instead of purchasing the worker's labour power, maintained him, as it maintained the fighting man, during the period of his service. The distribution of food rations to the factories through the trade unions emphasized this attitude; and in September 1919 an order was issued by the central council of trade unions for the supply to all manual workers in factories

[1] *Sobranie Uzakonenii, 1919*, No. 14, art. 163; this decree paved the way for the later extensive use of " labour armies " in the mines.

[2] N. Bukharin, *Ekonomika Perekhodnogo Perioda* (1920), p. 105.

and workshops of working clothes which remained the property of the institution — the counterpart of a military uniform.[1]

In such conditions, the development of fresh incentives to replace the " economic whip " of the capitalist system was a constant preoccupation of the authorities, since the possibility of arresting the decline in production depended on overcoming the chronic evils of absenteeism and inefficiency among the workers. The incentive most appropriate to the spirit of socialism was the natural revolutionary ardour which might be supposed to animate the worker in the factory no less than his comrade at the front. In May 1919, a month after the decree for the mobilization of labour, came the first of the " communist Saturdays ", when some hundreds of Moscow workers of the Moscow-Kazan railway volunteered to work an extra six hours after the end of work on Saturday in order to hasten the despatch of troops and supplies to the front. The practice spread and was hailed by Lenin in a special pamphlet as an outstanding example of " the new social discipline, socialist discipline ".[2] But this was a party enterprise of limited scope ; [3] and it was never seriously supposed that moral incentives, even when reinforced by material rewards, would be adequate without some specific organization for the marshalling of the labour force and the maintenance of labour discipline. To develop such an organization now became an urgent task.

The initial hypothesis that compulsion to work would have to be applied only to members of the former bourgeois and land-owning classes and that voluntary self-discipline would suffice to maintain the zeal of the workers was soon abandoned. The labour code of October 1918 merely repeated the general principle, already laid down in the constitution of the RSFSR, of a universal obligation to work ; and no provisions were made for its enforcement or for the exaction of penalties for failure to comply with it. But what was left of a voluntary system virtually ended with the

[1] *Proizvodstvo, Uchet i Raspredelenie Produktov Narodnogo Khozyaistva : Sbornik Dekretov* (n.d. [? 1921]), pp. 446-448.

[2] Lenin, *Sochineniya*, xxiv, 329.

[3] According to Bukharin i Preobrazhensky, *Azbuka Kommunizma*, ch. xii, § 100, the number of those working on " communist Saturdays " rose from 5000 to 10,000 in August and September 1919 : examples are quoted of skilled workers achieving 213 per cent of normal output and unskilled 300 per cent.

mobilization decree of April 10, 1919. In June 1919 the cautious
introduction of labour books for workers in Moscow and Petrograd
was another attempt to tighten up the controls.[1] But too much
reliance had been placed, no doubt because there was no available
alternative, on the machinery of the trade unions. Even for the
mobilization of skilled workers the unions proved ineffective.
Lenin in the winter of 1919–1920 complained bitterly to Tomsky
of a failure to transfer 10,000 skilled metal workers to the railway
repair shops.[2] From the end of 1919 the mobilization of unskilled
labour was taken entirely out of their hands and entrusted to
Narkomtrud and its local organs. In November the fuel crisis
inspired a decree instituting labour service " for the supply,
loading or unloading of all sorts of fuel ", as well as the so-called
" carting service " to be rendered by the peasants on the demand
of the local authorities, i.e. the obligation to provide horses and
carts or sleighs for the transport of timber, food, or military
supplies to stations or harbours. The decree applied to all
peasants not called up for military service up to the age of 50, or
for women up to 40.[3] In January 1920 a decree of Sovnarkom,
which solemnly invoked in its preamble the principle, established
by the constitution of the RSFSR and by the labour code, of the
citizen's obligation to perform " socially useful work in the
interests of the socialist society ", and the need to " supply
industry, agriculture, transport and other branches of the national
economy with labour power on the basis of a general economic
plan ", laid down general regulations for universal labour service.
Any member of the " working population " could be called up on
a single occasion or periodically for various forms of labour
service : fuel, agriculture (" on state farms or, in certain cases,
on peasant farms "), building, road-making, food supplies, snow
clearance, carting, and measures to deal with the consequences of
public calamities, were listed as examples. A chief labour committee (Glavkomtrud) was set up under STO to organize labour
service, with subordinate provincial, country and city labour committees.[4] These, together with the local organs of Narkomtrud

[1] See p. 200, note 1 above.   [2] Lenin, *Sochineniya*, xxix, 383-384.
[3] *Sobranie Uzakonenii, 1919*, No. 57, art. 543
[4] *Sobranie Uzakonenii, 1920*, No. 8, art. 49 ; a supplementary decree
required village Soviets to play their part in mobilizing rural workers for the
labour armies (*ibid.* No. 11, art. 68). A worker from the Kolomensky works in

which had replaced the labour exchanges, now became responsible for general labour mobilization.[1] There was even cause to regret the destruction by the revolution of " the old police apparatus which had known how to register citizens not only in the towns, but in the country ". Nevertheless the machinery was improvised, and large labour forces recruited for work in forestry, transport, building and other forms of employment calling for masses of unskilled labour.[2] " We supplied labour according to plan ", said a spokesman of Narkomtrud later, " and consequently without taking account of individual peculiarities or qualifications or of the wish of the worker to engage in this or that kind of work."[3] According to one authority nearly 6 million people were mobilized for labour service in the timber industry in the first half of 1920.[4]

At this time a new source of labour came into being which probably had at first a symbolical rather than a numerical significance. In April 1919 forced labour camps were instituted for offenders, who might be sentenced to this form of punishment by the Cheka, by revolutionary tribunals or by the ordinary people's courts. The initiative in creating such camps rested with the provincial Chekas; the administration of the camps was in the hands of a section of the People's Commissariat for Internal Affairs (NKVD); and prisoners in these camps were put to work " at the request of Soviet institutions ". Separate camps were set up for children and minors. An eight-hour working day was prescribed, overtime and night work being, however, permitted on the conditions laid down in the general labour code. Wages were

the spring of 1920 told the visiting British Labour delegation " that desertions from the works were frequent and that deserters were arrested by soldiers and brought back from the villages " (*British Labour Delegation to Russia, 1920 : Report* (1920), p. 18).

[1] The Moscow committee published in the summer of 1920 a weekly gazette *Izvestiya Moskovskogo Komiteta po Trudovoi Povinnosti*, which, studied in conjunction with the contemporary press, would throw much light on the working of the labour service. A decree of May 4, 1920 (*Sobranie Uzakonenii, 1920*, No. 35, art. 168) made Glavkomtrud and its local organs responsible for combating all forms of labour desertion.

[2] All the above information was given in a full and frank report to the third All-Russian Congress of Trade Unions in April 1920 (*Tretii Vserossiiskii S"ezd Professional'nykh Soyuzov* (1920), i (Plenumy), 50-51).

[3] *Stenograficheskii Otchet Pyatogo Vserossiiskogo S"ezda Professional'nykh Soyuzov* (1922), p. 83.

[4] L. Kritsman, *Geroicheskii Period Velikoi Russkoi Revolyutsii* (n.d. [? 1924]), p. 106.

to be paid to the prisoners at the trade union rates, but not more than three-quarters of the wages could be deducted to cover the maintenance of the prisoner and the upkeep of the camp.[1] The system had not, in this initial stage, the sinister significance which it later acquired as a major economic asset. At the same time a harsher form of punishment was instituted in the form of the " concentration camp " which purported to be reserved for those guilty of counter-revolutionary activities in the civil war.[2] These camps soon seem, however, to have been used for enemies of the régime in general. In a report prepared for the visiting British Labour delegation in the spring of 1920 it was stated that " the People's Commissariat provides labour detachments composed of persons confined in concentration camps (mainly members of the former ruling classes) for performing various kinds of difficult and unpleasant work ".[3]

The mobilization of labour reached its highest intensity in the first months of 1920 — at the moment when, thanks to the defeat of Denikin and Kolchak, the acute emergency which had made it necessary was already passing away. At the third All-Russian Congress of Councils of National Economy in January 1920 Trotsky devoted the greater part of his speech to a defence of labour conscription and labour discipline ;[4] and on the proposal of Tomsky, whose gloomy review of the depleted industrial labour force has already been quoted,[5] a far-reaching resolution was passed demanding *inter alia* the payment of bonuses, individual or collective, in kind, disciplinary courts for labour,[6] a labour book

[1] *Sobranie Uzakonenii*, *1919*, No. 12, art. 124 ; No. 20, art. 235.

[2] *Ibid.* No. 12, art. 130.

[3] Y. Larin i L. Kritsman, *Ocherk Khozyaistvennoi Zhizni i Organizatsiya Narodnogo Khozyaistvo* (1920), pp. 126-127 ; it was the identification of penal labour with the most arduous forms of labour needed by society that gave this institution its particularly brutal character.

[4] The proceedings of the congress were not published, but Trotsky's speech was printed as a pamphlet, and later in his collected works (*Sochineniya*, xv, 52-78).

[5] See pp. 194-195 above.

[6] In the middle of 1919 the first " workers' comradely courts of discipline " had been created in the factories (*Sobranie Uzakonenii*, *1919*, No. 56, art. 537) : these soon became a regular institution of factory discipline. Not much detailed information is available about the work of the workers' courts, but some figures of proceedings of the corresponding courts for factory officials and employees indicate the nature of the charges brought and of the penalties imposed. Of 945 recorded cases in 1920, the charge in nearly half was unpunctuality ; other

for all workers to prevent evasion of labour service, and the use of army recruiting machinery for the mobilization and transfer of labour.[1] Meanwhile the cessation of actual fighting at the front had suggested the diversion of units under military discipline to other urgent tasks. On January 15, 1920, a decree was issued transforming the third army in the Urals into a " first revolutionary army of labour ", enjoying military authority over the local civil authorities.[2] The precedent had been created. The stage was set for what came to be known as " the militarization of labour ".

This was the new issue which the ninth party congress had to face when it met towards the end of March 1920. Labour armies were appearing everywhere in the form of detachments of the Red Army employed, now that fighting was at an end, on heavy work of all kinds, including forestry and mining. Nor was there

common charges in order of frequency were " incorrect behaviour towards clients ", " absence from overtime on Saturdays ", " failure to obey trade union discipline ", " failure to obey orders ", " voluntary abandonment of work " and " propaganda for a shortening of the working day ". Acquittals followed in more than a quarter of the cases, dismissal in nearly a half ; in 30 cases the penalty of forced labour was pronounced, in 79 of labour in a concentration camp (D. Antoshkin, *Profdvizhenie Sluzhashchikh* (1927), p. 152). Years later, when war communism had become a painful memory, Tomsky recalled with shame that some trade unions had at that time gone so far as to " set up gaols " for recalcitrant members (*Vos'moi S"ezd Professional'nykh Soyuzov SSSR* (1929), pp. 42-44).

    [1] *Rezolyutsii Tret'ego Vserossiiskogo S"ezda Sovetov Narodnogo Khozyaistva* (1920), pp. 25-30.

    [2] *Sobranie Uzakonenii*, 1920, No. 3, art. 15 ; Trotsky, in a subsequent report to VTsIK, claimed that the first labour army had been formed out of the third army " on its own initiative " (*Sochineniya*, xv, 5 ; many documents relating to the first labour army are collected, *ibid.* xv, 263-342). Trotsky at the ninth party congress boasted of the high-handed action of the army in " turning ourselves into a regional economic centre " and claimed that what had been done was " in the highest degree excellent work, though it was illegal work " (*Devyatyi S"ezd RKP(B)* (1934), p. 114) ; immediately afterwards it was decided " to entrust to the revolutionary council of the first labour army the general direction of the work of restoring and strengthening normal economic and military life in the Urals " (*Sobranie Uzakonenii, 1920*, No. 30, art. 151). In August 1920 similar functions were conferred on the revolutionary council of the labour army of south-eastern Russia (*ibid.* No. 74, art. 344), and as late as November 1920 the council of the labour army of the Ukraine was recognized as " the local organ of the Council of Labour and Defence " (*ibid.* No. 86, art. 428). Trotsky's writings and speeches of the first months of 1920 (*Sochineniya*, xv, 3-206) are a copious source for the labour armies : one army provided labour to build a railway in Turkestan for the transport of oil, another manned the Donetz coal-mines (*ibid.* xv, 6).

any doubt what this implied. Trotsky, who believed that the problems of industry could be solved only by the methods and by the enthusiasm which had won the civil war, spoke of the need to " militarize the great masses of peasants who had been recruited for work on the principles of labour service ", and went on :

> Militarization is unthinkable without the militarization of the trade unions as such, without the establishment of a régime in which every worker feels himself a soldier of labour, who cannot dispose of himself freely ; if the order is given to transfer him, he must carry it out ; if he does not carry it out, he will be a deserter who is punished. Who looks after this ? The trade union. It creates the new régime. This is the militarization of the working class.[1]

And Radek concluded a speech devoted mainly to the affairs of Comintern with " an appeal to organized labour to overcome the bourgeois prejudice of ' freedom of labour ' so dear to the hearts of Mensheviks and compromisers of every kind ".[2] Though nobody else spoke this language, Trotsky had behind him the authority of the central committee and the Politburo ; and the congress was still sufficiently under the impression of military perils narrowly escaped, and of almost insuperable economic hazards ahead, to endorse the policy without overt dissent.[3] In a long resolution, which bore the marks of Trotsky's masterful style, it cautiously approved the employment of Red Army units on labour service " for so long as it is necessary to keep the army in being for military tasks ". About the principle of the militarization of labour it had no qualms. Help was to be given to " trade unions and labour sections " to " keep account of all skilled workers

---

[1] *Devyatyi S"ezd RKP(B)* (1934), p. 101.

[2] *Izvestiya*, April 2, 1920, which carries a much abbreviated report of the speech. The text of the speech was omitted from the official record of the congress on the ground that it would be published as a separate pamphlet (*Devyatyi S"ezd RKP(B)* (1934), p. 277) : according to a note in the second edition of the record (*ibid.* p. 575) the pamphlet never appeared.

[3] Before the congress Shlyapnikov had circulated theses distinguishing the Soviets as " the expression of political power " and the trade unions as " the only responsible organizer of the national economy " : these were intended as a counterblast to Trotsky's militarization of labour, and, though not formally discussed, were referred to at the congress by Krestinsky and Bukharin (*Devyatyi S"ezd RKP(B)* (1934), pp. 88, 225 ; see *ibid.* p. 564, note 32, for quotations from them). Shlyapnikov himself was not at the congress, having been sent — perhaps to keep him out of the way — on a trade union mission abroad (*ibid.* p. 62).

in order to direct them to productive work with the same accuracy and strictness as was done, and is done, with officer personnel [1] for the needs of the army ". As regards mass mobilizations for labour service, it was merely necessary to match the number of men available with the dimensions of the job and the tools required, and to have competent instructors ready as had been done " in the creation of the Red Army ". A worker leaving his job was to be treated as guilty of " labour desertion ", and a series of severe penalties was prescribed, ending with " confinement in a concentration camp ".[2]

The debate on labour conscription was resumed a few weeks later in the third All-Russian Congress of Trade Unions, where there was still a small but vocal Menshevik minority,[3] and where such opposition to the policy as still prevailed in Bolshevik ranks was likely to be strongest. Lenin, who a week earlier at the founding congress of an all-Russian mine-workers' union had declared that " we must create by means of the trade unions such comradely discipline as we had in the Red Army ",[4] now embarked on a more reasoned defence of the policy. He harked back to the " breathing-space " after Brest-Litovsk when, in April 1918, in

[1] The term *kommandnyi sostav* includes non-commissioned officers. The phrase reflects an idea current at the time of the possibility of creating an " officer corps " of skilled workers (what its opponents called a " labour aristocracy ") to organize and direct the mass of workers. The fullest exposition of the idea was in an article by Goltsman in *Pravda* of March 26, 1920, which was quoted at the ninth party congress (*Devyatyi S"ezd RKP(B)* (1934), p. 171), supported by Trotsky (*ibid.* pp. 210-212) and vigorously attacked by Ryazanov (*ibid.* pp. 247-249). Lenin made a vague but sympathetic reference to Goltsman's views (*Sochineniya*, xxv, 120). Zinoviev had denounced the idea in " theses " issued before the congress : " The task of communist workers in the trade union movement cannot consist in the separation and separate grouping of skilled workers who form a minority of the working class " (G. Zinoviev, *Sochineniya*, vi (1929), 344).

[2] *VKP(B) v Rezolyutsiyakh* (1941), i, 330, 335-336 ; immediately after the congress effect was given to the resolution on labour desertion by an official decree in the same terms (*Sobranie Uzakonenii, 1920*, No. 35, art. 168).

[3] The Menshevik delegates numbered 70 out of about 1000. The Menshevik spokesmen claimed that they still held a majority in the printers', chemical workers', metal workers' and textile workers' unions (*Tretii Vserossiiskii S"ezd Professional'nykh Soyuzov* (1920), i (Plenumy) 43, 110) ; except for the printers' union, the claim was of doubtful validity. The Menshevik case against the militarization of labour was stated in a memorandum on the trade unions handed to the visiting British Labour delegation (*British Labour Delegation to Russia, 1920 : Report* (1920), pp. 80-82).

[4] Lenin, *Sochineniya*, xxv, 135.

opposition to the Left communists, he had advocated in his theses
to VTsIK the " raising of labour discipline ". He admitted that
" two years ago there was no talk of labour armies ". But " the
forms of the struggle against capital change ". Now that another
breathing space had brought up the same problems, " labour
must be organized in a new way, new forms of incentives to work,
of submission to labour discipline, must be created ", though he
admitted that " to create new forms of social discipline is an
affair of decades ".[1] Lenin left the issue on these broad lines, and
in a brief resolution adopted at the end of his speech the congress
decided in general terms " to introduce immediately in all trade
union organizations severe labour discipline from below upwards ".[2] " We cannot live at the present time ", said Rykov
simply at a later stage of the congress, " without compulsion. The
waster and the blockhead must be forced under fear of punishment
to work for the workers and peasants in order to save them from
hunger and penury." [3] But it was left for Trotsky to offer a
theoretical defence of the Bolshevik position against the Menshevik
plea for the " freedom of labour " :

> Let the Menshevik spokesmen explain what is meant by
> free, non-compulsory labour. We know slave-labour, we know
> serf-labour, we know the compulsory, regimented labour of the
> mediaeval guilds, we have known the hired wage-labour which
> the bourgeoisie calls " free ". We are now advancing towards a
> type of labour socially regulated on the basis of an economic
> plan which is obligatory for the whole country, i.e. compulsory
> for every worker. That is the foundation of socialism. . . .
> And once we have recognized this, we thereby recognize fun-
> damentally — not formally, but fundamentally — the right of
> the workers' state to send each working man and woman to the
> place where they are needed for the fulfilment of economic
> tasks. We thereby recognize the right of the state, the workers'
> state, to punish the working man or woman who refuse to
> carry out the order of the state, who do not subordinate their
> will to the will of the working class and to its economic tasks. . . .
> The militarization of labour in this fundamental sense of which
> I have spoken is the indispensable and fundamental method for
> the organization of our labour forces. . . . We know that all

---

[1] *Ibid.* xxv, 137-142.
[2] *Tretii Vserossiiskii S"ezd Professional'nykh Soyuzov* (1920), i (Plenumy), 28.
[3] *Ibid.* i, 87.

labour is socially compulsory labour.   Man must work in order
not to die.   He does not want to work.   But the social organization compels and whips him in that direction.[1]

The argument for the permanent and unlimited conscription of
labour by the state, like the contemporary argument for the
abolition of money, reads like an attempt to provide a theoretical
justification for a harsh necessity which it had been impossible to
avoid.   But this frank speaking, though it represented accepted
party policy, and went unchallenged at the congress except by the
Mensheviks, was scarcely calculated to endear Trotsky to the rank
and file of the trade unions.   Later in the year Bukharin in his
Economics of the Transition Period argued that, while compulsory
labour service under state capitalism meant " the enslavement of
the working class ", the same measure under the dictatorship of
the proletariat was simply " the self-organization of the working
class ".[2]

Strenuous exertions to combine moral exhortation and example,
material inducements, and the fear of punishment as incentives to
work kept the system of labour discipline in being with increasing
difficulty throughout the period of the Polish war and the Wrangel
offensive.   The resolution of the ninth party congress, which so
resolutely endorsed measures of labour discipline, also advocated
the organization of " workers' emulation ", both collective and
individual, recommended a system of bonuses in kind and gave its
special blessing to the practice of " communist Saturdays "
spontaneously started in the previous summer.[3]   In April 1920 the
party printers set an example by bringing out a special one-day
newspaper *The Communist Saturday* to give a new impetus to the
movement ; and on the morning of May 1, which fell this year on a
Saturday, Lenin himself took part in a " communist Saturday "
in the Kremlin.   Later a party rule made participation in unpaid

[1] *Tretii Vserossiiskii S"ezd Professional'nykh Soyuzov* (1920), i (Plenumy),
88-90.   The argument had been anticipated in part in Trotsky's speech at the
ninth party congress (*Devyatyi S"ezd RKP(B)* (1934), pp. 104-105 ; a long
passage in L. Trotsky, *Terrorizm i Kommunizm* (1920), pp. 124-150 (reprinted
in *Sochineniya*, xii, 127-153), is a conflation of the two speeches.

[2] N. Bukharin, *Ekonomika Perekhodnogo Perioda* (1920), p. 107 ; Bukharin,
the most consistent exponent among the Bolshevik leaders of the principles of
war communism, was at this time associated with Trotsky on the trade union
issue (see pp. 222-226 below).

[3] *VKP(B) v Rezolyutsiyakh* (1941), i, 330-331, 336.

Saturday work obligatory for party members.[1] During the same year certain groups of specially active workers engaged in Trotsky's drive for the rehabilitation of transport were dubbed, by a military metaphor, *udarniki* or shock troops; and a substantive *udarnichestvo*, or " shock work ", was coined to designate particularly meritorious service on the labour front, teams of *udarniki* being assigned to specially difficult or specially urgent tasks. The scheme at first provided a valuable stimulus, but was later abused and rendered futile by too wide and constant use.[2]

The first *udarniki* worked entirely for glory, the incentives to extra effort being purely moral and psychological. This did not indicate a complete neglect of more material incentives in so far as these were available. How far the wage scales approved by the second All-Russian Congress of Trade Unions in January 1919 [3] were applied in practice cannot be estimated. But the third congress, meeting in April 1920, did not concentrate its whole attention of the major issue of the militarization of labour. It also held a debate on wages policy and approved a new wages scale. Shmidt, the People's Commissar of Labour, who put forward the new project, explicitly stated that " the changes in the construction of the wage scales have the purpose of attracting into industry a qualified working force "; and with this end in view wage differentials were sharply stepped up, the normal spread between the lowest and highest grade of " workers " being in the ratio of 1 : 2.[4] Thus, at the height of war communism and under the impetus of the need to provide stronger incentives to attract the skilled worker, the retreat had already begun from the policy of equalization professed, and to some extent practised, at the outset of the revolutionary period. What, however, foiled the new policy was the impending total eclipse of monetary payments by

[1] Lenin, *Sochineniya*, xxv, 612, note 92, 697-698.
[2] Y. S. Rozenfeld, *Promyshlennaya Politika SSSR* (1926), p. 138 ; a speaker at the fourth All-Russian Congress of Trade Unions in May 1921 remarked that " the conception of ' shock ' working has been so broadened that there are now more ' shock ' than non-' shock ' enterprises " (*Chetvertyi Vserossiiskii S''ezd Professional'nykh Soyuzov* (1921), ii (Sektsii), 48).
[3] See pp. 202-203 above.
[4] *Tretii Vserossiiskii S''ezd Professional'nykh Soyuzov* (1921), i (Plenumy), 112 : A. Bergson, *The Structure of Soviet Wages* (Harvard, 1944), pp. 183-184, quotes further evidence of the trend towards greater wage differentiation at this time.

supplies in kind, to which the emphasis was now transferred. Though there had been many variations in categories of rations adjusted to the status and occupation of the consumers,[1] no attempt had been made before 1920 to adjust rations to individual output. In January 1920, when money wages were becoming almost meaningless and rations were taking on the character of wages in kind, the proposal to institute bonuses in kind was made and endorsed at the third All-Russian Congress of Councils of National Economy;[2] and this recommendation was repeated by the ninth party congress in March 1920 and by the third All-Russian Congress of Trade Unions in the following month.[3] In June 1920 a decree was issued ordering the establishment of a system of bonuses both in money and kind " to raise the productivity of labour ". The practicability of the system admittedly depended on " the establishment of a general fund for bonuses in kind ";[4] and in October 1920 a fund of 500,000 puds of grain and corresponding quantities of other foodstuffs was accumulated for this purpose.[5] But the scheme, which was to have been administered by the trade unions, broke down owing to shortage of supplies, since the organs of Narkomprod " were frequently obliged to distribute the food not by way of bonuses, but as part of the ordinary regular ration ".[6] Now that money had almost lost its value, the effective part of the wages of workers was that constantly increasing part which was paid in kind. But, when the meagreness of supplies continually prevented any distribution being made in excess of the barest minimum ration, the material incentives to production which might have been afforded by bonuses or differential wages fell to the ground. The ultimate result of war communism in the field of labour policy was to leave no other incentives in operation except revolutionary enthusiasm and naked compulsion.

[1] See p. 232 below.

[2] See p. 211 above.

[3] *VKP(B) v Rezolyutsiyakh* (1941), i, 331; *Tretii Vserossiiskii S"ezd Professional'nykh Soyuzov* (1921), i (Plenumy), 112-114.

[4] *Sobranie Uzakonenii, 1920*, No. 55, art. 239.

[5] *Ibid.* No. 92, art. 497; Lenin called this decree "one of the most important decrees and decisions of Sovnarkom and STO " (*Sochineniya*, xxvi, 40).

[6] *Chetvertyi Vserossiiskii S"ezd Professional'nykh Soyuzov* (1921), i (Plenumy), 29, 114-115.

It was towards the end of 1920, when Wrangel had suffered defeat and the civil war was finally ended, that the labour front, like other aspects of the national economy, began to show signs of intolerable stresses. The " militarization of labour " had lost the justification which it seemed to possess so long as a fight for existence was in progress. The trade unions became once again the seat and the subject of acute frictions — friction within the central council, friction between the central council and the trade unions, and friction between the unions and Soviet organs. The questions at issue, which often appeared as questions of degree rather than of principle, were whether the main function of the unions was to stimulate production or to defend the immediate and sectional interests of their members, whether they should mobilize and organize labour by compulsory or solely by voluntary methods, and whether they should take orders from the state on matters of policy or maintain some degree of independence. No essential link existed between the issue of the " militarization of labour " and the issue of the relation of the trade unions to the state. But it was natural that those who regarded labour conscription as a permanent part of a socialist economy also sought to incorporate the trade unions in the state machine, while those who stood for independent trade unions assumed that the virtue of the unions resided in the voluntary nature of the discipline which they imposed. The vivid personality of Trotsky, who insisted without qualification on the compulsory mobilization of labour and on the complete subordination of the unions of the state, added point to the controversy and sharpened all its edges ; Tomsky emerged as the defender of the traditional " trade unionist " outlook.

The first All-Russian Congress of Trade Unions had laid it down in 1918 that the trade unions ought to become " organs of state power " ; the eighth party congress in the following year had declared in the relevant section on the party programme that the trade unions should " concentrate *de facto* in their hands the whole administration of the whole national economy as a single economic entity ". In the heat of the civil war the two points of view could be fused ; once it was over, the question was bound to arise whether vital decisions of policy were to be taken by the trade unions or by state organs. The occasion which forced the issue was more or less accidental. In the winter of 1919–1920 the conditions of the railways had become catastrophic and the economy was threatened with a breakdown owing to complete chaos in transport and Lenin telegraphed to Trotsky, then in the Urals, asking him to take charge of the question.[1]   Current methods of coercion were first thought of.   A decree of STO of January 30, 1920, declared all railway workers mobilized for labour service, and a week later a further decree conferred wide disciplinary powers on the railway administration; neither decree made any mention of the trade unions.[2]   At the beginning of March 1920, Trotsky secured the creation for the carrying out of his policy of a new organ of the People's Commissariat of Communications (Narkomput') called the " chief political railway administration " (Glavpolitput'), the function of which was to appeal to the political consciousness of the railway workers.[3]   One purpose, or at any rate one result, of its creation was to side-track the railwaymen's union, which, ever since the troubles of the first weeks of the revolution, had preserved a more stubborn tradition than most unions of independent action.   A special resolution of the ninth party congress at the end of March 1920 drew attention to the cardinal importance of transport, ascribed " the fundamental difficulty in the matter of improving transport " to " the weakness of the railwaymen's trade union ", and gave a special blessing to Glavpolitput', whose dual function was " urgently to improve transport through the organized influence of experienced communists . . . and at the same time to strengthen the railway trade union organization, to pour into it the best workers whom Glavpolitput' is sending to the railways, to help the trade union itself to establish iron discipline in its organization, and in this way to make the trade union of railwaymen an irreplaceable instrument for the further improvement of rail transport ".[4]   Jealousies were soon aroused, and open war broke out between Glavpolitput' and the railwaymen's union.   It came to a head in August, when the central committee of the party decided to depose the committee of the railwaymen's union and replace it by a new com-

---

[1] L. Trotsky, *Moya Zhizn'* (Berlin, 1930), ii, 198; see also pp. 373-374 below.

[2] *Sobranie Uzakonenii, 1920*, No. 8, art. 52; No. 10, art. 64.

[3] *Izvestiya Tsentral'nogo Komiteta Rossiiskoi Kommunisticheskoi Partii (Bol'shevikov)*, No. 13, March 2, 1920, p. 4.

[4] *VKP(B) v Rezolyutsiyakh* (1941), i, 335.

mittee, known in the subsequent controversy as Tsektran.[1] The unfinished Polish war and the new intervention by Wrangel in the south still seemed to justify any high-handed emergency measures which might keep transport moving. But at the end of September the trade unions had regained some of their prestige in the party central committee, which passed a resolution deprecating " all petty tutelage and petty interference " in trade union affairs, noting that the transport situation had " decidedly improved ", and declaring that it was now time to transform Glavpolitput' (and a corresponding body for river transport called Glavpolitvod) into trade union organs.[2]

When, therefore, an all-Russian trade union conference (not a full congress) assembled in Moscow in the first days of November 1920, feelings were already tense. The armistice had been signed with Poland, and the civil war and the worst of the transport crisis were virtually over. The Bolshevik delegates met as usual in advance to decide on their line at the conference. Trotsky, taking advantage of a discussion on production, launched a general attack on the trade unions which he described as in need of a " shake-up "; Tomsky retorted with asperity.[3] The quarrel was kept away from the floor of the conference, which was content with some non-committal theses of Rudzutak on the rôle of the trade unions in stimulating production.[4] But the situation in the party was now so embittered that the central committee had to take a hand. At a meeting on November 8, 1920, Lenin and Trotsky presented alternative drafts, and on the following day after some difficult discussions the committee by a majority of 10 to 4 (the dissentients being Trotsky, Krestinsky, Andreev and Rykov) adopted a resolution modelled on Lenin's draft. The resolution tactfully distinguished between " centralism and

---

[1] At the tenth party congress Trotsky twice stated without contradiction that the decision to create Tsektran (which presumably originated from him) was taken by the central committee of the party on August 28, 1920, being supported by Lenin, Zinoviev and Stalin against the protest of Tomsky (*Desyatyi S"ezd Rossiiskoi Kommunisticheskoi Partii* (1921), pp. 195, 214).

[2] *Izvestiya Tsentral'nogo Komiteta Rossiiskoi Kommunisticheskoi Partii (Bol'shevikov)*, No. 26, December 20, 1920, p. 2.

[3] *Desyatyi S"ezd Rossiiskoi Kommunisticheskoi Partii* (1921), p. 202 ; Lenin, *Sochineniya*, xxvi, 87-88, 631, note 49.

[4] These theses were praised by Lenin and quoted by him *in extenso* (*ibid.* xxvi, 77-80).

militarized forms of labour ", which were liable to degenerate into bureaucracy and " petty tutelage over the trade unions ", and " healthy forms of the militarization of labour ". On the substantive point it prescribed that Tsektran should participate in the central council of trade unions on the same footing as the central committees of other major unions, and decided to appoint a committee to draw up fresh general instructions for the trade unions.[1] This was followed by a split within Tsektran,[2] and on December 7, 1920, the central committee returned to the dispute in an atmosphere of increasing bitterness. On this occasion Lenin left Zinoviev to make the running against Trotsky. But feeling in the committee turned against both protagonists : and Bukharin formed a so-called " buffer group ", which included Preobrazhensky, Serebryakov, Sokolnikov and Larin, and carried by 8 votes to 7 a compromise resolution which had the effect of keeping every issue open till the party congress in the coming spring. Glavpolitput' and its companion organization Glavpolitvod were formally dissolved and their staffs and assets transferred to the trade unions. Tsektran was left in being, but on the understanding that new elections to it would take place at the forthcoming congress of transport workers in February 1921.[3]

From this time onwards it was impossible to maintain the original decision taken in November not to countenance public discussion of these differences within the party.[4] In the three months which separated the December session of the central committee from the opening of the tenth party congress on March

---

[1] The resolution is reprinted in *Protokoly X S"ezda RKP(B)* (1933), pp. 798-799. Trotsky's draft was published in *Partiya i Soyuzy*, ed. G. Zinoviev (1921), pp. 354-360. Some particulars of the two days' discussion, including the voting on the first day when Lenin's draft was approved in principle by 8 votes to 4, and Trotsky's rejected by 8 to 7, are given in Lenin, *Sochineniya*, xxvii, 88 (where Lenin admits that he " allowed himself in the course of the dispute certain obviously exaggerated and therefore erroneous sallies ") ; 624, note 35 ; 630, note 45 ; Trotsky refused to serve on the committee and was severely censured by Lenin for his refusal (*ibid.* xxvi, 88).

[2] *Izvestiya Tsentral'nogo Komiteta Rossiiskoi Kommunisticheskoi Partii* (*Bol'shevikov*), No. 26, December 20, 1920, p. 3.

[3] Lenin, *Sochineniya*, xxvii, 88-89, 630, note 45 ; the " buffer " resolution was published in *Pravda* of December 14, 1920, and reprinted in G. Zinoviev, *Sochineniya*, vi (1929), 599-600.

[4] The withdrawal of the ban by Zinoviev on Lenin's orders was recorded by Trotsky (*Desyatyi S"ezd Rossiiskoi Kommunisticheskoi Partii* (1921), p. 216).

8, 1921, an acrimonious debate on the rôle of the trade unions raged in party meetings and in the party press.[1] According to Trotsky and Tsektran, the railwaymen's union wanted to behave like a capitalist trade union, relegating the organization of production to a secondary place : Tomsky was being cast for the rôle of " the Gompers of the workers' state ". According to their opponents, " the apparatus of Narkomput' is swallowing the trade union apparatus, leaving nothing of the unions but the horns and the feet ".[2] Some half-dozen programmes or " platforms " were circulated. When the congress met, the situation had already to some extent simplified itself. Bukharin's " buffer group ", having failed to promote concord, had come to terms with Trotsky, and a common draft was submitted to the congress in the name of eight members of the central committee — Trotsky, Bukharin, Andreev, Dzerzhinsky, Krestinsky, Preobrazhensky, Rakovsky and Serebryakov.[3] On the opposite wing, a Left group took shape during the winter of 1920–1921 under the name of the " workers' opposition ". Its vague but far-reaching programme included the

[1] To give an impression of the unparalleled extent of the debate a few of its principal landmarks may be recorded : On December 24, 1920, Trotsky addressed a monster meeting of trade unionists and delegates to the eighth All-Russian Congress of Soviets : his speech was published on the following day as a pamphlet (*Rol' i Zadachi Profsoyuzov*) ; Tomsky and others also spoke at this meeting (Lenin, *Sochineniya*, xxvii, 625, note 35, 639, note 78). On December 30, 1920, another meeting of a similar character was addressed by Lenin, Zinoviev, Trotsky, Bukharin, Shlyapnikov and others : these speeches were published in a pamphlet *O Role Professional'nykh Soyuzov v Proizvodstve* (1921). A week later Zinoviev addressed a gathering in Petrograd (G. Zinoviev, *Sochineniya*, vi (1929), 403-431). Throughout January 1921 *Pravda* carried almost daily articles by the supporters of one or other platform. Stalin's contribution, a polemic against Trotsky, appeared on January 19 (*Sochineniya*, v, 4-14), Lenin's article, *The Crisis in the Party* (*Sochineniya*, xxiii, 87-94), on January 21. Lenin summed up at the end of January in a pamphlet *Once More About the Trade Unions*, bearing the sub-title *About the Mistakes of Comrades Trotsky and Bukharin* (*Sochineniya*, xxvii, 111-145). Before the congress met, the principal documents were published by order of the central committee in a volume edited by Zinoviev (*Partiya i Soyuzy* (1921)). That Stalin's rôle behind the scenes was more important than his one published article would suggest is indicated by the taunt of a delegate at the party congress who alleged that, while Zinoviev was active in Petrograd, " that war strategist and arch-democrat, comrade Stalin " was busy in Moscow drafting " reports that such and such victories had been won on this or that front, that so many had voted for the point of view of Lenin, and only six for the point of view of Trotsky . . . etc. etc." (*Desyatyi S"ezd Rossiiskoi Kommunisticheskoi Partii* (1921), pp. 52-53).

[2] *Partiya i Soyuzy*, ed. G. Zinoviev (1921), pp. 116-117, 126, 250.

[3] *Desyatyi S"ezd Rossiiskoi Kommunisticheskoi Partii* (1921), pp. 352-359.

control of industrial production by the trade unions, and it submitted proposals in this sense to the tenth party congress : its
leaders were Shlyapnikov and Kollontai.[1] This new element made
it all the easier for the Lenin-Zinoviev group to appear as a central
and moderating force : its point of view was presented to the
congress in the form of a draft resolution known as that of " the
ten " — Lenin, Zinoviev, Tomsky, Rudzutak, Kalinin, Kamenev,
Lozovsky, Petrovsky, Artem and Stalin.[2] The minor groups faded
away before the congress, or as soon as it met, leaving the three
major disputants in possession of the field.

The open debate in the tenth party congress was perfunctory.
It was confined to a single sitting, and much of it was occupied
with minor recriminations ; once the assembled delegates had
been canvassed, the result was known in advance. Lenin's personal influence and the weight of the party machine sufficed to
turn the scale. But the sympathy enjoyed by the alternative programmes was greater than the voting at the congress suggested.
The three main platforms showed clearly the issues of principle at
stake. The " workers' opposition ", like the former champions of
" workers' control ", took what was basically a syndicalist view of
the " workers' state ", appealing to the syndicalist strain in party
theory : Shlyapnikov at the congress quoted Engels' prediction
that the coming society would " organize industry on the basis of
a free and equal association of all producers ".[3] Since the trade
unions were the organization directly and exclusively representative of the workers, it was unthinkable that they should be subordinated to any political authority. At the centre, management
of the national economy should be vested in an all-Russian producers' congress ; at lower levels, in the trade unions. Political
functions were, by implication, left in the hands of the Soviets,
which, as the repositories of political power, were presumably
destined to die away. On immediate practical issues, the workers'
opposition sought an equalization of wages, free distribution of
food and basic necessities to all workers, and the gradual replace-

---

[1] *Desyatyi S"ezd Rossiiskoi Kommunisticheskoi Partii* (1921), pp. 360-364 ;
for the workers' opposition, see Vol. 1, pp. 196-197.

[2] *Ibid.* pp. 344-351 ; Lozovsky had rejoined the party in 1919.

[3] *Ibid.* p. 196 ; Lenin retorted (*Sochineniya*, xxvii, 236) that Engels was
speaking only of a " communist society ".

ment of money payments by payments in kind. It represented the workers in the restrictive sense of the term, and was, at any rate in theory, opposed to any concessions to the peasant. The workers' opposition, while rejecting anything that savoured of the militarization of labour, endorsed the most extreme economic and financial policies of war communism, thus holding its position on the Left wing of the party. It had no solution to offer of the crisis confronting the tenth congress, and mustered only 18 votes.

The Trotsky - Bukharin programme, which represented Trotsky's original view with some of its asperities slightly toned down, described itself as a " production " as opposed to a " trade union " platform. It called for " the transformation of the trade unions into production unions, not only in name, but in substance and method of work ". The party programme of 1919 had provided for a concentration in the hands of the trade unions " of the whole administration of the whole national economy considered as a single economic entity ". But this presupposed " the planned transformation of the unions into apparatuses of the workers' state ". As a corollary of this process a closer integration was to be achieved between Vesenkha and the central council of trade unions, and the People's Commissariat of Labour was to be abolished altogether. In practice " statization " of the unions had already gone extremely far : there seemed no reason not to carry it to its conclusion. The Trotsky-Bukharin programme possessed a high degree of logical consistency. But the underlying assumption that the industrial worker could have no interests distinguishable from those of the Soviet state as a whole, and therefore requiring the protection of independent trade unions, while it seemed to be justified by the current use of the term " dictatorship of the proletariat ", had little foundation in fact — if only because the existing state rested on a running compromise between the industrial worker and the peasant ; and the Trotsky-Bukharin programme was open to the same charge as the workers' opposition, though from a different angle, of ignoring the peasant component in the Soviet power. A more practical obstacle to its popularity was its known association with the policy of the compulsory mobilization of labour, which was indeed a logical deduction from its premises. In spite of its brilliant and influential sponsorship, the Trotsky-Bukharin draft received only 50 votes at the congress.

The field was thus clear for the resolution of " the ten " which was adopted by 336 votes against the 50 and the 18 votes for its two rivals. The main criticism to which it was exposed was that it remained inconclusive and left things much as they were. It rejected emphatically the workers' opposition proposal for a supreme all-Russian congress of producers, where, as Zinoviev frankly objected, " the majority at this grave moment will be non-party people, a good many of them SRs and Mensheviks ".[1] But it also declared, in opposition to Trotsky, that, while the unions already performed some state functions, " the rapid ' statization ' of the trade unions would be a serious mistake ". The important thing was to " win over these mass non-party organizations more and more for the Soviet state ". The distinguishing character of the trade unions was the use of methods of persuasion (though " proletarian compulsion " was not always excluded) ; to incorporate them in the state would be to deprive them of this asset.[2] The platform of " the ten " rested on considerations of practical expediency rather than of theoretical consistency. But that was its source of strength. On particular issues, the ten, while admitting that the equalization of wages was an ultimate objective, opposed its promulgation by the workers' opposition as an immediate goal of policy ; the trade unions must " use the payment of wages in money or in kind as a means of disciplining labour and increasing its productivity (system of bonuses, etc.) ". The trade unions must also enforce discipline and combat absenteeism through the operation of " comradely courts of discipline ". The proposals of " the ten " adopted by the tenth party congress as a solution of the trade union controversy were sensible rather than novel or sensational. But they did little to answer the underlying question how to give the trade unions a real function without turning them into agencies of the state.

Trotsky predicted at the congress that the victorious resolution would not " survive till the eleventh congress ".[3] The prediction

[1] *Desyatyi S"ezd Rossiiskoi Kommunisticheskoi Partii* (1921), p. 190.

[2] Lenin particularly insisted on this point in his short speech at the congress on the trade union question : " We must at all costs persuade first, and compel afterwards " (*Sochineniya*, xxvii, 235).

[3] *Desyatyi S"ezd Rossiiskoi Kommunisticheskoi Partii* (1921), p. 214.

was literally fulfilled. A further crisis came only two months later; and the party line in regard to the trade unions was once more substantially modified by a resolution of the central committee in January 1922.[1] If the further changes were accomplished without any revival of the bitterness which had marked the winter of 1920–1921, this was due to two factors. In the first place, the tightening up of party discipline at the tenth congress made impossible a renewal of controversy of the open and acrimonious kind which had preceded the congress. Secondly, the whole trade union controversy of the winter of 1920–1921 had been conducted under the system of war communism and on the economic presuppositions of that system. The abandonment of war communism and the introduction of NEP had repercussions in labour policy which rendered both the Trotskyist and the workers' opposition platforms obsolete, but fitted in well with the more flexible programme accepted by the congress, and could be plausibly represented as a continuation of it. The Trotskyist policy of the mobilization of labour by the state reflected the extreme tension of war communism and had to be relaxed when the emergency passed. It proved, however, to have a more lasting validity than some other features of war communism; the labour policy ultimately adopted under the five-year plans owed more to the conceptions propounded by Trotsky at this time than to the resolution adopted by the tenth party congress.

(d) Trade and Distribution

The break-down of the processes of trade between town and country had already driven the Soviet Government in the spring of 1918 to some new experiments — the organization of direct exchange of goods and the compromise with the cooperatives. From the summer of 1918 onwards the civil war made the problem increasingly urgent and, in some respects, simplified it by compelling concentration on the most immediate and elementary needs. The period of war communism had several distinctive characteristics in the field of trade and distribution: the extended use of methods of requisition rather than of exchange to obtain supplies urgently required by the state; the further development

[1] See pp. 326-327 below.

of exchange in kind; the widespread use of fixed prices and rationing; the assimilation of the cooperatives to the Soviet system as the main instruments of collection and distribution; and the growth of a black market existing side by side with the official channels of trade and finally eclipsing them in extent and importance.

The requisitioning of essential supplies — meaning, at this time, food and equipment for the Red Army and food for the urban population — was rendered imperative by the civil war and could be justified on grounds of military necessity. It could also be regarded as a foretaste of the future communist society to supersede methods of exchange where the power of the purse was the predominant factor, and substitute the principle of taking from each according to his capacity and giving to each according to his need. In theory the principle of distribution according to need might have come into conflict with the principle of distribution by way of exchange for supplies received: both principles had been recognized side by side in the original trade monopoly decree of April 2, 1918.[1]   But the conflict scarcely arose in relation to the peasant, since neither principle could be translated into practice in the absence of supplies. In the desperate effort to extract the maximum quantity of agricultural produce from peasants to whom little could be offered by way of return, the method of requisition by armed detachments, inaugurated in the summer of 1918 and further developed in decrees of August 1918,[2] continued to prevail during 1919 and 1920, so that throughout this period the chief instrument for obtaining supplies from the peasantry was not trade and exchange, but the forcible removal of surpluses by process of requisition. This was quickly established in popular opinion as a characteristic feature of war communism and the main cause of the resentment inspired by it among the peasants.

The relations of the state with industry under war communism were equally remote from the processes of trade. From the middle of 1918 onwards Vesenkha was rapidly extending its control over every important branch of Russian industry, and was bending every ounce of productive capacity to the needs of the civil war. As always in time of war, production for use rapidly drove out what was left of production for the market. A " war

[1] See p. 119 above.   [2] See p. 148 above.

contracts section " was established at the headquarters of Vesenkha with subordinate sections in the local Sovnarkhozy; [1] and the structure was crowned by an interdepartmental " extraordinary commission for the procurement of munitions ", of which Krasin became president on his return to Russia in September 1918 and which changed its name two months later to " extraordinary commission for the supply of the Red Army ".[2] This organization, reinforced in the summer of 1919 by the appointment of Rykov as an " extraordinary representative " of the Council of Workers' and Peasants' Defence to lend it the highest political authority,[3] took charge of all supplies for the Red Army other than agricultural products, and was the main user and controller of industrial production. To keep the Red Army supplied became, in Krasin's words, " the corner-stone of our economic policy ".[4] Throughout 1919 and 1920 a high proportion of the still active part of Russian industry was directly engaged on orders for the Red Army.

What was left of industry to keep up a supply of consumer goods to the civilian population was hardly less firmly harnessed to the war effort. The primary function of this limited supply was to induce the peasant by way of organized exchange to furnish the supplies of food without which the Red Army could not fight and the town populations would starve. Hence Vesenkha was scarcely less concerned to extend its control over consumer goods industries than over industries directly supplying the Red Army; and the ultimate destination of these goods was shown by the placing of Narkomprod in charge of their distribution. The wave of nationalization of industries in the autumn of 1918 was crowned by a decree of Sovnarkom of November 21, 1918, " On the Organization of Supply ", which was specifically designed to supersede " the apparatus of private trade ". This decree established what was in effect a state trading monopoly. It carefully

[1] *Sbornik Dekretov i Postanovlenii po Narodnomu Khozyaistvu*, ii (1920), 52-53.
[2] *Ibid.* ii, 721 ; for Krasin's own account of its functions see *Trudy II Vserossiiskogo S"ezda Sovetov Narodnogo Khozyaistva* (n.d.), pp. 78-80.
[3] *Sbornik Dekretov i Postanovlenii po Narodnomu Khozyaistvu*, ii (1920), 742-743 ; for the Council of Workers' and Peasants' Defence (later the Council of Labour and Defence (STO)), see Vol. 1, p. 216.
[4] *Trudy II Vserossiiskogo S"ezda Sovetov Narodnogo Khozyaistva* (n.d.), p. 75.

defined relations between Vesenkha and Narkomprod. All goods designed " for personal consumption or domestic economy " manufactured in factories nationalized or controlled by Vesenkha were to be transferred by the relevant *glavki*, centres or sections to Narkomprod for utilization according to the threefold plan. In the first place, the plan would determine the quantities to be set aside for export, the quantities to be kept in reserve and the quantities available for industrial consumption and for distribution to the population. Secondly, factory, wholesale and retail prices would be fixed. Thirdly, the plan would settle the method of distribution of the supplies destined for popular consumption. The first and third of these tasks were entrusted to a " commission of utilization " on which Vesenkha, Narkomprod and the People's Commissariat of Trade and Industry were all represented;[1] the second fell to the price committee of Vesenkha. For the exercise of its distributive functions, and for the collection of goods falling outside the scope of Vesenkha (the principal category of these would be the products of rural handicrafts), Narkomprod set up a special organ called Glavprodukt on which Vesenkha was to be represented. The cooperatives were to participate in the process of distribution throughout the country, which was to be covered with " a network of retail shops sufficiently dense for the convenience of the population ". Retail trade was to be " municipalized ", i.e. placed under the control of the local Soviets.[2] The decree was well conceived on paper. It corresponded to the aim of Bolshevik policy, defined in the party programme of 1919 as being " to continue on a planned, organized, state-wide scale to replace trade by distribution of products ".[3] But the system rested on a basis of rationing which presupposed two things : a powerful administrative machine and a reasonable sufficiency of goods to distribute. Neither of these things existed, or could be hoped for, in the Russia of 1919 and 1920. Yet, like other parts of war communism, the system was dictated not so much by theory as by urgent practical needs, and it is difficult to see what other

[1] The " commission of utilization " became for a brief period an important organ ; Y. S. Rozenfeld, *Promyshlennaya Politika SSSR* (1926), p. 125, calls it " the crown of the *glavki* system ". For its short-lived rôle in the pre-history of planning, see p. 369 below.

[2] *Sobranie Uzakonenii, 1917–1918*, No. 83, art. 879.

[3] *VKP(B) v Rezolyutsiyakh* (1941), i, 293.

system could have been applied at the height of the civil war.

Fixed prices for grain had been inherited, together with the grain monopoly, from the Provisional Government and since raised on more than one occasion. It was logical and inevitable that the establishment of state monopolies of other commodities which began in the spring and summer of 1918 should be followed by the fixing of prices for these commodities. Before the end of 1918 there were fixed prices for hides, leather and leather goods, for wool and woollen goods, for cotton yarns and cotton goods, for rubber goods, for soap, tobacco and tea and for many other products. In 1919 and the first part of 1920, as controls were extended and intensified, the list of fixed prices grew till almost every object of consumption was covered.[1] Fixed prices were regularly increased in a way which more than kept pace with periodical increases in the price of grain, so that the terms of trade were turned more and more against the peasant and in favour of the industrial worker.[2] But this had no great practical significance, since prices could never be increased drastically enough to take account of the rapidly falling value of the currency. Thus, in the course of time the fixed prices diverged more and more widely from the " free " prices at which the same commodities changed hands on the illegal but tolerated black market; by 1920 fixed

[1] The decrees for 1918 can be found in *Sbornik Dekretov i Postanovlenii po Narodnomu Khozyaistvu*, ii (1920), 473-656, later decrees in *Proizvodstvo, Uchet i Raspredelenie Produktov Narodnogo Khozyaistva* (n.d. [? 1921]), pp. 231-409.

[2] Milyutin explained to the all-Russian congress of financial officials in May 1919 that when, in the previous October, bread prices had been raised it had been necessary to make a corresponding increase in other fixed prices " bending the stick in favour of urban industry ". In January 1919, in connexion with a 50 per cent rise in wages, prices for manufactured goods had been put up to two and a half times the level of the previous autumn, though no change at all was made in bread prices. Prices for manufactured goods, which had been 25 times the 1914 level in October 1918, stood at 60 times that level in January 1919 (*Trudy Vserossiiskogo S"ezda Zaveduyushchikh Finotdelami* (1919), pp. 50-51). The same process continued, though less rapidly, till the introduction of NEP; an arshin of cloth which cost 1·3 pounds of rye bread in March 1919 cost 2·2 pounds two years later (L. Kritsman, *Geroicheskii Period Velikoi Russkoi Revolyutsii* (n.d. [? 1924], p. 212). Lenin again and again admitted that the peasant was not getting a fair return for his produce and was being asked to give a " credit " or " advance " to the urban proletariat as his contribution to the victory of the revolution (*Sochineniya*, xxiv, 409-410, 569, 696).

prices had become largely nominal and distribution at fixed prices virtually equivalent to gratis distribution, which was finally substituted for it. But by that time supplies in the hands of state organs available for distribution had also declined to negligible dimensions.

Rationing was the natural concomitant of fixed prices. Rationing for the principal foodstuffs was in force in Petrograd and Moscow under the Provisional Government; sugar and bread had been rationed before the February revolution. For the first nine months of the Soviet régime, during which the rations were more and more frequently unprocurable, and the gap between the fixed prices of the same articles on the free market progressively widened, no change was made in the system. But the acute scarcity of the summer of 1918, affecting first and foremost the workers in the large cities, and the adoption of the policy of requisitioning grain from the peasants, placed direct responsibility for distribution on the government. In August 1918 differential rations were first introduced for Moscow and Petrograd, the population being divided for the purpose into three categories, of which heavy manual workers formed the first, other workers and families of all workers the second, and members of the former bourgeoisie the third; the first category received rations four times, the second three times, as high as the third.[1] The differential system spread rapidly, and with innumerable variations. Manual workers always occupied the highest category, and were sometimes declared to be in receipt of an " iron-clad " ration enjoying absolute priority over all categories. Families of Red Army men were commonly included in the highest category. Presently, however, discrimination was introduced between different groups of manual workers and different groups of office workers on the supposed basis of the value of their services to the community; higher rations were offered to shock workers engaged in particularly vital or urgent work. The process of refinement was carried so far that in the autumn of 1919 there were in some places as many as twenty categories of rations.

This situation led not only to intolerable administrative complications, but to widespread anomalies, jealousies and discon-

---

[1] L. Kritsman, *Geroicheskii Period Velikoi Russkoi Revolyutsii* (n.d. [? 1924]), p. 110.

tents, which were publicly ventilated at a conference of representatives of Soviet organs of distribution in November 1919.
Vyshinsky, the future Public Prosecutor and Minister of Foreign
Affairs of the USSR, who was at this time an official of Narkomprod, made a report to the conference on this question.   He
attacked " the bourgeois principle of equality " which had
governed rationing in Hohenzollern Germany and Habsburg
Austria as well as under the Russian Provisional Government.
But, while discrimination against the bourgeoisie was right and
proper, a system of rationing which set " every privileged group
at war with its neighbours ", and was quite differently applied in
different cities and different regions, was indefensible.   Vyshinsky
proposed a return to three standard categories of manual workers,
other workers and non-workers, rations to be allocated between
them in the proportions of three, two and one.   A resolution in
this sense was unanimously adopted by the conference.[1]   A month
later the seventh All-Russian Congress of Soviets in December
1919 demanded a " single workers' ration ".[2]   In April 1920
there was a return to something like the three original categories,
with the proviso that special rations might be accorded to heavy
manual workers, as well as " for specially qualified forms of
intellectual work." [3]   But these changes lost their meaning as,
during 1920, the system of rationing was gradually replaced by
the payment of wages in kind.   This had the dual advantage of
eliminating the need for any attempt to calculate wages and prices
in terms of a depreciating currency, and of allowing the rewards of
labour to be adjusted to services rendered with far more precision
than could be dreamed of under a crude system of ration categories.   A system of wages for the industrial worker theoretically
based on distribution according to capacity was more appropriate
to the current crisis than a system of rationing theoretically based
on distribution according to need.[4]

In principle the rural population should have been rationed in
consumer goods on the basis of the decree of November 21, 1918,
which did not suggest any other criterion of distribution than that

[1] *Vserossiiskoe Soveshchanie Predstavitelei Raspredelitel'nykh Prodorganov*
(1920), pp. 13-16, 28, 51-52.
[2] *S"ezdy Sovetov RSFSR v Postanovleniyakh* (1939), p. 144.
[3] *Sobranie Uzakonenii, 1920*, No. 34, art. 165.
[4] For the payment of wages in kind, see, however, p. 218 above.

of need. But in practice the main motive of distributing supplies to the peasant was to procure agricultural products. Distribution proceeded on the basis of the decree of August 6, 1918, on "obligatory exchange ", i.e. on the principle that 85 per cent of the cost of goods supplied must be paid in kind;[1] and since the policy was to keep prices for manufactured goods proportionately higher than for agricultural products, this already represented a certain tax on the peasant.[2] When the 1919 harvest became available, this procedure was tightened up by a further decree of August 5, 1919. Under this decree Narkomprod was to " determine for each province or district separately the quantity of products of agriculture and rural handicrafts subject to obligatory delivery and the quantity of goods to be released for the supply of the rural population "; the latter would not be released until the former were delivered. The new decree marked an advance on that of the previous year in two respects. In the first place, the money element seems to have disappeared altogether : the calculation of equivalents was made by Narkomprod, apparently on the basis of amounts of grain and other products required and quantities of manufactured goods available. Secondly, the principle of collective responsibility, which had been left open in the decree of August 1918, was now clearly enunciated ; while the quantities of manufactured goods distributed depended on the amounts of agricultural products delivered, the " consumers' societies " which carried out the distribution were not allowed to discriminate against " proletarian or semi-proletarian elements living on wage payments or on allowances from the state ", so that, as far as the individual was concerned, the goods received stood in no necessary relation to the products delivered.[3] The official system of exchange between town and country as it developed in the latter stage of war communism thus approximated more nearly to a system of forced requisition of agricultural products compensated by free distribution of manufactured goods on a basis of rationing than to trade or exchange in any ordinary sense of the word. The element of

[1] See p. 149 above.

[2] Lenin, in advocating an increase in grain prices as an accompaniment of the obligatory exchange decree, was careful to add that prices of manufactured goods should be " proportionately (and even more than proportionately) raised " (*Sochineniya*, xxx, 991).

[3] *Sobranie Uzakonenii, 1919*, No. 41, art. 387.

individual incentive to production was still absent, and could not
be restored so long as the attempt was made to apply, however
imperfectly, the principle " from each according to his capacity,
to each according to his needs ".

Such results as were secured by the Soviet Government in its
distribution policy during the period of war communism were due
almost entirely to its success in making the cooperative movement
the main instrument of that policy. The impact of the civil war
hastened the process of harnessing the cooperatives to the Soviet
administrative machine and of using them to fill the gaps in the
machine. It compelled the Soviet Government to intervene far
more directly and vigorously than hitherto in promoting trade
between town and country ; and this function was concentrated
in Narkomprod, Vesenkha being finally relegated to the sphere
of industrial production. On the other hand, the discrediting
of the Left SRs and their expulsion from the Soviets deprived
the cooperatives of their political backing. Nothing remained
for them but to come to terms with the Bolsheviks, who on
their side no longer had any political motive for indulgence or
compromise. Thus the incorporation of the consumers' cooperatives in the Soviet administrative machine, tentatively begun by
the decree of April 11, 1918, could now proceed at an accelerated
pace.

The first overt symptom of the process was the " obligatory
exchange " decree of August 6, 1918. The original decree on
exchange with the peasants of April 2, 1918, had been concluded
before the agreement with the cooperatives, and made no mention
of them. The new decree set the cooperatives side by side with
official Soviet organs — one article even named them to the
exclusion of any official organ — as the instruments through which
the exchange would be carried out, and provided penalties in the
event of failure to comply with the regulations laid down : the
board of administrators of the offending cooperative would be
handed over to the courts, their successors would be appointed by,
or with the approval of, the Soviet Government, and the cooperative itself would be fined.[1] The decree of November 21, 1918, on

[1] *Sobranie Uzakonenii, 1917-1918*, No. 58, art. 638.

the nationalization of internal trade recognized the privileged position of the cooperatives. Their wholesale warehouses and retail shops were to remain " under their own management but under the control of Narkomprod "; where these had been nationalized or municipalized through an excess of zeal on the part of local Soviet organs, restitution was to be made. By way of counterpart Narkomprod received the right to nominate a representative with full powers to the presidium of Tsentrosoyuz and also to regional and provincial cooperative organs.[1] This represented a certain concession to the cooperatives, coinciding with the olive branch held out at the same moment to the Mensheviks and Left SRs and their short-lived readmission to the Soviets.[2] It provoked some grumbling in party circles [3] and was defended by Lenin on the plea that the petty bourgeois elements, which admittedly dominated the cooperatives, " know how to organize shops " and must therefore have the same indulgence as capitalist organizers of trusts.[4] The concession was more apparent than real. In the long run the effect of the decree was to turn the cooperatives, more thoroughly and more openly than before, into accredited agents of Soviet policy. The taking over of the Moscow Narodnyi Bank a few days later destroyed what was left of their financial autonomy.[5]

The record of the next two years, when war communism reached its climax, was merely the completion of what had already been set in motion by these encroachments. The Bolsheviks had at first hoped to capture the organization by splitting the coopera-

---

[1] *Sobranie Uzakonenii, 1917–1918*, No. 83, art. 879.
[2] See Vol. 1, pp. 171-172.
[3] Complaints made at the second All-Russian Congress of Councils of National Economy that local authorities had dissolved or " nationalized " the cooperatives met with the retort that the managers of the cooperatives had " fled to Ufa with the Czechs and the white guards ", and that to hand over distribution to the cooperatives was to " hand over the whole work to the elements against which you are fighting " (*Trudy II Vserossiiskogo S"ezda Sovetov Narodnogo Khozyaistva* (n.d.), pp. 110, 114).
[4] Lenin, *Sochineniya*, xxiii, 328.
[5] See p. 138 above ; the Narodnyi Bank was transformed into the cooperative section of the National Bank. The People's Commissar of Finance a few months later congratulated himself on the fact that nothing had really changed and the old employees remained, since this facilitated the drawing of the cooperatives into the Soviet system of control (*Trudy Vserossiiskogo S"ezda Zaveduyushchikh Finotdelami* (1919), p. 77).

tives of the workers against the general or " all-citizen " cooperatives. A congress of workers' cooperatives held at Moscow in
December 1918 voted by a small majority in favour of a demand to
alter the statutes of Tsentrosoyuz in such a way as to assure a
permanent majority on the presidium to delegates of the workers'
cooperatives.[1] At the full congress of the cooperatives in Moscow
in January 1919, where the Bolsheviks were still in a minority,
the majority attempted to compromise by offering the workers'
cooperatives five places out of thirteen in the board of administration of Tsentrosoyuz. The offer was refused, and the Bolshevik
delegates left the congress.[2] More direct methods were now tried.
The party programme adopted by the eighth party congress in
March 1919 declared it to be the policy of the party " to continue
the replacement of trade by a planned system of distribution of
commodities organized on an all-state scale " ; for this purpose
the whole population should be organized " into a single network
of *consumers' communes* ", though it was added that the foundation
for these consumers' communes should be provided by " the
existing general and workers' cooperatives, which are the largest
organization of consumers and the apparatus of mass distribution
most fully prepared by the history of capitalism ".[3] Party policy
was promptly translated into state action. A decree of March 16,
1919, issued while the congress was still in session, echoed the
demand for " a single distributive apparatus ". It announced the
transformation of all workers' and general consumers' cooperatives
as well as state organs concerned in distribution into a uniform
model of " consumers' communes ", in which the whole population would be included, the traditional distinction between the
two types of cooperatives being swept away. Consumers' communes were to elect representatives to provincial unions, and each
provincial union was to elect a delegate to Tsentrosoyuz, which
remained the directing organ of the system. The pyramidal
pattern of the Soviets was thus imitated in a slightly simplified

[1] According to Krestinsky (*Devyatyi S"ezd RKP(B)* (1934), p. 277) " our
party succeeded in winning a majority in the leading centre of ideas of the
workers' cooperatives " ; E. Fuckner, *Die Russische Genossenschaftsbewegung,
1865-1921* (1922), p. 116, accuses the Bolsheviks of rigging the mandates to
the congress.
[2] *Devyatyi S"ezd RKP(B)* (1934), p. 278.
[3] *VKP(B) v Rezolyutsiyakh* (1941), i, 293.

form. The official character of the system was emphasized by a clause assimilating the status of officials and employees of the cooperatives to that of employees of state supply organs. Finally local Soviet supply organs were entitled to be represented in all local cooperatives, and " the Council of People's Commissars may supplement the membership of the administration of Tsentrosoyuz with the necessary number of its representatives ". The execution of the decree on behalf of the Soviet Government was entrusted to Narkomprod; Vesenkha lost the last of its functions in this field by the closing down of its cooperatives section. The use throughout the decree of the term " consumers' communes " was significant of the desire to relegate even the name of the cooperatives to the past.[1]

The effects of this decree were far-reaching. The existing administration of Tsentrosoyuz consisted of four members of workers' cooperatives who were Bolsheviks or of Bolshevik sympathies and eight representatives of general cooperatives who were non-Bolshevik. By a curious compromise Sovnarkom used the right accorded by the decree to nominate three representatives to the administration of Tsentrosoyuz, thus still leaving the Bolsheviks in a minority; but one of the three, Frumkin, had a right of veto. This plan, which gave the Bolsheviks power to block anything but initiate nothing, soon broke down. In July 1919 Sovnarkom appointed three further representatives.[2] At the height of the civil war the coercion of the cooperatives must have been a singularly delicate business; and, even with the clear majority in Tsentrosoyuz, the process of assimilation was slow. But in November 1919 a local representative of Narkomprod noted that " the difference of principle between Soviet organs and cooperatives is falling away ", so that the cooperatives could be regarded as part of the " state apparatus ".[3] In January 1920, almost before the crisis of the civil war had been surmounted, the attack was extended to the much less important and powerful

---

[1] *Sobranie Uzakonenii, 1919*, No. 17, art. 191 ; three months later a further decree (*ibid*. No. 34, art. 339) altered the title " consumers' communes " back to " consumers' societies " — a symbol of the tenacity of the cooperative tradition.

[2] *Devyatyi S"ezd RKP(B)* (1934), pp. 280-281.

[3] *Vserossiiskoe Soveshchanie Predstavitelei Raspredelitel'nykh Prodorganov* (1920), p. 20.

credit and producers' cooperatives. With the virtual cessation both of deposits and of loans resulting from the collapse of the currency, the credit cooperatives had lost most of their original functions and appear to have been acting in certain cases as middlemen financing transactions of sale and purchase of goods. The producers' cooperatives were still performing a useful function in organizing the output of agricultural products and of rural handicrafts.[1] But a decree of January 1920 described them both as " lacking an all-Russian centre " and as " very often reflecting in their composition and structure the interests not of the toilers but of their class enemies ", transferred their assets to the consumers' cooperatives and placed them firmly under the authority of Tsentrosoyuz.[2] All forms of the cooperative movement were thus brought together under a single central organ, which had already been geared to the Soviet administrative machine.

So much having been achieved, the time might well seem ripe for carrying these processes to a logical conclusion and formally converting the cooperatives into state organs. This course was widely supported at the ninth party congress of March 1920. In the section of the congress which examined the question, Milyutin was the principal advocate of what was called the " statization " of the cooperatives, and secured a majority for a resolution which demanded that they should become " a technical apparatus of Narkomprod ". But Milyutin owed part of his success to the fact that the opponents of " statization " were not agreed among themselves and presented no less than three alternative proposals for the future status of the cooperatives ; and when the issue was brought up in plenary session, Lenin came out strongly against Milyutin and induced the congress to adopt a resolution standing

[1] The second All-Russian Congress of Councils of National Economy in December 1918 gave a guarded blessing to agricultural cooperatives, provided that they were included " in a general system of state regulation of the national economy ", and that the purpose was kept in view of developing agricultural cooperation " to the point of organizing agricultural producers' communes " (Trudy II Vserossiiskogo S"ezda Sovetov Narodnogo Khozyaistva (n.d.), p. 395) ; and the party programme of March 1919 pronounced for " full state support for agricultural cooperatives engaged in the working up of agricultural produce " (VKP(B) v Rezolyutsiyakh (1941), i, 292).

[2] Sobranie Uzakonenii, 1920, No. 6, art. 37 ; E. Fuckner, Die Russische Genossenschaftsbewegung, 1865–1921 (1922), p. 150, gives a list of producers' cooperatives " liquidated " on the strength of this decree, being transformed into sections either of Tsentrosoyuz or of Narkomzem.

in the name of Krestinsky.[1] His main argument was the familiar one of the need to propitiate the peasantry, which was unprepared for such a step : " We are dealing with a class that is less accessible to us and not at all amenable to nationalization ". The Krestinsky resolution, reaffirming the two basic decrees of March 20, 1919, and January 27, 1920, spoke quite clearly of consumers' cooperatives as being under the management of Narkomprod, and producers' cooperatives, agricultural and industrial, as under the management of Narkomzem and Vesenkha respectively; the subordination of the producers' cooperatives to Tsentrosoyuz was to have " only an administrative-political character ". The " statization " of the cooperatives was therefore effected in all but name ; and under the régime of war communism it could hardly be otherwise. But the fact that their formal independence was preserved proved to be of some importance in the ensuing period.[2] At the ninth party congress Khinchuk, the president of Tsentrosoyuz and an old Menshevik, was received into the party ; and several cooperative leaders who resisted the new organization were arrested in the following month and sentenced to terms of imprisonment.[3]

The most significant part of the history of internal trade in the period of war communism cannot, however, be written in terms of official decrees and official policies. The history of the period amply illustrates the persistence and ingenuity of human beings in devising ways and means to exchange goods when this becomes necessary to their survival. The initial and simplest form of these illicit expedients was the " bagging " which had been a matter of common talk and a thorn in the side of the new régime since the first days of the revolution.[4] But the illicit transportation of

[1] It is fair to suppose that Lenin was influenced in his attitude mainly by considerations of foreign policy. The blockade had been formally raised in January 1920, and at the end of March 1920 the British Government indicated its willingness to receive a delegation of Tsentrosoyuz to discuss a resumption of trade, carefully marking a distinction between negotiations with the cooperatives and negotiations with the Soviet Government ; at this moment, therefore, the Soviet interest in upholding the distinction was substantial.

[2] The discussion at the ninth party congress, including the text of several rival projects, is in *Devyatyi S"ezd RKP(B)* (1934), pp. 277-319, 381-400 ; Lenin's speech at the congress is in *Sochineniya*, xxv, 122-125, the congress resolution in *VKP(B) v Rezolyutsiyakh* (1941), i, 340-342.

[3] *Sovremennye Zapiski* (Paris), No. 1, 1920, p. 155.

[4] See pp. 117-119 above.

foodstuffs to the towns survived every persecution, including a decree ordering requisition squads on railways and waterways to confiscate all foodstuffs carried by passengers above trivial amounts.[1] In September 1918 bagging was tacitly recognized in orders allowing workers of Moscow and Petrograd to bring food into the cities in quantities not exceeding one and a half puds. The bagmen were hastily re-nicknamed " one-and-a-half-pud men " and, though the concession was nominally to expire on October 1, or according to a later amendment on October 10,[2] the licence to transport such amounts seems thereafter to have been taken for granted. In January 1919 VTsIK issued an order reproving railway requisition squads for handling passengers roughly and unjustifiably taking away foodstuffs intended for their personal use.[3] From the winter of 1918–1919 onwards the pressure was somewhat relieved by the legalization of methods of collective self-help for factories, trade unions and other organizations.[4] But, if the words " bagging " and " bagmen " fell largely out of use, this was mainly because the phenomenon had become too familiar to be talked about and was more or less openly tolerated by the authorities. Statisticians of the period attempted to estimate what proportion of the foodstuffs consumed by town-dwellers in 1919–1920 was supplied on ration at fixed prices and what proportion was obtained through extra-legal channels. According to one calculation, only from 20 to 25 per cent was supplied on ration ;[5] according to another, which distinguished between towns in " consuming " and towns in " producing " provinces, from 25 to 40 per cent of requirements in the former and 35 to 55 per cent in the latter were supplied on ration.[6] At the fourth trade union congress in April

---

[1] *Sobranie Uzakonenii, 1917–1918*, No. 57, art. 364 ; Makhno speaks in his memoirs (*Pod Udarami Kontrrevolyutsii* (Paris, 1936), p. 151) of " a crowd of thousands of bagmen " crossing the Ukrainian-Russian frontier in the summer of 1918.

[2] Quoted in Lenin, *Sochineniya*, xxiii, 590, note 147.

[3] *Izvestiya*, January 3, 1919.

[4] See pp. 155-156 above.

[5] G. Y. Sokolnikov, etc., *Soviet Policy in Public Finance* (Stanford, 1931), p. 82. This estimate was for the autumn of 1919, and the author states that the proportion increased in 1920.

[6] *Narodnoe Khozyaistvo*, No. 9-10, 1920, pp. 43-45 ; in the current terminology, " consuming " provinces were those which consumed more food than they produced, " producing " provinces those which produced more than they consumed.

1920, it was stated that the worker's necessary expenditure was from two and a half to three times what he received in wages, whether in money or in kind.[1] On any hypothesis it seems clear that, throughout the period of war communism, the urban population either went hungry or met more than half its basic requirements of food through what was nominally illicit trading. At the time of the introduction of NEP, workers in receipt of the highest category rations were stated to be getting only from 1200 to 1900 out of the 3000 calories which were recognized as a minimum for the manual worker.[2] A few weeks later Pyatakov asserted that " the miner of the Don basin . . . consumes only 50 per cent of the number of calories he needs in order to regain his full strength "; and Rykov admitted that " there are very few workers who do not buy goods on the free market " and that " in this form our bourgeoisie has already been growing for several years ".[3]

In what form was payment made for these illicit supplies? At first the bagmen accepted payment in currency, though at exorbitant prices; later, as the value of the currency dwindled, much trade had to be done on a basis of barter. Only the well-to-do had possessions to sell, and these were soon exhausted. Thus the illicit trade in foodstuffs brought into being an illicit trade in other goods. Soon after the revolution factories began to pay part wages in kind — in the form of a share in their own products; and what were at first doubtless intended for the personal use of the workers and their families quickly became objects of barter or were sold at the inflated prices of the free market. A speaker at the first All-Russian Congress of Councils of National Economy in May 1918 drew attention to this practice, which had already acquired the nickname " piece-selling ":

> Bagging is a terrible evil, piece-selling is a terrible evil; but it is an even greater evil when you begin to pay the workers in kind, in their own products . . . and when they themselves turn piece-sellers.[4]

[1] *Chetvertyi Vserossiiskii S"ezd Professional'nykh Soyuzov* (1921), i (Plenumy), 119.

[2] *Desyatyi S"ezd Rossiiskoi Kommunisticheskoi Partii* (1921), p. 237.

[3] *Trudy IV Vserossiiskogo S"ezda Sovetov Narodnogo Khozyaistva* (1921), pp. 40, 57.

[4] *Trudy I Vserossiiskogo S"ezda Sovetov Narodnogo Khozyaistva* (1918), p. 434.

But the practice persisted, and the second All-Russian Congress of Councils of National Economy in December 1918 even passed a resolution in favour of payment of wages to factory workers in kind.[1] Two years later the scandal had grown much worse, and the fourth trade union congress passed a resolution condemning the sale by workers of belts, tools and other equipment of factories where they worked.[2] Public institutions and nationalized industries often met their requirements by recourse to the free market, though this practice was formally prohibited.

Thus in the period of war communism two different systems of distribution existed side by side in Soviet Russia — distribution by state agencies at fixed prices (or, later, free of charge) and distribution through private trading. By decrees of April 2 and November 21, 1918,[3] trade in foodstuffs and in virtually all goods in common use had become a state monopoly. Such quantities of these commodities as were available were at first distributed by government agencies (including the cooperatives) at fixed prices on what was supposed to be a rationing principle, though regular rations were never established except for bread and a few staple foodstuffs. These forms of distribution were alone legally recognized : [4] " legal internal trade ", declared an authoritative statement drawn up in April 1920, " practically does not exist, and is replaced by an apparatus of state distribution ".[5] But side by side with this official system of distribution private trade, though legally prohibited, was busily carried on in all articles of consumption at prices 40 or 50 times as high as those fixed by the government. In Moscow the centre of this traffic was the market on the Sukharevsky Square, always crowded with these illicit traders and their customers. The police made raids from time to time, but in general seem to have turned an indulgent eye on this vast " black

---

[1] *Trudy II Vserossiiskogo S"ezda Sovetov Narodnogo Khozyaistva* (n.d.), p. 393.

[2] *Chetvertyi Vserossiiskii S"ezd Professional'nykh Soyuzov* (1921), i (Plenumy), 66, 119.   [3] See pp. 119, 229-230 above.

[4] In the winter of 1920-1921, 34,000,000 persons in all, including virtually the whole urban population and 2,000,000 rural handicraft workers, were said to be in receipt of rations (*Chetyre Goda Prodovol'stvennoi Politiki* (1922), pp. 61-62) ; but this figure probably represents intention rather than practice.

[5] Y. Larin i L. Kritsman, *Ocherk Khozyaistvennoi Zhizni i Organizatsiya Narodnogo Khozyaistva* (1920), p. 133 ; this pamphlet was originally written for the information of the visiting British Labour delegation.

market " ; and " Sukharevka " became the cant name for this
" free " sector of the Soviet economy.   Lenin never failed to
denounce it, arguing that " the capitalists are still undermining
the foundations of the Soviet power by way of bagging, the Sukharevka and so forth ".[1]   But there was no doubt on which side
victory lay.   Early in 1920 an official organ pointed the contrast
between " the yawning emptiness of the Soviet shops " and " the
busy activities of the Sukharevka, the Smolensk Market, the
Okhotny Ryad and other centres of private trade ".[2]   Throughout
this period an increasing proportion of the internal distribution of
goods in Soviet Russia passed through unrecognized and generally
illegal channels ; and the authorities, having long struggled in
vain to curb these expedients, came in practice to accept them,
first as a necessary evil, then as a positive contribution to the
national economy.   In certain respects NEP did little more than
sanction methods of trade which had grown up spontaneously, in
defiance of government decrees and in face of government repres-
sions, under war communism.

Foreign trade played virtually no part at all in the Soviet
economy during the period of war communism.   The ring
imposed by the allied blockade early in 1918 was completely closed
when the German collapse in November of the same year ended
relations with continental Europe, and the civil war severed the
last remaining link with Asiatic markets and sources of supply.
Imports and exports, which had shrunk to trivial dimensions in
1918, reached vanishing point in 1919, and Soviet Russia's
complete economic isolation at this time was a powerful contributory factor to economic experiments which could scarcely have
been attempted or persisted in except in a closed system.   The
removal of the blockade in January 1920 and the conclusion of
peace with Estonia a fortnight later opened the formal possibility
of international trade.   But the refusal of the allied countries to
accept Russian gold — the so-called unofficial " gold blockade " —
deprived the Soviet authorities of the one means of payment which
they might have used to secure much needed imports.   The first

---

[1] Lenin, *Sochineniya*, xxv, 155.
[2] *Ekonomicheskaya Zhizn'*, February 18, 1920.

Soviet trade delegation abroad left for Copenhagen under Krasin's leadership in March 1920; and an agreement concluded with a group of Swedish firms in May 1920 secured for Soviet Russia limited but valuable quantities of railway material and agricultural machinery. But, though Krasin proceeded to London, the Polish war once more brought down the curtain on the prospect of more far-reaching negotiations; and little more was achieved during 1920.[1] The decree of July 11, 1920, transforming the now virtually defunct People's Commissariat of Trade and Industry into a People's Commissariat of Foreign Trade with Krasin at its head,[2] was a declaration of policy and a preparation for the future rather than a response to any existing need. The trade statistics for 1920 showed a rise from the zero level of 1919, but did not register even the insignificant figures of the year 1918. Optimistic estimates of surpluses of timber, grain and flax for export did not materialize. An official journal showed more realism in an article of September 1920 entitled *Our External Trade*:

> It will be necessary to export what we need ourselves simply in order to buy in exchange what we need even more. For every locomotive, every plough, we shall be obliged literally to use pieces torn out of the body of our national economy.[3]

It was the realization of this stark necessity which impelled Sovnarkom in the autumn of 1920 to revert to a project already mooted in the spring of 1918 — the plan to attract foreign capital by the offer of concessions.[4] But this inspiration, which achieved no quick or immediate success, belonged not to the now almost bankrupt conception of war communism, but to the forthcoming NEP period.

(e) *Finance*

When the régime of war communism began in the summer of 1918, the initial impetus of the Bolshevik financial programme had

---

[1] The stages by which commercial relations between Soviet Russia and western Europe were re-established will be traced in Part V.

[2] *Sobranie Uzakonenii*, *1920*, No. 53, art. 235.

[3] *Ekonomicheskaya Zhizn'*, September 3, 1920.

[4] *Sobranie Uzakonenii*, *1920*, No. 91, art. 481; the circumstances of this revival of the concessions project will be described in Part V.

been exhausted. Its major item, the nationalization of the banks, had been duly enacted and in large measure carried out; its second point, the repudiation of the debts of preceding Russian governments, had also taken effect. The nationalization of the banks had not indeed fulfilled the vague hopes of socialist theory by providing an automatic instrument for the control and financing of industry. Nor had the repudiation of debts solved the problem of financing public expenditure; on the contrary, it had eliminated one method of obtaining revenue — the raising of loans. The printing of notes remained the sole serious available source of funds to meet current public expenditure and to make advances to industry. Continuous resort to this method intensified the headlong depreciation of the currency, and ultimately destroyed the willingness of sellers to accept now almost worthless notes in payment for their products, so that money lost its function of facilitating normal processes of trade and exchange. The financial characteristic of war communism was the virtual elimination of money from the economy. This was, however, in no sense the product either of doctrine or of deliberate design. In August 1918 Gukovsky, whose rigid and unimaginative financial purism ranged him with the extreme Right of the party, was replaced as People's Commissar for Finance by the more flexible and more intelligent Krestinsky, Commissar for the National Bank since January 1918, who had been in the ranks of the Left opposition on the Brest-Litovsk issue, though not in the subsequent economic debates. But it may be doubted whether even this change was intended as the herald of a new financial policy. It was the pressure of the civil war which forced the People's Commissariat of Finance into new and unexpected courses.

In the autumn of 1918 normal methods of raising revenue had been exhausted. On October 30, 1918, VTsIK issued two decrees which represented not so much a compromise between two different conceptions of fiscal or financial policy as a confused and hand-to-mouth attempt to try every conceivable expedient which might help in a desperate situation. The first decree prescribed an " extraordinary revolutionary tax " taking the form of a direct levy calculated to bring in a total sum of ten milliard rubles; the second established a " tax in kind ", which was in principle a levy from all cultivators of land of the surplus of their production over the needs of their household.[1] The first was the last serious attempt made in the early period of the Soviet régime to meet public expenditure by direct monetary taxation, the second the first experiment in taxation in kind which was a corollary of the flight from money under war communism. It was in this sense that Krestinsky contrasted them : " the extraordinary tax is our link with the past, the tax in kind our link with the future." [2]

The extraordinary revolutionary tax was to be borne, in proportions laid down in the decree itself, by all the provinces now remaining in Soviet hands : this meant the exclusion of the Ukraine and south-eastern Russia, of the Asiatic provinces and territories and of Archangel in the north, these all being in foreign or " white " occupation. Of the rest, the cities of Moscow and Petrograd with their respective provinces were assessed for half the total of 10 milliards ; the others were assessed according to their population and wealth for smaller amounts, Olonets, the poorest, being responsible for no more than 15 million rubles. Within these global amounts the assessment of districts and, ultimately, of individual payers of the levy, was left to the provincial executive committees. Persons possessing no property and earning not more than 1500 rubles a month were exempt ; so were nationalized and municipalized enterprises. A separate article declared that poor town-dwellers and poor peasants should be exempt, that the " middle strata " should be liable only for " small contributions ", and that the tax should " fall with its full weight on the rich part of the urban population and the rich peasants ".

The date originally fixed for the payment of the extraordinary tax was December 15, 1918. But throughout the winter enquiries and complaints poured into Narkomfin, and were answered in circulars and circular telegrams to the provincial authorities. When so much was left to local discretion and decision, differences of interpretation were bound to occur ; most of the complaints were of failure to honour the exemptions promised by the decree. A

---

[1] *Sobranie Uzakonenii, 1917–1918*, No. 80, art. 841 ; No. 82, art. 864. Lenin had already proposed a tax in kind three months earlier (*Sochineniya*, xxx, 392) ; according to Larin, who claims to have been the author of the proposal, it was approved by Sovnarkom, but rejected by VTsIK (*Narodnoe Khozyaistvo*, No. 11, 1918, p. 21).

[2] *Trudy Vserossiiskogo S"ezda Zaveduyushchikh Finotdelami* (1919), p. 20.

long circular of January 15, 1919, was devoted to the theme that
the tax had a class purpose as well as a fiscal purpose :

> If the tax were a brilliant success from the fiscal standpoint,
> but as the result of its incorrect enforcement a rapprochement
> occurred between the poor and the *kulak* elements in the
> country and town population on the ground of common dis-
> satisfaction with the tax, then we should have to register a
> failure.[1]

To combine the two purposes, or indeed to collect the tax at all,
proved excessively difficult. In April 1919 a decree, which began
by expressing special solicitude for the middle peasants (this was
the moment when policy had veered strongly in their favour [2]),
remitted all unpaid amounts on small assessments and reduced
medium assessments, while still stipulating that " the highest
assessments are not subject to the general reduction ".[3] Both the
methods and the results of the collection varied enormously from
province to province. In the provinces, as well as in the cities, of
Moscow and Petrograd, which had been assessed for half the total,
the yield was negligible. A few provinces furnished 50 per cent
and several 25 per cent of the sums for which they had been
assessed. But the total yield in May 1919 was less than 10 per
cent of the assessment, falling just short of a milliard rubles ; [4]
and it seems unlikely that much more was collected after that date.
The yield was perhaps no worse than that of other direct taxation
at the time. But the conclusion registered by Milyutin seemed
unescapable :

> Personally I put no hope in direct taxes. The experiments
> which we have made have yielded insignificant results. These
> taxes will no doubt be continued in the future, but no expecta-
> tions should be placed on them. Apart from their small results
> they create a mass of discontent and require a complicated
> apparatus to levy them.[5]

[1] These circulars are reprinted in *Sbornik Dekretov i Rasporyazhenii po
Finansam, 1917-1919* (1919), pp. 151-162.

[2] See pp. 159-161 above.

[3] *Sobranie Uzakonenii, 1919*, No. 12, art. 121.

[4] *Trudy Vserossiiskogo S"ezda Zaveduyushchikh Finotdelami*(1919), pp. 21-23,
33-35 ; according to another, probably exaggerated, estimate about 1·5 milliards
had been received when collection was abandoned in the middle of 1919 (G. Y.
Sokolnikov, etc., *Soviet Policy on Public Finance* (Stanford, 1931), p. 115).

[5] *Trudy Vserossiiskogo S"ezda Zaveduyushchikh Finotdelami* (1919), p. 50.

This plain failure of direct taxation in money rather than any addiction to theory drove the Soviet Government to rely on alternative expedients.

On the other hand, the first experiment in taxation in kind proved even less fruitful than the last large-scale attempt at direct monetary taxation. The decree of October 1918 instituting the tax in kind, like its counterpart on the extraordinary revolutionary tax, dwelt on the class aspect as well as the fiscal aspect of the measure. The tax was justified by the " extreme need of agricultural products " experienced by a state at war in a disorganized economy. But the subsidiary purpose was " the complete freeing of the poor from the burden of taxation by transferring the whole weight of taxation to the possessing and secure classes in such a way that in the country the middle peasants should be assessed only for a moderate tax and the chief part of state levies should fall on the *kulaks* and the rich ".[1] While the central administration of the tax was in the hands of Narkomfin (this being the only clear mark of its fiscal character), the collection was entrusted to the local executive committees and, in the rural districts and villages, to specially appointed commissions composed predominantly of poor peasants.[2] But, in spite of these provisions and of elaborate tables fixing the amounts of the levies, adjusted to the amount of land held, the province in which it was held and the number of members of the holders' family, the tax was a complete failure, and Lenin afterwards recalled it as one of the decrees of the period which " never entered into effect ".[3] The essence of the tax in kind as conceived at this time was that it was assessed not on production, but on supposed need. The only calculation made was of the needs of the " taxpayer " and his family; everything in excess of these was taken. It thus became indistinguishable from requisition. This desperate expedient was the main, if not the sole, means by which the Soviet Government throughout the years 1919 and 1920 obtained the essential supplies for the Red Army and for the city populations of the RSFSR. In these conditions the state budgets of the period of war communism could be no more than an empty formality. A budget was drawn

[1] *Sobranie Uzakonenii, 1917–1918*, No. 82, art. 864.
[2] *Sbornik Dekretov i Rasporyazhenii po Finansam, 1917–1919* (1919), p. 169.
[3] Lenin, *Sochineniya*, xxvi, 217.

up for the second half of 1918, as for the first half,[1] and formally approved towards the end of the period.[2] A budget for the first half of 1919 was approved by Sovnarkom on April 30, 1919.[3] Thereafter no budget estimates seem to have been submitted by Narkomfin until after the introduction of NEP in 1921, when formal budgets for the missing years were retrospectively approved. Throughout 1919 and 1920 the progressive devaluation of the currency and the flight from money rendered any kind of budget meaningless.[4]

The civil war had descended on the unfinished struggle between Narkomfin and the local Soviets over the fiscal rights of the Soviets. The constitution, while it recognized ultimate financial control from the centre, had left powers of taxation in the hands of the local Soviets, which exercised great persistence in maintaining their prerogative. During the whole of 1918 local taxation, mainly in the form of special levies and contributions, was probably more onerous and more effective over most of the country than taxes raised by the central government. When the extraordinary revolutionary tax was decided on in October 1918, Sovnarkom issued a further decree authorizing county, city and provincial Soviets to impose similar levies on their own account; and on December 3, 1918, a general and detailed decree regulated the fiscal powers of Soviets of different grades.[5] But during 1919 the balance shifted decisively against local initiative. The decree of December 3, 1918, by defining the sources of revenue of local Soviets, had in fact limited them; it had further established the principle that local needs should be met in part by local taxation, in part by subventions from the state. With the decline in the value of money which stultified all tax collection, and with the

[1] See p. 145, note 1 above.

[2] *Sbornik Dekretov i Rasporyazhenii po Finansam, 1917-1919* (1919), p. 291; the figures recorded 29 milliards of rubles expenditure, 12·7 milliards revenue (G. Sokolnikov, etc., *Soviet Policy in Public Finance* (Stanford, 1931), p. 126).

[3] *Sobranie Uzakonenii, 1919*, No. 23, art. 272.

[4] An article by an official of Narkomfin on the budgets for these years containing the accepted figures is in *Na Novykh Putyakh* (1923), ii, 1-49; no conclusions of value appear to emerge.

[5] *Sobranie Uzakonenii, 1917-1918*, No. 81, art. 846; No. 93, art. 931. Both these decrees encountered opposition from Narkomfin; Krestinsky afterwards described them as " a tribute to the past, a consequence of the keen controversies which preceded our arrival at the Commissariat of Finance " (*Trudy Vserossiiskogo S"ezda Zaveduyushchikh Finotdelami* (1919), p. 18).

progressive nationalization of industry which dried up the most prolific sources (nationalized enterprises were exempt from taxation, local as well as central), the revenues of local Soviets quickly fell off and dependence on central subsidies increased.[1] The congress of heads of financial sections in May 1919 delivered a frontal attack on the principle of local fiscal autonomy. It passed a resolution asking for the repeal of the decree of December 3, 1918, and announcing the intention of Narkomfin to propose at the next All-Russian Congress of Soviets an amendment of the budgetary chapter of the constitution. Meanwhile a further resolution laid down the general principles of a " single state budget " :

> All revenues, whether state or local, are poured into a single state treasury ; similarly, all expenditures to meet requirements, whether state or local, come out of the same single state treasury.
>
> All financial estimates, both of revenue and expenditure, are drawn up in accordance with the general budgetary rules.[2]

It was more than six months before the next All-Russian Congress of Soviets met in December 1919, and the amendment of the constitution was never formally mooted. But a decree of September 1919 set up an interdepartmental committee to which all applications from local Soviets for financial assistance were to be submitted and in which Narkomfin seems to have secured a preponderant voice ; [3] and this was probably the real moment when the centralization of fiscal and financial authority was finally secured. It was not till July 18, 1920, that the situation was regularized by a resolution of VTsIK :

> The division of the budget into state and local budgets is abolished ; in future local expenditure and revenue will be included in the general state budget. . . .
>
> Narkomfin is instructed to work out a system of monetary taxes defined by named purposes and collected for specific local needs, but included in and expended from the general budget.[4]

[1] No statistical information about local budgets at this time appears to have been published ; the process is described, by a writer who had had personal experience of it in the province of Smolensk, in G. Y. Sokolnikov, etc., *Soviet Policy in Public Finance* (Stanford 1931), pp. 133-137.

[2] *Trudy Vserossiiskogo S"ezda Zaveduyushchikh Finotdelami* (1919), pp. 130-131.

[3] *Sobranie Uzakonenii, 1919*, No. 59, art. 558.

[4] G. Y. Sokolnikov, etc., *Soviet Policy in Public Finance* (Stanford, 1931), p. 137.

But by this time monetary taxation had almost ceased, and nothing was done to carry this instruction into effect. A formal victory for complete centralization was accompanied by a decay of the whole budgetary system. It was not till after the introduction of NEP and the establishment of a stable currency that the policy was reversed and a system of local finance, as contemplated in the constitution of the RSFSR, once more brought into existence.

Not less acute than the problem of meeting public expenditure in the state budget was the problem of financing industry. The party programme of 1919 reflected current party beliefs when it declared that, as sources of direct taxation fell away with the nationalization of property, " the covering of state expenditure must rest on the immediate conversion of a part of the revenue of various state monopolies into revenue of the state ", in other words, on profits from nationalized industries.[1] But in the first year of the revolution this was still a remote ideal, and nationalized industries, exhausted by the war, stood in need of substantial capital investment as well as credits for current business. When in the winter of 1917–1918 the banks were nationalized and Vesenkha began to exercise control over the major industries, whether nationalized or not, the question arose from what source these credits were to be forthcoming. A decree of February 1918 set up a central committee of the National Bank, on which VTsIK, Vesenkha, the central council of trade unions and various People's Commissariats were represented to receive and examine applications for advances to industrial enterprises.[2] Similar committees were attached to local branches of the National Bank. But no uniform practice was immediately established, and advances seem to have been given without much scrutiny, and without regard for the policies of Vesenkha.[3] Cases were quoted in which owners of property about to be nationalized by Vesenkha had successfully mortgaged it with a branch of the National Bank on the eve of the

[1] VKP(B) v Rezolyutsiyakh (1941), i, 294.
[2] Sobranie Uzakonenii, 1917–1918, No. 24, art. 332.
[3] The National Bank and its branches had, before March 1918, " distributed advances of some hundreds of millions of rubles to private entrepreneurs " (Trudy Vserossiiskogo S"ezda Zaveduyushchikh Finotdelami (1919), p. 75).

act of nationalization.[1] It was clearly necessary to introduce some order and system into this haphazard process. The first concrete scheme, which was drawn up in the spring of 1918, and received support from Gukovsky and in Right circles, was for the creation of special banks to finance major branches of industry — a grain bank, a metal bank, a textiles bank and so forth — in which half the shares would be held by the state and half by the privatè interests in the industry concerned. This scheme, a financial counterpart of the projects for mixed companies negotiated with Meshchersky and others and a natural adjunct of the plan to restore the autonomy of the private banks,[2] was denounced equally with those projects by the Left opposition, which described it in its memorandum of April 4, 1918, as " denationalization of the banks in a disguised form ".[3] The defeat of the Meshchersky project also led to the abandonment of this scheme. But, with the final loss of independence by the banks and the drying up of all sources of credit other than the treasury, the field was open ; and Vesenkha took over the financing of Russian industry. By a decree issued on the eve of the first All-Russian Congress of Councils of National Economy in May 1918 all advances to nationalized industries were to be granted by the treasury on decisions of Vesenkha : the responsibility of checking and vouching for applications rested on the *glavki* and similar bodies or on the regional Sovnarkhozy.[4] At the congress Sokolnikov, who had vigorously denounced the Gukovsky scheme for a " diffusion of banks ", proposed that a fund of two-and-a-half or three milliards of rubles should be placed at the disposal of Vesenkha for the financing of industry in 1918.[5] This proposal was not pursued, and Vesenkha in its relations with the treasury continued to live from hand to mouth. But in practice its discretion seems to have been untrammelled, and during the second half of 1918 it became, so far as decrees could make it, the absolute controller of Russian industry. The second All-Russian Congress of Councils of

---

[1] A. Potyaev, *Finansovaya Politika Sovetskogo Pravitel'stva* (1919), p. 31.

[2] See pp. 88-89 and 137-138 above.

[3] Lenin, *Sochineniya*, xxii, 568 ; for the memorandum of April 4, 1918, see p. 89 above.

[4] *Sobranie Uzakonenii, 1917–1918*, No. 36, art. 477.

[5] *Trudy I Vserossiiskogo S"ezda Sovetov Narodnogo Khozyaistva* (1918), pp. 121-127.

National Economy in December 1918 demanded that the National
Bank should be transformed into " the technical organ for carrying
out settlements and accounting in accordance with decisions of
Vesenkha and of its organs ".[1]   Balance-sheets and profit and loss
accounts of industrial enterprises were presented to Vesenkha and
decisions of policy taken on them ; only the balances were carried
to the state budget.

Meanwhile the exclusive control over the financing of industry
established by Vesenkha in the latter part of 1918 was subject to
insistent criticism.   Socialist writers, down to and including Lenin,
had provided for a central bank as the accounting organ of a
socialist economy.   The National Bank had, however, abandoned
this function to Vesenkha, which attempted to combine the rôles
of an administrative and an accounting organ.   The combination
had fatal drawbacks.   The sole aim of Vesenkha was to stimulate
production by whatever methods and at whatever cost.   This was
defensible in the crisis of the civil war.   But the inefficiencies
inseparable from a time of acute emergency and the inexperience of the new bureaucracy made Vesenkha an easy target for
the jealous and relatively expert financiers of Narkomfin and the
National Bank.   It appeared that, in the accounts of Vesenkha,
revenue was not distinguished from credits employed in the
business — the working capital.[2]   Profits were reinvested in the
industry, and, generally speaking, only losses carried to the
budget.   Early in 1919 discussions took place between Vesenkha
and Narkomfin, and a compromise between them was recorded
in a decree of Sovnarkom of March 4, 1919.   The decree of
May 1918 recognizing the undivided authority of Vesenkha in
the financing of industry was rescinded.   All decisions by Vesenkha
and its organs on the granting of credits to state enterprises were
in future to be taken " with the participation of representatives of
the Commissariats of Finance and State Control " : irreconcilable
disagreements were to be referred to Sovnarkom.   All credits were

[1] *Trudy II Vserossiiskogo S"ezda Sovetov Narodnogo Khozyaistva* (n.d.)
p. 397.   The National Bank came in for some hard words at the congress ;
according to one delegate, " working through old employees, it still sticks too
slavishly to rules which have apparently not yet been abolished " (*ibid.* p. 272).
[2] *Trudy Vserossiiskogo S"ezda Zaveduyushchikh Finotdelami* (1919), pp. 26-
27 ; an attempt to remedy this was made in a decree of Vesenkha of November
2, 1918 (*Sobranie Uzakonenii, 1917-1918*, No. 96, art. 960).

to be granted through the National Bank to which all estimates and accounts of expenditure were to be submitted.[1] Another change still further limited the authority of Vesenkha and strengthened the hands of Narkomfin. It was laid down that, in the budget for the first half of 1919, all receipts of nationalized industries and of the *glavki* and centres controlling them, as well as of Narkomprod, should be paid to the account of Narkomfin and figure on the revenue side of the state budget.[2]

These measures deprived Vesenkha of its exclusive authority over the financing of industry, and gave the last word to Narkomfin. It can scarcely be doubted that this separation of finance from technical management was in principle a step towards a more efficient organization of industry. But the changes also had another aspect which experience failed to justify. The transfer to Narkomfin of the direct responsibility for the financing of industry, and the assimilation of items in the industrial balance-sheet to items in the state budget, meant that the financing of industry was conducted on budgetary principles and not on those of commercial credit. Such a system had no place for banking as a separate element; and it was a logical corollary of what had gone before when the National Bank was abolished in January 1920. The decree of Sovnarkom explained in some detail the reasons for the step :

> The nationalization of industry . . . has placed the whole of state industry and trade under the general system of estimates, which excludes any necessity for the further use of the National (State) Bank as an institution of state credit in the former sense of the word.
>
> Although the system of bank credit has retained its validity for small private industrial activity and for the needs of individual citizens, who deposit their savings in state savings banks, these operations, in view of their gradual loss of importance in the national economic life, no longer demand the existence of special banking institutions. These now secondary functions can successfully be discharged by new central and local institutions of Narkomfin.[3]

[1] *Sobranie Uzakonenii, 1919*, No. 10-11, art. 107 ; the " agreement " between Vesenkha and Narkomfin is referred to in *Trudy Vserossiiskogo S"ezda Zaveduyushchikh Finotdelami* (1919), p. 79.

[2] *Sobranie Uzakonenii, 1919*, No. 23, art. 273.

[3] *Sobranie Uzakonenii, 1920*, No. 4-5, art. 25. The savings banks had remained untouched till April 10, 1919, when they were merged in the National

Thus Narkomfin, taking advantage of the centralizing tendencies of war communism, succeeded in establishing for itself not merely an overriding financial authority, but an actual monopoly, at the expense both of local administration and of the banking system. In both spheres the process of concentration was to be revised under NEP.

The successes achieved by Narkomfin in the early part of 1919 in establishing its authority both over local public finances and over the financing of industry seemed an important step towards the introduction of order and common sense into the management of the national economy. They proved Pyrrhic victories, partly because neither political nor economic organizations were yet sufficiently well-knit to sustain the weight of so much centralized control, but mainly because the financial weapons wielded by Narkomfin broke in its hands with the headlong depreciation of the currency. The depreciation of the ruble came, from 1919 onwards, to dominate every aspect of Soviet financial and economic policy, and gave to the policies of war communism their final and characteristic shape. It was not until October 26, 1918, that, obeying some sudden scruple of legality, Sovnarkom issued a decree sanctioning an increase in the uncovered note issue by no less than 33·5 milliards of rubles,[1] thereby raising it from the limit of 16·5 milliards fixed by the last decree of the Provisional Government to an authorized total of 50 milliards. Here too the precedent set by the Provisional Government was closely followed. The decree merely gave retrospective sanction to what had already been done ; at the moment of its promulgation the new legal limit had been reached and was once more about to be passed.

From this time the growing needs of the civil war began to make themselves felt in an ever-increasing note issue and a more and more rapid rise in prices, which reflected the vanishing purchasing power of the ruble. The turning-point — which consisted in a psychological realization of the facts rather than in any specific change in the facts themselves — came in the early months of 1919. Some vague hope of salvation through the sub-

Bank (*Sobranie Uzakonenii, 1919*, No. 18, art. 200) ; it may be assumed that by January 1920 deposits had lost any real value.

[1] *Sobranie Uzakonenii, 1917–1918*, No. 90, art. 913.

stitution of a new currency seems to have dawned for a moment on the optimistic minds of the Bolshevik leaders.[1] Hitherto the Soviet Government had been content to print without change notes of the old patterns used by the Tsarist and Provisional Governments. In February 1919 notes of the RSFSR first made their appearance, but only in small denominations of one, two and three rubles " of a simplified type ".[2] Then on May 15, 1919, a decree was issued instituting new notes of a Soviet pattern for all denominations, and at the same time granting the National Bank the right to issue notes " above the level fixed by the decree of October 26, 1918, and within the limits of the real demand of the national economy for currency notes ".[3] For a long time these notes circulated both on the black market in Russia and on foreign exchanges at a lower rate than the notes of the Provisional Government, which in turn had a lower value than Tsarist notes. According to a Soviet authority, a 1000-ruble Tsarist note was at one time worth 50,000 to 60,000 Soviet rubles.[4]

When the decree of May 15, 1919, removed the last formal obstacle to an unlimited note issue, the note circulation exceeded 80 milliard rubles. Having more than doubled in volume in 1918, it more than trebled in 1919, and increased fivefold in 1920. The catastrophic and irreversible nature of the collapse could no longer be disguised, and began for the first time to have its full effects. The depreciation of the ruble in terms of gold or of foreign exchange was of little moment. Foreign trade in 1919 had virtually ceased ; and, when it began slowly to revive in the following year, the existence of the foreign trade monopoly assured that transactions would be conducted in stable foreign currency.[5]

[1] In May 1919 Krestinsky referred to " proposals of Lenin and myself for an exchange of money of the old pattern for new, coupled with the cancellation of a considerable part of the old money which was in the hands of large holders " (*Trudy Vserossiiskogo S"ezda Zaveduyushchikh Finotdelami* (1919), p. 29) ; by that time, however, such proposals had been abandoned as hopeless, though Krestinsky still spoke of the continued need of a " radical monetary reform " (*ibid.* p. 30).

[2] *Sobranie Uzakonenii, 1919*, No. 10-11, art. 102.

[3] *Ibid.* No. 16, art. 179.

[4] Z. S. Katzenellenbaum, *Russian Currency and Banking, 1914-1924* (1925), pp. 80-81.

[5] Speculation in the exchange value of the ruble, which varied widely from time to time, continued none the less both in Moscow and in foreign centres ; a decree of October 8, 1918 (*Sobranie Uzakonenii, 1917-1918*, No. 72, art. 781),

The depreciation of the purchasing power of the ruble on the home market was, however, significant and catastrophic. In the first stage of an inflationary process, prices increase less rapidly than the volume of the currency, so that the purchasing power of the total currency in circulation rises, and the issue of notes is an effective, though temporary, means of financing public expenditure. In the second stage, when people at large have become conscious of the fact of inflation and confidence in the currency has been sapped, prices begin to increase more rapidly than the volume of currency, so that they can no longer be overtaken by fresh issues and the purchasing value of the total currency in circulation falls. This second stage had already been reached in Russia at the time of the February revolution of 1917. In the eight months which separated the February and October revolutions, while the volume of currency notes had barely doubled, prices had trebled. When the Soviet Government came into power, inflation was far advanced in this second stage, with prices multiplying more rapidly than volume of currency. The rate of decline in the first years of the revolution is illustrated by a published estimate of the purchasing power of the total currency in circulation at the dates named, calculated in terms of the official cost of living index based on 1914 prices :

Nov. 1, 1917	2,200 million rubles	
July 1, 1918	488	,,
July 1, 1919	152	,,
July 1, 1920	62	,,
July 1, 1921	29	,, [1]

Another calculation depicted the same process in a different form. State revenue from currency emission, which stood at 523 millions of gold rubles in 1918–1919, fell to 390 millions in 1919–1920, and 186 millions in 1920–1921.[2] By the middle of 1919 the value in

prohibited Soviet citizens or enterprises from holding foreign exchange or from transferring funds abroad or to occupied territory in any form, except with the specific authority of Narkomfin.

[1] L. N. Yurovsky, *Currency Problems and Policy of the Soviet Union* (1925), p. 27.

[2] *Bol'shaya Sovetskaya Entsiklopediya*, xii (1928), 374, art. " Voennyi Kommunizm ". According to the same source, grain requisitions in the same three periods were valued at 121, 223, and 480 millions of gold rubles respectively; in proportion as currency inflation was no longer effective as a means of draining off peasant supplies, it became necessary to resort to direct requisition.

terms of goods of a rapidly increasing volume of rubles was already approaching extinction. But force of habit and the inescapable need for some conventional medium of exchange kept the almost worthless ruble alive for another three years. The printing presses worked to capacity. At the end of 1919, " the demand for currency was so great that factory tokens issued on bits of ordinary paper with the stamp of some responsible person or local institution or president of some committee or other passed as money ".[1] In 1920 the business of note-printing was being carried on in four different establishments, at Moscow, Penza, Perm and Rostov, and gave employment to upwards of 10,000 persons.[2]

The practical consequences of the collapse of the ruble were progressive and cumulative. Since official prices were not raised anything like frequently enough or steeply enough to keep pace with the falling value of money, the gap between fixed and free market prices widened to fantastic dimensions; and, in those parts of the economy where official prices still ruled, various forms of barter and payment in kind quickly made their appearance to supplement and replace meaningless monetary transactions. Thus, suppliers of raw materials to nationalized factories, who could only invoice the materials at official prices, received payment in kind in the form of the products of the factory.[3] The workers were paid in part in the products of the factory in which they worked (or of some other factory with which it had exchange arrangements), so that in place of almost worthless currency they received goods for their own use or for barter.[4] The depreciation of the currency produced other examples of this return to a natural economy which seemed particularly consonant with the spirit of socialism. With the ever-widening gap between fixed and free market prices, the distribution of rationed goods at fixed prices approximated more and more closely to gratis distribution. From this it was only a

[1] *Dva Goda Diktatury Proletariata, 1917–1919* (n.d.), p. 56.

[2] *Finansovaya Politika za Period s Dekabrya 1920 g. po Dekabr' 1921 g.: Otchet k IX Vserossiiskomu S"ezdu Sovetov* (1921), p. 140.

[3] V. P. Milyutin, *Istoriya Ekonomicheskogo Razvitiya SSSR* (2nd ed., 1929), p. 197, quotes some of the rates current early in 1920: a kilo of soap for a kilo of crude fat, 5·92 metres of linen yarn for 100 kilos of flax, 2·5 kilos of starch for 100 kilos of potatoes.

[4] See pp. 242-243 above; the system was so far regularized that permits for it were issued first by Narkomprod, later by a section of the All-Russian Central Council of Trade Unions (*Sobranie Uzakonenii, 1920*, No. 84, art. 415).

short step to the abolition of all payment for basic goods and services; and this step was progressively taken in 1920. Since May 1919 food rations for children under 14 had been supplied gratis.[1] In January 1920 it was decided to provide " free common dining-rooms " to serve in the first instance the workers and employees of Moscow and Petrograd.[2] On October 11, 1920, a decree of Sovnarkom instructed the Commissariat of Finance to draw up regulations for the abolition of payment by Soviet institutions or by their workers and employees for public services such as post, telegraph and telephone, water and drainage, light and power and public housing.[3] On December 4, 1920, all payments for rationed foodstuffs were abolished; on December 23, 1920, all payments for fuel supplied to state institutions and undertakings and to all workers and employees employed by them; on January 27, 1921, all house rents " in nationalized and municipalized houses ".[4] The levying of taxes in money had become meaningless. Stamp duties and customs duties were abandoned in October 1920.[5] On February 3, 1921, VTsIK had before it a draft decree proclaiming the abolition of all taxation in money; the introduction of NEP came just in time to prevent this logical step being taken.[6]

Far from being any part of the original Bolshevik design, the collapse of the currency had, in its earlier stages, been treated by every responsible Soviet leader as an unmixed evil against which all possible remedies should be invoked. But, when no remedy could in practice be found, and when in the later stages of war communism money had been almost eliminated as an effective element

---

[1] *Sobranie Uzakonenii, 1919*, No. 20, art. 238.
[2] *Sobranie Uzakonenii, 1920*, No. 4-5, art. 21.
[3] *Ibid.* No. 85, art. 422; the benefits of the decree were extended, as affecting institutions, to Comintern, the All-Russian Central Council of Trade Unions and Tsentrosoyuz and, as affecting individuals, to Red Army men and war invalids and their families, and to all persons enjoying benefits from the People's Commissariat of Social Security. The decree was specifically designed to abolish not only monetary payments, but all forms of monetary accounting, for such services.
[4] *Ibid.* No. 93, art. 505; No. 100, art. 539; *Sobranie Uzakonenii, 1921*, No. 6, art. 47.
[5] *Sobranie Uzakonenii, 1920*, No. 84, art. 413.
[6] *Pyat' Let Vlasti Sovetov* (1922), p. 393.

in the Soviet economy, a virtue was made of necessity and the view became popular that the destruction of the currency had been a deliberate act of policy. This view rested on two different arguments. The first was summed up in a famous dictum of Preobrazhensky, who described the printing press as "that machine-gun of the Commissariat of Finance which poured fire into the rear of the bourgeois system and used the currency laws of that régime in order to destroy it ".[1] It was true that the unlimited issue of paper money was a method of expropriating the capital of the bourgeoisie for the benefit of the state. But the method was clumsy, and this particular result unpremeditated. There was no analogy to the situation in Germany after 1919, where inflation served the interests of a small but influential group of industrialists and provided a dramatic excuse for the non-fulfilment of foreign obligations. The thesis that the depreciation of the ruble was engineered or tolerated by the Soviet Government in order to compass the ruin of the bourgeoisie by destroying the bourgeois monetary system was an *ex post facto* justification of a course which was followed only because no means could be found of avoiding it.

The second and more popular argument afterwards invoked to explain and justify the inflation was derived from the familiar doctrine of the eventual disappearance of money in the future communist society. Here, too, a certain taint of discredit attaching to money in the eyes of ardent Bolsheviks may have weakened the traditional respect accorded to it and made it more vulnerable to attack. But no serious communist at first treated the disappearance of money as an immediate goal. As late as March 1919 the revised party programme adopted by the eighth party congress roundly declared that " in the first period of transition from capitalism to communism . . . the abolition of money is an impossibility " ;[2] and two months later Krestinsky, despairing of any radical reform to save currency, still hoped for " palliatives " which would " postpone the moment of the final collapse of our

[1] E. Preobrazhensky, *Bumazhnye Den'gi v Epochy Proletarskoi Diktatury* (1920), p. 4. At the tenth party congress of March 1921, Preobrazhensky half humorously congratulated the congress on the fact that, whereas the *assignats* of the French revolution depreciated only 500-fold, the ruble had depreciated 20,000-fold : " This means that we have beaten the French revolution by forty to one " (*Desyatyi S"ezd Rossiiskoi Kommunisticheskoi Partii* (1921), p. 232).

[2] *VKP(B) v Rezolyutsiyakh* (1941), i, 293 ; the point was already in Lenin's draft (*Sochineniya*, xxiv, 103).

monetary system and help us to hold out till the socialist revolution in the west ".[1] The supreme necessity of keeping the ruble alive was implicit in Lenin's appeal at this time to the peasant to deliver grain in exchange for paper money " for which he cannot receive goods ", but which would serve as " the token of a credit given to the state ".[2] In the famous *ABC of Communism* published in the autumn of 1919, Preobrazhensky insisted on the need for money " in the socialist society which is inevitable as an intermediate stage between capitalism and communism ".[3] The abolition of money would come when society passed from socialism (or the " lower stage of communism ") to communism proper ; and no Bolshevik in 1919 believed that this ultimate transition could be effected in Russia without the support of a proletarian revolution in Europe. Certain obeisances were, indeed, made to the still distant vision of a moneyless economy. The party programme, while rejecting the abolition of money as impracticable, none the less recommended measures which would " prepare the way for the abolition of money "; and the *ABC of Communism* further developed this theme. As war communism moved into its last phase, consolation for the headlong downfall of the ruble was more and more often sought in the reflection that this was part of the road that led to the moneyless communist order of the future. At the end of 1919 a Soviet financial expert noted with satisfaction that " the rôle of money in the material circulation of the economy has largely come to an end ", and that this would save a lot of " unnecessary work ".[4] Zinoviev used the argument as a retort to German social-democrats who pointed a finger of scorn at the valueless Russian currency :

> When the value of money drops in Russia it is certainly difficult for us to bear : that we need not conceal. But we have a way out, a hope. We are moving towards the *complete*

[1] *Trudy Vserossiiskogo S"ezda Zaveduyushchikh Finotdelami* (1919), p. 30. About the same time Krestinsky made the same point to a foreign journalist without referring to revolution in the west : " You can fairly say that our ruin or salvation depends on a race between the decreasing value of money (with the consequent need for printing notes in ever greater quantities) and our growing ability to do without money altogether " (A. Ransome, *Six Weeks in Russia in 1919* (1919), p. 89).

[2] Lenin, *Sochineniya*, xxiv, 409.

[3] Bukharin i Preobrazhensky, *Azbuka Kommunizma* (1919), ch. xv, § 120.

[4] *Dva Goda Diktatury Proletariata, 1917–1919* (n.d.), p. 57.

abolition of money. We pay wages in kind, we introduce free trams, we have free school teaching, free (though at present bad) dinners, free lodging, lighting, etc.[1]

But none of these expressions of faith in war communism as a foretaste of the higher and final stage of communism can be legitimately read back as an explanation of the policy of unlimited inflation.

The campaign for the abolition of money which gradually gathered strength during 1919 and 1920 received a spurious reinforcement from a far more legitimate demand, which was much canvassed at this time, for " moneyless settlements " in relations between Soviet institutions and between nationalized industrial establishments. The argument was, however, vitiated by a latent ambiguity in the use of the word " money ". The theses of the Left opposition of April 1918 included a demand for " the organization of centralized social book-keeping and the abolition of capitalist forms of finance " ;[2] and, when in May 1918 all public institutions including nationalized enterprises were instructed to keep their accounts and deposit their cash holdings with the National Bank and settle all transactions by cheque or by book entry,[3] these arrangements, which in no way departed from ordinary capitalist practice,[4] were hailed by many as a step towards the elimination of money from a socialist economy. At the second All-Russian Congress of Councils of National Economy in December 1918 Larin argued that the business of Vesenkha was to place orders with nationalized industrial undertakings for products required and to see to it that the undertaking in question received the raw materials, fuel and other supplies necessary for the execution of the order. It was pointless that the undertaking should pay for these materials or receive payment for the finished product, or that the state railways should charge freight for transporting them. Money must be advanced to undertakings for the payment of wages to their workers, but need

---

[1] G. Zinoviev, *Zwölf Tage in Deutschland* (1920), p. 74.

[2] Lenin, *Sochineniya*, xxii, 568.

[3] *Sobranie Uzakonenii, 1917–1918*, No. 35, art. 460 ; the instruction was further amplified in a decree of August 1918 (*ibid.* No. 63, art. 691).

[4] A writer in *Narodnoe Khozyaistvo*, No. 1-2, 1920, p. 7, actually compared the system of " moneyless settlements " used by Soviet institutions with the clearing system of the English banks.

play no other part in such transaction. But the whole argument concealed a fundamental ambiguity. Larin seems to have passed delicately over the question whether his proposals meant merely that no monetary payments should actually be made, or that these transactions should not be invoiced at all in terms of monetary values. When, therefore, a spokesman of Narkomfin insisted on the function of the National Bank to exercise a book-keeping control over the movement of goods from factory to factory, " even though these are expressed in the former monetary units ", he assumed or pretended to assume that the only real dispute between Larin and himself turned on the precise relations between the National Bank and the accounting section of Vesenkha. Other speakers were less conservative in their interpretation. A representative of the metal workers argued that there was " no need for these book-keeping entries and this accountability in settlements which is being observed up to the present ", and that, under the scheme proposed by the National Bank, " we shall be slaves of superfluous accounting " ; and another delegate thought that the trade unions would in the near future introduce a system of wages in kind, so that even there the need for money would no longer remain and " we shall come in the end to doing without any calculations in rubles, reckoning the energy used by number of days and hours ". But nobody in authority was yet prepared to face this fundamental issue.[1]

As the sequel to this debate, the congress passed a long and ambiguous resolution on the financing of industry which was explicitly stated to represent an agreement with Narkomfin.[2] It opened with a high-sounding declaration of principle :

> The development of the socialist reconstruction of economic life necessarily demands the renunciation of the former reciprocal relations of private capitalism in production and the elimination in the last resort of all influence of money on the relations between economic factors.
> The abolition of private financial institutions, the concentration of the fundamental branches of production in the hands of

---

[1] *Trudy II Vserossiiskogo S"ezda Sovetov Narodnogo Khozyaistva* (n.d.), pp. 266-286 ; the debate took place, not in plenary session, but in the " section on the financing of industry ", and was reported only in a much abbreviated form.

[2] *Ibid.* p. 192.

the state and the centralization of distribution under the management of state organs are a sufficient basis for the consistent elimination from economic life of monetary circulation in the dimensions which it has assumed up to the present.

The resolution which followed this prelude laid it down among other things that freight belonging to state enterprises should be carried without charge on state railways and state-owned ships; that outstanding debts of state enterprises to one another should be cancelled, the documents being handed to Narkomfin for " liquidation "; that no payments should be made to or by state enterprises for goods furnished by or to them on the orders of Vesenkha; and that state enterprises should use money payments only for purposes, such as the payment of wages, which could not be met by supplies in kind.[1]

The resolution was voted unanimously by the congress. Some of the more enthusiastic delegates may well have supposed that in future, when one state enterprise supplied goods or services to another, the transaction would not be recorded in monetary terms or, since no alternative standard was proposed, in any terms expressive of value. Encouragement was given on all sides to the view that the end of the monetary system was in sight. The revised party programme of March 1919, which described the early abolition of money as an impossibility, none the less recommended " a number of measures which will widen the sphere of moneyless settlements and pave the way for the abolition of money: obligatory holding of money at the National Bank, the introduction of budget books, the replacement of money by cheques and by short-term vouchers giving the right to receive goods etc."; [2] and, while the question of monetary accounting was still not explicitly raised, its defenders were placed more and more on the defensive. This was apparent at the congress of heads of financial sections which met in May 1919. Krestinsky opened the proceedings on a modest note by admitting that under communism there would be " no separate department of finance or separate financial policy ", and that any such conception was " foreign to a developed society ". Even now there could be " no purely financial policy "; finance was the servant of economics.[3] But

[1] *Ibid.* pp. 396-400.   [2] *VKP(B) v Rezolyutsiyakh* (1941), i, 293.
[3] *Trudy Vserossiiskogo S"ezda Zaveduyushchikh Finotdelami* (1919), pp. 9-10.

the clear-headed Milyutin, after celebrating " the transition to moneyless settlements which put our monetary system on a sound footing ", stated in the most categorical terms the relation of finance to nationalized industry :

A system without money is not a system without payments. On the contrary. The revenue of an enterprise, like its expenditure, must be entered and accounted for in monetary symbols ; money must not pass from hand to hand, but must be recorded to the requisite number of millions of rubles ; the account must show that a given enterprise is spending so many millions and has delivered goods to the amount of so many millions. . . . Thanks to this method of settlement by book-keeping we shall have the possibility of judging whether an enterprise is developing or falling behind, for what reasons, where the trouble lies, what needs remedying. But, I repeat, with such settlements between individual enterprises for purchases and delivery of goods the circulation of monetary tokens is completely unnecessary.[1]

At a later stage of the proceedings Krestinsky himself cautiously admitted that " the ruble may remain as a unit of account even when money has ceased altogether to exist in a material form ".[2] But what nobody explained was how the function of providing " monetary symbols " for a system of book-keeping which would enable value to be measured could be satisfactorily performed by a currency in process of headlong depreciation. The failure of the ruble to perform its function not merely as a circulating medium, but as a stable unit of account, stimulated the strong theoretical drive for the supersession of money as a condition of the development of a socialist economy.

Sooner or later, therefore, apart from the failure of an unstable ruble to serve as an efficient medium of exchange, its unsuitability as a unit of account was bound to prompt the search for an alternative ; and for Marxists there would be little doubt where to look for it :

Accounting requires another constant unit [wrote a financial expert at the end of 1919] ; this will probably be the unit of labour time, which in the future can be converted into a universal unit of account of living energy — the calory.[3]

[1] *Trudy Vserossiiskogo S"ezda Zaveduyushchikh Finotdelami* (1919), pp. 51-52.
[2] *Ibid.* p. 84.   [3] *Dva Goda Diktatury Proletariata, 1917-1919* (n.d.), p. 58.

In January 1920 the third all-Russian congress of Sovnarkhozy at length faced this issue. It accepted a thesis which declared that, " in view of the excessive instability of the monetary unit and unit of account (the ruble) ", it was desirable to establish a new unit of economic accountancy " adopting as a basis of measurement the unit of labour ".[1] This proposal was referred to a commission. It occupied for many months the best economic brains of the country; and the term " labour unit " became familiar enough to be known by a current abbreviation as tred (*trudovaya edinitsa*). Robert Owen had issued " labour money " for his model settlements; and the adoption of labour as the source of value seemed a tribute to orthodox Marxism. It also seemed to be based on sheer common sense. Larin had propounded the underlying principle as long ago as December 1918:

> Today when the whole national economy must be regarded as one whole, the conception of comparative profit or loss becomes senseless. Today the only question can be how many days must be spent to produce how many articles in a given branch of production.[2]

In a resolution of June 1920 VTsIK spoke of the importance of extending moneyless settlements " with a view to the total abolition of the monetary system — a solution which is fully in harmony with the fundamental problems of the economic and industrial development of the RSFSR ".[3] But this contributed nothing to the practical problem of finding an alternative unit of account; and accountants continued to work in terms of the declining ruble, however inconvenient and misleading their calculations might appear. On July 15, 1920, a decree of Sovnarkom yet again provided that all settlements between state institutions or undertakings and cooperatives should be conducted through the National Bank by way of book entries and should not involve the passing of currency, drafts or cheques from one institution to another.[4] But this was a mere repetition of what had been prescribed in previous decrees and still took for granted the

[1] Quoted in L. N. Yurovsky, *Currency Problems and Policy of the Soviet Union* (1925), p. 34; it was not included in the published resolutions of the congress.
[2] *Trudy II Vserossiiskogo S"ezda Sovetov Narodnogo Khozyaistva* (n.d.), p. 96.
[3] Quoted in L. N. Yurovsky, *Currency Problems and Policy of the Soviet Union* (1925) pp. 33-34.
[4] *Sobranie Uzakonenii, 1920*, No. 67, art. 305.

survival of money as the unit of account. None of several schemes for replacing money by tred or by some other unit had won acceptance when the introduction of NEP caused the whole project to be relegated once more to the realms of academic speculation.[1]

[1] The discussion occupied an enormous place in the economic literature of 1920 and the first months of 1921 ; a rival to tred was propounded in the form of a " unit of energy " (*ened*). A detailed study of the discussion would have some theoretical interest, but it had little or no influence on future developments. It was influenced by two works of the German economist Otto Neurath which were much studied by Soviet writers of the period : *Durch die Kriegswirtschaft zur Naturalwirtschaft* (Munich, 1919), and *Von der Nächsten und Übernächsten Zukunft* (Jena, 1920).

CHAPTER 18

FROM WAR COMMUNISM TO NEP

THE first eight months of the revolution had failed to effect the transition from the bourgeois to the socialist economic order. The main achievement hitherto had been to break the economic power of the feudal landowner and of the bourgeoisie rather than to lay the foundations of the economy of the future. None of the key measures of that period bore the authentic stamp of socialism — or, less still, of communism — in the Marxist sense of the term. The land was nationalized in form — a measure preached by many advanced bourgeois radicals; in fact it was divided for purposes of cultivation into a multiplicity of small peasant holdings — the programme of the Social-Revolutionaries which Marxists had always treated as essentially petty bourgeois. In industry, a slow and somewhat reluctant beginning had been made with a policy of nationalization; but this was carried out as part of a programme of state capitalism, and the necessity of " learning from the capitalists " was still preached. In trade and distribution nothing was done except to extend and organize the grain monopoly set up by the Provisional Government. In finance the banks had been nationalized — once more a measure perfectly compatible with bourgeois radicalism; but in other respects it was difficult to detect any departure from orthodox capitalist practice. Lenin more than once went out of his way to emphasize the moderation of Soviet intentions at this time. Where more drastic measures had been applied, the fault lay elsewhere : " the tactics adopted by the capitalist class forced us into a desperate struggle which compelled us to smash up the old relations to a far greater extent than we at first intended ".[1] In the main the precept of the April theses of 1917 had been observed :

[1] Lenin, *Sochineniya*, xxvii, 63-64.

269

Not the " introduction " of socialism as an *immediate* task, but immediate transition merely to *control* by the Soviet of Workers' Deputies over the social production and distribution of products.

Lenin summed up the position in May 1918 in commenting on the prospective title of the RSFSR :

The expression " Socialist Soviet Republic " indicates the intention of the Soviet power to realize the transition to socialism, not at all a recognition of the new economic dispositions as being already socialist.[1]

It was thus left to the ensuing period to take the plunge into the economic policies of socialism, and to take it under the impetus of a desperate civil war. What came to be called " war communism " was, as its chief contemporary historian wrote, " an experiment in the first steps of the transition to socialism ".[2] The period from 1918 to the end of 1920 was in every way a testing time for the new régime ; and, while it defeated with impressive ease enemies whose only programme was to restore the old order, the exigencies of the civil war threw into relief the fundamental dilemma confronting it. The economic backwardness of Russia had smoothed the path for the political triumph of the revolutionaries, since they had been opposed only by the survivals of an obsolete feudalism and by an undeveloped and still inefficient capitalism. But the same fact made the subsequent work of socialist construction infinitely difficult, since they were called on to build a new socialist order without the solid democratic and capitalist foundation which Marxist theory had treated as indispensable. These peculiar conditions dictated, as Lenin fully realized, a certain slowness and caution in approaching the positive tasks of socialism. In theoretical terms, it was necessary to complete the bourgeois revolution before moving forward to the socialist revolution ; and the uncertainties in the minds of the party leaders, including Lenin, about the precise moment of the transition reflected this underlying embarrassment. The civil war removed all hesitations by driving the régime forward willy-nilly at breakneck speed along the socialist road. But war communism in

---

[1] Lenin, *Sochineniya*, xxii, 513.
[2] L. Kritsman, *Geroicheskii Period Velikoi Russkoi Revolyutsii* (n.d. [? 1924]), p. 75.

Russia had much of the artificial and unstable character of what was sometimes called " war socialism " in Germany.[1] It was the product of a special emergency, and lacked a sufficiently solid social and economic basis to ensure its full survival (even though some of its legacies were likely to remain) when the emergency was over.

The victorious ending of the civil war with the overthrow of Wrangel in November 1920, and the consequent easing of tension sealed the fate of war communism. So long as the war lasted, hand-to-mouth policies were inevitable ; the end of the war dictated a review of these policies in the light of longer term considerations. This was particularly true of the requisitioning of grain, a policy whose *raison d'être* lay in the continuous and inexorable need to meet today's emergency even at the expense of tomorrow's prospects. The decisive factor was the attitude of the peasants, whose loyalty to the Bolshevik régime and reluctant submission to the requisitions had been inspired mainly by fear of a " white " restoration and the loss of their lands. Once this fear was finally removed, the way was open for a revival of normal resentments at oppressive exactions whose only justification had now disappeared. The outbreaks of peasant unrest, which had begun with the demobilization in September 1920,[2] increased in extent and violence throughout the winter, till Lenin in March 1921 admitted that " tens and hundreds of thousands of disbanded soldiers " were turning to banditry.[3] These widespread disorders were the background and the prelude to the Kronstadt rising of March 1921 — the first concerted internal revolt against the Soviet régime since the summer of 1918. The demands of the peasants had an important place in the first resolution of the assembly of mutineers of the naval squadron : " to give full right of action to the peasant over all the land . . . and also the right to own livestock, which he must maintain and manage by his own resources, i.e. without employing hired labour ", and " to allow free small-scale production by individual labour ".[4]

[1] The analogy is developed in L. Kritsman, *Geroicheskii Period Velikoi Russkoi Revolyutsii* (n.d. [? 1924], p. 69).
[2] See pp. 167-170 above.
[3] Lenin, *Sochineniya*, xxvi, 204.
[4] *Izvestiya Revolyutsionnogo Komiteta Matrosov Krasnoarmeitsev i Rabochikh gor. Kronstadta*, No. 1, March 3, 1921, reprinted in *Pravda o Kronstadte*

The economic consequences of war communism, whose bank-ruptcy was revealed by these events, formed a vicious circle offer-ing no defined starting-point for analysis.   A catastrophic decline in industrial production, due in part to the destruction of plant, in part to the disorganization of labour, in part to the cumbrous system of centralized administration represented by the *glavki*, had been followed by a virtual breakdown of state or state-controlled distribution of commodities at fixed prices, leading to a rapid growth of illicit private trade at runaway prices and a wild currency inflation; and this in turn had prompted the refusal of the peasant, in the face of a goods famine and a worthless currency, to deliver necessary supplies of grain to the towns, so that popula-tion was progressively drained away from the industrial centres, and industrial production brought still nearer to a standstill.   The antidote, familiarly known to history as NEP,[1] was also a series of measures not conceived at a single stroke, but growing gradually out of one another.   It began, by striking at the point of greatest danger, as an agricultural policy to increase the supply of food by offering fresh inducements to the peasant ; it developed into a com-mercial policy for the promotion of trade and exchange, involving a financial policy for a stable currency ; and finally, reaching the profoundest evil of all, it became an industrial policy to bring about that increase in industrial productivity which was a condition of the building up of a socialist order.   The essential feature of NEP was the negation or reversal of the policies of war com-munism.   Everyone, once the first shock of surprise was over,

---

(Prague, 1921), pp. 46-47. The common statement that the impulse to NEP came from the Kronstadt rising is, however, incorrect ; the NEP resolution had been submitted to the party central committee on February 24, 1921, five days before the rising (see p. 281 below).

[1] The phrase " new economic policy " (without capitals or inverted commas) seems to have been used for the first time in the resolution of a party conference in May 1921 (*VKP(B) v Rezolyutsiyakh* (1941), i, 405), but was not yet in popular use. In Lenin's article in *Pravda* of October 14, 1921, written in preparation for the fourth anniversary of the revolution, it appeared in inverted commas (*Sochineniya*, xxvii, 30) ; and in a resolution of the party conference of December 1921 it was referred to as " the so-called ' new economic policy ' " (*VKP(B) v Rezolutsiyakh* (1941), i, 411). The abbreviation NEP appeared in March 1922 in Lenin's notes for his report to the eleventh party congress and in a conversa-tional passage of the report itself (*Sochineniya*, xxvii, 207, 241), but the full for... continued to be used in the formal passages of the report and in the resolutions of the congress. Later NEP came into common use everywhere.

accepted NEP as a necessity. But it was accepted by some willingly, by others with an uneasy conscience; and the justification of NEP was a theme of prolonged argument reaching back to the beginnings of the régime and pointing forward to the economic controversies of the future.

War communism was made up of two major elements — on the one hand, a concentration of economic authority and power, including centralized control and management, the substitution of large for small units of production and some measure of unified planning; on the other hand, a flight from commercial and monetary forms of distribution, including rationing and supply of basic goods and services free or at nominal prices, payments in kind, and production for direct use rather than for a hypothetical market. Between these two elements, however, a fairly clear distinction could be drawn. The processes of concentration and centralization, though they flourished exceedingly in the forcing-house of war communism, were a continuation of processes already set in motion during the first period of revolution. Lenin had long ago insisted that socialism was the logical next step forward from state capitalism,[1] and that forms of organization inherent in the one were equally indispensable for the other. Here war communism was building on a foundation of what had gone before, and many of its achievements stood the test; only in their detailed application, and in the extended scope given to them, were its policies afterwards subject to criticism and reversal. The second element of war communism, the substitution of a " natural " for a " market " economy, had no such foundations. Far from developing logically out of the policies of the initial period of the revolution, it was a direct abandonment of those policies — an unprepared plunge into the unknown. These aspects of war communism were decisively rejected by NEP; and it was these aspects which most of all discredited war communism in the eyes of its critics.

Between the two major elements of war communism there was, however, a further distinction. The policies of concentration and centralization were applied almost exclusively in industry (attempts to transfer them to agriculture met with no success); and it was here that the revolution had the main social basis of its support

[1] See pp. 91-92 above.

and that the Russian economy showed some of the features of a developed capitalism. The policies of the flight from money and the substitution of a " natural " economy arose from inability to solve the problems of a backward peasant agriculture which occupied some 80 per cent of the whole population. They were the expression of the fundamental difficulty of the attempt to run in double harness the anti-feudal revolution of a peasantry with petty bourgeois aspirations and the anti-bourgeois, anti-capitalist revolution of a factory proletariat, and of the conflict between town and country inherent in the attempt. These were the incompatibilities which eventually brought the revolt against war communism and destroyed it.

These differences within the conglomeration of policies collectively known as war communism go far to explain the divergent interpretations of it current in the party. According to one school of thought, it was a logical development of the policies of the preceding period, a series of steps correctly conceived though unduly hastened as a result of the civil war; the error inherent in war communism was one of degree and timing rather than of substance. This was the view of those who had hailed even the most extreme measures of war communism as victories for socialist principles. According to the other school of thought, war communism constituted a rash and dramatic reversal of the policies of the first period of the régime, and a plunge into untried and utopian experiments which objective conditions in no way justified. War communism was, on this view, not an advance on the road to socialism, but a forced response to the civil war emergency. The distinction between the two schools was neither rigid nor constant. The first view tended to be identified with the attitude of the former Left opposition and the recently founded workers' opposition, which deplored the increasing pressures on the proletariat and stressed the overriding importance of industry in a revolutionary economy; it received some support from Bukharin who, in his *Economics of the Transition Period*, had treated war communism as a process of transition, appropriate to the special Russian conditions from capitalism to socialism. The second view was taken by the other principal party leaders, including Lenin and Trotsky, who had become convinced of the necessity of giving greater weight to the wishes and interests of the

peasantry. But Lenin was not wholly consistent in his diagnosis
of the driving forces behind war communism. In one of the two
speeches which introduced NEP to the tenth party congress he
ascribed war communism to " dreamers " who supposed that it
would be possible in three years to transform the " economic
base " of the Soviet order ; in the other he described war communism as " dictated not by economic, but by military needs,
considerations and conditions ".[1] When, in the crisis atmosphere
of March 1921, the substitution of NEP for the more extreme
policies of war communism was unanimously accepted as a welcome
and necessary relief, these underlying divergencies were shelved,
but not wholly reconciled. In so far as war communism was
thought of as an aberration dictated by military and not by
economic necessities, by the requirements of the civil war and
not by those of socialism, NEP was a retracing of steps from a
regrettable, though no doubt enforced, digression and a return
to the safe path which was being followed before June 1918.
In so far as war communism was treated as an over-rash, over-
enthusiastic dash forward into the higher reaches of socialism,
premature, no doubt, but otherwise commendable, NEP was a
temporary withdrawal from positions which it had proved impossible to hold at the moment, but which would have to be regained
— and regained sooner rather than later. The unspoken premise
of the first view was the practical necessity of taking account of a
backward peasant economy and peasant mentality ; the unspoken
premise of the second was the need to build up industry and not
further depress the position of the industrial workers who formed
the main bulwark of the revolution.

[1] Lenin, *Sochineniya*, xxvi, 239, 253. What may be called the final official
verdict was pronounced in the article " Voennyi Kommunizm " in *Bol'shaya
Sovetskaya Entsiklopediya*, xii (1928), 374 : " It would be a great error not to
see, behind the obvious economic utopianism of the attempt at war communism
to realize an immediate marketless-centralized reorganization of our economy,
the fact that fundamentally the economic policy of the period of war communism was imposed by the embittered struggle for victory. . . . The historical sense of war communism consisted in the need to take possession of the
economic base by relying on military and political force. But it would be
incorrect to see in war communism only measures of mobilization imposed by
war conditions. In working to adapt the whole economy to the needs of the
civil war, in building a consistent system of war communism, the working class
was at the same time laying the foundations for further socialist reconstruction."

Both views left their traces in Lenin's speeches and writings as well as in the policies of NEP. The first was strongly argued in a pamphlet, *On the Food Tax* (*The Significance of the New Policy and its Conditions*), which Lenin published early in April 1921. Here, dropping the faintly apologetic tone which had occasionally crept into his exposition of NEP at the tenth congress, he boldly described NEP as a resumption of the true line laid down by him in the spring of 1918 and interrupted only by the civil war emergency. He began with a long quotation from *On "Left" Infantilism and the Petty-Bourgeois Spirit* — his broadside of May 1918 against the Left opposition. He reiterated that, in the backward Russian economy, state capitalism (and NEP as formulated in March 1921 represented a recognition of small-scale capitalism in the country-side under state control) was an advance on the straight road to socialism :

> The food tax is one of the forms of transition from a peculiar " war communism " dictated by extreme need, destruction and war to a correct socialist exchange of goods. And this last is one of the forms of transition from socialism, with the peculiarities called for by the predominance in the population of a small peasantry, to communism.[1]

The restoration of freedom to trade was a return to capitalism. But what he had said in 1918 he repeated now in italics : " *There is much that can and must be learned from the capitalists* ".[2] This suggested a comparatively long interval before the transition to socialism could be safely and successfully completed. At the party conference of May 1921 summoned to expound the new course to party workers, Lenin insisted that NEP had been adopted " seriously and for a long time " ; and the conference resolution described it as " established for a long period to be measured in terms of years ".[3] On the other hand, Lenin on the same occasion referred to it as a " retreat " ; a few months later he called it " a defeat and retreat — for a new attack " ;[4] and such descriptions seemed to encourage the view of NEP as a temporary evil to be

---

[1] Lenin, *Sochineniya*, xxvi, 332.   [2] *Ibid.* xxvi, 341.

[3] *Ibid.* xxvi, 408 ; *VKP(B) v Rezolyutsiyakh* (1941), i, 396.

[4] Lenin, *Sochineniya*, xxvi, 408, xxvii, 35 ; in another passage, he compared war communism with the first Japanese attempts to take Port Arthur by storm — a costly mistake, but indispensable for the discovery and application of the correct tactics of indirect approach (*ibid.* xxvii, 58-59).

overcome as quickly as possible, a blot to be erased from the party scutcheon. At the end of 1921 Lenin was still speaking of the need for further retreat.[1] In February 1922 he suddenly announced that " this retreat, in the sense of what concessions we make to the capitalists, is at an end "; and the same declaration was repeated more formally to the eleventh party congress a month later, when it was stated to have received the approval of the central committee.[2] But the declaration had no immediate effect on policy, and can perhaps be best understood either as an attempt to strengthen wavering morale within the party or as an intimation to the world at large that Soviet Russia would not come cap in hand to the impending international conference at Genoa.

These uncertainties and inconsistencies in the attitude of the party and of Lenin himself towards NEP reflected the persistent duality of aims that lay behind it — the need at all costs to create a workable economy by way of agreement with the peasantry, and the desire to effect the long-delayed transition to a socialist order, which could be realized only through a radical transformation of the peasant economy. It involved the fundamental problem which had dogged the Bolshevik revolution from the outset — the problem of building a socialist order in a country which had missed the stage of bourgeois democracy and bourgeois capitalism. When Lenin introduced NEP to the tenth congress he reverted to the two conditions for the transition to socialism which he had first propounded as long ago as 1905.[3] Only " in countries of developed capitalism " was it possible to make an " immediate transition to socialism ". In Russia there was still " a minority of workers in industry and a vast majority of small cultivators ". Lenin went on :

A socialist revolution in such a country can be finally successful only on two conditions. First, on the condition of its support at the right moment by a socialist revolution in one or several leading countries. As you know, we have done very much compared with what was done before to bring about this condition, but far from enough to make it a reality.

The other condition is a compromise between the proletariat which puts its dictatorship into practice or holds the state power in its hands and the majority of the peasant population.[4]

[1] *Ibid.* xxvii, 70. [2] *Ibid.* xxvii, 175, 238.
[3] See Vol. 1, pp. 54-55. [4] Lenin, *Sochineniya*, xxvi, 237-238.

Neither now nor later did Lenin discuss the relation between the two conditions or hint that either one or the other of them could be dispensed with. But the introduction of NEP, coming at a moment when the high hopes of the summer of 1920 had been rudely dashed, and when faith in an early international socialist revolution was dimmer than at any time since 1917, seemed inevitably to portend a certain shift of emphasis from the first condition to the second. It was because the international revolution still tarried, because the proletariat of western Europe had failed to come to the rescue, that the Russian revolution was still at the mercy of the peasant, and that NEP had become necessary. " Only an agreement with the peasantry can save the socialist revolution in Russia until the revolution has occurred in other countries ", said Lenin at the tenth congress; and Ryazanov neatly reminded the congress of an earlier context of the same argument when he called NEP a " peasant Brest ".[1] The essence of NEP was to keep in being the " link " between peasantry and proletariat by which the civil war had been won.

> The proletariat is the leader of the peasantry [Lenin told a party conference in May 1921], but that class cannot be driven out as we drove out and annihilated the land-owners and the capitalists. It must be transformed with great labour and great privations.[2]

Two months later he expounded the same view in an international setting to the third congress of Comintern. Apart from the class of exploiters, nearly all capitalist countries had their small producers and their small cultivators; in Russia these formed a large majority. " The chief question of the revolution now consists in the struggle against those two last classes." These could not be dealt with by the simple measures of expropriation and expulsion which had been applied to the exploiters : other methods would be necessary. The other methods were embodied in NEP, the principle of which was " the maintenance of the alliance of the proletariat with the peasantry, in order that the proletariat may keep the rôle of leadership and state power ". The equivocal position of a peasantry, which was at one and the same time an

---

[1] Lenin, *Sochineniya*, xxvi, 239 ; *Desyatyi S"ezd Rossiiskoi Kommunisticheskoi Partii* (1921), p. 255.
[2] Lenin, *Sochineniya*, xxvi, 400.

essential ally and the object of a struggle directed to overcome it, lay at the root of many future problems. " In any case ", added Lenin by way of afterthought, " the experiment we are making will be useful to future proletarian revolutions ".[1] At the eleventh party congress in March 1922 Lenin still reiterated the same axiom : " the new economic policy is important to us above all as a test of the fact that we are really achieving the link with the peasant economy ".[2] But NEP had in this respect certain obscure and still unrealized, yet vital, implications. Its inherent tendency was to relegate to the background the first of the two conditions of the transition to socialism — the condition of an international socialist revolution — which Soviet power had proved unable to realize, and to concentrate on the second condition — the winning over of the peasantry — whose fulfilment seemed to depend exclusively on the ingenuity and strength of Soviet policy. Three years later, when the impracticability of the first condition had been still more plainly revealed, Lenin's insistence on NEP as the true road to socialism was revealed as an unavowed forerunner of the doctrine of " socialism in one country ".

[1] *Ibid.* xxvi, 455, 460.
[2] *Ibid.* xxvii, 228 ; a few minutes later he added that they had " not yet " achieved the " link with the peasant economy " (*ibid.* xxvii, 229).

CHAPTER 19

NEP: THE FIRST STEPS

(a) Agriculture

THE initial and cardinal measure of the New Economic Policy — the substitution of the tax in kind for the requisitioning of surpluses — was no new conception. The tax in kind had been first introduced in the autumn of 1918; but the requisitions had continued, and the tax been abandoned.[1] In February 1920, before the ninth party congress, at a moment when the civil war already seemed over, Trotsky had proposed in the Politburo to replace requisitioning of surpluses by a tax in kind calculated on a percentage of production, and to put the exchange of goods with the peasantry on an individual rather than a collective basis. But he had been opposed by Lenin, and obtained only 4 of the 15 votes.[2] Such projects were once more in the air after the final defeat of Wrangel, and had been ventilated by SR and Menshevik delegates at the tenth All-Russian Congress of Soviets in December 1920.[3] Hitherto they had been dismissed as an inadmissible and impracticable derogation from Bolshevik principles — a return to " free trade " and petty bourgeois capitalism. But just a year after Trotsky's original initiative, on February 8, 1921, a discussion of agrarian policy in the Politburo prompted Lenin himself to put forward a recognizably similar project. A rough draft made by Lenin and submitted to

---

[1] See p. 249 above.
[2] These facts were stated by Trotsky without challenge at the tenth party congress (*Desyatyi S"ezd Rossiiskoi Kommunisticheskoi Partii* (1921), p. 191). Later he reprinted the " main part " of his memorandum to the Politburo of February 1920 under the title " Fundamental Questions of Supply and Agricultural Policy " in L. Trotsky, *Novyi Kurs* (1924), pp. 57-58, adding that it had been written " under the influence of the moods of the army and of the experience of a journey to the Urals " (*ibid.* p. 53).
[3] See pp. 170-171 above.

a committee of the Politburo for elaboration defined it in the following terms :

1. To satisfy the desire of the non-party peasantry for the replacement of the requisition (meaning the taking of surpluses) by a grain tax ;
2. To reduce the level of this tax in comparison with last year's requisition ;
3. To approve the principle of bringing the level of tax into relation with the effort of the cultivator in the sense of lowering the percentage of tax in proportion to an increase of effort by the cultivator ;
4. To extend the freedom of the cultivator to use his surplus over and above the tax for local economic exchange, on condition of prompt and full payment of the tax.

On February 17 and 26 inspired articles appeared in *Pravda* advocating and explaining the suggested change.   On February 24 a detailed draft, worked out by the committee on the basis of Lenin's notes, was submitted to the central committee of the party.   After further discussion and the appointment of another drafting committee, the central committee approved a revised project on March 7, 1921.   On the following day it was introduced by Lenin, though cautiously and not as a principal topic, in his general policy speech at the tenth party congress.   On March 15 Lenin in a further speech formally submitted the proposal to the congress, which unanimously approved it and appointed yet another drafting committee to prepare the text of a law ; and this text was referred back to the Politburo which made further changes.   On March 20 the matter was transferred for the first time from the party to the governmental machine.   The decree, in the form in which it had been finally approved by the Politburo, was formally adopted by VTsIK on the following day.[1]

---

[1] Particulars of the proceedings in the Politburo, together with the text of Lenin's draft, taken from unpublished party archives, are in Lenin, *Sochineniya*, xxvi, 651-653, note 11.   The debates in the party congress were confined to one session on the last day but one (*Desyatyi S"ezd Rossiiskoi Kommunisticheskoi Partii* (1921), pp. 221-224) after 140 delegates had left for Kronstadt and others had gone home (*ibid.* p. 184).   Nearly half the session was occupied by Lenin's introductory and concluding speeches (Lenin, *Sochineniya*, xxvi, 237-256) ; Lenin was followed by Tsyurupa, People's Commissar for Supply, who agreed in principle, but expressed dissent on the degree of freedom to be accorded to the cooperatives (see p. 337 below).   The rest of the debate was limited to six speakers chosen by the presidium, who were allowed ten minutes each ; none

The guarded phraseology of the decree did not conceal the revolutionary quality of the change. The tax in kind, calculated as a percentage of crops harvested, was to be progressive in the sense of being graduated to fall more lightly on middle and poor peasants and on the farms of " town workers ". So far the principle of levies adjusted to capacity and to need was maintained. But Lenin's original draft was followed in giving tax rebates to peasants who increased the area of land sown or the productiveness of their land as a whole ; and in other respects the changes made by the Politburo after the party congress and embodied in the final text of the decree were all designed to accentuate the strictly commercial character of the new policy. Collective responsibility, which had still been recognized in the congress draft, was explicitly abolished, and the individual peasant was made responsible for discharge of the tax falling on him ; a state fund was to provide consumer goods and agricultural equipment, no longer for the " poorest part of the population ", but solely in exchange for surpluses voluntarily delivered in excess of the amount of the tax ; and freedom to trade surpluses " within the limits of local economic exchange " was made more specific by the addition of the words, " both through cooperative organizations, and on markets and bazaars ". A few days later a decree of Sovnarkom cancelled whatever limitations were implicit in the term " local exchange " by authorizing " free trade, sale and purchase " and removing restrictions on the movement of foodstuffs by road, rail and water.[1] In May 1921 a party conference solemnly declared that the " new economic policy " had been " established for a long period to be measured in terms of years ", and that its " fundamental lever " was the exchange of goods.[2]

The introduction of NEP required not so much the creation of

---

of these challenged the proposal in principle, though some made criticisms of detail. The subject was evidently blanketed by the Kronstadt rising, and by the exciting controversies on party unity and on the trade unions which occupied the main attention of the congress, and its full significance was scarcely realized at the time by most of the delegates. The text approved by the party congress on March 15, 1921, is in *VKP(B) v Rezolyutsiyakh* (1941), i, 388-389 ; the decree as published in *Izvestiya* on March 23, 1921, is in *Sobranie Uzakonenii, 1921*, No. 26, art. 147.

[1] *Ibid.* No. 26, art. 149.

[2] *VKP(B) v Rezolyutsiyakh* (1941), i, 396-397 ; for the extension of trade under NEP see pp. 332-333 below.

new institutions as the transformation of existing institutions from instruments of compulsion into instruments of the new policy of encouraging the individual initiative of the peasant.   A first attempt was made with the " sowing committees " set up by the decision of the eighth All-Russian Congress of Soviets in December 1920.[1] A joint decree of VTsIK and Sovnarkom of May 26, 1921, declared that the functions of the committees as hitherto defined were " too narrow " and that, " in the interests of the further development of the independence of the peasantry ", the sphere of their activity should be broadened ; in addition to increasing the sown area, they should concern themselves with improving methods of cultivation, assisting rural industries, and encouraging local exchanges of goods and the development of cooperatives.[2]   A month later a further long decree drafted by Lenin himself placed the system of village committees, through intermediate stages of county and provincial " economic conferences " (a return to the old will-o'-the-wisp of " economic Soviets ") under the authority of the Council of Labour and Defence.[3] But this elaborate structure was never realized, and left no trace on subsequent developments.   Centralized control smacked too much of war communism to be compatible with the spirit of NEP, which purposed to limit the relation of the state to the peasant to the rôle of tax-collector.

The original conception of NEP — that agricultural production could be increased by guaranteeing to the peasant freedom to dispose of his surpluses and freedom and security in the tenure of his land — was correct.   But time was required to apply and develop it ; and the decision of March 1921, hurriedly taken in response to a grave emergency, came too late to forestall or mitigate a great natural catastrophe.   The initial calculations were made on the apparently cautious basis of the achievements of the previous year.   A decree of Sovnarkom of March 28, 1921, fixed the total assessment of grain to be levied under the tax in kind " on the basis of an average harvest " at 240 million puds against an assessment of 423 million under the requisition of 1920, of which

[1] See pp. 171-172 above.
[2] *Sobranie Uzakonenii, 1921*, No. 57, art. 364.
[3] *Ibid.* No. 44, art. 223 ; Lenin's original draft, dated May 21, 1921, is in *Sochineniya*, xxvii, 364-381, and constitutes a summary of the scope of NEP as conceived by Lenin at this time.

about 300 million puds were in fact collected.[1] The process of
trade and exchange was relied on to supply a further 160 million
and thus make up the estimated minimum requirement of 400
million.[2] The announcement of a change in policy scarcely came
in time to affect the sowing programme. It may have been due in
part to the incentives held up by NEP that the sown area in the
northern and central provinces increased by from 10 to 15 per cent
in 1921. These, however, " consumer " provinces which
did not even fully supply their own needs ; and in the much more
important southern and south-eastern provinces the sown area
actually declined by a similar percentage.[3] But what destroyed all
calculations was the catastrophe of a second successive year of
drought, afflicting most severely the " producer " provinces of the
Volga basin. The first note of warning was sounded at the end of
April 1921 in an announcement by the Council of Labour and
Defence of measures for the " struggle against drought ".[4] In
July 1921 the magnitude of the disaster was disclosed by the
sensational appointment of a non-party All-Russian Committee
for Aid to the Hungry, followed a month later by the scarcely less
sensational agreement with Hoover's American Relief Administration (ARA) for famine relief from abroad.[5] In July decrees had
been issued for the evacuation to Siberia of 100,000 inhabitants
of the stricken regions.[6] A few days later authority was given
to exempt from the tax in kind peasants suffering from major
disasters to their crops.[7] At the end of the year it was officially
stated that, out of 38 million desyatins of sown land in the
European provinces of the RSFSR, the harvest of 1921 had

[1] Sobranie Uzakonenii, 1921, No. 26, art. 148. According to Tsyurupa's
statement at the tenth party congress in March 1921, the collection was then
" approaching this figure " (Desyatyi S"ezd Rossiiskoi Kommunisticheskoi Partii
(1921), p. 228) ; a more cautious estimate on the same occasion was 265 millions
" so far " (ibid. p. 236). Corresponding assessments for potatoes (60 million
puds against 112 million), oil-seeds (12 million puds against 24 million), and
eggs (400 million against 682 million) were contained in two decrees of April 21,
1921 (Sobranie Uzakonenii, 1921, No. 38, arts. 204, 205).
[2] Lenin, Sochineniya, xxvi, 302, 409, 417-418 ; these figures were several
times repeated in Lenin's speeches in the spring of 1921.
[3] Otchet Narodnogo Komissariata Zemledeliya IX Vserossiiskomu S"ezdu
Sovetov (1921), pp. 70-75.
[4] Sobranie Uzakonenii, 1921, No. 49, art. 250.
[5] See Vol. 1, p. 178.
[6] Sobranie Uzakonenii, 1921, No. 59, arts. 396, 397.
[7] Ibid. No. 64, art. 484.

totally failed over more than 14 million desyatins.[1] Instead of the estimated 240 million puds, the tax in kind for 1921–1922 realized only 150 million puds, or half the total collection for 1920–1921.[2]

The horrors of the famine of 1921 which devastated the whole Volga basin have been vividly described by many witnesses, notably by members of the foreign relief missions which ministered to the suffering. Estimates of those who perished are unreliable, more especially since hunger is more often an indirect than a direct cause of death ; nor can the losses in livestock be even approximately computed. The decree constituting the all-Russian committee estimated the number of those in need at 10 millions. Five months later, at the ninth All-Russian Congress of Soviets in December 1921, the official estimate was 22 millions, and Kalinin gave reasons for thinking that this was at least 5 millions too low. At this time about one and a quarter million people were believed to have trekked from the stricken regions into the Ukraine or into Siberia, some of them making journeys of weeks or months. The famine had been more widespread, more severe and more serious in its effects on an already much tried and enfeebled population than the last great famine of 1891–1892. Kalinin estimated the total of relief supplies up to December 1921 at 1,800,000 puds of grain and 600,000 puds of other foodstuffs from home stocks, and 2,380,000 puds, including about 1,600,000 puds of grain, from abroad.[3] For the collection and distribution of these supplies a major share of credit went to ARA, the only officially sponsored foreign organization in the field. According to a contemporary article by Kamenev, " the support of the American Government gave ARA the possibility to carry out a systematic work of assistance on a large scale and to exceed everything that was done by other organizations ".[4]

---

[1] *Otchet Narodnogo Komissariata Zemledeliya IX Vserossiiskomu S"ezdu Sovetov* (1921), p. 80.

[2] *Pyat' Let Vlasti Sovetov* (1922), p. 373.

[3] *Devyatyi Vserossiiskii S"ezd Sovetov* (1922), pp. 23-33 ; accounts of the famine were given to the congress by eye-witnesses from the Saratov province and from the German Volga republic (*ibid.* pp. 110-117, 135-136). Kalinin made a further report to VTsIK in May 1922 (*III Sessiya Vserossiiskogo Tsentral'nogo Ispolnitel'nogo Komiteta IX Sozyva*, No. 1 (May 22, 1922), pp. 1-5).

[4] *Itogi Bor'by s Golodom v 1921–1922 gg.* (1922), p. 24 : Kamenev's article goes on to express doubt " precisely what interests of internal policy or what calculations of external policy " inspired American aid, and adds that " America,

The crop failure and famine concentrated all attention on the next harvest; and in December 1921 a party conference and the ninth All-Russian Congress of Soviets announced the opening of " the agricultural campaign of 1922 ", in which " the whole party organization from top to bottom " was called on to play its part.[1] In addition to the regular measures of admonition and organization, including the provision of seeds and other material aid, the principle of personal and collective incentives was, for the first time, freely invoked. An all-Russian agrarian congress at the beginning of December — no longer a congress of peasants, as in the early days of the revolution, but a congress of agrarian officials — had urged that " every achievement in raising the level of the economy should in particular be more regularly rewarded with the order of the Banner of Labour and with money prizes ".[2] The ninth All-Russian Congress of Soviets later in the month decided that " in order to record the successes and failures of the agricultural campaign of 1922 and to give public encouragement to provinces, counties and districts ", an agricultural exhibition should be held in Moscow in the autumn of 1922 " with economically useful rewards for the most successful (e.g. the equipment of an electrical station or a fleet of tractors as a reward for a province) ".[3] By this time the stimulus of NEP had begun to work, though it is difficult to know whether to attribute to NEP or to the consequences of the famine the new land hunger, the " veritable struggle for land ", which an official of Narkomzem described at the end of 1921.[4] By March 1922 the authorities had sufficient confidence in the prospects to announce a reduction of the tax in kind to a standard 10 per cent of production, and to prohibit the seizure of

thanks to the important help given by her, was in a better position than any other country to become acquainted with the economic and other conditions of Russia ". Details of American relief supplies are in F. M. Surface and R. L. Bland, *American Food in the World War and Reconstruction Period* (Stanford, 1931), pp. 244-257.

[1] *VKP(B) v Rezolyutsiyakh* (1941), i, 408-409 ; *S"ezdy Sovetov RSFSR v Postanovleniyakh* (1939), pp. 212-213 (also published in *Sobranie Uzakonenii, 1922*, No. 4, art. 41).

[2] *Novoe Zakonodatel'stvo v Oblasti Sel'skogo Khozyaistva : Sbornik Dekretov* (1923), p. 64.

[3] *S"ezdy Sovetov RSFSR v Postanovleniyakh* (1939), pp. 213-214 ; the exhibition was later postponed till the autumn of 1923 (*Novoe Zakonodatel'stvo v Oblasti Sel'skogo Khozyaistva : Sbornik Dekretov* (1923), p. 452).

[4] *O Zemle*, i (1921), 6.

livestock from peasants as a penalty for non-payment.[1] The spring of 1922, when the disaster of the famine had run its course and the new sowings were in progress, was the turning-point of NEP in the countryside : only a good harvest was now required to crown the recovery.

The distribution of the former landowners' estates among the peasants had virtually come to an end in 1918 ; and, once this was completed, the period of war communism saw no further substantive changes in the system of land tenure. The official encouragement given to new forms of collective agriculture had been more important in theory than in practice. Even at the height of war communism no attempt had been made to impose measures of collectivization on the peasant. The *mir*, with its periodical redistribution of land among its members and the individual peasant holding, continued to exist side by side without official discrimination between them. But the attitude of the authorities was equivocal.[2] The legal prohibition on the leasing of land (buying and selling was, in any case, precluded by the theory of public ownership) and on the hiring of labour prevented the individual peasant holder from adjusting himself to changing family conditions — a function automatically performed by redistribution under the *mir* system — and thus militated against the individual holding ; nor under a régime of the requisitioning of surpluses had the enterprising peasant much inducement to set up on his own account. Broadly speaking, war communism had two different effects on the burning question of land tenure. On the one hand, it tended to fix existing forms of tenure through lack of any incentive or opportunity to change them. On the other hand, apart from the demoralizing consequences of repeated requisitions, it created a sense of complete insecurity, since the whole future of land tenure obviously depended on the issue of the civil war, and

---

[1] *Novoe Zakonodatel'stvo v Oblasti Sel'skogo Khozyaistva : Sbornik Dekretov* (1923), pp. 432-433.

[2] An instruction from the central land committee of May 16, 1919, reaffirmed the right of peasants to abandon communal cultivation in favour of individual holdings (the so-called *khutor* and *otrub*). But the question of the need for consent by all members of the commune was never cleared up ; different local authorities adopted different attitudes, and some continued to put obstacles in the way of all forms of individual cultivation (*O Zemle*, i (1921), 7).

even the assumption of a Bolshevik victory provided no guarantee against further revolutionary changes.

An important function of NEP was therefore to give to the peasant two things on which he set the highest value : freedom to choose the form in which the land should be cultivated, and security of tenure. This, however, at once raised the moot point of the prohibitions on the leasing of land and the hiring of labour, which, if enforced, would make the choice in large measure illusory. If these prohibitions had not been extensively evaded under war communism, this was because there was no sufficient inducement to do so. Now that commercial incentives began once more to operate under NEP, evasions were inevitable. In October 1921 Narkomzem reported that " leasing exists surreptitiously " ; [1] and the same was certainly true of the hiring of labour. The question of land tenure was a main preoccupation of the all-Russian agrarian congress of December 1921, which, " in order to remove any unclearness in existing legislation ", enumerated the different systems of tenure in force and confirmed the right of free choice between them.[2] The ninth All-Russian Congress of Soviets a fortnight later took up the theme in a long and confused debate. Osinsky complained that the issue was dealt with " very indefinitely and obscurely in the existing law " and that " our peasantry has no legal guarantees for its exploitation of the land ". He admitted the anomaly of allowing the peasant to lease land given him not in ownership, but for use, and proposed by way of compromise to limit leases to six years — the equivalent of two rotations on the three-year system.[3] The congress, conscious of the difficulties but divided or uncertain about the method of solving them, instructed VTsIK to embody these principles in a decree, and further commissioned Narkomzem to review existing agrarian legislation " with a view to bringing it into full agreement with the foundations of the new economic policy " and to prepare " a coherent, clear collection of laws about the land, accessible to the understanding of every cultivator of the soil ".[4]

---

[1] *O Zemle*, i (1921), 16 ; the same publication carried a long argument by an official of Narkomzem in favour of the legalization of leasing (*ibid.* i, 105-115).

[2] *Novoe Zakonodatel'stvo v Oblasti Sel'skogo Khozyaistva : Sbornik Dekretov* (1923), p. 40.

[3] *Devyatyi Vserossiiskii S"ezd Sovetov* (1922), pp. 103-104.

[4] *S"ezdy Sovetov RSFSR v Postanovleniyakh* (1939), p. 209.

The decree of VTsIK in the form of a " Fundamental Law on the Exploitation of Land by the Workers " in 37 articles appeared in May 1922.[1] The artel, the commune, the *mir*, the isolated holding in the form of the *otrub* or the *khutor*, or some combination of these, were equally recognized : freedom of choice rested with the peasant concerned, subject to a not very clearly defined right of the local authorities to fix rules in cases of dispute. The maintenance of the *mir* with its periodical redistribution of land was not prohibited or directly discouraged. But the peasant, at any rate in theory, was free to leave it and take his land with him, and the decree helped to make this possible by permitting both the leasing of land and the hiring of labour, though professedly by way of exception to meet particular needs. Households that had been " temporarily weakened" by natural disasters or loss of labour power could lease part of their land for a maximum period of two rotations. Labour could be hired provided members of the household also worked " on an equal footing with the hired workers ". Thus the effect of NEP was to put an end to what was left of the equalizing tendencies of the revolutionary period. It recognized, so far as was compatible with the theory of the public ownership of land, the right of the peasant to treat his holding as his own, to increase it, to cultivate it with the help of hired labour or to lease it to others. His obligations to the state were those of a taxpayer. The state in return offered him, for the first time since the revolution, security of tenure to develop his holding and to crop it for his own and the common good.

The introduction of NEP did not theoretically affect the official encouragement given to current voluntary forms of collective cultivation, such as the Sovkhozy (including farms " assigned " to factories, Soviet institutions or trade unions), the agricultural commune or the artel. In one of his early speeches in defence of NEP, Lenin repeated that the future development of agriculture depended on the prospect that " the least profitable, most backward, small and scattered peasant farms should gradually amalgamate and organize large-scale agriculture in common "; and he added significantly : " That is how socialists have always imagined all this ".[2] The only change in principle was that the

---

[1] *Novoe Zakonodatel'stvo v Oblasti Sel'skogo Khozyaistva : Sbornik Dekretov* (1923), pp. 441-446.   [2] Lenin, *Sochineniya*, xxvi, 299.

new commercial principles applied to state industry under NEP [1] were extended to the Sovkhozy, which were now called on to show a profit from their operations. All Soviet farms were to be considered vested in the People's Commissariat of Agriculture, " assigned " farms being leased by a legal contract to the institution exploiting them, which paid rent in kind to the commissariat.[2] Later instructions were drawn up permitting the leasing of Sovkhozy to certain favoured categories of private persons.[3] On the analogy of what was being done in industry, the Sovkhozy of each province were grouped together in a provincial " trust ", and the edifice was crowned by a " state farm syndicate " (Gossel'-sindikat) attached to Narkomzem. Active support was still accorded to producers' cooperatives whether in the form of agricultural communes or of artels.[4] But as NEP gradually reopened normal channels of exchange between country and town, the impetus which had originally created the system of " assigned " farms died away ; and other Sovkhozy eked out an unhonoured and precarious existence. The new emphasis on individual enterprise was clearly inimical to state-organized forms of collective cultivation.[5]

The mood of acquiescence and relief in which NEP had been received by the party in March 1921 could not be expected to last. A change so radical and so contrary to the hopes and expectations of an advance into socialism which had been confidently shared by the whole party, a change which looked at first sight like a capitulation not only to capitalism, but to the pessimistic views long expressed by the SRs and Mensheviks, a change which shifted the emphasis of policy from the industrial proletariat, the bearer and spearhead of the revolution, to the backward and mainly petty-

---

[1] See pp. 303-305 below.

[2] *Novoe Zakonodatel'stvo v Oblasti Sel'skogo Khozyaistva : Sbornik Dekretov* (1923), pp. 42-47. [3] *Ibid.* p. 167.

[4] *Ibid.* pp. 47-49 ; *S"ezdy Sovetov RSFSR v Postanovleniyakh* (1939), pp. 230-231.

[5] The fullest account of Soviet farms under the NEP is in *Na Novykh Putyakh* (1923), v, 582-618. The mass of detailed information provided does not conceal the general picture of inefficiency and neglect : it is perhaps significant that the editors of the volume disclaim responsibility for the statistics cited by the author of the article.

bourgeois peasantry, was bound to arouse apprehension and resentment.[1] Since the new attitude to the peasant was the foundation of NEP, it was the new policy in agriculture which bore the brunt of the first attacks. A new and critical spirit spread in party circles, and found expression along two different lines.

The first criticism of NEP in agriculture related to its effect on the social structure of the peasantry. For three years Soviet agrarian policy had had a consistently levelling effect: it had sought with some success both to level up and to level down.[2] Its hostility to the *kulak* had been the counterpart of its desire to extend the holdings and improve the status of the poor peasant. Now it appeared that the aim of NEP was to rehabilitate and encourage the *kulak* at the expense of the poorer peasants. Lenin when he introduced NEP admitted the fact, and had no answer to the critics but the plea of necessity :

> We must not shut our eyes to the fact that the replacement of requisitioning by the tax means that the *kulak* element under this system will grow far more than hitherto. It will grow in places where it could not grow before.[3]

The free play of the market was bound to increase the differentiation between the successful and well-to-do and the unsuccessful and poor, and to open the possibility for the former to exploit the latter. This was the price to be paid, whether under the Stolypin reform or under NEP, for the extension of capitalism to the countryside. In the terrible famine conditions of 1921 the *kulak* was slow to emerge : in the stricken areas the only difference that mattered was the difference between survival and starvation. But in other areas the symptoms were more obvious. At the party conference of December 1921 Preobrazhensky drew attention to

---

[1] These were vividly expressed by Maxim Gorky in a conversation in the summer of 1921 with a French visitor : " Hitherto the workers are masters, but they are only a tiny minority in our country : they represent at most a few millions. The peasants are legion. In the struggle which, since the beginning of the revolution, has been going on between the two classes, the peasants have every chance of coming out victorious. . . . The urban proletariat has been declining incessantly for four years. . . . The immense peasant tide will end by engulfing everything. . . . The peasant will become master of Russia, since he represents numbers. And it will be terrible for our future " (A. Morizet, *Chez Lénine et Trotski à Moscou* (n.d. [? 1922]), pp. 240-242). Such feelings were certainly shared, though less openly expressed, by many Bolsheviks.

[2] See p. 168 above.   [3] Lenin, *Sochineniya*, xxvi, 246.

the danger of a development of the *kulak*-farmer type of economy.[1] In March 1922 he submitted to the central committee, in preparation for the eleventh party congress, an elaborate set of theses which constituted the first serious treatment of the question. The stratum of the peasantry which had " preserved its economic stability throughout the civil war and strengthened itself in the period of the most acute dependence of the town on the country " was establishing its predominance under NEP " in the form of intensive small-scale farming with regular or occasional hired labour or in the form of a strengthening of large-scale general farming in Siberia and other borderlands with regular hired labour ". At the other end of the scale, " in consequence of the decrease in draught animals, the draining off of workers for the front in the imperialist and civil wars and repeated bad harvests, the stratum of peasants without horses, without ploughed land, without cows . . . has increased ". Thus the general picture of a reversal of earlier tendencies was beginning to take shape :

> The levelling of class contradictions in the country has been stopped. The process of differentiation has begun anew and grown stronger, and is strongest of all where the revival of the peasant economy is most successful and the area under the plough is being increased. . . . In the midst of the immense decline of the peasant economy as a whole and the general impoverishment of the countryside the emergence of an agricultural bourgeoisie is going on.

Preobrazhensky's long review of existing evils ended with a return to the old ideals of Bolshevik theory — " to develop the Sovkhozy, to support and extend proletarian agriculture on holdings allocated to factories, to encourage the development of agricultural collectives and to bring them within the orbit of a planned economy as the basic form of the transformation of a peasant economy into a socialist economy ". He followed a fashionable will-o'-the-wisp of the moment by suggesting the introduction of foreign capital and foreign workers " to create great agricultural factories " and to apply modern technical methods of large-scale cultivation.[2]

Lenin read Preobrazhensky's theses with unconcealed impatience as one of those theoretical exercises in long-term planning

---

[1] *Vserossiiskaya Konferentsiya RKP (Bol'shevikov)*, No. 3 (December 21, 1921), p. 20.   [2] Lenin, *Sochineniya*, xxvii, 440-446.

which seemed to have little relation to the practical possibilities of the moment. He dismissed them in a highly critical note to the Politburo as " unsuitable ". He proposed that the forthcoming congress should confine itself to the setting up of a commission which would be instructed " not to fall into a repetition of common-places, but to study exclusively and in detail local . . . *practical experience* ". The party central committee accepted Lenin's views.[1] The proceedings of the congress were organized on these lines, Preobrazhensky's request for a general debate on economic policy being rejected ; and the short congress resolution, adopted on the recommendation of the commission, merely marked time, avoiding all reference to an evil for which, so long as the pre-suppositions of NEP held good, no remedy could be found.[2] With the fate of the harvest hanging in the balance it was no time to open a campaign against the *kulak*.

The second criticism rested on a broader basis and was more immediately threatening. When NEP was introduced as a neces-sary concession *to* the peasant, nobody was in a hurry to raise the question *from* whom the concession was demanded ; it could be plausibly and truthfully argued that any measure calculated to raise agricultural production and the supply of food to the towns was at least as imperative an interest of the industrial worker as of anyone else. But, as the year 1921 went on, concessions to the peasant were multiplied and the situation of the industrial worker, threatened with the loss of guaranteed rations and with the hazards of unemployment, steadily deteriorated. The party conference and the ninth All-Russian Congress of Soviets in December 1921 continued to focus attention on the peasant to the neglect of the growing discontents of industry. The original workers' opposition which was condemned at the tenth party congress belonged to the days before NEP ; and, when it complained of the predominance of " non-proletarian " elements in the party, the reference was not to the peasantry. But, now that complaints began to be heard that NEP meant the sacrifice of the industrial worker to the peasant,

---

[1] For Lenin's note to the Politburo see *ibid.* xxvii, 191-194 ; for the decision of the central committee, *ibid.* xxvii, 524, note 81.

[2] *Odinnadtsatyi S"ezd RKP(B)* (1936), p. 88 ; *VKP(B) v Rezolyutsiyakh* (1941), pp. 428-429. Lenin's share in the drafting of the resolution may be traced in a letter to Osinsky in which he deprecated " ignorant interference " pending critical study (*Sochineniya*, xxvii, 273-274).

it was natural that they should be taken up by circles in which former members of the workers' opposition were active. It was Shlyapnikov who blurted out at the eleventh party congress in March 1922 that the purpose of NEP was to provide " a cheaper government for the peasant ", and that this was being done at the expense of the workers.[1] Lenin avoided any direct retort to the criticism of Shlyapnikov as he had done to that of Preobrazhensky. He reiterated the argument of the indispensable " link " with the peasantry, and specifically added that " everything must be subordinated to this consideration ". He spoke briefly and confusedly about industry, and apologized for his failure " for a variety of reasons, in large part through illness " to elaborate this section of his report. He announced the ending of the retreat.[2] But nothing in the speech suggested any vital change of policy. The fundamental issues that lay beneath the surface of NEP were not yet ripe.

The waiting policy which Lenin was content to follow at the eleventh party congress was amply justified by the sequel. Thanks in part to the incentives to peasant production offered by NEP, in part to the favourable season, the harvest of 1922 was by far the most prolific since the revolution,[3] and provided a complete vindication of the new relation of the Soviet power to the peasant. Not only had the peasant for the first time since the revolution a surplus to sell and legal authority and encouragement to sell it, but the terms of trade were exceptionally favourable to him. The towns, after years of semi-starvation, were hungry for food, and compulsion was simultaneously placed on industry, for quite different reasons,[4] to liquidate a high proportion of its stocks of finished products. Thus prices moved in the summer and autumn of 1922 to an unprecedented degree in favour of agriculture and against industry. Both the avowed purposes and the hidden implications of NEP were suddenly realized to an extent which had

[1] *Odinnadtsatyi S"ezd RKP(B)* (1936), p. 108.
[2] Lenin, *Sochineniya*, xxvii, 230, 233, 238.
[3] At the twelfth party congress in April 1923 Zinoviev officially estimated the harvest of 1922 as being " three-quarters of an average harvest of the pre-war period " ; industrial production was 25 per cent of the pre-war level (*Dvenadtsatyi S"ezd Rossiiskoi Kommunisticheskoi Partii (Bol'shevikov)* (1923), p. 25). A later estimate in terms of value quoted in Y. S. Rozenfeld, *Promyshlennaya Politika SSSR* (1926), p. 432, put agricultural output at this time at 75 per cent and industrial output at one-third of the 1913 figures.
[4] See pp. 312-313 below.

scarcely been foreseen : partly by design, partly by accident, the peasant had become the spoilt child of the proletarian dictatorship. Lenin was fully justified in his boast to the fourth congress of Comintern in November 1922 of the success of NEP :

> The peasant risings which formerly, before 1921, were, so to speak, a feature of the general Russian picture, have almost completely disappeared. The peasantry is satisfied with its present position. . . . The peasantry may be discontented with this or that side of our governmental work, it may complain. That is of course possible and inevitable, since our administrative machine and our state economy are still too defective to prevent that; but any serious disaffection against us on the part of the peasantry as a whole is in any event completely excluded. This has been achieved in the course of a single year.[1]

It was true that what happened in the summer of 1922 added point both to the criticism of Preobrazhensky and to the criticism of Shlyapnikov. The flow of merchandise from towns and factories to the countryside, now resumed in however limited a volume after an almost total interruption of six or seven years, was primarily directed to the most efficient and most prosperous peasants, who had acquired the largest and most fertile holdings and contributed most to the success of the harvest. The revival of prosperity which NEP was bringing to the countryside was accompanied by no comparable advance in heavy industry, and was achieved to some extent at the expense of the industrial worker. But, though these arguments were theoretically correct, the impetus given by NEP to the whole economy was for the moment strong enough to outweigh them. If the major profits of the revival of agriculture flowed into the pockets of the *kulak* and would-be *kulak*, the poorer peasant was at least relieved of some of the intolerable pressures of the past few years. If the country was profiting at the expense of the town, the town was deriving visible benefits, however unequal the distribution and however high the eventual cost, from the greater abundance of supplies. The reanimating influence of NEP spread over every part of the economy ; and, while on the long view it was bound to create new

---

[1] Lenin, *Sochineniya*, xxvii. 347.

stresses and inequalities, these were for the present eclipsed by a general sense of increased welfare.

In the autumn of 1922, when NEP seemed to have reached the summit of its achievement, and before fresh clouds began to gather, the Soviet Government decided to stabilize the situation in the form of a series of legal codes. The agrarian code which was formally approved by VTsIK on October 30, and came into effect on December 1, 1922,[1] contained no innovations. Indeed, its purpose was to give the peasant a sense of security in existing arrangements. The principle of the nationalization of the land was solemnly reaffirmed : " The right of private property in the land, in deposits under the soil, in waters and in forests within the territory of the Russian Socialist Federal Soviet Republic is abolished for ever ". All land which was used, or could be used, for agricultural purposes constituted " a single state fund ". The right of " exploitation by the workers " could, however, be exercised in any of the familiar forms — the rural community of the *mir*, with or without strip cultivation and periodical redistribution, the individual peasant holding, the voluntary association in the form of agricultural commune, the artel or the Sovkhoz. The right of the dissentient individual or minority to leave the community with an appropriate allocation of land was recognized, subject to provisions (which had been more carefully elaborated since the law of May 1922) to prevent excessive fragmentation of holdings.[2] Apart from these restrictions, serious practical limitations on the rights of the peasant landholder were almost entirely removed. The crucial rights to lease land and to employ hired labour were conceded in terms virtually identical with those of the law of May 1922. The right to the exploitation of land for agricultural purposes was enjoyed equally by " all citizens (without distinction of sex, creed or nationality) desirous of working it with their own labour ". The code recognized no rights in perpetuity, but implied that the rights accorded by it were of indefinite

---

[1] *Sobranie Uzakonenii, 1922*, No. 68, art. 901.

[2] The right of the individual to leave the *mir* was the most strongly contested issue of the code and had to be referred to Sovnarkom for decision (*IV Sessiya Vserossiiskogo Tsentral'nogo Ispolnitel'nogo Komiteta IX Sozyva*, No. 1 (October 25, 1922), p. 33). The *rapporteur* on the code in VTsIK admitted that it had been impossible to deal adequately with the problem of fragmentation : provinces had been left to fix their own lower limits for units of cultivation (*ibid.* pp. 35-36).

duration. In the struggle to retain the principle of small peasant agriculture and the traditional pattern of cultivation by the rural community against the threatened encroachments of the large-scale modernized collective unit, the peasant seemed to have won as striking and complete a victory as for the right to dispose of his surplus products on the open market. In the autumn of 1922 NEP was still unchallenged in the countryside, and it seemed unlikely that, in this respect at any rate, it could ever be seriously altered. But the agrarian code of December 1922 set the pattern of rural Russia for rather less than ten years ; and these were years of almost unceasing controversy on the fundamental issue on the relations between peasant agriculture and large-scale industry in the Soviet economy. The " scissors crisis " of 1923 already marked a beginning of this controversy.

(b) Industry

The New Economic Policy was, in its inception, a policy for agriculture, and, by implication, for internal trade, but not for industry. The problems of industry were not discussed by the party congress which adopted it; and the resolution " On the Replacement of the Requisition by a Tax in Kind " referred to industry only in the context that " the revival of transport and industry " would " permit the Soviet power to receive the products of agriculture in the normal way, i.e. by exchange for the products of factories and of home industries ".[1] Two months later Lenin, in the article which was his fullest exposition of NEP, for the first time faced the practical issue :

> Want and destruction have gone so far that we cannot *at once* restore large-scale, factory, state, socialist production . . . that means that it is indispensable in a certain measure to help the restoration of *small* industry [2] which does not require machines,

---

[1] *VKP(B) v Rezolyutsiyakh* (1941), i, 388.

[2] " Small " industry included three main categories : artisans working independently for themselves, single-handed or with at most one or two hired workers ; " home " or " rural " industry (*kustarnaya promyshlennost'*) carried on by part-time labour of peasants and members of their families ; and industrial cooperatives, combining and organizing the workers of either of the first two categories. " Small " industry worked with only the simplest machines and was predominantly rural, being contrasted with the factory industry of the towns.

does not require either state-owned or large stocks of raw material, fuel and food, and can immediately render some aid to the peasant economy and raise its productive powers.[1]

But this relegation of large-scale industry to a secondary rôle also had its difficulties. In a draft which was written a few weeks later in the middle of May 1921 and subsequently appeared as a resolution of VTsIK the question was more discreetly left open :

Let experience show how far we shall succeed in setting this exchange in motion by increasing the production and deliveries of the state products of large socialist undertakings, how far we shall succeed in encouraging and developing small local industry.[2]

When, however, this draft was submitted to the fourth All-Russian Congress of Councils of National Economy and the fourth All-Russian Trade Union Congress, both of them bodies reflecting the interests of large-scale nationalized industry, doubts came quickly to the surface. One speaker thought that the peasant would supply his needs mainly from home industries so that " the link between town and country " would be broken ; and Milyutin reported at the end of the debate that dozens of notes sent up to the platform had expressed anxiety lest " this new turn in the direction of free competition, of encouraging small industry, may destroy the fundamental basis of our big industry ".[3] At the fourth All-Russian Congress of Trade Unions Lozovsky urged that the trade unions should take part in the " regulation " of small industry ; and Shmidt foresaw in the new conditions a danger that the working class would " be inclined to drift away from its fundamental work towards small industry ".[4]

The party conference at the end of May 1921 gave Lenin an opportunity to turn the edge of criticism with his customary skill. If the predominant place of large-scale industry in any socialist

---

[1] Lenin, *Sochineniya*, xxvi, 332-333.

[2] *Ibid.* xxvii, 365-366 ; *Sobranie Uzakonenii, 1921*, No. 44, art. 223.

[3] *Trudy IV Vserossiiskogo S"ezda Sovetov Narodnogo Khozyaistva* (1921), pp. 42, 53.

[4] *Chetvertyi Vserossiiskii S"ezd Professional'nykh Soyuzov* (1921), i (Plenumy), 49, 115. A delegate from South Russia at the fifth trade union congress in September 1922 complained that while the large cigarette factory at Rostov was discharging its workers, local small-scale manufacture of cigarettes was increasing by leaps and bounds (*Stenograficheskii Otchet Pyatogo Vserossiiskogo S"ezda Professional'nykh Soyuzov* (1922), pp. 91-92).

society had not been emphasized, this was because it was a universally accepted postulate. He invoked what was now his favourite *deus ex machina*, the plan of electrification :

> We have a quite precisely calculated plan, calculated with the help of the work of the best Russian specialists and men of learning, which gives us an exact notion how and with what resources, taking account of Russia's natural peculiarities, we can, must and shall put this foundation of large-scale industry under our economy. Without this it is not possible to speak of a really socialist basis of our economic life.

But large-scale industry could not be revived without more abundant supplies of food and raw material ; these could not be obtained except by process of exchange ; to encourage the development of small industry was to get this process started. " In order seriously and systematically to pass over to the revival of this large-scale industry, we need a revival of small industry." [1] The resolution of the conference put the desiderata of industrial policy in what was from this point of view the logical order. First came " support of small and medium undertakings, private and cooperative " ; secondly, " permission to lease state enterprises to private persons, cooperatives, artels and associations " ; thirdly, " a partial review of the programmes of big industry in the direction of strengthening the production of objects of popular consumption and everyday peasant use " ; and lastly, " a broadening of the independence and initiative of every large-scale enterprise in the matter of disposing of its financial and material resources ".[2] This was the order to be followed in Soviet enactments.

The initial steps of NEP in industry were two decrees issued by Sovnarkom on May 17, 1921. The first announced the intention of the government to " take necessary measures to develop rural and small industries, whether in the form of private enterprises or of cooperatives ", and to " avoid the excessive regulation and excessive formalism which crush the economic initiative of individuals or groups of the population " ; [3] the second cancelled several previous decrees limiting the scope and powers of producers' cooperatives, and put an end to the operation of the decree of

[1] Lenin, *Sochineniya*, xxvi, 390-391.
[2] *VKP(B) v Rezolyutsiyakh* (1941), i, 397.
[3] *Sobranie Uzakonenii, 1921*, No. 47, art. 230.

November 29, 1920, nationalizing all industrial enterprises, while stipulating that nationalizations effected before May 17, 1921, were not annulled.[1] Throughout the summer of 1921 a series of decrees marked the almost ostentatious encouragement now given to industrial cooperatives. They enjoyed the rights of juridical persons, they could employ hired workers in numbers not exceeding 20 per cent of their membership, and were not subject to control by the People's Commissariat of Workers' and Peasants' Inspection, thus escaping from the disability of state institutions; on the other hand, they were entitled to obtain long- and short-term credits from the cooperative section of Narkomfin.[2] Rural industries and small industrial enterprises, defined as those " in which not more than 10 or 20 hired workers are employed, including workers at home ", received substantial, though less signal tokens of favour, being promised freedom from nationalization or municipalization and the cooperation of the organs of Vesenkha.[3] The broad result of these measures was to accord to the small artisan and the petty industry of the countryside the same legal security and the same opportunity to trade which NEP offered to the peasantry.

The second step laid down in the resolution of the party conference of May 1921 was the return to private management and control, by way of leasing, of industrial enterprises which had already been nationalized and taken over, but which the state in the new conditions could not profitably retain. Rumours of an impending restoration of such concerns to their former owners

---

[1] *Sobranie Uzakonenii, 1921*, No. 48, art. 240. This decree provides an excellent illustration of the ambiguity of the term nationalization as used at this period. All industrial undertakings (with insignificant exceptions) had been " nationalized " in the legal sense of the term by the decree of November 29, 1920; what the decree of May 17, 1921, evidently meant was that enterprises not hitherto taken over administratively would not be taken over. On June 14, 1921, the People's Commissariat of Justice issued an " interpretation " in this sense, concluding that enterprises not taken over before May 17, 1921, "must be regarded as not nationalized " (*Novaya Ekonomicheskaya Politika v Promyshlennosti: Sbornik Dekretov* (1921), pp. 38-40). A further attempt to clear up the muddle was made in a decree of December 1921 which laid it down that a decision by the presidium of Vesenkha whether a particular enterprise should be regarded as nationalized or not was binding (*Sobranie Uzakonenii, 1921*, No. 79, art. 684); the same decree provided for the denationalization of enterprises employing less than 20 workers which had already been nationalized if they were not being sufficiently utilized by state organs.

[2] *Ibid*. No. 53, art. 322; No. 58, art. 382.   [3] *Ibid*. No. 53, art. 323.

were so strong that a brisk business was done in Moscow in the form of a sale of titles by these owners or their heirs.[1] The resolution of the party conference recognized the right of " local economic organs " to lease enterprises under their administration " without permission of the higher authorities ". Local authorities hastened to act on this recommendation without awaiting the formal promulgation of a Soviet decree. Provincial councils of national economy began to unload the unwelcome responsibility of administering nationalized enterprises of the third category [2] (which were under their exclusive control) by leasing them to any applicant on whatever terms could be secured.[3] It could probably have been pleaded that these proceedings, rough and ready though they may have been, were a means of resuscitating many concerns that had come to a standstill. But thus challenged, Sovnarkom issued a decree on July 6, 1921, laying down the conditions on which the leasing of nationalized enterprises was desirable. Preference was given to cooperatives, though leasing to private persons was not ruled out. The lessees were answerable under both civil and criminal law for the maintenance of the leased properties, and took over sole responsibility for supplying the enterprises and the workers in them.[4] Leases were generally granted for periods of from two to five years, and rent was paid in kind in the form of a percentage of goods produced. The fact that the decree resulted from local initiative suggests that it was applied mainly to small local enterprises. This is confirmed by statistics for September 1, 1922, when the scheme had been working for a year. The industries showing the highest number of leased enterprises were the food and leather industries. Of 7100 enterprises scheduled at this time for leasing, 3800 had been leased; these employed altogether 68,000 workers, an average of less than 20 each. Figures which cover only about half the leased enterprises show that rather less than 50 per cent were leased to private persons, the majority of

---

[1] *Trudy IV Vserossiiskogo S"ezda Sovetov Narodnogo Khozyaistva* (1921), p. 12.

[2] See pp. 181-182 above.

[3] A telegram and a circular from Vesenkha to provincial councils warning them against indiscriminate leasing and asking them to await the issue of the decree are in *Novaya Ekonomicheskaya Politika v Promyshlennosti: Sbornik Dekretov* (1921), pp. 45-46.

[4] *Sobranie Uzakonenii, 1921*, No. 53, art. 313.

whom were the former owners ; the rest were leased to cooperatives, to artels of workers and to state institutions. It is clear that
they were, for the most part, small concerns working with little
capital for a limited and mainly local consumers' market.[1]

These proceedings continued to cause perturbation in orthodox
party circles where the return of some industrial enterprises to
private ownership and the leasing of others was regarded as a
betrayal of the stronghold of socialism. How strongly this attitude
was reflected even in the inner counsels of the party is suggested by
an instruction to provincial party committees issued in November
1921 over the signature of Molotov as secretary of the central
committee. Members of the party were warned that it was
inadmissible for a communist to become the owner or lessee of any
economic organization employing hired labour or to participate in
any private economic organization working for profit. Communists
might participate in an artel or other collective economic organization, but only if it was working for the state or for the cooperatives, not if it was " pursuing specific aims of enrichment ".[2] The
question of principle was more important than the issue of substance. Kamenev stated, at the tenth All-Russian Congress of
Soviets in December 1922, that state industry, including transport,
employed 3,000,000 workers, as against 70,000 employed in private
and leased industries.[3] A census of 165,000 so-called industrial
enterprises taken in March 1923 showed that 88·5 per cent of them
were in private ownership or leased to private persons, state-run
enterprises accounting for only 8·5 per cent and cooperative enterprises for 3 per cent. But 84·5 per cent of all industrial workers
were employed in the state enterprises, which employed an average
of 155 workers each, while the cooperative enterprises employed
on an average 15 hired workers each and privately run enterprises
only 2. Moreover, since the productivity of labour was highest
in the state enterprises, these accounted for 92·4 per cent of all
production by value, leaving only 4·9 per cent for private concerns

[1] The statistics quoted are taken from an informative account by Milyutin
in *Na Novykh Putyakh* (1923), iii, 69-84 ; statistics quoted at the eleventh
party congress in March 1922 (*Odinnadtsatyi S"ezd RKP(B)* (1936), p. 268)
show a higher number of leased enterprises employing a lower average number
of workers.
[2] *Izvestiya Tsentral'nogo Komiteta Rossiiskoi Kommunisticheskoi Partii
(Bol'shevikov)*, No. 34, November 15, 1921, p. 10.
[3] *Desyatyi Vserossiiskii S"ezd Sovetov* (1923), p. 20.

and 2·7 per cent for the cooperatives.[1] Lenin, many months later, defending NEP from attacks at the fourth congress of Comintern, boasted that " all the commanding heights " had remained in the hands of the state.[2] The defence was cogent and well founded. The main importance of the new industrial policy resided not in the recognition of private ownership or private management in a mass of small enterprises which for the most part never had been, and could not at this time have been, effectively nationalized, but in the change of attitude towards the administration of large-scale nationalized industry. This change followed the third and fourth of the industrial directives of the party conference in May 1921: to strengthen the consumer goods sector of large-scale industry, and to develop the " independence and initiative " of industrial enterprises.

A so-called " instruction " of Sovnarkom of August 9, 1921, " On the Carrying into Effect of the Principles of the New Economic Policy ", was the first major NEP decree devoted primarily to large-scale industry. It recognized " rural and small industry as subsidiary to large state industry " and sought to establish a systematic classification of enterprises :

> The state, in the person of Vesenkha and its local organs, concentrates under its direct administration separate branches of production and a limited number of individual enterprises which are either large or for some reason important to the state, or subsidiary to such enterprises, mutually complementing one another.

Enterprises which did not fall into any of these categories were to be leased to cooperatives or other associations, or to private persons : those for which lessees could not be found were to be closed. But enterprises brought under the direct administration of state organs were to be " conducted on principles of precise economic accounting (*khozraschet*) ".[3] Two principles were

---

[1] Y. S. Rozenfeld, *Promyshlennaya Politika SSSR* (1926), pp. 211-212.

[2] Lenin, *Sochineniya*, xxvii, 350.

[3] *Sobranie Uzakonenii, 1921*, No. 59, art. 403. The " instruction " was drafted by Vesenkha (*Pyat' Let Vlasti Sovetov* (1922), p. 318) and may be regarded as the first " come-back " by large-scale industry after the shock of NEP. It took the form of a policy directive rather than of a legislative enactment ; but such pronouncements were commonly included in the official collection of decrees, and had an equally binding character.

simultaneously recognized, one of centralization, the other of decentralization. Enterprises engaged in the same " branch of production " were to be " concentrated " in what were known at this time as " unions " and later as " trusts " ; on the other hand, both these " unions " and such industrial enterprises as were large or important enough to escape unification were to be " separated " in the sense of being made independent and released from the direct administrative control of Vesenkha and its organs. These were the twin themes of a resolution of STO of August 12, 1921 :

> The largest technically equipped, practically organized and suitably situated enterprises in a given branch of industry may be united . . . into a special union, organized on the principles of *khozraschet*. Individual enterprises may also be " separated " on the same principles.[1]

The " separation " of large-scale nationalized industry from direct state management and its independent operation on commercial principles was the counterpart of the encouragement given to all forms of small industry, non-nationalized or leased, and formed the corner-stone of the industrial policies of the new economic order. " Separation " had vital consequences in labour policy, where industrial enterprises became directly responsible for the maintenance of the workers employed by them, and where all forms of maintenance, whether in kind or in money, were henceforth treated as wage payments ; [2] in the field of trade and distribution, where the major part of industry, instead of relying on state organs as its suppliers and its customers, became a buyer and seller on an open market ; [3] and in financial policy, where industry received credit, no longer from the treasury on a basis of budget estimates, but from a state bank, and later from other banking institutions, on a basis of profitability.[4] The introduction of *khozraschet*, which Lenin described as a " transition to commercial principles ", was an inescapable corollary of NEP : it was impossible to combine private capitalist agriculture with state industry in the same economy unless the state sector accepted the conditions of the market.[5] The function of *khozraschet* was, in the first place, to ensure that state enterprises should cease to be a burden on the

---

[1] *Sobranie Uzakonenii, 1921*, No. 63, art. 462.
[2] See pp. 320-321 below.   [3] See pp. 308-309 below.
[4] See pp. 348-349 below.   [5] Lenin, *Sochineniya*, xxvii, 76.

state, and, secondly, to enable the authorities to determine what enterprises deserved to retain the privilege of state ownership and administration. But in the autumn of 1921 the tools available were scarcely delicate enough for this exacting task. In its report to the ninth All-Russian Congress of Soviets in December 1921 Vesenkha reminded the congress that some of the most elementary decisions about the definition of profit had still to be taken :

> There are so far no guiding instructions to explain what is meant by profit and whether it should be accounted for in full, or whether any deduction should be made from it in order to provide capital for the enterprise, how to deal with profit represented in the form of unrealized products remaining in the enterprise, etc.[1]

Nor were these simple or purely formal questions. Nearly two years later a competent writer in a publication of STO pointed out that different trusts were computing their costs of production and therefore their profits in very different ways.[2]

The formation of trusts was a method of carrying out the transition of industry to *khozraschet* and of enabling industry to face the stresses which the change brought with it. In one sense it was a policy of self-help. Industry, and especially heavy industry whose needs had been a first priority while the civil war lasted, now had to bear the main brunt of the concessions to the peasant and the return to a market economy. Yet, if large-scale industry was no longer the favourite child of the proletarian state, it must organize to meet the new and unfamiliar stresses of open competition. In another and more immediate sense, the trusts were an answer to the problem of rationalization. It had long been apparent that an immense amount of waste both of material and of labour could be eliminated by the closing down of inefficient units and the concentration of production on the most efficient. Under the system of *glavki* administering each enterprise separately, and subject to a strong trade union influence which did nothing to mitigate managerial conservatism in this respect,

---

[1] *Finansovaya Politika za Period s Dekabrya 1920 g. po Dekabr' 1921 g.: Otchet k IX Vserossiiskomu S"ezdu Sovetov* (1921), pp. 60-61 ; Rykov, a former president of Vesenkha, wrote at this time that existing statistics were inadequate for any " genuine *khozraschet* " and that " we even lack figures to determine fixed capital " (A. I. Rykov, *Stat'i i Rechi*, ii (1928), 97).

[2] *Na Novykh Putyakh* (1923), iii, 133-137.

hardly anything had been achieved. Attempts to group together small enterprises in the same line of production in what was sometimes called a trust and sometimes a *kust* or " bundle " had enjoyed little success. In May 1921, in the first flush of NEP, the central committee of the party had recommended to the fourth All-Russian Congress of Trade Unions " an extremely rapid contraction of the number of enterprises and workers by concentrating the latter in a minimum number of the best and largest enterprises ", and had repeated the recommendation in similar terms to the fourth All-Russian Congress of Councils of National Economy.[1] But progress was slow. Only in one vital sector had the fuel crisis dictated drastic measures. In the summer of 1920 a technical commission inspected the coal mines of the Donetz basin, recently delivered from the ravages of successive military campaigns, and found 959 pits in operation, including 338 so-called " peasants' pits " working without machinery. The labour armies of the last period of war communism had been extensively used in the Donetz mines, and this no doubt made concentration relatively easy. By July 1, 1921, the number of pits working had been reduced to 687.[2]

The new industrial policy, by favouring everywhere the formation of trusts, made possible a wider application of this principle. The two first trusts (still at this time referred to as unions), one of linen mills, the other of timber-working concerns of the White Sea region, were brought into existence by decrees of STO in August 1921, with statutes which obliged them to keep profit-and-loss accounts and permitted them (though professedly as an exception) to buy supplies, and sell products, on the open market.[3] These were held up as models for imitation; and from October 1921 the formation of trusts proceeded rapidly. At the ninth All-Russian Congress of Soviets in December, Bogdanov, the new president of Vesenkha, announced that 15 major trusts (the word was now freely employed) had been created.[4] In September 1921 a further commission had been despatched by

[1] *Izvestiya Tsentral'nogo Komiteta Rossiiskoi Kommunisticheskoi Partii (Bol'shevikov)*, No. 32, August 6, 1921, pp. 3-4.

[2] *Na Novykh Putyakh* (1923), iii, 49-50.

[3] *Novaya Ekonomicheskaya Politika v Promyshlennosti: Sbornik Dekretov* (1921), pp. 95-103, 110-120.

[4] *Devyatyi Vserossiiskii S"ezd Sovetov* (1922), pp. 72, 89.

STO to the Don. As the results of its work only 288 pits were retained by the state (267 of them being in operation) and combined into a new trust, Donugol; the remaining 400 were leased or abandoned.[1] In the summer of 1922 the other coal-producing regions and the oil-producing areas were formed into trusts on the same pattern. These industries were the most thoroughly trustified and concentrated. But the same processes of rationalization were applied to light industry. Out of more than 1000 enterprises in the leather industry formerly administered by Glavkhozh, 124 were taken over and combined into a group of leather " trusts ", the remainder being leased or abandoned; but these 124 accounted for from 70 to 88 per cent of the total output of the industry in their respective branches.[2] By the end of August 1922, when the trust-building process was virtually complete, 421 trusts had been formed, including over 50 each in the textile, metallurgical and food industries, over 40 in the leather industry, 35 in the chemical industry and 20 in the electrical industry. The average number of enterprises grouped in each trust was about 10. The 380 trusts of which detailed statistics were available employed 840,000 workers, of whom 525,000 were in textile and metallurgical trusts. These figures did not include the great coal and oil trusts.[3] The largest of the trusts was the Ivanovo-Voznesensk textile trust, employing 54,000 workers,[4] and the Gomza and Yugostal metallurgical trusts employing 48,000 and 41,000 respectively : there were 21 trusts employing over 10,000 workers each.[5] The state trust had become the main form of organization for factory industry in the Soviet republics.

The transition to *khozraschet* lagged at first behind the process

---

[1] *Na Novykh Putyakh* (1923), iii, 51.   [2] *Ibid.* iii, 11.

[3] *Ibid.* iii, 27-30 : a volume published to commemorate the fifth anniversary of the revolution in November 1922 gives a total of 430 trusts (65 in the food industry, 57 in the metal industry and 52 in the textile industry) grouping 4144 enterprises employing almost a million workers (*Pyat' Let Vlasti Sovetov* (1922), p. 321). Slightly higher figures for 1923 are quoted in Y. S. Rozenfeld, *Promyshlennaya Politika SSSR* (1926), pp. 216-220.

[4] A delegate to VTsIK in 1922 gave some particulars of the formation of this trust. The larger local textile factories were included in it ; the smaller were at first leased, but later combined under the management of the trade and industry department of the local Soviet (*IV Sessiya Vserossiiskogo Tsentral'nogo Ispolnitel'-nogo Komiteta IX Sozyva*, No. 2 (October 26, 1922), pp. 25-26).

[5] Y. S. Rozenfeld, *Promyshlennaya Politika SSSR* (1926), p. 220.

of trustification. A decree of October 27, 1921, drew a distinction between two categories of state enterprise — those which no longer received supplies or subsidies from the state in any form, and those still dependent on state support, the most common and important form of which was the direct supply of rations to the workers from Narkomprod. The first category, which was soon to include a majority of state enterprises, was at liberty to dispose of its products on the market without restriction ; the second category, mainly confined to the essential sectors of heavy industry, might be allowed under special arrangements to dispose of up to 50 per cent of its products on the market, though it was bound in all cases to give preference to state institutions, and then to cooperatives, over private buyers.[1] Permission to dispose of a proportion of products on the market was readily accorded, and the practice received the specific blessing of the party conference of December 1921.[2] On March 21, 1922, a far-reaching step was taken : the fuel industry was placed on a commercial footing. This meant that industrial undertakings no longer received fuel supplies from the state, but were obliged to purchase them from the Chief Fuel Administration ; on the other hand, workers in the fuel industry no longer received food from state organs.[3] This drastic order was apparently subject to some exceptions. The decree itself provided for a continuation of free deliveries of fuel to the railway administration ; and provision was later made for the continued supply of food to the miners of the Donetz basin.[4] But over the greater part of the industrial field the transition to " commercial principles " was substantially complete before the end of 1922.

It was in the autumn of 1922 that the drawing up of the new civil code brought about the first serious attempt to define the legal status of the new trusts. They differed from the state industrial enterprises, or groups of such enterprises, under war communism, in being independent of direct administration by an organ of government (Vesenkha or its *glavki* and centres), and in being responsible for their own separate profit-and-loss account.

[1] *Sobranie Uzakonenii, 1921*, No. 72, art. 577.
[2] *VKP(B) v Rezolyutsiyakh* (1941), i, 410.
[3] *Novoe Zakonodatel'stvo v Oblasti Sel'skogo Khozyaistva* : *Sbornik Dekretov* (1923), pp. 216-218.
[4] *Na Novykh Putyakh* (1923), iii, 53.

On the other hand, they had at this time no fixed capital and were not juridicial persons. Article 19 of the civil code created a special category of " state enterprises and unions of such enterprises placed under a régime of autonomous management and not financed out of the state budget ". Such entities were entitled to " participate in economic transactions as independent juridicial persons " and were subject to the ordinary processes of law; current assets, including working capital, could be pledged as security for debts, but not fixed assets, which remained national property. Finally, a decree of April 10, 1923, defined and regulated the status of trusts on these lines.

> State trusts [ran article 1 of the decree] are state industrial enterprises, to which the state accords independence in the conduct of their operations in accordance with the statute laid down for each enterprise, and which operate on principles of commercial accounting with the object of earning a profit.

The state accepted no responsibility for debts of the trust (except in the case of the trust being taken over by the state) and was not obliged to cover any losses incurred. Profits accrued to the state after certain statutory deductions. A sum was now assigned to every trust as its fixed capital, and amortization calculated as a percentage of capital was to be charged against the profits of each year; one-quarter of profits earned went to the trust, 22 per cent to a welfare fund to improve the conditions of the workers, 3 per cent for distribution in bonuses to managers, employees and workers. The trusts had complete liberty to buy and sell on the open market, and were required to give preference to state organs as customers or suppliers only if the prices offered or asked were equally favourable.[1] The element of profit-making implicit in *khozraschet* was emphasized throughout: what had been at first conceived as an instrument of rationalization and a criterion of value was being developed as a new incentive to industrial production.

In agriculture NEP quickly provided the indispensable stimulus to production which launched Soviet Russia on the path of economic rehabilitation. In industry achievements were slower,

---

[1] *Sobranie Uzakonenii, 1923*, No. 26, art. 336.

less direct and dangerously one-sided. Its initial aim was to offer the peasant a quick and sufficient return for his products, and its advance lay along the line of the party resolution of May 1921. In conformity with this outlook, it stimulated first and foremost those small rural and local industries which produced directly for the peasant, which called for little or no capital investment to supply or renew plant, and whose products could be rapidly exchanged for those of agriculture. In the field of factory industry, it encouraged consumer industries, whose products could be quickly mobilized for exchange, as against capital goods industries whose benefits to the economy were more remote. All these purposes were served by the return to private enterprise and a free market, which in the primitive conditions of the Russian economy could reflect only immediate and elementary consumer demand to the exclusion of any long-term capital requirements. Almost everywhere industrial production reached its lowest level in 1920, registering a total of 16 per cent of the 1912 figure.[1] But the recovery from that level was very uneven. The output of small industry — rural and artisan — which stood in 1920 at just over a quarter of the output of 1912, had risen in 1921 to 35 per cent and in 1922 to 54 per cent. Large-scale factory industry, on the other hand, which in 1920 had fallen to 15 per cent of the 1912 level of production, recovered in 1921 only to 17 per cent and in 1922 to 20 per cent. Within large-scale industry by far the best results were shown by the light consumer industries which catered directly for the peasant. The leather industry was the one industry which throughout these years returned figures of output equal to those of 1912.[2] But textiles also made a good recovery, woollen goods rising from 36 per cent of the 1912 total in 1920 to 55 per cent in 1922, linen goods from 35 per cent in 1920 to 72 per cent in 1922, and cotton goods (whose main source of raw material, Turkestan, was inaccessible for more than two years)

---

[1] The calculations which follow were made in gold rubles at 1912 prices and are taken from *Na Novykh Putyakh* (1923), iii, 186-189 ; they obviously represent only a rough approximation. The figures for 1922 were estimated from the actual results of the first nine months, and tend to under-state slightly the final results for the year.

[2] This surprising result is attributed to the fact that small leather concerns which " did not enter into the statistics of 1912 ", or were perhaps included in small " artisan " industry, had now been nationalized (*ibid.* iii, 185).

from 6·5 per cent in 1920 to 15·5 per cent in 1922. Among the heavy industries mining recorded 33 per cent of the output of 1912 in 1920, fell to less than 30 per cent in 1921 and rose only to 36 per cent in 1922. Only the oil industry made a striking recovery from 16 per cent of the 1912 output in 1920 to 39 per cent in 1922 ; and here the low figure of 1920 was due directly to the military events of the two preceding years. But the most significant results were those of the metallurgical industry, the greatest of Russia's pre-revolution industries, and the foundation of all large-scale industry. Here the output in 1920 was no more than 6 per cent of 1912, rose in 1921 to 9 per cent and fell back again in 1922 to 7 per cent. According to a statement at the twelfth party congress in April 1923 industry as a whole, in spite of measures of rationalization, was still only working at 30 per cent of capacity.[1]

Soviet industry in the initial period of NEP was exposed to two adverse influences. In the first place, NEP at the outset meant a policy not only of concessions to the peasantry, but of concessions at the expense of the proletariat, or at any rate of concessions which left no room for corresponding favours to industry; its first impact on industry as a whole was therefore bound to be discouraging.[2] Secondly, by stimulating the demand for consumer goods it disturbed the balance within industry itself.

The first of these effects showed itself almost at once in a crisis of industrial prices. Throughout the period of war communism the official fixed prices had been consistently regulated in such a way as to favour the producer of manufactured goods. On the illegal free market, on the other hand, the acute demand for foodstuffs shifted the balance in the opposite direction, so that, say, a pud of rye exchanged for a larger quantity of leather or of cotton textiles than before the war. When, therefore, controls were abandoned, a tendency of prices to move in favour of the agricultural producer was to be expected. That this movement not only occurred, but occurred in a more violent and extreme form than

---

[1] *Dvenadtsatyi S"ezd Rossiiskoi Kommunisticheskoi Partii (Bol'shevikov)* (1923), p. 339.

[2] Kamenev, at the party conference of December 1921, noted the fundamental dilemma of NEP : " only at the expense of the peasant, or of the worker, or of one and the other, can we revive industry and consequently our economy as a whole " (*Vserossiiskaya Konferentsiya RKP (Bol'shevikov)*, No. 1 (December 19, 1921), p. 20).

anyone had foreseen, was due to special conditions both in country and in town. In the country, the exactions of war communism had denuded the peasant of all reserves, and the catastrophic harvest of 1921 prevented many parts of the country from reaping the advantages of NEP, so that effective demand for industrial goods proved unexpectedly low, whereas the demand of the towns for depleted supplies of foodstuffs was even more acute than before. The peasant had been placed by NEP in a position, for the first time for many years, to sell his surplus production, after meeting the requirements of his family and of the tax-collector, at his own price. Those peasants who, in the winter of 1921–1922, had surpluses to sell were conscious of their strength and not unwilling to recoup themselves for what they had suffered at the hands of the cities under war communism.

The situation of industry was more complex. The freedom of trade and loosening of state controls under NEP, which stimulated and encouraged the peasant, meant something quite different for large-scale industry which found itself suddenly thrown on its own resources and on the tender mercies of *khozraschet* : from the autumn of 1921 onwards, more and more enterprises were cut off from state credits and state supplies of raw materials and food, and told to shift for themselves. The prospect was bleak, even for the strongest. After seven years of neglect, equipment had run down to its lowest point, and renewals could scarcely be postponed much longer. Financial resources were nil, and credit was almost unobtainable.[1] Resources had to be found to cover running costs, and to provide in cash or kind the wages of the workers, now for the most part deprived of direct state supplies. Assets were virtually confined to stocks of raw material, which could only be replaced at open market prices, and stocks of finished products ; in a majority of enterprises the latter were in fact the only liquid assets.[2] Hence the urgent need for working capital, created by

[1] The new State Bank, which had powers to make advances to industry on a commercial basis, was only opened on November 16, 1921, and with quite inadequate resources (see p. 349 below).

[2] According to a table in *Na Novykh Putyakh* (1923), iii, 15, which can hardly lay claim to much precision but will serve as a rough indication, stocks of finished products on January 1, 1922, were in excess of stocks of raw materials in all industries except the metallurgical and textile industries. A further estimate, which must be still more speculative, shows that these stocks were quite inadequate to cover the requirements of the industries in working capital.

the cessation of state support, could be met only by selling stocks of finished products on an extensive scale. The process of liquidation was a sufficiently conspicuous phenomenon by the end of 1921 to have acquired the cant name *razbazarovanie* (" scattering through the bazaars ").[1]

This forced attempt to liquidate stocks on an obstinate and inelastic market produced the natural result — a collapse in prices of manufactured goods. As a result of NEP, state industry no longer operated under a single authority but was divided into " separate economic units having almost no connexion with one another " ; and " unrestricted competition " between these units, which in obedience to the new commercial spirit underbid each other in the effort to dispose of their goods, aggravated the collapse.[2] Its extent was partially and momentarily masked by the continuing currency inflation, but became apparent from a comparison between industrial and agricultural prices, the latter being simultaneously driven up by the prevailing scarcity. For example, on January 1, 1921, an arshin of cotton cloth was worth 4 lb. of rye flour, a box of matches 0·23 lb., and a pound of sugar 11·55 lb. ; during the first four months of 1921 the value of these goods in terms of flour declined by more than 50 per cent, the corresponding figures for May 1, 1921, being 1·68 lb., 0·09 lb. and 5·07 lb. respectively.[3] Index numbers based on 12 agricultural and 12 industrial products showed that the value of agricultural products rose from 104 on January 1, 1922 (taking 100 to represent the 1913 level), to 113 on May 1, 1922, while the value of industrial products fell during the same period from 92 to 65.[4] Thus the disparity between the values of agricultural and industrial products which

---

[1] The term, prefaced by " so-called ", was in use at the ninth All-Russian Congress of Soviets in December 1921 (*Devyatyi Vserossiiskii S"ezd Sovetov* (1922), p. 95).

[2] *Na Novykh Putyakh* (1923), iii, 34, 138.

[3] These figures are taken from a table in an article by Kondratiev in *ibid.* (1923), i, 11 ; similar figures, with slight variations characteristic of Soviet statistics of this period, are in S. G. Strumilin, *Na Khozyaistvennom Fronte* (1925), p. 211. The difference of substance between the two tables is that Kondratiev used official prices for 1920 and January 1, 1921, whereas Strumilin used the then illegal open market prices, so that in Kondratiev's table the fall in value of goods in terms of rye flour begins only with January 1, 1922, whereas in Strumilin's tables the January 1, 1922, values already show a decline from the open market values of the pre-NEP period.

[4] S. G. Strumilin, *Na Khozyaistvennom Fronte* (1925), p. 212.

reached its extreme point in May 1922 was caused to a minor extent by the rise in agricultural values and to a major extent by the fall in industrial values. The plight of industry was voiced by Shlyapnikov at the eleventh party congress in March 1922 :

> The conjuncture of the market is such that it is beating us down, we cannot stand up to the flood of goods. We need money at once, and in the search for it we create such an anarchic competition, even on the market for metal products, that we have nothing to pay the wages with, so low are the prices for our products falling.[1]

According to one current calculation, cotton cloth was selling in May 1922 at considerably less than half its cost of production ;[2] and the textile industry was financially in a stronger position than many others. It was the period, as a Soviet economist afterwards wrote, of " the dictatorship of rye and the dissipation of our state industrial capital ".[3]

These results may have been consonant with the the immediate purpose of NEP, which was to offer the peasant a tolerable return for his labour. But they were a disaster for Soviet industry, whose leaders and directors were bound to react strongly to them. The response was remarkably similar to that evoked by such situations in more normal forms of capitalism. In March 1922, when the collapse had gone far and Lenin was proclaiming that the "retreat" was at an end, began the formation of " syndicates " whose function was to combine and monopolize the whole selling machinery of a single industry. During the next three months the trusts in all the leading industries united to form syndicates of this pattern, covering from 70 to 100 per cent of the production of the industry concerned.[4] The increased bargaining power acquired by industry through these organizations was the main factor which stayed the persistent fall in industrial prices and, after May 1922,

---

[1] *Odinnadtsatyi S"ezd RKP(B)* (1936), p. 111.
[2] *Na Novykh Putyakh* (1923), iii, 17.
[3] Y. S. Rozenfeld, *Promyshlennaya Politika SSSR* (1926), p. 428.
[4] *Ibid.* pp. 230-237 : by the end of 1922 there were 18 syndicates, of which the textile, Ural mining, leather, sewing thread, tobacco and agricultural machinery syndicates were the most important (*Na Novykh Putyakh* (1923), i, 336-342) ; for a list of the syndicates, see *ibid.* iii, 36. In contrast with previous experience, it was consumer industries rather than the heavy industries which in the early NEP period lent themselves most readily and thoroughly to the formation of syndicates.

turned the movement in the opposite direction. The president of Vesenkha frankly described the syndicates as having been " created to defend in the first instance the commercial interests of the trusts ", and claimed that they had " fulfilled their function in particular cases and done away with competition, thus allowing prices to be raised for a whole range of products ".[1] By August 1922 the loss had so far been made good that industrial and agricultural prices stood in approximately the same relation to each other as in 1913. From that time, under the combined influence of the better organization of industry and an abundant harvest, prices once more began to move apart, but in the opposite sense, i.e. in favour of industrial and against agricultural products. The stresses set up by this fresh divergence were to become familiar in Soviet history as the " scissors crisis " of 1923.

The second adverse influence of NEP in the industrial field was the encouragement given by the market to light consumer industries at the expense of heavy industry ; and this, though less immediately disconcerting, carried graver long-term implications. The effect of NEP had been not only to expand those forms of small-scale or individual industrial production which remained in private hands and stood nearest to the petty-bourgeois economy of the peasant and furthest from the large-scale industry of the factories, but also, within the domain of large-scale industry, to stimulate those light industries whose products were immediately consumed at the expense of the heavy industries which were the traditional stronghold of the industrial proletariat and the ultimate key to the industrialization of the country and to socialist reconstruction. Before the end of 1922 a note of alarm about the future of heavy industry was being sounded on all sides. The fifth All-Russian Congress of Trade Unions in September 1922, while noting a revival in " a number of branches of production that rely on a free commodity market ", recorded that " the basic branches

---

[1] *Desyatyi Vserossiiskii S"ezd Sovetov* (1923), p. 42. A few months later, at the twelfth party congress, Bogdanov offered a more cautious version of the function of the syndicates, which may have been an attempt to qualify his previous frankness ; according to this version " the syndicates and trusts have now begun to cut down their overhead expenses, and the watchword of a reduction of costs is the fundamental watchword of our syndicates, which act in this sense on the trusts, compelling them to take account of market requirements " (*Dvenadtsatyi S"ezd Rossiiskoi Kommunisticheskoi Partii (Bol'shevikov)* (1923), p. 332).

of industry which by themselves determine the course of development of the national economy as a whole " — transport, mining, and the metallurgical, machine-building and electrical industries were named — " continue to experience a most severe crisis ", and proclaimed " the restoration of large-scale industry and transport as the immediate task of the republic ".[1] Two months later Lenin, devoting his speech at the fourth congress of Comintern to a defence of NEP, drew the same contrast between the " general revival " of light industry and the " very difficult position " of heavy industry, and pointed the moral :

> Russia cannot be saved only by a good harvest in a peasant economy — that is not enough — or only by the good condition of light industry which supplies articles of consumption to the peasantry — that also is not enough; *heavy* industry is also indispensable. . . .
> Heavy industry needs state subsidies. Unless we find them we are lost as a civilized state — let alone, as a socialist state.[2]

Lenin's last public utterance on economic affairs had put in the simplest and most unequivocal terms the fundamental problem created by the first two years of NEP.

The implications of these anxieties were too uncomfortable and too far-reaching to be readily accepted. In the autumn of 1922 the malaise of heavy industry expressed itself in a series of complaints against the niggardly credit policy of the State Bank. Bogdanov, the president of Vesenkha, in an attack on Narkomfin in VTsIK alleged that the mines of the Donetz basin were so starved of credits that they had been compelled to dismiss miners in default of cash to pay their wages ; [3] and the shortage of credit was a main theme of his report on industry to the tenth All-Russian Congress of Soviets in December.[4] Official spokesmen at the congress still professed a rather easy optimism. Kamenev firmly declared that " the time for political disputes on matters

---

[1] *Stenograficheskii Otchet Pyatogo Vserossiiskogo S"ezda Professional'nykh Soyuzov* (1922), pp. 507-509 : Tomsky, who made the principal speech at the congress, quoted Lenin as saying that " without heavy industry there can be no construction and therefore no socialism, not even bad socialism " (*ibid.* p. 114).

[2] Lenin, *Sochineniya*, xxvii, 348-349.

[3] *IV Sessiya Vserossiiskogo Tsentral'nogo Ispolnitel'nogo Komiteta IX Sozyva*, No. 5 (October 29, 1922), p. 5.

[4] *Desyatyi Vserossiiskii S"ezd Sovetov* (1923), pp. 36, 40.

of principle is over " and that " the question of the new economic policy has ceased to be a question of principle, has ceased to be contentious, has ceased to require explanation " ; and, though he admitted a little later that " NEP struggles against state industry ", he was confident that the Soviet power was strong enough to keep NEP well in hand.[1] Sokolnikov, the People's Commissar for Finance, reiterated an unwavering faith in *khozraschet*. Industry could no longer be carried on the budget ; the state could no longer be responsible for paying the wages of industrial workers or for providing them with rations ; the relation of the state to industry could only be that of a customer paying the full price for what it bought. Thus a complete divorce had been effected between the state and industry which, " whether it sells on the market or to the state, must sell on conditions which permit it not only to produce, but to replace its capital ". Sokolnikov even developed the argument that, since industry depended on the purchasing power of the peasant, the best way of supporting industry was to support the peasant.[2] Larin opposed Sokolnikov in the name of heavy industry, and another delegate called industry " the step-child of Narkomfin ".[3] But no relief was possible under the current interpretation of NEP. In restoring a market economy, NEP had restored the interdependence of the various elements of the economy on the familiar lines of the capitalist order. Direct state intervention to support heavy industry was contrary to the new principles. The controversies which were to determine the fate of industry and the course of industrial production were to be fought out in the fields of commercial and financial policy.

(c) *Labour and the Trade Unions*

The effects of NEP in labour policy, like its implications for industry as a whole, were not at once revealed, but gradually became apparent through the summer and autumn of 1921, and finally took shape in the spring of 1922. Under war communism labour, like other factors of production, had been treated as an obligatory state service, the rendering and rewarding of which

---

[1] *Ibid.* pp. 17-18, 29.   [2] *Ibid.* pp. 101-102, 110-111.
[3] *Ibid.* pp. 121, 136.

were not governed by commercial considerations. This attitude had to be radically revised under a system where some industrial enterprises employing labour were once more under private owner-ship and management, and those which remained in state owner-ship and control were enjoined to conduct their business on commercial principles. If the goods produced either by private or by state-owned industry were to be treated as market com-modities, the logical conclusion was that labour-power was also once more a market commodity. The return to a free market under NEP meant also the return to a free labour market; and, though this conclusion was not immediately drawn, it seemed to underlie the changed attitude towards labour.

The bulwark of war communism which fell most quickly was the compulsory mobilization of labour. The reaction against this had set in at the end of the civil war with the demobilization of the armies, and already found expression in the trade union resolution of the tenth party congress in March 1921.[1] It had arisen inde-pendently of the main considerations leading to the adoption of NEP, though it was an important part of the general *malaise* that had made the change of front necessary. The first decree after the congress abolished Glavkomtrud and its local organs, trans-ferring its functions to Narkomtrud; but this measure, while it dismantled the machinery of compulsion, kept the compulsory powers in being and had in fact been prepared before the congress.[2] A few days later an elaborate decree appeared regulating the functions of the " comradely courts of discipline ".[3] On April 6, 1921, a further decree removed the main restrictions on the movement of workers from one job to another, thus paving the way for the return to a labour market.[4] But this negative measure took effect slowly, and seems at first to have had no widespread effect on conditions of employment in state enterprises. Even the labour armies, though now transferred to Narkomtrud,[5] were not dissolved for some time. In June 1921, labour service was prescribed for the beet harvest in the event of sufficient voluntary labour not being available.[6] In July 1921 a detailed decree regu-

---

[1] See p. 226 above. [2] *Sobranie Uzakonenii, 1921*, No. 30, art. 164.
[3] *Ibid.* No. 23-24, art. 142 ; for the courts, see p. 211, note 6 above.
[4] *Ibid.* No. 36, art. 188. [5] *Ibid.* No. 27, art. 155.
[6] *Ibid.* No. 55, art. 337.

lated the calling up of peasants for forestry work.[1]   The turning point came with a decree of November 3, 1921, which strictly limited the categories of persons liable to be called up for labour service (these were now confined to persons not employed in any state organ, institution or enterprise) and the purposes for which such service would be employed (these were restricted to major natural emergencies).[2]   Even then a further decree of February 9, 1922, was required before the ghost of labour conscription as practised under war communism was finally laid, and the procedures of hiring and dismissal substituted as the normal methods of obtaining workers and of moving them from place to place.[3]

A more difficult issue was that of the remuneration of labour. Under war communism, where labour was a state service, wage-payments could be regarded in either of two ways : they were a necessary outlay from public funds to keep the worker fit and efficient (like the rations of a soldier), or they were a social right of the worker balancing his social obligation to work for the community (" he that does not work, neither shall he eat "), but not specifically linked with the particular work on which he was employed.   Both these conceptions fitted in with the growing practice of wage-payments in kind — a practice dictated by the collapse of the currency rather than by theoretical considerations, and not readily to be abandoned.   When the fourth All-Russian Congress of Trade Unions met in May 1921, Shmidt still assumed that " the workers cannot be compelled to part with the idea of guaranteed supplies to which the working class has grown accustomed ".   The congress by a large majority adopted a resolution arguing that the coming of NEP had made a policy of support for heavy industry all the more imperative, and that this required a further " replacement of the monetary form of supplying the needs of the working class by supplies from the state in kind ".[4]   Moreover, this form of wage-payments, which amounted in the last days of

---

[1] *Ibid.* No. 55, art. 343.

[2] *Ibid.* No. 74, art. 607. The initiative, according to Shmidt (*Stenograficheskii Otchet Pyatogo Vserossiiskogo S"ezda Professional'nykh Soyuzov* (1922), p. 83), came from Narkomtrud ; the decision of principle was taken by VTsIK on a report from Narkomtrud (*Sobranie Uzakonenii, 1921*, No. 72, art. 591).

[3] *Sobranie Uzakonenii, 1922*, No. 17, art. 179.

[4] *Chetvertyi Vserossiiskii S"ezd Professional'nykh Soyuzov* (1921), i (Plenumy), 116, 134.

war communism to a system of free rations, also fitted in with the broad concept of equality in distribution as an ideal to be aimed at ; the trade union resolution of the tenth party congress still rather surprisingly paid tribute to the continued strength of egalitarian sentiment by observing that, while " for a variety of reasons differences in wages corresponding to qualifications must be temporarily maintained, wages policy none the less must be built up on the greatest possible equality between wage rates ".[1] The trade union congress of May 1921, while maintaining its formal recommendation of bonuses in kind, was once more obliged to record the impracticability of any such system in face of the chronic shortage of supplies.[2]

It was some time before the introduction of NEP to industry produced its logical results. The application of *khozraschet* required the return to a monetary economy and was incompatible with any conception of wages as a system of free rationing or as a social service rendered by the state to the citizen. The labour philosophy of war communism was obsolete. The party conference of May 1921 propounded the principle of appealing to " the interest of the worker in production " and insisted that " the calculation of the part of the wages paid in kind should correspond to the monetary prices of the products ".[3] But the carrying out of this difficult change was delayed for some months. A decree of September 10, 1921, broke new ground by describing the wage system as " a fundamental factor in the development of industry ". Wages were now primarily a matter of the relation between the worker and the undertaking in which he worked. The decree demanded " the removal from the undertaking of everything which is not connected with production and has the character of social maintenance " : this was henceforth to be the affair of the state in its capacity as a public authority. It was emphasized that this change would permit the reward of different forms of labour according to their value. " Any thought of egalitarianism must be excluded." Wages were linked to productivity ; engineers and skilled workers must no longer be employed on unskilled tasks because the wage system recognized no differentiation.[4]

[1] *VKP(B) v Rezolyutsiyakh* (1941), i, 376.
[2] *Chetvertyi Vserossiiskii S'ezd Professional'nykh Soyuzov* (1921), i, 30.
[3] *VKP(B) v Rezolyutsiyakh* (1941), i, 410.
[4] *Sobranie Uzakonenii, 1921*, No. 67, art. 513.

After November 1921 the distribution of rations gratis or at nominal prices was replaced by the distribution of food to workers, calculated at market prices, in part payment of wages.[1] This continued for more than a year longer.[2] Thus, from the autumn of 1921, when the wage system was being step by step re-established and when surplus labour was being dismissed under the compelling discipline of *khozraschet*, the hiring of labour by voluntary contract between worker or trade union on the one side and employer on the other came to be the recognized typical form of employment, the only survival of the old system being the fixing by the state of an obligatory minimum wage. With the growth of the industrial trusts in the autumn of 1921[3] came the return to collective labour agreements concluded by the trade union on behalf of its members. The first important collective labour contract of the NEP period was concluded between Severoles, the first large state trust, and the union of timber-workers in November 1921.[4]

The change from payments in kind to a monetary wage system was too unpopular to be introduced except by slow stages. The worker, unconcerned with theory, was alive to the consequences of receiving, in the place of his guaranteed ration, payment in a currency of uncertain and constantly declining purchasing-power. The release from the hardships of compulsory labour mobilization which might have seemed a *quid pro quo* for this material loss[5] proved largely illusory; for this crude form of labour discipline was quickly replaced by the old " economic whip " of capitalism. The end of the civil war and the introduction of NEP inaugurated

[1] *Ibid.* No. 76, art. 617.

[2] It was still current in September 1922, and was incorrectly referred to at the fifth trade union congress as " the old rationing system " (*Stenograficheskii Otchet Pyatogo Vserossiiskogo S"ezda Professional'nykh Soyuzov* (1922), p. 97). A table in *Na Novykh Putyakh* (1923) iii, 108 shows that the money element in wage payment which fell as low as 6 per cent in 1921 had risen only to 32 per cent in the first quarter of 1922.

[3] See p. 306 above.

[4] *Stenograficheskii Otchet Pyatogo Vserossiiskogo S"ezda Professional'nykh Soyuzov* (1922), p. 47.

[5] The relation was not purely theoretical : the promise of supplies in kind was the inducement which under war communism made compulsory direction of labour tolerable and even palatable. As late as December 1921 a speaker at the ninth All-Russian Congress of Soviets remarked that he had taken part in two mobilizations of labour for the Donetz coal-mines but would not care to attempt a third " since we have no supplies " (*Devyatyi Vserossiiskii S"ezd Sovetov* (1922), p. 86).

a period of serious and widespread unemployment, due to drastic dismissals of workers both by public services and by industrial enterprises reorganizing themselves in response to the dictates of *khozraschet*. It was a sign of the times when, in the autumn of 1921, a decree was issued bringing up to date the half-forgotten legislation of 1918 on unemployment insurance, and provision was made in a further decree to pay half a month's salary by way of compensation to workers dismissed from state enterprises and institutions " through no fault of their own ".[1] The process of dismissing superfluous staffs proceeded at a cumulative rate. The number of railway workers was reduced from 1,240,000 in the summer of 1921 to 720,000 in the summer of 1922 ;[2] the number of workers and employees per 1000 spindles in a leading textile factory was reduced from 30 in 1920–1921 to 14 a year later (compared with 10·5 before 1914).[3] In the first half of 1918, unemployed industrial workers had flowed back to the country and were easily absorbed, so that unemployment merely took the form of a decline in the members of the proletariat. In 1921 famine had overtaken the countryside, and surplus industrial workers congregated in the cities, creating for the first time an unemployment problem of the kind familiar in western industrial countries. The creation in this way of the " reserve army of labour " of classical economics set up pressures sufficiently strong to direct labour to the points where it was required, and made further legal regulation superfluous. Work as a legal obligation (which had been one of the central conceptions of the Declaration of Rights of the Toiling and Exploited People and of the constitution of the RSFSR) was succeeded by work as an economic necessity, fear of legal penalties replaced as a sanction by fear of hunger. When the decree of February 9, 1922, finally substituted " hiring and firing " for the compulsory mobilization of labour,[4] it was abandoning an already obsolete weapon. The eleventh party congress of March 1922 even heard from Shlyapnikov the complaint, long familiar in capitalist countries, of workers being put out of work at home owing to imports from abroad.[5] In less

[1] *Sobranie Uzakonenii, 1921*, No. 68, art. 536 ; No. 77, art. 646.
[2] S. G. Strumilin, *Na Khozyaistvennom Fronte* (1925), p. 86.
[3] *Na Novykh Putyakh* (1923), iii, 14.
[4] See p. 319 above.   [5] *Odinnadtsatyi S"ezd RKP(B)* (1936), p. 111.

than a year NEP had reproduced the characteristic essentials of a capitalist economy.[1]

The status of the trade unions was logically affected in two ways by the abandonment of war communism and compulsory labour service. In the new conditions of licensed private enterprise and *khozraschet* in public concerns, the duty of trade unions to protect the interest of worker against employer seemed unequivocal, and the movement to incorporate the unions in the state lost its most plausible justification. When the fourth All-Russian Congress of Trade Unions met in May 1921, the first of these issues was not yet ripe for discussion. The organization of industry under NEP had scarcely begun ; and the resolution of the congress was vitiated by the assumption, which subsequent developments did not justify, of a sharp distinction between the attitude of the trade unions towards state-owned industries and towards those reverting to private management.[2] The second issue — the relation of the unions to the state — had been closed for party members by the decision of the tenth party congress two months earlier. But this decision automatically gave new significance to an old, but hitherto subsidiary, issue — the relation of the party to the unions. The independence of the unions from the state was a logical consequence of NEP. But this made it all the more essential to leave no doubt about the control of the unions by the party. This had been firmly, if cautiously, asserted by the resolution of the party congress :

> The Russian Communist Party, through its central and local organizations, as before unconditionally directs the whole ideological side of the work of the trade unions. . . . The choice of the leading personnel of the trade union movement

---

[1] Unemployment figures were 150,000 for October 1921, 175,000 for January 1922, 625,000 for January 1923 and 1,240,000 for January 1924 (Y. Gindin, *Regulïrovanie Rynka i Bor'ba s Bezrabotitsei* (1928), pp. 13, 18) ; unemployment was worse in Moscow than in the provinces, and worst of all in Petrograd (*Stenografícheskii Otchet Pyatogo Vserossiiskogo S"ezda Professional'-nykh Soyuzov* (1922), p. 101). By the spring of 1924, owing to the break-down of the finances of social insurance, only from 15 to 20 per cent of the unemployed were " in regular receipt of benefit " (*Report of the British Labour Delegation* (1924), p. 154).

[2] *Chetvertyi Vserossiiskii S"ezd Professional'nykh Soyuzov* (1921), i (Plenumy), 66-67.

must, of course, take place under the directing control of the party. But party organization should be particularly careful to apply normal methods of proletarian democracy in the trade unions, where most of all the choice of leaders should be made by the organized masses themselves.[1]

The fourth All-Russian Congress of Trade Unions was convened for May 17, 1921 ; and the usual theses " On the Rôle and Tasks of the Unions " had been prepared by the central committee of the party for consideration and adoption by the congress. These theses did not, however, repeat the emphasis on the use of "normal methods of proletarian democracy in the trade unions " which had appeared in the resolution of the party congress ; and when they were submitted, a few hours before the congress met, to the Bolshevik fraction, Ryazanov proposed an amendment recalling the terms of this resolution. Tomsky, taken aback by the amendment or not regarding it as important, did not resist it with sufficient vigour, and it was carried by a large majority of the fraction. The congress was duly opened the same evening with a formal speech from Tomsky. But, when the central committee discovered what had taken place, a severe reprimand was administered to Tomsky for his failure to carry the theses through the fraction, and he was suspended from further participation in the congress. The regular report on the work of the All-Russian Central Council of Trade Unions since the previous congress was made by Shmidt ; and the theses " On the Rôle and Tasks of the Unions ", restored to their original form after a further meeting of the fraction attended by Lenin in person, were presented by Lozovsky.[2] Neither Tomsky nor Rudzutak, who was made to share the responsibility for his mistake, was elected to the presidium of the congress at the opening of the second session ; and at the elections for the central council which took place at the end of the congress, while Rudzutak was re-elected a full member of the council, Tomsky

[1] *VKP(B) v Rezolyutsiyakh* (1941), i, 372-373.

[2] The main source for this episode is the report of the special commission set up by the party central committee under the presidency of Stalin to investigate Tomsky's lapse (*Izvestiya Tsentral'nogo Komiteta Rossiiskoi Kommunisticheskoi Partii (Bol'shevikov)*, No. 32, August 6, 1921, pp. 2-3) ; Ryazanov referred to his share in the matter at the eleventh party congress in an unsuccessful appeal against the decision of the central committee excluding him from further participation in trade union work (*Odinnadtsatyi S"ezd RKP(B)* (1936), pp. 277-279).

was relegated to the status of a candidate.[1]   Within a few weeks Tomsky and Rudzutak found themselves appointed members of a special commission to proceed to Tashkent to supervise the affairs of the newly formed Turkestan SSSR.[2]

One surprising sequel of these changes was the reinstatement of Andreev, who had been a supporter of Trotsky's platform at the tenth party congress and had not been re-elected to the central committee.   Andreev was now chosen to make the official report " On the Question of Organization ", which turned out to be the most controversial business of the fourth trade union congress. Now that the independence of the trade unions had become a recognized part of NEP, it was necessary not only that the party should be in full control of the central trade union organization, but that the central organization should be able to control individual unions.   This purpose was subtly achieved by Andreev's resolution.   Under cover of a necessary measure of decentralization in trade union organization precisely the opposite result was achieved.   Under the guise of a measure of devolution local inter-union organs which were directly dependent on the All-Russian Central Council of Trade Unions were to have authority over the local organs of particular unions : the resolution, taking up an idea already launched at the third congress, even looked forward to the day when the unions and their organs would be combined into " a single union with industrial sections ".   These proposals were bitterly contested.   One delegate said that the question at stake was " whether the industrial unions should continue to exist " ; and another declared that the result of the resolution would be to " set up a trade union commissariat with local sections ".   In a congress where there was only a tiny handful of non-Bolshevik delegates, an amendment of substance to Andreev's resolution none the less secured 453 votes against 593.[3]

---

[1] *Chetvertyi Vserossiiskii S"ezd Professional'nykh Soyuzov* (1921), i (Plenumy), 18, 185.   [2] See Vol. 1, p. 338.
[3] *Chetvertyi Vserossiiskii S"ezd Professional'nykh Soyuzov* (1921), i (Plenumy), 153-162, ii (Sektsii), 202 ; since members' dues had generally ceased to be collected under war communism with its system of wage payments in kind, and the trade unions subsisted mainly on state subsidies paid through the central council, the weapons of authority in the hands of the council were admittedly strong (*Stenograficheskii Otchet Pyatogo Vserossiiskogo S"ezda Professional'nykh Soyuzov* (1922), pp. 44-45).

The majority, though relatively narrow, was decisive. The control of the party over the All-Russian Central Council of Trade Unions, as over the organs of the Soviet state, was absolute. Once the control of the central council over the unions was firmly established — a process in which the resolution of the fourth trade union congress was an outstanding landmark — the fusion of party, state and unions in a single complex of power was well advanced. The issue of the " statization " of the trade unions was dead. But every fresh step in economic policy helped to deprive the trade unions of a little more of the importance and independence which they had formerly enjoyed. Under war communism they had at least been indispensable and partially autonomous organs of state power. Under NEP they could no longer occupy this position ; and, since it was necessary to curb any potential tendency under the new conditions to pit themselves against the authority of the state, the precaution was taken to tighten the already strict control of the party over the trade union apparatus. After the fourth trade union congress, Andreev succeeded Tomsky as president of the central council.

Towards the end of 1921, as the industrial aspects of NEP gradually unfolded themselves, symptoms of restiveness reappeared in the trade unions. About this time Tomsky and Rudzutak were recalled from Turkestan and an agreement effected between them and Andreev, apparently not without the intervention of the highest party authorities. On December 28, 1921, the central committee of the party listened to reports on the rôle of the trade unions presented by Rudzutak, Andreev and others.[1] On January 12, 1922, the Politburo adopted a detailed resolution drafted by Lenin on the basis of the theses submitted by Rudzutak and Andreev ; and this was published five days later in *Pravda*. The resolution diagnosed " a series of contradictions between different tasks of the trade unions ". These contradictions were " not accidental and would not be removed for several decades " — so long, indeed, as " remnants of capitalism and of small-scale production " persisted. Thus there was contradiction between the usual trade union methods of persuasion and education and the occasional acts of compulsion to which, as " sharers of state power ", the unions were committed ; between " the defence of

[1] Lenin, *Sochineniya*, xxvii, 515, note 56.

the interests of the toiling masses " and the " pressure " which they had to exercise as " sharers of state power and builders of the national economy as a whole " ; between the rigours of class warfare and the measures of conciliation proper to trade unions. These contradictions reflected the contradictions of the period of transition to socialism. But the practical paragraphs of the resolution were more significant. Since the application of *khozraschet* to state enterprises inevitably led to " an opposition in the consciousness of the masses between the administrations of these enterprises and the workers employed in them ", Soviet trade unions under NEP performed a function, and enjoyed a status, in some respects analogous to those of their prototypes under capitalism. The obligation rested on them " unconditionally " to protect the interests of the workers. On the other hand, membership of the trade unions must be voluntary (though the state would " encourage the unionization of the workers, both legally and materially ") ; and the unions must not interfere in factory administration. Both these points were concessions to what might be called an out-and-out capitalist view of trade unions. Even strikes in socialized enterprises — and *a fortiori* in private enterprises — were not prohibited, though the trade unions were to make it clear to the workers that " strike action in a state with a proletarian government can be explained and justified only by bureaucratic perversions in that state and by survivals of capitalism ". The normal way to settle disputes was by negotiation between the trade union and the economic administration concerned, and the establishment of conciliation commissions was recommended for this purpose.[1]

The resolution of the Politburo was, of course, mandatory to the overwhelmingly Bolshevik membership of the All-Russian Central Council of Trade Unions ; and in February 1922 the council met to give effect to it. This occasion was afterwards referred to by Tomsky at the fifth trade union congress as " our trade union revolution " and the beginning of a " new course in the trade union movement ".[2] It was in fact the first consistent

[1] *Ibid.* xxvii, 147-156.
[2] *Stenograficheskii Otchet Pyatogo Vserossiiskogo S"ezda Professional'nykh Soyuzov* (1922), p. 105 ; Andreev's speech at the same congress (*ibid.* pp. 40-54) significantly dwelt on the elements of continuity in the new course and on the

application of the principles of NEP in labour policy. The dependence of wages on productivity was confirmed, and the collective contract approved as the normal basis of employment; eight months later it was recorded that " the immense majority of workers in state or private enterprises come under the régime of collective contracts ". It was the business of the trade unions to secure for the workers wages as far as possible above the state minimum, and so bring home the benefits of unionization to thousands of unorganized workers in small, predominantly rural, industries. The admissibility of strikes was cautiously reaffirmed, and arrangements made to set up the proposed conciliation commissions. Membership of the trade unions was to become voluntary and individual; this was a corollary of the withdrawal of the state subsidies of the period of war communism, the unions being now once more dependent on members' dues.[1] A month later the eleventh party congress formally adopted the resolution of the Politburo, and, by way of making party control secure, laid it down in a further resolution that only party members of several years' standing could be elected to leading posts in the trade union organization, the length of qualification required being graded to the importance of the post.[2] The fate of the trade unions was an excellent illustration of the way in which NEP, by conceding a measure of economic freedom, provoked a strengthening of direct political control by the party over individuals or organs which might be tempted to abuse this conditional freedom. A month after the party congress the withdrawal of state functions from the trade unions, which was implicit in NEP and in the party resolution, was carried a step further by a decree transferring the adminis-

extent to which the changes had been anticipated in the latter part of 1921, i.e. while Andreev was still responsible for the policy of the central council.

[1] *Stenograficheskii Otchet Pyatogo Vserossiiskogo S"ezda Professional'nykh Soyuzov* (1922), pp. 48, 88-89, 109. It was admitted that the introduction of voluntary membership had caused " hesitations " among the leaders (*ibid.* p. 34); but these proved groundless. Indirect pressure and the system of the deduction of dues from wages were sufficient to keep the workers in the unions. The fall in trade union membership from 8,400,000 in July 1921 to 6,700,000 in January 1922 and 5,800,000 in April 1922 (two months after the introduction of the voluntary rule) was easily explained by the growth of unemployment. These figures are, however, subject to the same qualification as earlier ones (see p. 205 above).

[2] *VKP(B) v Rezolyutsiyakh* (1941), i, 424.

tration of social insurance against sickness and unemployment from the trade unions to Narkomtrud.[1]

The fifth All-Russian Congress of Trade Unions, which met in September 1922, was marked by the complete public reinstatement of Tomsky. Andreev made the report on the work of the central council since the previous congress. But Tomsky delivered the main speech of the congress under the title " Results of the New Trade Union Policy and Current Tasks of the Trade Union Movement "; and Tomsky and Rudzutak headed the list of those elected by the congress to the central council.[2] The development of NEP was now reaching its peak, and little was required but to repeat and underline what had been said by the Politburo in January, by the central council of the unions in February, and by the party congress in March. Only on two points was it thought prudent to sound a note of caution. For all their insistence on securing the best terms for the workers, the trade unions could not, in the words of the resolution proposed by Tomsky, " abandon the establishment of a guaranteed level of production ", and must be constantly concerned to raise the productivity of labour. The other difficult issue was that of strikes. According to Andreev, 102 strikes involving 43,000 workers had occurred in the past year : the number was trivial in comparison with what occurred in capitalist countries, but must be reduced. The resolution of the congress declared that every potential strike must be " treated as a strictly individual case in relation to the significance of the sector of the economy concerned and the dependence on it of the whole economic life "; Tomsky specifically said that a strike of railway workers, for example, would be intolerable " from the point of view of the general tasks of the working class ". The resolution went on to point out that it was the duty of the unions to undertake the " speedy liquidation " of any strike which broke out " spontaneously or against the wish of the organs of the unions ".[3]

[1] *Sobranie Uzakonenii, 1922*, No. 29, art. 338 ; by a decree of November 15, 1921 (*Sobranie Uzakonenii, 1921*, No. 76, art. 627), provision had been made for cash contributions for these services, which thus became for the first time insurance services properly so called.
[2] *Stenograficheskii Otchet Pyatogo Vserossiiskogo S"ezda Professional'nykh Soyuzov* (1922), pp. 511-512.
[3] *Ibid.* pp. 51, 109, 529-530.

While the congress was in session discussions were already proceeding on the drafting of a new state labour code which was to replace the outmoded labour code of 1918 [1] and give effect to the principles established by NEP. Its character was explained by Shmidt who, as People's Commissar for Labour, piloted it through VTsIK at the end of October 1922. The code of 1918 had been " constructed mainly on the basis of universal labour service "; the code of 1922 was based, in accordance with the spirit of NEP, on voluntary agreement. In 1918 the state had sought to fix and limit wages and conditions of employment; now the function of the state was merely to fix a minimum wage which could be, and normally was, exceeded, and to insist on certain minimum conditions (the eight-hour day, paid holidays, restrictions on juvenile labour, etc.). The collective contract concluded by the trade union became the usual, though not an obligatory, form of engagement. Engagement must in principle pass through the labour exchanges, though fairly wide exceptions to this rule were admitted for responsible posts requiring specialist or " political " qualifications. The trade unions retained a monopoly of the protection of labour and of the interests of the workers; elections of factory committees were to be conducted in accordance with the rules of the trade union concerned and had to be confirmed by it. Tomsky welcomed the code on behalf of the trade unions. " State regulation of wages ", he declared, " obviously does not work and is absolutely inappropriate to the conditions of the New Economic Policy "; and the trade unions were praised as " private organizations defending the interests of the workers ".

It was, however, also in the spirit of NEP that the rights of employers, public or private, should not be overlooked. The functions of the unions included the encouragement of production: the obligations placed on factory committees included " collaboration in the normal process of production in state undertakings, and participation through the intermediary of the appropriate trade unions in the regulation and organization of the national economy ". The failure of the worker to reach the required norm of production might be penalized by deductions from wages, which must not, however, fall below two-thirds of

[1] See pp. 198-199 above.

the standard rate. A long list of grounds on which the worker was liable to dismissal without compensation for failure to fulfil his contract was the one point in the code which aroused serious criticism in VTsIK : one speaker described it with some show of reason as " a trump card in the hands of private employers ".[1] Lenin, in his speech at the session of VTsIK which adopted the code — one of his last public utterances and his last appearance at VTsIK — was far from echoing the official optimism of Shmidt and Tomsky :

> We have to count with the fact that in comparison with all the states in which mad capitalist competition is now in progress, in which there are millions and tens of millions of unemployed, in which the capitalists are organizing with all their might powerful capitalist alliances, organizing a campaign against the working class — in comparison with them we are less cultured, our resources are less developed than any, we know less than any how to work. . . . But I think that, just because we do not conceal these things in fine phrases and official panegyrics, but confess them openly, just because we are conscious of this and are not afraid to say from the platform that more energy is required to correct this than in any other state, we shall succeed in catching up the other states with a rapidity of which they have not yet dreamed.[2]

Labour and trade union policy was an integral part of the whole problem of the efficiency of national economy. Whatever forms might seem to be dictated by the logic of NEP, to stimulate industrial production was still the basic need of the Soviet economy — a need all the more vital now that industry was placed at a disadvantage by the privileges which NEP had accorded to the agricultural sector ; and labour policy must somehow or other and at all costs help to meet this requirement.

(d) Trade and Distribution

The corollary of the substitution of taxation in kind for requisitioning as a method of extracting surplus agricultural products

---

[1] The code which came into force on November 15, 1922, is in *Sobranie Uzakonenii, 1922*, No. 70, art. 903. The debate in VTsIK is in *IV Sessiya Vserossiiskogo Tsentral'nogo Ispolnitel'nogo Komiteta IX Sozyva*, No. 1 (October 28, 1922), pp. 1-20 ; the adoption of the code is reported *ibid.* No. 7 (November 1, 1922), p. 6.   [2] Lenin, *Sochineniya*, xxvii, 318.

from the producers was a return to private trade. The reduced quantities of grain which would now be collected by the state made the maintenance of the system of state rationing impossible;[1] and the new incentive offered to the peasant was the right to sell the residue of his crop for whatever he could get on an open market instead of being compelled to sell to the state at a fixed price. This conclusion, however shocking at first sight to party stalwarts,[2] could not be evaded. Lenin, in commending the new policy to the party congress, admitted that "the slogan of free trade will be unavoidable", since it "answers to the economic conditions of the existence of small-scale production".[3] The decree in which the new policy was embodied was, however, couched in terms of barter rather than of trade properly so called :

> All stocks of foodstuffs, raw material and fodder remaining in the hands of the cultivators after they have discharged the tax are at their exclusive disposal, and can be used by them to supplement and strengthen their own economy, or to raise their personal consumption, or to exchange for the products of factory or rural industry or of agricultural production.
> Exchange is permitted within the limits of local circulation of goods both through cooperative organizations and in markets and bazaars.[4]

Moreover the granting of this incentive to the peasant implied a similar facility for the industrial worker who would be his partner in the exchange : the process of barter had to be extended to what the peasant wanted to buy as well as to what he had to sell. A fortnight later a further decree authorized the workers in industrial enterprises to set aside a "fund for exchange" out of output, the goods thus reserved being exchanged for the agricultural products of the peasant : workers' cooperatives were to be set up to organize

---

[1] The total of 34,000,000 persons said to be in receipt of rations before the introduction of NEP was reduced in the autumn of 1921 to 7,000,000 workers who received rations in part payment of wages (*Chetyre Goda Prodovol'stvennoi Politiki* (1922), pp. 61-62).

[2] "We did not learn to trade in our prisons", an old revolutionary bitterly remarked (Lenin, *Sochineniya*, xxvii, 74) ; Lenin, in condemning this "socialism of sentiment", was nevertheless careful to commend trade only as "an economically transitional form" (*ibid.* xxvii, 84).

[3] Lenin, *Sochineniya*, xxvi, 216-217.

[4] *Sobranie Uzakonenii, 1921*, No. 26, art. 147.

this exchange. Industrial workers were likewise allowed to set aside a portion of their output for their own personal consumption, allocating to this purpose a proportion of their working time or, alternatively, the full time of a certain proportion of the workers in a given enterprise.[1] In effect this was perhaps mainly an attempt to legalize and control an illicit traffic which had already assumed alarming dimensions under war communism.[2] It was described at the fourth All-Russian Congress of Trade Unions as an " experiment ";[3] and Lenin called it a " concession " prompted by psychological reasons :

> A privilege has been given to the peasants : it is necessary on the same ground to treat the workers in the same way.[4]

This exchange of goods was not only " the chief method of collecting foodstuffs ", but " the test of a correct mutual relation between industry and agriculture ".[5] It was, declared the party conference at the end of May 1921, " the fundamental lever of the new economic policy ".[6]

What was often spoken of as a return to private trading was in fact not so much an innovation as an official recognition and encouragement of what had never ceased to exist, the legalization of a common, though hitherto illegal, practice. The chief function of the government in the early stages of NEP was not merely to stimulate a desired volume of internal exchange, but to regulate and, if necessary, to dam its flow in such a way as to avert a threatened submersion of all socialist construction and a restored ascendancy of private capital throughout the whole economy. Lenin had recognized frankly that " freedom of trade means in a certain measure a development of capitalism ", but had added that " this capitalism will be under the control, under the supervision, of the state ".[7] The first attempts at regulation were,

---

[1] *Ibid.* No. 28, art. 156.   [2] See p. 243 above.
[3] *Chetvertyi Vserossiiskii S"ezd Professional'nykh Soyuzov* (1921), i (Plenumy), 117-118 ; the experiment was apparently limited at first to the period ending May 31, 1921, but continued sporadically until the full restoration of a monetary economy.
[4] Lenin, *Sochineniya*, xxvi, 392-393.
[5] *Sobranie Uzakonenii, 1921*, No. 44, art. 223 ; this detailed pronouncement by VTsIK on the principles of NEP was drafted by Lenin (*Sochineniya*, xxvi, 364-381).   [6] *VKP(B) v Rezolyutsiyakh* (1941), i, 397.
[7] Lenin, *Sochineniya*, xxvi, 307.

however, unsuccessful. What exactly had been intended by the permission given in the original NEP decree of March 21, 1921, to trade " within the limits of local circulation of goods ", is not clear. But, whatever the intention, it was quickly defeated. An attempt was made in a decree of Sovnarkom of March 28, 1921, on trade in grain, forage and potatoes to maintain the principle of regulation by provinces. But, since the decree cancelled all restrictions on transport, it acted in effect as a removal of local barriers.[1] Once the principle of private exchange had been admitted, the attempt to restrict it to local markets or to exchange in kind was bound to break down. A decree of May 24, 1921, accorded to individual citizens and the cooperatives the right of " exchange, purchase and sale " of agricultural products remaining after the payment of the tax in kind.[2]

By the autumn of 1921 Lenin frankly admitted defeat on this point :

It was intended throughout the state to exchange the products of industry in a more or less socialist manner for the products of agriculture and, through this exchange of goods, to restore large-scale industry as the only possible basis of a socialist organization. What was the result ? The result was—you now understand all this perfectly well in practice, and you can even see it in the whole of our press — that the exchange of goods broke loose ; it broke loose in the sense that it turned into buying and selling. And we are now obliged to confess it, if we do not want to pose as people who do not see their own defeat, if we are not afraid to look danger in the face. We must confess that our retreat turned out to be not enough, that it is indispensable for us to carry out a supplementary retreat, another step backwards, when we pass from state capitalism to the setting up of state regulation of buying and selling, of monetary circulation. Nothing came of the exchange of goods ; the private market turned out stronger than we ; and instead of exchange of goods we have got ordinary buying and selling, ordinary trade.

Be so good as to adapt yourselves to it, otherwise the element of buying and selling, of monetary circulation, will overwhelm you.[3]

---

[1] *Sobranie Uzakonenii, 1921*, No. 26, art. 149.   [2] *Ibid.* No. 40, art. 212.
[3] Lenin, *Sochineniya*, xxvii, 67-68 ; later Lenin compared the Soviet state under NEP to a machine which has got out of hand : " It is as if a man were sitting there to drive it, but the machine does not travel in the direction in which it is being driven " (*Ibid.* xxvii, 237).

The conference of communists of the Moscow province to which Lenin addressed this warning passed a resolution which declared it urgent, " starting from the existence of a market and taking account of its laws, to master it and, by means of systematic and carefully considered economic measures founded on an accurate appreciation of market processes, . . . to take control of the regulation of the market and of monetary circulation ".[1] Two months later the ninth All-Russian Congress of Soviets heard Lenin explain once more that trade was " the touchstone of our economic life ", and that the essence of the new economic policy was to learn — to learn from the private merchant who was clever enough to do for 100 per cent profit what no communist or trade unionist could do at all.[2] Kamenev repeated once more the plea of *force majeure* :

> Having, thanks to the tax in kind, created a market, having accorded the possibility of trading in grain, we have created an environment which will keep on changing. The market is not a logical phenomenon which can be fixed in its existing form. It is a phenomenon which develops and continually begets new and ever new phenomena.[3]

And the resolution of the congress, noting that the " formation of an internal market "and the" development of monetary exchange " were the characteristic features of the economic landscape, con-tained the first of those paradoxical panegyrics of free competition which became familiar in the NEP period :

> Now the struggle between communist and private manage-ment is transferred to the economic plane, to the market, where nationalized industry, concentrated in the hands of the workers' state, must, by applying itself to the conditions of the market and to methods of competition in it, win for itself the decisive mastery.[4]

The institutional organization of trade under NEP was three-fold ; trade was conducted by private traders, by cooperatives,

---

[1] Quoted *ibid.* xxvii, 430 : for the monetary reform advocated in the resolu-tion see p. 348 below.

[2] Lenin, *Sochineniya*, xxvii, 135-136.

[3] *Devyatyi Vserossiiskii S"ezd Sovetov* (1922), p. 60.

[4] *S"ezdy Sovetov RSFSR v Postanovleniyakh* (1939), pp. 222, 225-226.

and by state organs.   While all professedly competing against one
another on equal terms, a certain division of competence naturally
established itself.   The private trader was mainly active in retail
trade, though he also appeared, as time went on, in wholesale trade
as an agent of state trusts or other state organs.   State organs
confined their main commercial activities to wholesale trade,
though state retail shops were also set up.   The cooperatives
followed their old tradition in combining the functions of wholesale
and retail traders.

The encouragement of retail trading by private individuals was
a conspicuous reversal of previous policy.   A decree of July 1921
made it possible for any person over 16 to obtain a licence to carry
on trade in shops, public places, markets or bazaars in any product
or article other than goods manufactured from raw materials
supplied by the state : the aim of the restriction was presumably
to exclude the products of nationalized industries from private
trade.[1]   Here, too, the first result was to legalize and extend what
already existed rather than to create anything new.   Private
trading had never ceased to be carried on surreptitiously or in
semi-legal markets of which the Sukharevka in Moscow was
merely the most famous.   This petty private trading now came out
into the open.   The itinerant pedlar or the small huckster selling
his wares in more or less organized markets or bazaars was the
characteristic figure of private trade in the first year of NEP ; but,
far from being the creation of NEP, he was the heir of the " bagman " of war communism and scarcely distinguishable from him
except by the official recognition which he had now secured.
Once, however, private trade was officially tolerated and encouraged, this primitive pattern could not survive.   It was bound to be
driven out as soon as sufficient capital and sufficient enterprise had
been mustered to organize more developed and more efficient forms
of trade.   By the middle of 1922 this new process was already well
on the way ; and the State Universal Store (GUM), an emanation
of Vesenkha, with branches in all the principal cities, was soon
only the largest of a growing number of retail shops.   In 1922 two
famous Russian fairs were revived for the first time since 1917 —
the Irbit fair in Siberia in the spring, and the Nizhny Novgorod

---

[1] *Sobranie Uzakonenii, 1921*, No. 57, art. 356.

fair in the late summer.[1]   The vast mass of small retail trade remained almost entirely in private hands ; it was only in the larger enterprises that state organs obtained an important footing.[2]

The introduction of NEP had been designed to favour the cooperatives even more than the private trader ; for the organization of the cooperatives was at any rate founded on a collective principle which seemed less antipathetic to Bolshevik orthodoxy than competitive individualism.[3]   Lenin, in commending NEP to the tenth party congress in March 1921, briefly proposed to annul the resolution of the preceding congress which had insisted on the strict subordination of the cooperatives to Narkomprod : [4]   now that agricultural surpluses, after the collection of the tax in kind, were to be extracted from the peasant by processes of barter and trade, the consumers' cooperatives had an important part to play.

---

[1] For an account of the revival of the fairs see *Na Novykh Putyakh* (1923), i, 272-280 ; the revival came through decisions of STO, and state trade predominated.   According to a participant in the Nizhny Novgorod fair, turn-over reached 75 per cent of that of 1917 and 50 per cent of that of 1913 (*Stenograficheskii Otchet Pyatogo Vserossiiskogo S"ezda Professional'nykh Soyuzov* (1922), pp. 160-162).

[2] A detailed investigation on the basis of trading licences issued in 1921 and 1922 gives some interesting though not very precise information about the relative importance of the respective forms of trade.   Trading licences for 1921 were divided into three categories — licences for pedlars, for open markets and bazaars, and for "closed premises", i.e. shops ; in 1922 the third category was subdivided into three according to the size of the establishment concerned, making five categories in all.   The first category was in practice confined to private traders, the second to private traders and cooperatives.   The first category declined after 1921 as trade became more organized ; the second category always accounted for the largest number of licences.   But the important categories in respect of volume of trade, though not of the number of licences, were the third, fourth and fifth, where the three forms of trade competed against one another.   An estimate for 1922, based on statistics from three provincial cities only, gives 84 per cent of licences of all categories to private enterprises, 15 per cent to cooperatives and less than 1 per cent to state enterprises ; these figures do not distinguish between categories of licence.   In Moscow the corresponding figures for 1922 gave 95·1 per cent to private traders, 3·6 per cent to cooperatives and 1·3 per cent to state enterprises ; but in the fourth category 12·9 per cent of the licences went to state enterprises and in the fifth (and numerically smallest) 45·9 per cent (*Na Novykh Putyakh* (1923), i, 179-185).

[3] Lenin wrote at this time : " Freedom and rights for cooperatives in present conditions in Russia mean freedom and rights for capitalism. . . . But ' cooperative ' capitalism, as distinct from private commercial capitalism, is under Soviet power a species of state capitalism, and as such is beneficial and useful to us at present — of course, in a certain degree " (*Sochineniya*, xxvi, 336).

[4] *Ibid.* xxvi, 242-243 ; for the resolution of the ninth party congress, see p. 240 above.

A decree of April 7, 1921, restored to them a measure of the formal independence which they had lost two years earlier, subject only to the right of Narkomprod to direct the carrying out by them of their " obligatory state tasks " and of VTsIK to appoint members of the administration having equal rights with elected members.[1] The following month saw a series of agreements between government and cooperatives, including what was referred to as a " general treaty " with the consumers' cooperatives of May 17, 1921, under which Tsentrosoyuz became the sole agent of the government for the wholesale distribution of consumer goods throughout the country.[2] The conception prevailing in the first months of NEP emerged clearly from these arrangements. Food was to be extracted from the peasants by two levers — the tax in kind and exchange of goods. The first of these was to be operated directly by the Soviet authorities, the second by the cooperatives acting as agents for Narkomprod.

This conception failed to work. It failed partly because Narkomprod[3] was not in a position to furnish the promised supplies of consumer goods for purposes of exchange, so that recriminations quickly began between Narkomprod and Tsentrosoyuz, but mainly because, in the absence of a highly organized machinery, the whole clumsy process of an exchange of goods " broke loose ", in Lenin's phrase, and " turned into buying and selling ". The forces of NEP, overwhelming its creators and sweeping away the plan of an orderly state-marshalled system of exchange in kind, forced a reconsideration of the status and functions of the cooperatives; and this revision, a further tribute to the hold of cooperative institutions on the loyalty of the masses, was undertaken in a decree of Sovnarkom of

[1] *Sobranie Uzakonenii, 1921*, No. 26, art. 150.

[2] *Na Novykh Putyakh* (1923), i, 143; Lenin, *Sochineniya*, xxvi, 401-402 (referring to it as a " treaty "). The report on the cooperatives to the party conference of May 1921 was made by Khinchuk (see p. 240 above); the resolution of the conference described the cooperatives as a " fundamental apparatus for conducting the exchange of goods " (*VKP(B) v Rezolyutsiyakh* (1941), i, 397).

[3] With the gradual abandonment of rationing and of supplies in kind under NEP, Narkomprod lost the prestige and importance which it had enjoyed under war communism (*Dvenadtsatyi S"ezd Rossiiskoi Kommunisticheskoi Partii (Bol'shevikov)* (1923), p. 334); for its eventual disappearance, see p. 344 below.

October 26, 1921. All property belonging to the cooperatives which had been nationalized or municipalized was to be returned to them (this was an old grievance dating back to 1919); the right to buy and sell without the intervention of any government authority was recognized; Soviet industrial organs, including trusts, *glavki* and sections of Vesenkha, were instructed to offer their goods in the first instance to Tsentrosoyuz or to the appropriate local cooperative institution, and only in the event of refusal were free to offer them, on not more favourable terms, on the open market.[1] Simultaneously an instruction from the party central committee to all party members emphasized the new independent rôle assigned to the cooperatives under NEP and the obligation for communists to play an active part in this " in order to master these organizations ".[2]

This decree continued in theory to govern the status of consumers' cooperatives and the relations between Tsentrosoyuz and the Soviet Government throughout the ensuing period. In practice disputes and complaints were constant. Negotiations dragged on interminably with Vesenkha for the return of nationalized property claimed by the cooperatives; government departments and trusts (as well as the syndicates which began to be founded in April 1922) continually by-passed the cooperatives and preferred to sell to private traders. Nevertheless such figures as are available appear to show that in the first half of 1922 the cooperatives were still drawing more than three-quarters of their supplies from state organs, including the trusts.[3] Nor, however obstructive individual departments or institutions might be, could either party or government afford to dispense with the cooperatives. A party conference in August 1922 passed a long resolution on the attitude to be adopted to the cooperatives. It considered that the principle of obligatory membership ought not to " transform consumers' cooperatives merely into the technical apparatus for the exchange of goods and distribution by the state ". The intervention of

---

[1] *Sobranie Uzakonenii, 1921*, No. 72, art. 576.

[2] *Izvestiya Tsentral'nogo Komiteta Rossiiskoi Kommunisticheskoi Partii* (*Bol'shevikov*), No. 33, October 1921, pp. 33-34; this was the counterpart of the strengthening of party control over the trade unions (see pp. 323-326 above).

[3] Some of the complaints, as well as the statistics, are quoted in *Na Novykh Putyakh* (1923), i, 144-146, a source apparently biased in favour of the cooperatives.

private trade as the intermediary between state-controlled industry and the peasant was a " contradiction " ; the task of the cooperatives was " to drive private capital out of trade, and by this measure to forge a solid link between the peasant economy and socialist industry ".[1] This optimistic assessment of the rôle of the cooperatives was not realized. The relation between state and cooperatives remained uneasy and unstable. The Soviet Government, or some of its organs, were too mistrustful and jealous of the cooperatives to work whole-heartedly with them. In wholesale trade the cooperatives themselves often found it difficult to meet the private trader in open competition — even in competition for the favour of trusts and official selling organs. In retail trade their long tradition of popularity among consumers enabled them to retain their position. Lenin, in one of the very last articles written by him at the beginning of 1923, stressed the " exceptional importance " of the cooperatives under NEP.[2] At the twelfth party congress in April 1923 Khinchuk reported the existence of nearly 25,000 consumers' cooperative societies and 30,000 cooperative shops.[3]

The introduction of NEP created a vacuum in the organs of state, since it had not hitherto been admitted that the conduct or administration of internal trade was any part of the task of the Soviet Government. Foreign trade with capitalist countries stood in a class by itself and was managed by a special organization. The original People's Commissariat of Trade and Industry had never concerned itself with internal trade ; and the organs of Narkomprod and Vesenkha which controlled supplies to the population were organs not of trade, but of distribution. When NEP began, the idea — if it ever existed — that trade could be left exclusively to cooperatives and private individuals was quickly dissipated. A central trading section was set up in Vesenkha, which, in addition

---

[1] *VKP(B) v Rezolyutsiyakh* (1941), i, 460-463 ; the concluding part of the resolution, from which the second quotation in the text is taken, is omitted from this volume, and will be found in *Direktivy VKP(B) v Oblasti Khozyaistvennoi Politiki*, ed. M. Saveliev (1928), pp. 356-364.

[2] Lenin, *Sochineniya*, xxvii, 391.

[3] *Dvenadtsatyi S"ezd Rossiiskoi Kommunisticheskoi Partii (Bol'shevikov)* (1923), p. 328.

to its incursion into retail trade through GUM, had under its control wholesale " trading establishments " (*gostorgi* or simply *torgi*) attached to the provincial Sovnarkhozy. Narkomprod and several other commissariats also set up trading sections to deal in commodities with which they were concerned.[1] More important were the industrial trusts, which were the major producers of manufactured goods; these, having been instructed to act on commercial principles, sought to organize the sale of their products sometimes through the cooperatives and sometimes (in defiance of the assurances given to the cooperatives under the decree of October 26, 1921) through private traders. It had at first not been foreseen that state trading organs or state organs would purchase supplies required by them on the market. But, as the system of centralized supplies of raw materials and goods gradually broke down, permission was accorded to them to buy on the open market, first by way of exception, and later, by the decree of October 4, 1921, as a regular practice, though they were instructed to give preference to the cooperatives as suppliers.[2] But none of these institutions was well equipped either by tradition or by experience to embark on the complicated processes of trade. Once the policies of " exchange of goods " and supplies in kind receded into the background, and " buying and selling " began in earnest, an urgent need arose of men thoroughly at home in the habits, procedures and expedients of the market, men ready to find buyers and sellers at the right moment, to advise on prices, and in general to act as brokers and go-betweens for principals who were ill at ease in this unfamiliar world.

The gap was filled by the more ambitious and more successful grade of Nepmen, some of them once reputable — or not so reputable — business men emerging from the underworld where they had lived since the revolution, others newcomers to the scene who quickly adapted themselves to the new tricks of the trade. The strength of the Nepman was his success in making himself indispensable to state trading institutions and to the great industrial

[1] *Na Novykh Putyakh* (1923), i, 107-128, lists government institutions which set up trading sections during the first months of NEP; these included the People's Commissariats of Health and Education and the State Bank.

[2] *Sobranie Uzakonenii, 1921*, No. 68, art. 527; at the same time they were authorized to sub-contract with private contractors where necessary for the fulfilment of orders from state organs (*ibid.* No. 68, art. 529).

trusts. In the words of a semi-official account, " the characteristic trait of contemporary private wholesale trade lies in the powerful infiltration of private capital into state trading organs and in their mutual interpenetration ". The Nepmen travelled with mandates from state institutions and claimed and obtained privileged treatment everywhere; their profits were doubtless large enough to enable them to resort to direct and indirect forms of corruption. They found their way into the cooperatives, some of which apparently became mere façades for private trading concerns. Thus " private capital envelops the state organs from all sides, feeding on them and living at their expense ".[1] The comparatively harmless phenomenon, noted by a speaker at the ninth All-Russian Congress of Soviets in December 1921, of " the petty capitalism of speculators, bagmen and money-lenders which is now celebrating its resurrection in the form of café-chantants, delicatessen-shops and pastry-cooks "[2] soon developed into the picture of Moscow under NEP as a luxury city for private agents of the new state capitalism which was criticized by many foreign visitors during 1922 and 1923.[3] It was part of the price which had to be paid in following Lenin's injunction to " learn to trade ".

It was in the autumn of 1922 when the first phase of NEP was complete that the Soviet Government, simultaneously with its agrarian and labour codes,[4] decided to introduce a civil code. Lenin described it as an embodiment of " that policy which we have firmly established and in regard to which we can have no vacillations ", and an attempt " to preserve the boundary between what is legitimate satisfaction of the individual citizen under the present economic system of exchange and what represents an

[1] Na Novykh Putyakh (1923), i, 185-188 ; besides local reports, this account refers to the " very rich material on this question " in a volume issued by Rabkrin, Nasha Trestirovannaya Promyshlennost', which has not been available.

[2] Devyatyi Vserossiiskii S"ezd Sovetov (1922), p. 93.

[3] The Menshevik Dan, who knew Moscow and had a factual mind, noticed on emerging from prison in January 1922 that foodstuffs of all kinds were fairly plentiful at prices which only the new rich could afford ; that " speculators " were everywhere in evidence ; that the word barin was once more in common use by waiters, cab-drivers, etc. ; and that prostitutes had reappeared on the Tverskaya (F. Dan, Dva Goda Skitanii (Berlin, 1922), pp. 252-255). Krasin wrote to his wife from Moscow in September 1922 : " Moscow looks all right, in some parts as it was before the war " (Lyubov Krasin, Leonid Krasin : His Life and Work (n.d. [1929]), p. 202).

[4] See pp. 296-297, 330-331 above.

abuse of NEP ".[1]   The *rapporteur* who presented the code to VTsIK for enactment described its aim as being " to give guarantees that those conquests, those commanding heights, which it [i.e. the state] keeps for itself even under the concessions of the New Economic Policy, shall remain inviolable in the hands of the workers' and peasants' state, and at the same time to give the possibility for private initiative to develop within the limits permitted by the interests of the workers' and peasants' state ".[2] But, now that lapse of time had brought forgetfulness of the fearful crisis which necessitated the introduction of NEP, and some of its less agreeable implications had become notorious, complaints against it, though rarely articulate in high places, began to be widely heard.   A spokesman of Narkomfin in VTsIK referred indignantly to talk in country districts " that ' the centre has gone too far to the Right ', that there is no need to spare ' speculators ' and ' marauders ', that they are outside Soviet law ", whereas in fact these " speculators " were precisely the traders whom " NEP seeks to protect ".   The same delegate went on :

> The rumours current even in Moscow that the position of NEP is not secure have some foundation in the fact that nowadays, though we talk a lot about " revolutionary legality ", respect for the laws does not extend far enough.[3]

The civil code set the stamp on the new cult of legality, the main purpose of which was to defend and consolidate the achievements of NEP.

As has already been pointed out, the RSFSR had entered the NEP period without any official machinery for the conduct or regulation of internal trade.   The philosophy of NEP, while it encouraged state institutions to engage in trade, insisted that trade should be conducted on market principles without state interference; it was therefore as inimical as the practice of war communism had been, though for a different reason, to the creation of any supervisory organ.   Complete official detachment could not, indeed, be maintained.   Once the clumsy attempts to establish the exchange of goods by barter gave way everywhere to monetary transactions, the demand was bound to be heard for an

---

[1] Lenin, *Sochineniya*, xxvii, 319.
[2] *IV Sessiya Vserossiiskogo Tsentral'nogo Ispolnitel'nogo Komiteta IX Sozyva*, No. 3 (October 27, 1922), pp. 7-8.   [3] *Ibid.* No. 5 (October 29, 1922), p. 3

attempt to control prices. A price committee was set up by Narkomfin as early as August 5, 1921, to fix prices of all commodities dealt in by state organs or state enterprises.[1] But this proved a complete fiasco and prices moved everywhere in response to market conditions.[2] From the autumn of 1921 onwards the policy of Narkomfin was directed towards the re-establishment of a stable currency and a balanced budget, and was opposed to any form of interference with the free market economy of NEP.[3] Nor was any other department equipped to assume this rôle. An attempt was made to transform the central trading section of Vesenkha into an " administration for the regulation of trade ".[4] But this extension of the functions of an organ rightly regarded as representing the industrial sector of the economy was unlikely to be accepted by other organs concerned in trade policy. In May 1922 Sovnarkom created, and attached to STO, a commission for internal trade with powers to draft decrees on trade for confirmation by Sovnarkom or STO, and to make regulations on its own authority within the limits of existing decrees.[5] The powers of the commission do not, however, seem to have been very widely or effectively exercised. In spite of the warning given by the *razbazarovanie* crisis of the consequences of unregulated commerce, the development of internal trade, at any rate till the autumn of 1923, was governed almost exclusively by the competing forces of the market. It was not till May 1924 that the commission for internal trade was amalgamated with what was left of Narkomprod to form a People's Commissariat of Trade.[6]

[1] *Sobranie Uzakonenii, 1921*, No. 60, art. 406.

[2] An account of its failure is given in *Finansovaya Politika za Period s Dekabrya 1920 g. po Dekabr' 1921 g.: Otchet k IX Vserossiiskomu S"ezdu Sovetov* (1921), pp. 112-116.

[3] The objections of Narkomfin to price regulation, conceived on strictly orthodox financial lines, are recorded in *Na Novykh Putyakh* (1923), i, 47.

[4] *Ibid.* i, 386-387.

[5] *Sobranie Uzakonenii, 1922*, No. 34, art. 400.

[6] It was under NEP that foreign trade began for the first time to have some importance in the Soviet economy : the Anglo-Soviet trade agreement which was the token of its revival was signed on the day after the announcement of NEP by Lenin to the tenth party congress. The attempt to attract foreign capital by the offer of concessions, though inaugurated earlier (see p. 245 above), was frequently referred to as a feature of NEP, but led to no material results in this period. Both foreign trade and the offer of concessions were at this time significant primarily in relation to foreign policy, and the discussion of them is reserved for Part V.

(e) Finance

The New Economic Policy was launched without any thought of its financial implications. The original project of barter in local markets seemed to offer nothing incompatible with the movement towards a moneyless economy or with the long continued process of monetary inflation. Only Preobrazhensky, who had so often hymned the virtues of inflation, had some inkling of what would happen. His speech at the tenth party congress which adopted NEP was a mixture of penetrating common sense and far-fetched fantasy. He warned the congress that it was " impossible to trade with a ruble rate which fluctuates on the market not only in the course of days, but in the course of hours "; but the only concrete solution which he offered was a new currency based on silver. Neither his arguments, nor the sensible proposal with which he concluded for a committee to review the whole range of financial policy " in its application to the new economic conditions on which we are entering ", made any impression on the congress.[1] The lesson would be learned not from theory but from experience; and the moment was not yet ripe. It occurred to nobody to foresee a return to orthodox banking to finance industry, or to the orthodox fiscal policy of a balanced budget to be achieved through the drastic curtailment of government spending. These conclusions were all reached in a piecemeal and roundabout way from the initial premise that the peasant was to be at liberty to trade his surpluses of agricultural produce for the goods which he might require. The course of financial policy under NEP provides an excellent illustration of the necessary interrelation of parts in a single economic structure.

When the original conception of local barter broadened into buying and selling in a nation-wide market, monetary policy became an indispensable part of NEP. The return to capitalism — even to " state " capitalism — made the return to a money economy inevitable. Party prejudices were strong enough to make the initial moves slow and halting. On June 30, 1921, a decree of Sovnarkom, which expressed in its preamble the desire " to remove the limitations which hamper economic exchange and to promote a healthy monetary circulation by way of a development of deposits

---

[1] *Desyatyi S"ezd Rossiiskoi Kommunisticheskoi Partii* (1921), pp. 232-234.

and transfers ", abolished all limits on sums which might be held
by private persons or organizations. Deposits in the savings banks
of Narkomfin or of the cooperatives were not liable to confiscation
and must be paid out to holders on demand ; and no information
would be disclosed about them except to the holders or to the
judicial authorities.[1] This measure — a first step on the long road
back to financial orthodoxy — was evidently designed to rehabilitate money in popular esteem. But it thrust into the foreground
the question, awkwardly raised by Preobrazhensky at the congress,
how to create a stable currency which would inspire confidence and
perform the elementary functions of a medium of exchange. This
could plainly not be done so long as the printing press continued
to turn out an unlimited supply of rubles ; the printing press could
not be checked till the government could find some other way of
making both ends meet ; and to bring government expenditure
within the limits of any revenue it could conceivably raise was
unthinkable till the state relieved itself of the immense costs of
maintaining state industry and the workers engaged in it. The
need of a stable unit of account was still more urgent in an economy
whose nationalized industry had been instructed to conduct its
business on the principles of *khozraschet*. The decree of August 8,
1921, setting up the linen factories trust prescribed that the value
of the assets acquired should be taken into the accounts " at
1913–1914 prices " ;[2] a few days later a decree on the development
of large-scale industry stipulated that " stocks and raw materials
are valued approximately at the middle prices of the west European
(especially the London) market ".[3] But these surprising provisions
were to be read as distress signals rather than as considered solutions
of a problem.

All these questions forced themselves piecemeal in the summer
of 1921 on leaders who were still unwilling to draw financial conclusions from NEP, and isolated steps were taken in response to
particular emergencies and without any coherent plan. The
approach to the budgetary issue came from both sides. Under
war communism the very notion of a budget had been allowed to

[1] *Sobranie Uzakonenii*, *1921*, No. 52, art. 301.
[2] *Novaya Ekonomicheskaya Politika v Promyshlennosti : Sbornik Dekretov*
(1921), p. 94.
[3] *Sobranie Uzakonenii*, *1921*, No. 63, art. 462.

lapse. Budget figures had been drawn up for the second half of 1919 and for 1920, but had never received formal approval. The incorporation of the balance-sheet of industry in the state budget put an end to the conception of specifically governmental revenue and expenditure; and the draft decree of February 3, 1921, abolishing all monetary taxation [1] would, if it had ever come into effect, have been a logical part of the advance towards a natural economy. Now under NEP all this was reversed. The unloading of industry from the state budget started in July and August 1921, when the leasing of enterprises began and enterprises retained by the state were instructed to pass over to *khozraschet*. A tax on industry, comprising a licensing fee, varying with the number of workers employed, as well as a tax on turnover, was introduced in July 1921.[2] A few weeks later a decree of Sovnarkom laid down the sweeping principle that all goods or services supplied by the state or state organs must be paid for in cash.[3] Then, on August 21, 1921, Sovnarkom restored the principle of a state budget. It went through the formality of approving the almost meaningless figures of budgets for the second half of 1919 (28 milliards of rubles revenue, 164 milliards expenditure) and for 1920 (159 milliards revenue, 1215 milliards expenditure), and went on to issue instructions to departments to prepare their estimates for 1921 not later than October, for 1922 not later than March of that year, and for 1923 not later than December 31, 1922.[4] On the following day it took a first step towards restoring the financial autonomy of the local authorities — another measure designed to lighten the load on the central budget; it authorized the deduction of a percentage of the tax on industry to meet the financial

[1] See p. 260 above.
[2] *Sobranie Uzakonenii*, *1921*, No. 56, art. 354.
[3] *Ibid*. No. 59, art. 394. On July 9, a new railway tariff was introduced by a decree, the first clause of which proclaimed the principle of obligatory payment for transportation, though exceptions were still admitted in favour of state enterprise and cooperatives (*ibid*. No. 54, art. 327); the effect of the new tariff was to multiply existing charges by 20,000, raising them to about 40 per cent of pre-war charges in terms of pre-war rubles (*Pyat' Let Vlasti Sovetov* (1922), p. 401). In August 1921, a new tariff was published for postal telegraphic services (*Sobranie Uzakonenii*, *1921*, No. 56, art. 351). As from September 15, 1921, payment once more became obligatory for all public services and facilities, ranging from drainage to chimney-sweeping (*ibid*. No. 62, art. 445); the decree of January 27, 1921, on rents (see p. 260 above) was repealed.
[4] *Sbornik Dekretov i Rasporyazhenii po Finansam*, iv (1921), 120-121.

requirements of the provincial executive committees.[1] When, therefore, at the beginning of October 1921 VTsIK undertook the first systematic review of financial policy since the inception of NEP, much of the groundwork had been done. In a resolution of October 10 VTsIK instructed Narkomfin to take measures to " increase state revenues ", to carry out a policy of " restraint and the strictest economy in the expenditure of currency ", and to " develop the banking operations necessary to improve the national economy ", and decided to " abolish the unification of state and local budgets ". These were desiderata which had already been settled in principle, and only required — it was a large require- ment — to be carried out. But the resolution also contained a new and vital instruction to Narkomfin to " contract the note issue ".[2] The way was being pointed to the measure which was to crown the whole edifice of financial reform but was not as yet specifically mentioned : the establishment of a stable currency.

The most spectacular of the financial reforms of October 1921, however, received its initial impetus from another source. The withdrawal of state credits left industry in a parlous condition, cut off from the source to which it had learned to look for its working capital. Initially Soviet industry had received credits from the National Bank. Then commercial credit had been replaced by advances from the state budget ; and the National Bank had logically terminated its existence in January 1920. When NEP was introduced, no credit institution of any kind existed in Soviet Russia other than the cooperative section of Narkomfin, which continued to give a more or less formal support to what was left of the credit cooperatives. Now that trade was to be restored, and industry was no longer to be financed by treasury advances, some credit institution had to be resuscitated. On October 12, 1921, as a sequel to its general financial resolution, VTsIK con- firmed a draft resolution of Sovnarkom for the creation of a state bank, and on the following day formally approved its statutes. The bank was instituted " for the purpose of promoting by credit and other banking operations the development of industry, agriculture and exchange of goods ", and was itself to operate on the principles of *khozraschet*. Its initial capital of 2000 milliards

[1] *Sobranie Uzakonenii, 1921*, No. 62, art. 446.
[2] *Sbornik Dekretov i Rasporyazhenii po Finansam*, iv (1921), 121-122.

of rubles was furnished by the state, and the members of its administration were appointed by Narkomfin, the appointment of the president being confirmed by Sovnarkom.[1] The new State Bank of the RSFSR (Gosbank)[2] opened its doors on November 16, 1921. The beginnings were not encouraging. Its resources, being at the outset confined to its foundation capital, were limited and its rates exorbitant; in addition to interest it safeguarded itself against currency depreciation by charging on its advances an " insurance percentage " calculated at 8 per cent per month for government institutions, 10 per cent for cooperatives and 12 per cent for private concerns.[3] It is not surprising that its help was neither prompt nor generous enough to assuage the credit hunger of large-scale industry[4] or to avert the *razbazarovanie* crisis of the ensuing winter. The bank itself was faced with the difficulty of operating in terms of a rapidly falling currency, which progressively depreciated its capital and frustrated any credit policy. Just as the stabilization of the currency was impracticable till the budgetary situation had been cleared up, so the necessary credit system could not be made to work till the currency had been stabilized. The financial reforms projected in October 1921 and crowned by the creation of the State Bank were all interdependent parts of a single policy.

By the autumn of 1921, therefore, it had become transparently clear that a stabilized currency and a balanced budget were the fundamental items in any financial reform and essential conditions of NEP itself. The introduction of NEP had been followed in the summer of 1921 by a temporary pause in the now chronic general rise of prices, so that from July 1921 onwards, for the first time since the October revolution, prices rose at a less rapid rate than the volume of currency in circulation, and a certain slowing up

---

[1] *Sobranie Uzakonenii, 1921*, No. 72, arts. 593, 594; No. 75, art. 615.

[2] Its name was changed two years later to " State Bank of the USSR " (*Sobranie Uzakonenii, 1923*, No. 81, art. 786).

[3] *Na Novykh Putyakh* (1923), ii, 192.

[4] On January 1, 1922, advances of Gosbank to industry totalled only 10 million rubles (1922 pattern) equivalent to 400,000 pre-war rubles; credits against goods accounted for another 10 million rubles; discounting of bills did not begin till May 1922 (*ibid.* ii, 201-205). Thereafter advances and credits slowly grew, but did not reach significant figures till the autumn of 1922.

occurred in the work of the printing press.[1] A commission was
appointed to advise on currency policy. On November 3, 1921,
it was decided to inaugurate in the following year a new currency
issue, of which one ruble would be equivalent to 10,000 rubles of
previous issues; the new notes were described no longer as
" settlement notes " but as " money notes " — a return to the
usage of the pre-revolutionary period and presumably an attempt
to restore prestige and respectability to the word " money ".[2] On
November 5, 1921, Sovnarkom took two important decisions about
the forthcoming budget for 1922. It was to be drawn up for nine
months only, so that in the future the budget year would begin
on October 1 ; and it was to be drawn up in pre-war rubles.[3] An
instruction of the same date from Narkomfin fixed the rate of conversion of current rubles into pre-war rubles at 60,000 Soviet
rubles for one pre-war ruble.[4] The conversion rate was thereafter
changed month by month to take account of rising prices, reaching
a figure of 200,000 by March 1922.[5] This was, in effect, a price
index currency and was sometimes referred to as a " goods
ruble ". But the inconveniences and the logical absurdity of
using the fluctuating relation between the current and the 1913
price-level as a permanent standard of measurement were quickly
pointed out by economists ; and in the controversy that arose on
this point the " goods ruble " was gradually ousted from favour
by the " gold ruble ". A decree of November 14, 1921, laid it
down that the rental payable for leased enterprises should be calculated in terms of gold rubles.[6] A curious document of this
phase in the evolution of policy was Lenin's customary article in
Pravda on the anniversary of the October revolution. On this,
the fourth, anniversary the article bore the unexpected title *On*

[1] *Za Pyat' Let* (1922), p. 331.
[2] *Sobranie Uzakonenii, 1921*, No. 77, art. 643 ; whatever psychological effect
may have been expected from the reduction in the numerical denomination of
the currency seems to have miscarried, since the old denominations were
retained in common parlance. A year later a decree was issued (*Sobranie
Uzakonenii, 1922*, No. 66, art. 867) providing that one ruble of the 1923 issue
should be equivalent to 100 1922 rubles or 1,000,000 rubles of the earlier issues.
[3] *Sbornik Dekretov i Rasporyazhenii po Finansam*, iv (1921), 126.
[4] *Ibid.* iv, 127.
[5] *Novoe Zakonodatel'stvo v Oblasti Sel'skogo Khozyaistva : Sbornik Dekretov*
(1923), pp. 273-274.
[6] *Sbornik Dekretov i Rasporyazhenii po Finansam*, iv (1921), 136.

*the Significance of Gold Now and After the Complete Victory of
Socialism.* It was devoted to NEP in general rather than to the
question of gold in particular. It contained the famous prediction
that, " when we conquer on a world scale, we shall . . . make the
public lavatories in the streets of some of the greatest cities in the
world out of gold "; but it went on to insist that for the RSFSR
in present conditions the important thing was to " economize
gold " and to " master trade ".[1]

The financial decisions of October and November 1921 concentrated the attention of the Soviet leaders on financial policy,
and for a time made Narkomfin and Gosbank the most sensitive
nerve-centres of NEP. It was a curious reversal of the attitudes
of the period of war communism, when it had been loudly proclaimed that finance could never be more than the handmaid of
economic policy, and the spokesman of Narkomfin had apologetically looked forward to its early demise. The change was sym-
bolized by a series of new appointments. Krestinsky, who had
once been a member of the Left opposition and had, since March
1919, combined the no-longer-very-onerous duties of People's
Commissar for Finance with the rôle of secretary of the central
committee of the party, had been disgraced at the tenth party
congress in March 1921 for his failure in this second rôle.[2] Shortly
afterwards he was despatched on a mission to Germany, where he
became Soviet Ambassador, and was succeeded at Narkomfin by
Sokolnikov. Sokolnikov, an old party member who had returned
to Petrograd with Lenin in the sealed train, was also a practical
man of business who had participated with authority and effect
in early discussions of financial policy.[3] He now threw himself
with vigour into the financial aspects of NEP, and especially
the creation of a stable currency, and for the next few years
made Narkomfin a key-point of the conservative or Right tendencies in Soviet policy. A hitherto little-known party member
named Sheiman, said to be the son of a banker, became director of
Gosbank. But a far more sensational move was made early in 1922
when Kutler, a former financier and industrialist, who had held

---

[1] Lenin, *Sochineniya*, xxvii, 79-85.
[2] See Vol. 1, p. 204; for his appointment as People's Commissar for Finance
in 1918 and his *obiter dicta* on finance see pp. 246, 265 above.
[3] His speech at the first All-Russian Congress of Councils of National
Economy is quoted on p. 145 above.

ministerial positions in Witte's cabinet and joined the Kadet party after 1905, was appointed to the board of Gosbank. From this time till his death in 1924, Kutler was beyond doubt an influential force behind the scenes at Gosbank, — and perhaps also at Narkomfin — and played an important part in the stabilization of the currency.[1]

The foundation of Gosbank became the starting-point for a campaign which, making the establishment of a stable currency its immediate and overriding goal, was directed to the re-establishment of the main principles, of " orthodox " capitalist finance, with a state bank as the central regulator of the national economy. On November 20, 1921, a conference was held at Gosbank to consider the report of the commission on the currency question, and adopted a set of theses which six months earlier would have made a sensation. It advocated free markets, support for light rather than for heavy industry as more likely to promote a rapid development of internal trade, a modification of the monopoly of foreign trade, a renewed attempt to obtain foreign loans, and an eventual return to a gold currency.[2] These were the views of the financiers and, though they had won the support of Narkomfin, were too far-reaching to command universal acceptance in the party. But the party conference of December 1921 proclaimed that " the restoration of monetary circulation on a metallic basis (gold), the first step towards which is the inflexible carrying out of a plan to limit the issue of paper money, must be the guiding principle of the Soviet power in the matter of finance " ;[3] and this programme was repeated at the ninth All-Russian Congress of

---

[1] In the heyday of NEP no need was felt to mask the cooperation of experts of the pre-revolutionary régimes : V. N. Ipatieff, *The Life of a Chemist* (Stanford, 1946), p. 402, relates how in the autumn of 1922 Sheiman and Kutler addressed a public meeting in the Conservatorium to celebrate " the first anniversary of the State Bank and the introduction of a stable currency ". On the other hand, the influences at work in Narkomfin made it a target for attack by industrial circles which were opposed to its policy. According to the sometimes well-informed Menshevik journal published in Berlin, *Sotsialisticheskii Vestnik*, No. 2, January 17, 1923, p. 16, Larin at the tenth All-Russian Congress of Soviets in December 1922 described Sokolnikov as being led by the nose by " former Tsarist ministers, Kutlers, etc." ; but the remark does not appear in the official record.

[2] *Finansovaya Politika za Period s Dekabrya 1920 g. po Dekabr' 1921 g.: Otchet k IX Vserossiiskomu S"ezdu Sovetov* (1921), pp. 35-43.

[3] *VKP(B) v Rezolyutsiyakh* (1941), i, 407.

Soviets later in the month, where Kamenev pointed out that neither an economic plan nor a state budget could be effectively drawn up so long as money consisted simply of " coloured pieces of paper ".[1] At the eleventh party congress, which met in March 1922, Sokolnikov made a detailed plea for the new financial policy, significantly noting that this was the first occasion on which a party congress had occupied itself with matters of finance ;[2] and Lenin, in his only speech to the congress, devoted a rather incoherent but remarkable passage to the coming " financial crisis " and its effects in industry :

> If it [i.e. the crisis] is too severe and overwhelming, we shall have once again to revise much, and to concentrate all our forces on one thing. But if it is not too overwhelming, it may even be useful : it will purge the communists from all sorts of state trusts. Only we must not forget to do this. A financial crisis shakes up institutions and enterprises, and the inefficient among them crack first. Only we must remember not to put all the blame on the specialists and pretend that the communists in responsible positions are very good, fought at the front and have always worked well. So that, if the financial crisis is not excessively severe, good can be extracted from it, and we shall be able to purge, not as the central control commission or central verification commission purges,[3] but thoroughly purge, as should be done, all the responsible communists in economic institutions.[4]

There was no doubt an element of conscious hyperbole in this eulogy, couched in terms of orthodox capitalist finance, of the salutary effect of a financial crisis, as well as in the defence of specialists as contrasted with communists. But the passage, taken from the same speech in which Lenin had proclaimed the ending of the " retreat ", was a symptom of the party mood of the moment on the financial issue. The congress clinched the matter by a long resolution on financial policy which sought " a broadening

---

[1] S"ezdy Sovetov RSFSR v Postanovleniyakh (1939), p. 222 ; Devyatyi Vserossiiskii S"ezd Sovetov (1922), p. 53.

[2] Odinnadtsatyi S"ezd RKP(B) (1936), p. 312.

[3] See Vol. 1, pp. 205-207. As was there pointed out, the conventional English translation " purge " is stronger than the Russian chistka or chistit' ; the meaning here is not that all communists should be dismissed, but that they should all be closely scrutinized and the inefficient eliminated.

[4] Lenin, Sochineniya, xxvii, 257.

of the sphere of monetary circulation at the cost of a contraction of the natural part of the state economy ", spoke of the
" struggle with the budget deficit ", and thought it indispensable
to " establish firmly that our economic and financial policy is
decisively directed to a restoration of a gold backing for money ".[1]

The summer of 1922 saw the slow ripening of this policy. The
budget estimates for the first nine months of 1922 approved in
December 1921, the first to be drawn up in pre-war rubles, showed
a deficit which was only 40 per cent of estimated expenditure ; the
corresponding percentages for the problematical budgets of 1920
and 1921 had been 86 and 84 respectively.[2] Vigorous efforts were
made to cut expenditure by reducing the staffs of state institutions
and taking more and more industrial enterprises and workers off
the budget. The return to a monetary economy had as its logical
corollary a transition from taxation in kind to monetary taxation.
But this change in a primitive peasant economy came very slowly.
A first step was taken in March 1922 when the series of taxes in
kind which had been substituted a year earlier for requisitioning
were reduced to a single uniform tax in kind calculated in terms of
rye.[3] But taxation in kind on agricultural products continued
throughout 1922 : at the end of that year more than one-third of
the total revenue was still being received in that form.[4] Meanwhile
new sources of monetary taxation were also tapped, taxes on wines,
spirits, tobacco, beer, matches, honey and mineral waters all being
imposed between August 1921 and February 1922. In January
1922 the decision to draw up the budget in pre-war rubles was
supplemented by a decree prescribing the assessment of all taxes
in pre-war rubles, payment to be made at the current rate of
exchange.[5] In February 1922 there followed a poll-tax (a so-
called " general citizens' tax ") earmarked for the relief of the
victims of the famine,[6] and in the autumn of 1922 a much more
important experiment in an income-tax designed to catch the
earnings of the so-called " free " professions (doctors, lawyers,
writers, etc.), as well as Nepmen and highly paid employees of

[1] *VKP(B) v Rezolyutsiyakh* (1941), i, 425-428.
[2] *Na Novykh Putyakh* (1923), ii, 2.
[3] *Sobranie Uzakonenii, 1922*, No. 22, art. 233.
[4] *Desyatyi Vserossiiskii S"ezd Sovetov* (1923), p. 138.
[5] *Sobranie Uzakonenii, 1922*, No. 6, art. 75.
[6] *Ibid.* No. 16, art. 167.

state institutions or industrial trusts — those whom Sokolnikov referred to as " elements of the urban bourgeoisie and the urban bourgeois and technical intelligentsia, which forms the top layer of our trust organizations ".[1]   Thanks to all these expedients the yield from monetary taxation became for the first time a serious item in the budget.   Of all governmental receipts in the first nine months of 1922, only 10 per cent were derived from monetary taxation and 60 per cent from the note issue.   But some encouragement could be derived from the monthly figures, which showed that the proportion derived from monetary taxation had risen between January and September from 1·8 to 14 per cent, while the proportion derived from the note issue fell from 90 to 56 per cent.[2] By the last quarter of 1922, Sokolnikov was able to announce that one-third of the revenue was being derived from monetary taxation, less than a third from the note issue and the remainder from taxation in kind.[3]

In the summer of 1922 another tentative step was taken towards the re-establishment of orthodox public finance.   The Soviet Government invited subscriptions to its first state loan to a total amount of 10 million puds of rye.   Bonds of the value of 100 puds were to bear no interest, but were put on the market at 95 and were repayable at par between December 1, 1922, and January 31, 1923. Payment and repayment were to be made in currency at the market rate of rye : the loan was to be guaranteed by a deposit of gold specie in the state treasury to the value of 10 million rubles.[4] The persistence of prejudice against state loans, and scepticism of the ability of the Soviet Government to float one with success, were reflected at the session of VTsIK which approved the loan : Sokolnikov quoted the precedent of the French revolution to prove that past defaults did not preclude the possibility of raising loans.[5]   In October 1922 Sokolnikov was able to announce the success of the loan, 85 per cent of the total amount offered for subscription having been taken up, though the main inducement

---

[1] *Ibid.* No. 76, art. 940 ;   *Desyatyi Vserossiiskii S"ezd Sovetov* (1923), pp. 138-139.
[2] *Na Novykh Putyakh* (1923), ii, 134-135.
[3] *Desyatyi Vserossiiskii S"ezd Sovetov* (1923), p. 138.
[4] *Sobranie Uzakonenii, 1922*, No. 36, art. 430.
[5] *III Sessiya Vserossiiskogo Tsentral'nogo Ispolnital'nogo Komiteta IX Sozyva,* No. 7 (May 21, 1922), pp. 16-17.

was apparently the right to tender the bonds at par in payment of the tax in kind.[1] This was followed by the issue of a loan for 100 million gold rubles at 6 per cent for the declared purpose of preparing the way for currency stabilization.[2] The loan was probably taken up in the main by state institutions and state industrial trusts. But the intention was also to mop up some of the private wealth which was being accumulated under NEP, and moral pressure to subscribe was strongly exerted.[3] The return to a policy of public borrowing and the encouragement of private savings were further signalized by a revival of state savings banks which was approved by Sovnarkom on December 26, 1922.[4] The first two savings banks, in Moscow and Petrograd, opened in February 1923. The deposits were calculated at their equivalent in gold rubles and were repayable at the current rate. The savings banks were probably used at first rather as a method of insurance against currency depreciation than as a form of investment, but they were effective in re-creating a habit and a tradition. By October 1923 there are said to have been 300 banks with 60,000 depositors, and more than ten times that number six months later.[5] The announcement of a state lottery to open in February 1923 was another return to the financial methods of the past.[6]

The re-establishment of a State Bank was naturally followed by an attempt to rebuild the whole banking system. Just as the first move for the creation of a State Bank had been inspired by the need to provide a source of credits for industry when direct financing from the state treasury was withdrawn, so the first important move to extend the system came from Vesenkha as the spokesman of industry at the beginning of 1922, and was strongly endorsed both by Gosplan and by the new industrial trusts. The

[1] *IV Sessiya Vserossiiskogo Tsentral'nogo Ispolnitel'nogo Komiteta IX Sozyva*, No. 4 (October 28, 1922), p. 26.

[2] G. Y. Sokolnikov, *Gosudarstvennyi Kapitalizm i Novaya Finansovaya Politika* (1922), pp. 31-34.

[3] At the tenth All-Russian Congress of Soviets in December 1922 Sokolnikov observed that, " if a man has the possibility of supporting the loan and does not support it, we can and shall interpret this as a refusal to support the Soviet Government in general " (*Desyatyi Vserossiiskii S''ezd Sovetov* (1923), p. 140).

[4] A. Z. Arnold, *Banks, Credit and Money in Soviet Russia* (N.Y., 1937), p. 324 : the old savings banks had been taken over by the National Bank on April 10, 1919 (see p. 255, note 3 above).

[5] *Ibid.* pp. 325-326.

[6] *Sobranie Uzakonenii, 1922*, No. 81, art. 1029.

project for a Bank for Industry (Prombank), with powers to grant
to industry both short-term commercial credit and loans up to
three years' duration, was approved by STO on September 1,
1922. Its capital was subscribed by state institutions, including
Vesenkha and the People's Commissariats concerned, and state
industrial enterprises.[1] The initial impulse was beyond doubt
to render industry independent of the State Bank and of what was
regarded as the niggardly policy of the financial authorities towards
industry. But Prombank was never really strong enough to escape
from the leading-strings of the State Bank and Narkomfin, and
took its place as a unit in a closely knit banking system. Meanwhile in February 1922, the cooperatives had re-established a
Consumers' Cooperative Bank (Pokobank), which in January 1923
was enlarged into an All-Russian Cooperative Bank (Vsekobank).[2]
Municipal banks to finance local industries and local government
projects,[3] and mutual credit associations designed to meet the
needs of the small private trader under NEP,[4] also made their
appearance during 1922.

The financial progress of NEP continued to be marked by a
rapid growth in the influence of Gosbank, the temple of the new
financial orthodoxy. The price-index by which Narkomfin calculated the conversion of the current into the pre-war ruble fell
before the critical scrutiny of the financiers. In March 1922 this
system was abolished, and replaced in the following month by a
gold ruble system based on the rate at which Gosbank purchased
gold, the rate of conversion being announced monthly no longer
by Narkomfin, but by Gosbank : all state revenue and expenditure
was henceforth to be calculated not in pre-war, but in gold,
rubles.[5] The prestige of gold as the basis of money, and of

---

[1] A. Z. Arnold, *Banks, Credit and Money in Soviet Russia* (N.Y., 1937),
pp. 287-288. The first director of Prombank was Krasnoshchekov, formerly
Prime Minister of the Far Eastern Republic (see Vol. 1, pp. 355-356) ; in 1924
he was sentenced to imprisonment for misuse and embezzlement of bank funds
(V. N. Ipatieff, *The Life of a Chemist* (Stanford, 1946), pp. 402-403).

[2] *Sobranie Uzakonenii, 1922*, No. 16, art. 163 ; A. Z. Arnold, *Banks, Credit,
and Money in Soviet Russia* (N.Y., 1937), pp. 296-297.

[3] *Ibid.* pp. 307-308.   [4] *Ibid.* pp. 318-319.

[5] *Sobranie Uzakonenii, 1922*, No. 26, art. 310 ; No. 31, art. 377. In August
1922 a further change was made ; the rate of conversion was determined by a
special commission on which both Narkomfin and Gosbank were represented on
the basis of the rate of exchange for stable foreign currencies (*ibid.* No. 55, art.
692). The budget for 1922-1923 was drawn up not in pre-war, but in gold, rubles.

Gosbank as its custodian, was correspondingly enhanced, and one more step taken along the path that led to currency reform. After the brief slowing up of the inflationary process in the summer of 1921, the still uncurbed forces of economic disequilibrium once more took charge, and all attempts to reduce the rate of the note emission were abandoned as hopeless. From a figure of 3500 milliards on September 1, 1921, the total of ruble notes in circulation rose by January 1, 1922 (continuing to reckon in the 1921 denomination) to 17,500 milliards, by May 1, 1922, to 130,000 milliards, and by the end of the year 1922 to just short of 2 million milliards.[1] The solution of a currency issue backed by gold and under the supervision of a state bank, in close imitation of western models, seemed to commend itself with irresistible force. The argument was heard (though this afterwards proved to be of doubtful and limited validity) that the development of foreign trade required a stable monetary unit.[2] On July 25, 1922, Sovnarkom authorized Gosbank to issue bank-notes in a new monetary unit to be called the chervonets, one chervonets being equivalent to ten gold rubles ; the issue was to be covered as to 25 per cent by precious metals and as to 75 per cent by short-term obligations and other liquid assets.[3] After more detailed provisions had been laid down in a further decree of October 11, 1922,[4] the first chervonets notes appeared towards the end of November. After years of financial anarchy and a disordered currency, the attractions of stabilization seemed irresistible. Opposition was not formidable, and was branded by the spokesman of Narkomfin in VTsIK as a revival of " the infantile disease of Leftism ".[5] The initial issue was extremely small, and for a long time the new chervonets served not as a medium of exchange, but rather as a store of value or a unit of account. For fifteen months the stable but limited chervonets circulated side by side with the unlimited and constantly depreciating ruble currency. Major transactions were

[1] A. Z. Arnold, *Banks, Credit and Money in Soviet Russia* (N.Y., 1937), pp. 128-129.

[2] G. Y. Sokolnikov, *Gosudarstvennyi Kapitalizm i Novaya Finansovaya Politika* (1922), p. 6.

[3] *Sobranie Uzakonenii, 1922*, No. 46, art. 578.

[4] *Ibid.* No. 64, art. 827.

[5] *IV Sessiya Vserossiiskogo Tsentral'nogo Ispolnitel'nogo Komiteta IX Sozyva*, No. 5 (October 29, 1922), p. 2.

more and more regularly expressed in terms of chervontsy; but cash payments continued to be made in rubles at the current rate.

Thus at the end of 1922 a short-lived and in some degree illusory equilibrium had been achieved in financial, as well as in economic, policy. The impetus given by NEP and confirmed by the good harvest of 1922 had opened up a prospect, still somewhat remote, of balancing the state budget and of replacing, if not revivifying, the almost defunct ruble. But these ambitions, so sharply at variance with those of the first revolutionary years, could be pursued only at the expense of severe shocks inflicted on other sectors of the economy. The fresh crisis of 1923 had to be surmounted before they were finally fulfilled.

CHAPTER 20

THE BEGINNINGS OF PLANNING

THE Marxist analysis which contrasted the unplanned, irrational capitalist economy with the planned, rational economy of the future socialist order had had little or nothing to say of the process of transition from one to the other. Only Engels towards the end of his life, commenting on a passage in the Erfurt programme of the German Social-Democrat Party which referred to " the lack of planning inherent in the existence of private capitalist production ", let fall the pregnant remark that share companies had already put an end to private production, and that, " if we pass from share companies to trusts which subordinate to themselves and monopolize whole branches of industry, there is an end not only to *private production*, but to the *lack of planning*".[1] The growth of planning was thus inherent in capitalism itself and in the constantly increasing size of the unit of capitalist production. Hilferding in his book *Das Finanzkapital*, published in 1909, carried the analysis a step further by showing how, in the early years of the twentieth century, the major part of the capital of industry in leading capitalist countries had passed into the hands of the great banks, so that industrial capital had been still more closely concentrated in the form of finance capital. This strikingly confirmed the traditional socialist conception of the banking system as a central lever for the control and organization of industry, and appeared to demonstrate that capitalism had taken a further step on the path which would, according to the Marxist analysis, lead to its final break-down under the impact of the socialist revolution.

---

[1] Marx i Engels, *Sochineniya*, xvi, ii, 105-106 ; Marx refers to " capitalist joint-stock companies " side by side with workers' industrial cooperatives as " forms of transition from the capitalist to the social mode of production " (*Das Kapital*, iii, ch. xxvii).

Lenin's *Imperialism as the Highest Stage of Capitalism* was a further elaboration of this text.[1]

The war of 1914 acted as a forcing-house for all these processes. By subjecting the capitalist economies of the principal belligerent countries to intensive concentration and centralized planning, it was bound, in the eyes of Marxists, to hasten the disintegration of private capitalism and pave the way for a planned economy. These developments were most conspicuous in Germany, not so much because Germany was exposed to the most drastic economic stresses (in this respect both Austria-Hungary and Russia were just as severely tried), but because the Germans had advanced furthest in these directions before the war. During 1915 Larin, then still a prominent Menshevik living in Stockholm, wrote a noteworthy series of articles for the Petrograd journal *Vestnik Evropy* on the German war economy. The first article, published in April 1915, concluded:

> Contemporary Germany has given the world a pattern of the centralized direction of the national economy as a single machine working according to plan. In contemporary Germany the keys of the machine are held by Siemens, Börsig, Gwinner, Bleichröder — representatives of the biggest banks and the biggest accumulations of industrial capital in the country. He who holds the keys of the machine runs it according to his own conception; but the experience in the practical life of a vast country of the possibility of constructing such a unified machine within the complicated framework of modern civilization retains its theoretical interest and all its social scientific significance.

And four months later, after Helfferich's appointment as Minister of Finance, Larin summed up again:

> The German economy is moving towards the planned and organized domination of big capital realized through cooperation of the state with the big banks.[2]

---

[1] For Lenin's emphasis on the rôle of the banks and his reference to Saint-Simon, see p. 132 above.

[2] *Vestnik Evropy*, April 1915, p. 303; August 1915, p. 300; Larin's articles were republished in book form in Moscow in 1928 (the year of the first Five-Year Plan) under the title *Gosudarstvennyi Kapitalizm Voennogo Vremeni v Germanii*.

Whatever other sources were open to him, Lenin must certainly have read Larin's articles ; and, when he returned to Russia after the February revolution, the state-controlled war-time German economy increasingly influenced his economic thinking. This was the economic system which Lenin designated as a " state monopoly capitalism " or, simply, " state capitalism " — the equivalent of what came to be called in German *Planwirtschaft*, in French *une économie dirigée* and in English " planning ".

> Compulsory trustification [he wrote], i.e. compulsory unification into associations under state control, that is what capitalism has prepared, that is what the *junker* state has carried out in Germany, that is what will be fully carried out in Russia for the Soviets, for the dictatorship of the proletariat, that is what will be given us by our universal, modern, non-bureaucratic " *state apparatus* ".[1]

Lenin emphasized that it was not socialism : " What the German Plekhanovs (Scheidemann, Lentsch, etc.) call ' war socialism ' is in fact war state monopoly capitalism ". But the attainment under the stress of war of this final stage of capitalism meant that the socialist revolution was now at hand :

> The dialectic of history is such that the war, by enormously hastening the transformation of monopoly capital into state monopoly capital, has *by that very means* brought mankind enormously nearer to socialism.
>
> The imperialist war is the eve of the socialist revolution. And that not only because war with its horrors begets the proletarian uprising — no uprising can bring socialism if it is not yet economically ripe — but because state monopoly capitalism is the fullest *material* preparation for socialism, the *ante-chamber* to it, the step on the ladder of history between which and the step called socialism *there are no intermediate steps left*.[2]

Planning, under the name of state capitalism, thus occupies a cardinal place in the transition from capitalism to socialism. " Socialism ", as Sorel once paradoxically remarked, " has no longer any need to concern itself with the organization of industry, since capitalism does that." [3] Capitalism itself evolves an element

---

[1] Lenin, *Sochineniya*, xxi, 261-262.   [2] *Ibid.* xxi, 186-187.
[3] G. Sorel, *Reflections on Violence* (Engl. transl., 1916), p. 35.

of planning by way of a necessary antidote to its own anarchic propensities. The final stage in the evolution of capitalism becomes the first stage in the creation of socialism. Historically, Friedrich List preceded Marx as the father of the theory of planning; Rathenau, who organized the first modern planned economy in the Germany of the first world war, preceded Lenin, whose approach to the problem of planning in Soviet Russia was consciously based on the German precedents. But when a Menshevik writer in the autumn of 1917 proposed to introduce planning to Russia and thought that this involved " not the replacement of the apparatus, but only its reform ", Lenin, while defending the conception of a " plan " (the word was still sufficiently unfamiliar to keep its inverted commas), made clear the difference between planning which was the last line of defence of the capitalist order and planning which was to become the instrument of the transition to socialism :

> The proletariat will do this when it conquers : it will set economists, engineers, agronomists, etc., *under the control* of workers' organizations to work out a " plan ", to check it, to seek out means of economizing labour by centralization. . . . We are for centralism and for a " plan ", but for the centralism and the plan of the *proletarian* state, of proletarian regulation of production and distribution in the interests of the poor, the toilers, and the exploited, *against* the exploiters.[1]

These distinctions contained the germ of Lenin's remark some months after the revolution that socialism had already been realized — one-half, the material, economic half, in Germany in the form of state monopoly capitalism, the other half, the political half, in Russia in the form of the dictatorship of the proletariat.[2]

The fundamental dilemma of the Bolshevik revolution — the attempt to build a socialist society in an economically backward country — affected the issue of planning in two different ways. On the one hand, the poverty of Russia, the meagreness of its capital resources, the low efficiency of its industry, had from the outset fostered the growth of state capitalism at the expense of

---

[1] Lenin, *Sochineniya*, xxi, 268-270 ; this first discussion by Lenin of planning was closely bound up with his advocacy of " workers' control " (see p. 65 above).

[2] *Ibid.* xxii, 517 ; on the other hand, Lenin in March 1917 had described the German system as " hunger organized with genius " (*ibid.* xx, 19).

private capitalism. Industry in Russia had been largely built up by governmental action to serve the purposes of the state and to strengthen its power; dependent on the state both directly as a customer and indirectly through the great banks, it never altogether lost its public and quasi-military character. The vested interests of private enterprise, which were so formidable a source of opposition to planning in the western countries, scarcely existed in Russia, and the higher degree of concentration prevailing in the major industries made state intervention technically easy. If, during the first world war, planning made no great progress in Russia,[1] this was due to the lack of ability and initiative conspicuously displayed by the Russian public services rather than to the unripeness of the economy for centralized direction.

On the other hand, the absence of any widespread development of private capitalist enterprise in Russia, while it facilitated some of the approaches to planning, faced Soviet planners with several grave drawbacks. It compelled them to operate in conditions of extreme material scarcity, which associated the régime of planning with acute hardship and privation. It deprived them of the resources in trained personnel and organization which efficient planning demanded. Even the limited number of Russian bourgeois specialists of all kinds, economic and technical, boycotted the régime in its early years and were boycotted by it; and it was not until a qualified reconciliation was effected in 1920 and 1921 that serious planning became a possibility at all. Most important of all, the backwardness of the Russian economy was summed up in the predominance of primitive peasant agriculture — an economic form more recalcitrant than any other to planning. Hence planning in Russia inevitably began from an attempt to introduce a new balance into the economy through the development of industry, and became an incident in the age-long struggle between town and country. Towards the end of his last published article in the spring of 1923, Lenin wrote of the need to " change over, figuratively speaking, from one horse to the other, namely from the starveling, peasant, *muzhik* horse . . . to the horse of heavy

[1] War committees of the principal industries and the Economic Council and Chief Economic Committee set up by the Provisional Government (see pp. 56-57 above) were not in themselves very serious contributions to planning, though they provided a foundation on which subsequent Soviet organs were built.

machine industry ",[1] and called this " the general plan of our work, of our policy, of our tactics, of our strategy ".   Russian conditions made this from the outset, and for many years to come, the essential theme of Soviet planning.

The principle of planning inherent in the Marxist conception of a socialist economy had received Lenin's cautious blessing on the eve of the October revolution.   The first tentative approach to a concrete application of the principle followed the conclusion of the Brest-Litovsk treaty, when it seemed for the moment as though the way were open for economic reconstruction.   It was at this time that Lenin began to grasp the magnitude and novelty of the task :

> We have knowledge of socialism, but as for knowledge of organization on a scale of millions, knowledge of the organization and distribution of commodities — that we have not.   This the old Bolshevik leaders did not teach us. . . . Nothing has been written about this yet in Bolshevik text-books, and there is nothing in Menshevik text-books either.[2]

A few weeks later he added a longer explanation :

> All that we knew, all that had been precisely indicated to us by the best experts, the most powerful brains, of capitalist society who had foreseen its development, was that a transformation must, by historical necessity, take place along a certain broad line, that private ownership of the means of production had been condemned by history, that it would break, that the exploiters would inevitably be expropriated.   This was established with scientific exactitude.   We knew it when we raised in our hands the banner of socialism, when we declared ourselves socialists, when we founded socialist parties and when we set out to transform society.   We knew it when we seized power in order to embark on socialist reorganization.   But the forms of the transformation and the rapidity of the development of the concrete reorganization we could not know.   Only collective experience, only the experience of millions, can give decisive indications in this respect.[3]

---

[1] Lenin, *Sochineniya*, xxvii, 417.   [2] *Ibid.* xxii, 484.
[3] *Ibid.* xxiii, 40.

Having learned that the Academy of Sciences was already investigating the country's natural resources,[1] he suggested that it might appoint a commission of specialists to work out a " plan for the reorganization of industry and the economic revival of Russia ", including the location of industry, the concentration of production in a few large enterprises, and the electrification of transport and agriculture ;[2] and about the same period he looked forward to " the positive or creative task of the adjustment of the extraordinarily complicated and delicate network of new organizational relations covering the planned production and distribution of goods necessary for the existence of tens of millions of people ".[3]

Meanwhile the newly created Vesenkha had made a first tentative approach to the problems of " planning ", not yet under this name but in terms of " public works ". At a meeting in March 1918 Larin enumerated as the three most urgent public works to be undertaken the development of the Kuznetsk coal basin, the electrification of the industry of Petrograd and the irrigation of land for cotton-growing in Turkestan.[4] About the same time Vesenkha appointed a committee on public works whose president, Pavlovich, reported at length to the first All-Russian Congress of Councils of National Economy in May 1918. Its aim was nothing less than the full utilization of Russia's natural resources. It was proposed to draw up projects for the construction of railways, canals and roads, of electric power stations, elevators and cold storage plants, for the regulation and use of water power, and for irrigation and land reclamation. Pavlovich was prepared to be equally precise about the scope and functions of the organization :

> On its foundation the committee on public works set itself first and foremost two tasks : first, to draw up a general plan of constructional works for the whole of Russia, and, secondly, to

[1] In May 1915 the Imperial Academy of Sciences set up a Commission for the Study of the Natural Productive Resources of Russia; it survived the revolution, and from 1918 received funds from the Soviet Government (*Obzor Nauchnoi Deyatel'nosti Komissii po Izucheniyu Estestvennykh Proizvoditel'nykh Sil Rossii*, ed. G. P. Blok (1920), p. 6; this pamphlet contains a long list of scientific publications of the commission, and a later account of its work is in *Raboty Akademii Nauk v Oblasti Issledovaniya Prirodnykh Bogatsv Rossii* (1922)).

[2] Lenin, *Sochineniya*, xxii, 434. [3] *Ibid.* xxii, 451.

[4] *Byulleteni Vysshego Soveta Narodnogo Khozyaistva*, No. 1, April 1918, p. 27.

bring about the unification of all constructional operations of state importance in a single department. . . .

The tasks of construction should be taken away from the commissariats and transferred to a special organ which would do the building, being guided by general considerations and purposes and taking account of the international and the domestic policy of the country.

It was perhaps evidence of the common sense of a majority of the delegates that the congress voted to postpone a debate on this report and apparently passed no resolution on it.[1] Vesenkha claimed in September 1918 to have passed from " the organization of administration to the organization of production ", and ordered all *glavki* and centres to " draw up programmes of production for the forthcoming working year ".[2] In the same month it created a special section on electro-technical construction under the committee on public works.[3] But as the realities of civil war grew more and more menacing such grandiose projects could only remain on the files. The committee on public works receded into the background ; [4] and there was something fantastic about Larin's complaint at the second All-Russian Congress of Councils of National Economy in December 1918 that the presidium of Vesenkha was neglecting " general questions of the economy " and devoting its time and attention exclusively to " current business ".[5] The congress still spoke hopefully of the possibility of " constructing a single economic plan in 1919 ".[6] The revised programme of the party, adopted at its eighth congress in March

---

[1] *Trudy I Vserossiiskogo S"ezda Sovetov Narodnogo Khozyaistva* (1918), pp. 180-181, 202 ; the report, which covers 25 pages of the proceedings of the congress (*ibid.* pp. 176-202) is, however, a remarkable early instance of planning on paper.

[2] *Narodnoe Khozyaistvo*, No. 10, 1918, p. 42.

[3] *Sbornik Dekretov i Postanovlenii po Narodnomu Khozyaistvu*, ii (1920), 45-46 ; about the same time Sovnarkom, on the motion of Krasin, created a " central electrical council " (*Trudy 8 Elektrotekhnicheskogo S"ezda* (n.d. [? 1921]), i, 128-129). Few of the innumerable organs created at this time ever became effective.

[4] A. Ransome, *Six Weeks in Russia in 1919* (1919), pp. 65-72, records a visit of February 1919 to Pavlovich, who complained that " war spoils everything ", and that " this committee should be at work on affairs of peace, making Russia more useful to herself and the rest of the world ".

[5] *Trudy II Vserossiiskogo S"ezda Sovetov Narodnogo Khozyaistva* (n.d.), p. 19.   [6] *Ibid.* p. 319.

1919, demanded " the maximum union of the whole economic activity of the country in accordance with one general state plan ".[1] But this remained, for the time being, a pure aspiration. No single organ supervised the whole field of economic policy, Vesenkha having tacitly renounced this function. Such planning as was done was virtually confined to rather primitive attempts to organize the nationalized industries. Economic activity was devoted exclusively to the exacting and sometimes almost hopeless day-to-day task of organizing supplies for the Red Army in the civil war.

It was not till the beginning of 1920, when the assaults of Kolchak and Denikin had been broken and the war seemed all but over, that thoughts could turn back to the work of economic reconstruction. Two different conceptions of planning then began to emerge, and planning developed slowly along two parallel and sometimes rival lines. According to the first conception, a plan was a broadly defined long-term economic policy, and the main essential of planning was a central organ responsible for the formulation of general economic policy (the " plan ") and for the direction of the commissariats engaged in the day-to-day execution of economic policy. According to the second conception, a plan was a project or series of projects which, while designed in a general way to promote increased productivity and a revival of the national economy as a whole, contained specific and detailed proposals for stated work to be carried out in stated quantities within a given period. The first conception was general, the second specific; but neither of them as yet remotely approached the later view of a plan as a comprehensive and detailed budget of the whole national economy.

The first view of planning turned on the creation, as an essential preliminary, of a single central economic authority. The experience of the civil war revealed the practical necessity of a central department strong enough to impose its authority on the existing economic organs of government and to direct economic policy in the light of a single plan of campaign. In the autumn of 1918 the centre of the economic scene had been occupied by the war contracts section of Vesenkha, with sub-sections attached to provincial and local Sovnarkhozy, and by the extraordinary com-

[1] *VKP(B) v Rezolyutsiyakh* (1941), i, 290.

mission for the supply of the Red Army presided over by Krasin.[1] But these subordinate bodies were clearly unable to exercise a function of supreme direction and control. What turned out to be a decision of lasting significance was taken on November 30, 1918, when VTsIK created a Council of Workers' and Peasants' Defence with full powers for " the mobilization of the resources and means of the country in the interests of defence ". Its president was Lenin, and among its members were Trotsky as People's Commissar for War and president of the military-revolutionary council, Krasin as president of the extraordinary commission of supply and Stalin as representing VTsIK;[2] and the new council thus constituted quickly became the supreme authority in all except military matters. So long as the civil war continued, it had the status of an *ad hoc* body concerned with a passing emergency, did not obviously trench on the permanent attributions of Vesenkha, and was unconcerned with planning except in the day-to-day sense of the term. This state of affairs continued throughout the year 1919. The third All-Russian Congress of Councils of National Economy in January 1920 passed the usual routine resolution in favour of a " single economic plan " and of the " coordination of the production programmes of all branches of industry in accordance with the material resources of the republic ", and even decided to set up under Vesenkha a " permanent central commission of production ".[3] But when the civil war seemed to be over in the spring of 1920, the issue of planning arose

---

[1] For the war contracts section and the extraordinary commission, see pp. 228-229 above. The organ through which Vesenkha attempted to carry out a rudimentary planning policy was the " commission of utilization " (see p. 230 above). The theory rather than the practice of this body was described by Milyutin in 1920 : " A plan of distribution is settled by the commission of utilization and goes for confirmation to the presidium of Vesenkha ; then begins the execution of the plan by the appropriate production sections, which receive from central stores the necessary quantity of raw material and distribute it to the factories and workshops " (*Istoriya Ekonomicheskogo Razvitiya SSSR* (2nd ed., 1929), p. 197). The commission is said to have approved " plans " for 19 products in 1918, for 44 in 1919 and for 55 in 1920 (*Bol'shaya Sovetskaya Entsiklopediya*, xxiii (1938), 619, art. " Komissiya Ispol'zovaniya "). In March 1921 this commission was transferred from Vesenkha to STO, and in December 1921 abolished altogether (see p. 379 below).

[2] *Sobranie Uzakonenii, 1917–1918*, No. 91-92, art. 924.

[3] *Rezolyutsii Tret'ego Vserossiiskogo S"ezda Sovetov Narodnogo Khozyaistva* (1920), pp. 42-44.

for the first time in an acute form in the shape of open rivalry between Vesenkha and the Council of Workers' and Peasants' Defence.

The ninth party congress of March 1920 first brought Trotsky on the scene as a protagonist of planning. Being much concerned at the time with the mobilization for industry of the labour released by the ending of the civil war, he was charged with the report to the congress " On Current Tasks of Economic Construction ". The resolution which he presented contained a section, not originally drafted by him but inserted during the discussion of the draft in the central committee, advocating the introduction of " *a single economic plan* designed for the coming historical period ".[1]   The project differed from previous vague aspirations by enumerating " a series of consistent basic tasks which condition one another " as falling within the scope of the plan.   Trotsky, in his report, argued that the mobilization of labour could " make sense only if we have an apparatus for the correct allocation of labour power on the basis of a single economic plan embracing the whole country and all branches of the economy ", and that the main purpose of the plan must be not to yield immediate benefits, but " to prepare conditions for the production of the means of production ". He went on :

> We have as yet no single economic plan to replace the elementary work of the laws of competition.   This is the origin of the difficulties of Vesenkha.   There is a certain economic plan.   This plan is dictated by the views of our economic tasks taken at the centre, but in practice is carried out on the spot to the extent of only 5-10 per cent.[2]

Trotsky's military duties had associated him closely with the Council of Workers' and Peasants' Defence;   and Rykov and

[1] Trotsky's original draft resolution is in *Devyatyi S"ezd RKP(B)* (1934), pp. 511-512 ; he admitted at the congress that his failure to include any mention of planning in it was " a serious and important omission " (*ibid.* p. 102).   What member of the central committee proposed the insertion does not seem to be recorded.

[2] *Ibid.* p. 103.   Some remarks of Trotsky three years later throw significant light on his original approach to planning : " What are the basic supports of planned economy ? First, the army ; the army never lives on a market basis. The army is a planned economy.   Secondly, transport ; our (railway) transport belongs to the state.   Thirdly, heavy industry which works either for the army, or for transport, or for other branches of state industry " (*Dvenadtsatyi S"ezd Rossiiskoi Kommunisticheskoi Partii (Bol'shevikov)* (1923), pp. 306-307).

Milyutin rightly saw in these new and radical proposals a threat to the ambitions of Vesenkha. Rykov attacked Trotsky's " plan " as " an abstract composition remote from life ", and added that, " if we have to construct machines in order to equip our whole industry, tens of years will be needed ". But Rykov in turn incurred a sharp rebuff from Lenin and was told that " the attempt of Vesenkha to organize itself in some kind of separate bloc of economic commissariats " had " provoked a negative attitude " in the party central committee.[1] The resolution of the congress instructed the party central committee to work out in the near future a scheme for " an organizational link between Vesenkha and the other commissariats directly concerned with the economy . . . for the purpose of guaranteeing complete unity in the carrying out of the economic plan confirmed by the party congress ".[2] The resolution disposed of the pretensions of Vesenkha by firmly putting it on a level with " other commissariats " and implied that the " organizational link " would be found elsewhere. Immediately after the congress the Council of Workers' and Peasants' Defence received a new lease of life. The demobilization and allocation of labour being the crucial economic issue of the moment, it was renamed the Council of Labour and Defence (Soviet Truda i Oborony or STO);[3] and in this new guise it gradually emerged as the permanent central figure in the economic landscape, the arbiter of economic policy and the future planning authority. But the resumption of war in the summer of 1920 once more relegated the " single economic plan " to the background and postponed the issue of competence.

Meanwhile the alternative approach to planning through the treatment of specific problems had begun to gain ground, and another organ had come into being which was destined to play a distinguished part in the history of Soviet planning. In April 1918 Lenin had casually written of the electrification of transport and of agriculture as desiderata in a long-term plan for the Russian

---

[1] *Devyatyi S"ezd RKP(B)* (1934), p. 139 ; *Lenin, Sochineniya*, xxv, 120.
[2] *VKP(B) v Rezolyutsiyakh* (1941), i, 337.
[3] The decree making this change was recapitulated in the resolution of the eighth All-Russian Congress of Soviets in December 1920 (*S"ezdy Sovetov RSFSR v Postanovleniyakh* (1939), p. 181) ; see also Lenin, *Sochineniya*, xxvi, 619-620, note 23.

economy.[1]   In February 1920, when planning had once more
become a practical issue, Lenin, in a speech before VTsIK, again
" dwelt on the question of the electrification of the country, thus
linking it with the town ".[2]   At the end of the session VTsIK
resolved that the moment had now come to " take steps towards a
more regularly planned economic construction, towards the
scientific working out and consistent execution of a state plan for
the whole national economy ".   Taking into account the " primary
significance " of electrification for industry, agriculture and transport, it instructed Vesenkha to prepare a project for the building of
a " network of electric power stations " and to set up a commission
for the electrification of Russia (Goelro).[3]   The commission, which
had a membership of over 100, contained many *bourgeois* specialists
and was presided over by the old Bolshevik Krzhizhanovsky.[4]   The
project began to have a particular personal fascination for Lenin.
He wrote eagerly to Krzhizhanovsky about getting publicity for
the work of the commission.[5]   The ninth party congress, at which
Lenin administered his snub to Rykov and to the pretensions of
Vesenkha, gave direct encouragement to the specific approach
to planning ; for in once more demanding " *a single economic plan*
designed for the coming historical period ", it added that the plan
" naturally falls into a series of consistent basic tasks which
condition one another ".   Among these were the improvement of
transport and the construction of machinery.   The technical
foundation of the whole plan was " the working out of a plan of
electrification of the national economy ", involving the " electrification of industry, transport and agriculture ".[6]   Lenin still connected
electrification especially with the crucial problem of agriculture.
In the theses on the agrarian question which he drew up for the
second congress of Comintern in the summer of 1920, and which
were adopted by it, he declared it urgent to " reorganize the whole

---

[1] See p. 366 above.

[2] Lenin, *Sochineniya*, xxv, 22 (only a newspaper report of this speech has
survived).

[3] *Izvestiya*, February 8, 1920 : no official records of this session of VTsIK
appear to have been published, and the decision is not in the official collection of
laws and decrees.

[4] Lenin, *Sochineniya*, xxvi, 620, note 24 : Krzhizhanovsky with Lenin's
encouragement published in *Pravda* on January 30, 1920, an article on *Tasks of
the Electrification of Industry* (ibid. xxix, 432-433).

[5] *Ibid.* xxix, 434-435.   [6] *VKP(B) v Rezolyutsiyakh* (1941), i, 329.

of industry on the principle of large-scale collective production and on the most modern (i.e. founded on the electrification of the whole economy) technical basis " : only thus could help be brought by the town to the " backward and dispersed countryside " and the productivity of peasant labour raised.[1] Reconstruction of industry and agriculture, he told an all-Russian congress of communist youth, depended on electricity, the " last word " in modern science.[2] In 1919 a German socialist professor had published a work in which he estimated that the whole German economy could be electrified in three or four years. The book was quickly translated into Russian,[3] and Lenin was thinking of this estimate when he told a Moscow party conference in November 1920 that it would take not less than ten years to carry out a plan of electrification in Russia. It was on this occasion that Lenin coined the aphorism : " Communism is Soviet power plus electrification of the whole country ".[4] This was the revised version of the old quip about one half of socialism having been realized in Russia, the other half in Germany ; it was electrification which would create the conditions hitherto lacking in Russia for the transition to socialism.[5]

The year 1920 had also witnessed another specific " plan " which, though less far-reaching than Lenin's plan of electrification, had more immediate results. The resolution of the ninth party congress had referred to the improvement of transport as one of the basic tasks of planning.[6] Immediately after the party congress, a transport commission composed of representatives of the People's Commissariat of Communications (Narkomput') and of Vesenkha (as responsible for the railway construction and repair shops) was established with Trotsky as president, and issued, on

[1] Lenin, *Sochineniya*, xxv, 276 ; *Kommunisticheskii Internatsional v Dokumentakh* (1933), pp. 137-138.
[2] Lenin, *Sochineniya*, xxv, 389.
[3] K. Ballod, *Der Zukunftstaat* was first published in 1906 ; the revised edition containing the electrification programme was published in 1919, the Russian translation in 1920. It was first mentioned by Lenin in February 1921 (*Sochineniya*, xxvi, 171) ; but he had certainly read it before his speech of November 1920, since the estimate of ten years there given was subsequently related by Lenin himself (*ibid.* xxvi, 462) to Ballod's estimate of three or four years for Germany.
[4] *Ibid.* xxv, 491.   [5] *Ibid.* xxvi, 338.
[6] For the transport crisis at this time, see pp. 192, 219-220 above.

May 20, 1920, its famous " Order No. 1042 ". The order was a
detailed plan for the restoration of the locomotive park to its
normal condition by the end of 1924. Thanks to the impetus given
by the needs of the Polish war and by the " shock " organization
of labour, the work proceeded so well that, when Trotsky eventually reported on it to the eighth All-Russian Congress of Soviets
in December 1920 (by which time a plan for wagons had been
added to the locomotive plan), he was able to announce that the
original five-year plan could be fulfilled in three and a half years.[1]
This success at once enhanced the popularity of planning. Where
Lenin and Trotsky led the way, imitators were quickly found. It
was the period, as Milyutin records, of " broad economic plans "
in the plural :

> Questions of electrification, questions of new construction,
> questions of increasing the output of fuel or the supply of raw
> materials, of the fixing of higher norms of work, etc., seemed the
> most serious and important of absorbing questions, on the
> solution of which the best forces of Soviet Russia were concen-
> trated.[2]

Even the cautious Rykov[3] produced some highly optimistic
estimates, presumably drawn up in Vesenkha, according to which
the production of timber would rise in 1921 from 10 to 19 million
cubic *sazhen'*, coal from 431 to 718 million puds, oil from 71 to

---

[1] Order No. 1042 is in Trotsky, *Sochineniya*, xv, 345-347 ; for its fulfilment,
see Trotsky's speech to the congress (*Vos'moi Vserossiiskii S"ezd Sovetov* (1921),
pp. 174-175), reprinted with other documents of the period in Trotsky, *Sochineniya*, xv, 348-485. Lenin also commented on it in his speech at the congress
(*Sochineniya*, xxvi, 42, 47).

[2] V. P. Milyutin, *Istoriya Ekonomicheskogo Razvitiya SSSR* (2nd ed., 1929),
p. 192.

[3] Rykov, who throughout this time was moving towards the Right, was one
of the most consistent opponents of planning in the broader sense. At the
eighth All-Russian Congress of Soviets he thought that " we shall not for many
years achieve such a plan of production as would embrace all sides of our
economic life ", and jested at " those who suppose that a plan of production is
to be found on the pen-point of some literary man, whence the plan can be
taken and put on to paper " (*Vos'moi Vserossiiskii S"ezd Sovetov* (1921), pp.
101-102). The thirteenth party conference in 1924 found him in a reminiscent
vein : " When I was in Vesenkha in the time of war communism, it was so
arranged that you could call by telephone, and in three hours they would give
you a plan with figures, decorated with red and blue circles, squares, etc."
(*Trinadtsataya Konferentsiya Rossiiskoi Kommunisticheskoi Partii (Bol'shevikov)*
(1924), p. 18).

298 million puds, sugar from seven and a half to 25 million puds, cotton textiles from 135 to 780 million arshins and so forth. The most modest item in the list was an estimated increase in the production of electric power from 180 to 244 million kilowatts. Jealousy of the Krzhizhanovsky plan was perhaps not without influence on the calculations of the Vesenkha statisticians.[1]

When therefore the eighth All-Russian Congress of Soviets — the only important Soviet gathering between the end of the civil war and the inception of NEP — met in December 1920, planning was in the air, though different and to some extent conflicting meanings were attached to the term. The congress was in a mood to give its blessing to them all. It endorsed the electrification plan as " the first step in a great economic principle " and instructed the organs concerned " to complete the elaboration of this plan " in the shortest possible time. It approved Trotsky's report, and attached " great importance to the working out of a single plan for the exploitation of transport ". It confirmed the status and functions of STO, constituting it as a commission of Sovnarkom, to be composed of the principal People's Commissars, a representative of the trade unions and, in a consultative capacity, the director of the Central Statistical Administration. Among its other functions, STO " establishes the single economic plan of the RSFSR, directs the work of the economic People's Commissariats in accordance with the plan, watches over its fulfilment and establishes in case of necessity exceptions to the plan ";[2] for the first time the RSFSR had a general planning organ with clearly defined functions.

Lenin himself was so deeply committed to the scheme for electrification that he displayed a certain lukewarmness towards the conception of a general plan. At the congress he repeated the quip that " communism is Soviet power plus electrification ", and added another : " the electrification plan was our second party programme ".[3] On the other hand, he went out of his way to attack a pamphlet by a well-known old Bolshevik named Gusev, which propounded " a far-reaching plan for the creation of a Council of Labour and Defence, including the transfer to it of

---

[1] *Vos'moi Vserossiiskii S"ezd Sovetov* (1921), pp. 110-111.
[2] *S"ezdy Sovetov RSFSR v Postanovleniyakh* (1939), pp. 181-182.
[3] Lenin, *Sochineniya*, xxvi, 45-46.

many prominent party workers, among whom we find the names
of Trotsky and Rykov ".[1] While Lenin seems to have supposed
that he had clipped the wings of STO by insisting on its formal
status as a mere commission of Sovnarkom, the fact that Lenin,
as president of Sovnarkom, was its president and Trotsky, Rykov,
and the other principal People's Commissars its members, put its
position as the supreme economic organ beyond challenge; and
the existence of such an organ opened up far wider possibilities of
comprehensive planning than had existed under Vesenkha. Lenin,
however, remained mistrustful. In an unusually impatient article
" On the Single Economic Plan" in *Pravda* on February 22, 1921, he
attacked Kritsman, Milyutin and Larin by name for articles about
planning which he described as " idle talk " and " boring pedantry
. . . now in the literary, now in the bureaucratic, style ". The
electrification plan of Goelro was " the one serious work on the
question of the single economic plan ", and any idea of a planning
commission other than Goelro was mere " ignorant conceit ".[2]
In spite, however, of this vigorous article, Lenin sustained something of a defeat in Sovnarkom, which, on the very day on which
the article appeared, decided to set up a " state general planning
commission " attached to STO.[3] By way of compensation Lenin
persuaded the central committee of the party to nominate Krzhizhanovsky as president of the commission, thus securing continuity
with the work of Goelro, which was to function as a sub-commis-
sion of the new body. But he was unable to exclude Larin, whom
he now regarded as the principal enemy of practical and accurate
planning as he conceived it, and wrote an anxious letter to Krzhizhanovsky on ways and means of neutralizing his obnoxious
influence.[4] Under these rather unpromising auspices the " state
general planning commission ", henceforth familiarly known as
Gosplan, was born.

[1] Lenin, *Sochineniya*, xxvi, 43-44.

[2] *Ibid.* xxvi, 168, 173 ; a month later Stalin, having read the Goelro plan for
the first time, wrote a letter to Lenin attacking Trotsky and Rykov and concluding that " the *one and only* ' single economic plan ' is the ' plan of electrification ', and all the other ' plans ' mere chatter, idle and harmful " (Stalin,
Sochineniya, v, 50-51).

[3] *Sobranie Uzakonenii, 1921*, No. 17, art. 106 ; according to V. P. Milyutin,
Istoriya Ekonomicheskogo Razvitiya SSSR (2nd ed., 1929), p. 303, Lenin,
Milyutin and Larin all made reports at the meeting of Sovnarkom which took
this decision.   [4] Lenin, *Sochineniya*, xxix, 445-446.

In the major controversies of the tenth party congress and the introduction of NEP, the debate on planning lapsed into the background. In April 1921 Gosplan began work. Its staff consisted of thirty-four officials, most of them " learned technicians and professors whose names enjoy a deserved reputation as a result of their specialized work "; only seven of them were party members. Specialists working for Gosplan received a monthly salary of 1,000,000 rubles, rations of the highest category and clothing for themselves and their families, together with free passes and priority on the railways on the same footing as members of VTsIK.[1] Planning commissions were also attached to Vesenkha and to the principal economic commissariats, so that Gosplan could work through them on particular questions.[2] Lenin was now mollified. He told Krzhizhanovsky that, just as he had formerly thrust the noses of " communist ' know-alls ' ", who chattered about " the plan in general ", into the electrification plan, he was now prepared to thrust the noses of workers in Goelro into " questions of current economic plans ".[3] In May 1921 he was writing again to Krzhizhanovsky on the details of the work and expressing the hope that Gosplan would " work out at any rate in time for the harvest the foundations of a general state economic plan for the coming period — a year or two ", though grumblings were still heard about " bureaucratic utopias ".[4] But it was Trotsky who emerged at this time as the most influential advocate of planning. On August 7, 1921, when NEP was being applied for the first time to industry, Trotsky circulated a memorandum to the party central committee, protesting against the " contradictory zigzags " of recent policy and demanding the establishment of a " central economic authority " and an autonomous Gosplan reorganized on the basis of large-scale industry.[5] The sequel, two days later, was a decree which, while not conceding formal autonomy to Gosplan, authorized it not only to " institute a single economic plan embracing the whole of Russia ", but

---

[1] V. N. Ipatieff, *The Life of a Chemist* (Stanford, 1946), p. 308 ; Ipatiev was appointed to Gosplan in May 1921.

[2] *Trudy IV Vserossiiskogo S"ezda Sovetov Narodnogo Khozyaistva* (1921), pp. 83-84 ; the decree establishing these planning commissions is in *Sobranie Uzakonenii, 1921*, No. 38, art. 203.

[3] Lenin, *Sochineniya*, xxvi, 296.   [4] *Ibid.* xxvi, 359, 466.

[5] Memorandum of August 7, 1921, in the Trotsky archives.

to " harmonize the plans of the economic departments, including the commissariats, and superintend the operation of the plan in general and in the actual details ".[1] Meanwhile Goelro settled down comfortably as a department of Gosplan. In October 1921 an all-Russian electro-technical congress with 1000 delegates met in Moscow,[2] and gave its blessing to the work of Goelro.[3] Two months later Lenin announced to the ninth All-Russian Congress of Soviets that 221 electrical stations had been opened during the past two years with a capacity of 12,000 kilowatts, and that two large new stations, one on the outskirts of Moscow and the other of Petrograd, would be opened early in 1922.[4]

These achievements notwithstanding, the logical consequence of NEP was to relegate planning to a secondary place. The ninth All-Russian Congress of Soviets in December 1921, while it approved the progress made and promised in the work of electrification, and discussed a " fuel plan " of which Smilga was placed in charge,[5] was silent about the " single economic plan " ; [6] nor was the omission repaired at the eleventh party congress in the following March. But it was at this congress that Lenin announced the ending of the " retreat " inaugurated by NEP. It was fundamental that Soviet planning must be directed to increasing the rôle of industry in the national economy ; in this sense it was an instrument in the struggle of the industrial prole-

[1] *Sobranie Uzakonenii, 1921*, No. 59, art. 403.

[2] The decision to convene this congress " for the general discussion of technical-economic questions connected with the realization of the plan for the electrification of Russia " had been taken as long ago as February 1921 (*Sobranie Uzakonenii, 1921*, No. 10, art. 66). It was officially called the " eighth all-Russian electro-technical congress " to establish formal continuity with its predecessor of 1913 : a message from Lenin was read to it (Lenin, *Sochineniya*, xxvii, 21). Its proceedings (*Trudy 8 Vserossiiskogo Elektrotekhnicheskogo S"ezda*) were published by Gosplan in 2 volumes (n.d.).

[3] The resolution was reported to the ninth All-Russian Congress of Soviets by Krzhizhanovsky, who also mentioned two achievements forecast at the congress as soon likely to be within the reach of science — television and the development of energy by splitting the atom (*Devyatyi Vserossiiskii S"ezd Sovetov* (1922), p. 219).

[4] Lenin, *Sochineniya*, xxvii, 134.

[5] *S"ezdy Sovetov RSFSR v Postanovleniyakh* (1939), pp. 236-239 ; for the fuel plan see Lenin, *Sochineniya*, xxvii, 132-133.

[6] Lenin at this time wrote that " the new economic policy *does not change* the single state economic plan . . . but changes the approach to its realization " (*Sochineniya*, xxix, 463).

tariat against peasant predominance, of socialism against petty capitalism.[1] Since NEP marked a retreat into capitalism and a concession to the peasant, any reaction against it, or belief that it had gone far enough, was likely to be expressed in a renewed emphasis on the importance of planning. This new antithesis began to emerge in 1922 with the development of the industrial crisis. In terms of the Soviet bureaucracy it expressed itself in a keen rivalry between Gosplan, now the chief champion of industry, and Narkomfin, the most influential of the departments interested in carrying NEP to its logical conclusion. Among secondary leaders, the most ardent supporters of war communism, Preobrazhensky, Larin and Kritsman, now raised their voices against " the weakening of the planned economy " under NEP; as early as March 1922 Larin attributed the industrial crisis to this factor.[2] In the inner circles of the party leadership there was greater reluctance to assume clear-cut positions. But Trotsky continued to insist more and more vigorously on the vital need for a central plan and the development of industry. The campaign to strengthen Gosplan continued intermittently throughout 1922, and on June 8 a further decree re-defined its functions and powers : the functions included the drawing up both of a long-term plan (the *perspektivnyi plan*) and of an immediate plan of production (the *eksploatatsionnyi plan*), and Gosplan was to be consulted on drafts of important economic and financial decrees submitted to Sovnarkom or STO by the commissariats concerned.[3] But in general any substantial extension of the powers of Gosplan was resisted by Lenin both before his first stroke in May of that year and after his return to work in the autumn, and found no other supporters in the Politburo. In the autumn Trotsky's attack

---

[1] Bukharin had already written in 1920 : " In the towns the main struggle for the type of economy *is ending* with the victory of the proletariat. In the country it is ending so far as concerns the victory over large-scale capitalism. But at the same time it is *beginning again* in other forms as a struggle between state planning for a proletariat embodying socialized labour, and the mercantile anarchy, the speculative licence, of a peasantry embodying small-scale property and elements of the market. But, as a simple mercantile economy is nothing but the embryo of a capitalist economy, so the struggle between the above-mentioned tendencies is in essence a continuation of the struggle between communism and capitalism " (N. Bukharin, *Ekonomika Perekhodnogo Perioda* (1920), p. 86).

[2] *Odinnadtsatyi S"ezd RKP(B)* (1936), p. 118 ; the occasion of the protest of the three was the abolition of the utilization commission (see p. 369 above).

[3] *Sobranie Uzakonenii*, 1922, No. 40, art. 468.

crystallized into two specific proposals : that Gosplan should be given legislative powers, and that a deputy president of Sovnarkom should become president of Gosplan. On December 27, 1922, Lenin dictated from his sick-bed a memorandum to the Politburo in which he declared himself converted to the first proposal, but resisted the second. He accepted Trotsky's general view of the necessity for comprehensive planning, but still held that the head of Gosplan should be an " educated technician ", and defended the combination of Krzhizhanovsky as president with Pyatakov as his deputy.[1] But, with Lenin now finally withdrawn from the scene, Trotsky was completely isolated in the top rank of the party hierarchy. His request to publish Lenin's memorandum was rejected by the Politburo, and the reform of Gosplan once more shelved.[2]

The section devoted to planning in the resolution on industry adopted by the twelfth party congress of April 1923 summed up the position which had now been reached, and bore clear traces of the uneasy truce between the rival leaders on fundamental issues of economic policy.[3] Every statement which might be taken to represent Trotsky's positive attitude was qualified by a correspond-

---

[1] The course of this controversy, which became involved with a controversy about the proposed appointment of further deputy presidents of Sovnarkom during Lenin's illness (hitherto Rykov was the sole deputy), can be traced, with many lacunae, in the Trotsky archives. It was particularly active in December 1922. Lenin's memorandum of December 27, 1922, recording his partial acceptance of Trotsky's views, was quoted by Trotsky in his letter to members of the Politburo of October 22, 1923, long extracts from which were published in *Sotsialisticheskii Vestnik* (Berlin), No. 11 (81), May 28, 1924, p. 11. At one point the suggestion seems to have been made that Trotsky, who had already refused to become a deputy president of Sovnarkom, should be appointed president of Gosplan : his enemies evidently suspected him, with or without reason, of nourishing this ambition. Lenin's loyalty to Krzhizhanovsky, whom Trotsky regarded as inefficient, was clearly a factor in the situation.

[2] The record of the Politburo decision not to publish Lenin's memorandum is in the Trotsky archives. Trotsky's last move in the Gosplan controversy appears to have been a letter of January 25, 1923, to all members of the central committee ; in February 1923 he turned his attention to the question of credit for industry (see pp. 316-317 above).

[3] Trotsky states (*Stalin*, N.Y., 1946, p. 366) that he informed Stalin before the congress that he had " serious differences on economic questions " with the majority of the central committee. These differences, which were not brought into the open at the congress, will be discussed in a later instalment of the present work ; Trotsky's views on planning were in some degree a reflection of them.

ing expression of the caution and scepticism of his colleagues in the Politburo. While the aim was " a real socialist economic plan, embracing all branches of industry in their relations to one another and the mutual relations between industry as a whole and agriculture ", this could only be realized " as a result of prolonged preparatory economic experiment ", so that the immediate programme was " one of general direction and, to a large extent, preparatory ". The views of Trotsky on Gosplan were recorded in a paragraph of the resolution which could only have been drafted by him :

> It is perfectly clear that the fundamental planning of the economy cannot be achieved within industry itself, that is by the isolated efforts of the administrative organ controlling it, Vesenkha, but must form the task of a separate planning organ standing above the organization of industry and linking it with finance, transport, etc. Such an organ, in virtue of its position, is Gosplan.

But this was followed by a refusal to accord any " special administrative rights " to Gosplan, which, where compulsory powers were required, must still act through the commissariats or through STO or Sovnarkom.[1] The independent and authoritative planning organ of Trotsky's ambitions still eluded him.

More significant than this compromise resolution were the restatements of the two positions made by Zinoviev and Trotsky respectively at the congress, though the statements were made independently at different stages of the proceedings and any direct clash of opinion was studiously avoided. Zinoviev in his initial report on the work of the central committee, ignoring the substantial change in Lenin's attitude to planning during the past two years and the views expressed in his unpublished memorandum of December 1922, quoted Lenin's article of February 1921 " On the Single Economic Plan " in which, attacking the planning fantasies of Kritsman, Milyutin and Larin, he had described the electrification plan as the one serious contribution to planning and Goelro as the only effective planning organ. The moral for Zinoviev was obvious : to praise individual " plans ", but to throw cold water on Trotsky's advocacy of comprehensive planning and of the

---

[1] *VKP(B) v Rezolyutsiyakh* (1941), i, 478-480.

supremacy of Gosplan.[1] Trotsky went deeper. Under capitalism there were individual plans for particular enterprises and industries, but no general plan for the economy : this was replaced " by the market, the free play of forces, competition, demand, supply, crises, etc. etc.". It was because socialism meant the overcoming of the market and market phenomena that planning was the essence of socialism. The current industrial crisis called imperatively for planning: " if we condemned heavy industry to the free play of the market, it would run on the rocks ". He attempted — it was the most delicate point in the speech — to define his attitude to NEP. He too picked up a catchword of Lenin of two years ago, but in order, not to exalt its authority, but to qualify it. Lenin had said that NEP had been introduced " seriously and for a long time ". NEP, Trotsky now repeated, had been " established seriously and for a long time, but not for ever " ; it had been adopted " in order on its own foundation and to a large extent by using its own method to overcome it ". In other words, " our successes on the basis of the new economic policy automatically bring us nearer to its liquidation ".[2] In the peroration of a long speech he described the coming period as that of " primitive socialist accumulation " — the counterpart of Marx's " primitive capitalist accumulation " ;[3] to bring about this accumulation — Trotsky implied it without saying it — was the essential function of the plan. It was not the first time that Trotsky had thought ahead of his party colleagues or raised issues for whose solution the time was not yet ripe. It was not the first time that, in so doing, he had seemed to stake out for himself a claim to party leadership. In the spring of 1923 nobody was eager to take up the challenge of planning ; few perhaps understood it. The passages on planning in Trotsky's speech were the least criticized in the ensuing debate on the floor of the congress ; in the commission the section on planning in the resolution was the only one to which no amend-

---

[1] *Dvenadtsatyi S"ezd Rossiiskoi Kommunisticheskoi Partii (Bol'shevikov)* (1923), pp. 26-27 ; Zinoviev returned to the attack again, once more involving Lenin's authority, at the end of his speech (*ibid.* p. 45). For Lenin's article of February 1921 see p. 376 above : this was perhaps the earliest instance of misuse of Lenin's authority by selective quotation from his writings.

[2] *Ibid.* pp. 306, 313.

[3] *Ibid.* p. 321. Trotsky attributed the phrase to Smirnov, who worked in Gosplan ; it became famous at a later stage of the controversy on planning.

ments were proposed.[1] Nobody contested — indeed no Marxist could contest — the principle of planning. But the abstract calculations and abstract projects which in this initial period occupied the attention of the experts of Gosplan were not allowed to impinge on policy. Gosplan continued to operate and experiment in a vacuum. Two or three more years of preparatory work were required before it became an effective instrument in the hands of the planners. It was later still when the issue of planning finally emerged into the grim limelight of the struggle for power.

[1] *Ibid.* p. 373.

NOTE C

MARX, ENGELS AND THE PEASANT

THE attitude of Marx and of Marxists towards the peasantry has been the subject of a vast amount of controversy and misunderstanding. The core of Marxism was the analysis of the transition from capitalism to socialism. Capitalism was the creation of the bourgeoisie, the ruling class of capitalist society; the socialist revolution which would be primarily the work of the proletariat would usher in a future society in which all classes would be merged and finally disappear. The peasantry as a class was, on the other hand, a characteristic social form of the feudal order, and belonged neither to the world of bourgeois capitalism nor to that of proletarian socialism. When Marx, in the first volume of *Capital*, embarked on his analysis of the capitalist order, using what was admittedly an abstract model and not the picture of any existing society, he found no place for the peasant or the small craftsman: these were not typical figures of capitalism, but incidental survivals of an obsolete or obsolescent social order.

It was an essential part of this view that the peasantry, bearing the stigmata of its feudal origin, was a backward element in contemporary society — backward in relation not only to the capitalist bourgeoisie, but also *a fortiori* to the proletariat. It followed that, where capitalism was most advanced, the peasantry as a class was already in decay. In the *Communist Manifesto* Marx, thinking primarily in terms of western Europe, treated the peasantry as doomed, like other petty bourgeois groups (he lumped together " the small manufacturer, the shopkeeper, the artisan and the peasant "), to disappear in the advancing torrent of large-scale capitalism. In the meanwhile all these groups were conservative, even reactionary, trying " to roll back the wheel of history " :

> If by chance they are revolutionary, they are so only in view of their impending transfer into the proletariat; they thus defend not their present, but their future, interests; they desert their own standpoint to place themselves at that of the proletariat.

Flocon had warned Engels that 11 million small French farmers were " passionate property-owners " and sworn enemies of anything that smacked of communism.[1] The diagnosis of the conservative and

[1] Marx i Engels, *Sochineniya*, xxi, 91.

reactionary character of the peasantry seemed to be confirmed everywhere in western Europe, and notably in France, by the experience of
1848, when the peasants either remained passive spectators of the
revolution or actively assisted the authorities to crush the revolt of the
proletariat.

In eastern Europe (Germany occupying an intermediate position
between west and east) the peasantry was in a still less advanced stage
of the historical process. Down to 1848 its feudal status remained
almost intact; and the bourgeois revolution which would sweep away
the last strongholds of feudalism still lay in the future. But here a grave
dilemma arose. This revolution could not hope to succeed if the brunt
of it fell exclusively on the bourgeoisie and proletariat, which became
weaker and less numerous the further one went east; it could not hope
to succeed unless it were also an agrarian revolution and were actively
supported by the peasants. In the *Communist Manifesto* Marx's vision
was concentrated mainly on western Europe; but in the short last
section devoted to the relations of the communists to " various existing
opposition parties ", communist support was offered both to the
" agrarian reformers " in the United States and to the Polish party
which " insists on agrarian revolution as the prime condition of national
emancipation ". A few months later Marx stated the principle still
more clearly :

> The great agricultural countries between the Baltic and Black
> Seas can save themselves from patriarchal-feudal barbarism only by
> way of an agrarian revolution which would convert the serf or bonded
> peasants into free proprietors — a revolution precisely similar to
> that which occurred in 1789 in the French countryside.[1]

Thus, where the bourgeoisie and the proletariat, severally or jointly,
were too weak to complete the bourgeois revolution and the overthrow
of feudalism, it was legitimate for communists to give their support to
peasant parties making the revolution in the name of individual peasant
ownership, even though this remained " an agrarian form seemingly
opposed to any kind of communism ".[2] The distinction between the
policies to be followed in countries where the bourgeois revolution had
already been achieved and in countries where it had still to be achieved
was perfectly logical. But it was not free from embarrassment when it
involved offering to the peasants of eastern Europe the privileges of
peasant ownership which the peasants of western Europe were described
as " barbarians " for seeking to defend.

[1] *Karl Marx - Friedrich Engels: Historisch - Kritische Gesamtausgabe*, 1er
Teil, vii, 302.
[2] *Ibid.* vi, 12.

It was against this difficult background that the notion of a revolutionary alliance between proletariat and peasantry first began to take shape. Engels ended a long article of 1850 on the German peasant war of 1525, full of implied and explicit analogies, with a description of the fate of the German petty bourgeoisie in 1848 :

> The mass of the nation — the petty bourgeoisie, craftsmen and peasants — was left to its fate by its hitherto natural ally the bourgeoisie, as being too revolutionary, and in places also by the proletariat, as not being yet sufficiently advanced ; shattered in its turn into fragments, it was reduced to nullity and stood in opposition to its neighbours on both Right and Left.[1]

This passage plainly suggested that the peasantry, deserted by the bourgeoisie, would advance towards alliance with the proletariat : it also contained the germ of the idea, later to bear fruit, of a split between those peasants who would cling to the bourgeois alliance and those who would join the proletariat. Marx and Engels never abandoned their belief in the large-scale organization of production, in agriculture as in industry, as an essential condition of socialism ; and it followed that the peasants could become the allies of the proletariat in the socialist revolution only when they had been weaned from their faith in peasant ownership. In Germany this stage had not yet been reached. A much quoted passage of a letter to Engels of 1856, in which Marx wrote that everything in Germany turned on being able " to back the proletarian revolution by some second edition of the peasant war ",[2] shows that he still reckoned Germany among the predominantly peasant countries of eastern Europe, where the bourgeois revolution against the feudal order had not yet been completed, and where the proletarian minority might thus lend temporary tactical support to a programme of peasant proprietorship.[3]

Marx and Engels passed the remainder of their lives after 1850 in the one country where the peasant question had lost its acuteness with the process of wholesale industrialization and the conversion of what

[1] Marx i Engels, *Sochineniya*, viii, 197.
[2] *Karl Marx - Friedrich Engels : Historisch - Kritische Gesamtausgabe,* III[er] Teil, ii, 131-132 (the words quoted are in English in the original).
[3] On the large Prussian estates cultivated by agricultural labourers in semi-serf conditions the situation was once again different ; Engels wrote in a letter of 1865 that " in such a predominantly agricultural country as Prussia, it is mean to attack the bourgeoisie exclusively in the name of the industrial proletariat and at the same time not to say a single word about the patriarchal big-stick exploitation of the agricultural proletariat by the big feudal aristocracy ". Here Engels already makes the jump from the feudal exploitation of serfs to the capitalist exploitation of a rural proletariat of wage-labourers (Marx i Engels, *Sochineniya*, xxiii, 239).

was left of the peasantry into a rural proletariat. Nor did practical possibilities of revolution in Europe arise to compel them to reconsider the tactical issue. The two decades which separated the final extinction of the conflagration of 1848 from the Paris commune registered no change in their attitude to the peasant; nor did the heroism of the Paris commune inspire the peasant rising which alone might have saved it from defeat. But the impulse to a reconsideration of the peasant question in the last decade of Marx's life came from a more remote and unexpected source — Russia.

It was towards the end of the eighteen-sixties that Marx and Engels became interested in Russian affairs, and learned the language in order to read Russian economic literature. The moment was an important turning-point in Russian history. In the eighteen-fifties a new current of thought — for the *narodniks* were a group of intellectuals rather than an organized party — had arisen in Russia, combining the belief of the Slavophils in the peculiar destiny of Russia and her rôle as a bringer of light to Europe with western socialist doctrines, mainly of a somewhat utopian brand. The most concrete item in the *narodnik* creed was the conviction that the Russian peasant commune with its system of communal ownership was essentially socialist and capable of forming the basis of a future socialist order, so that Russia might indeed lead the rest of Europe on the road to socialism. The emancipation of the serfs in 1861 did not destroy this belief. This measure was inspired by the impulse to modernize the Russian economy after the disasters of the Crimean War and, like the English enclosures, by the need to create a reserve labour army for the industrialization of the country. It broke up the feudal relation of master-landowner and peasant-serf and went far to open the countryside to the infiltration of capitalism. But, since it did not formally disrupt the peasant commune (which continued to be the dominant form of organization for agriculture), its significance was not fully understood and it had little effect on *narodnik* doctrine. The activities of the *narodniks*, reinforced by terrorist groups professing *narodnik* doctrine, reached their height in the eighteen-seventies. The first Russian translation of the first volume of *Capital*, which appeared as early as 1872, was the work of a *narodnik* named Danielson.

The struggle against Bakunin drew Marx and Engels further into the field of Russian controversies. In 1875, replying to an attack by the Russian *narodnik* Tkachev, Engels published an article on *Social Relations in Russia* in which he pointed out, acutely enough, that the emancipation had " dealt the strongest blow at communal property ", and that " communal property in Russia has long outlived the time of its prosperity, and according to all appearances is approaching its dissolution." But he added some further considerations which opened a long controversy :

> None the less, it is incontestable that the possibility exists of transforming this communal form into a higher one, if only it is preserved until such time as the conditions are ripe for this transformation, and if it is capable of development in such a way that the peasants begin to work the land not separately but in common ; then the Russian peasants will pass over to this higher form, avoiding the intermediate stage of bourgeois small-scale ownership. But this can occur only in the event of the victorious proletarian revolution breaking out in western Europe before the final collapse of this common property — a revolution which will assure to the Russian peasant the essential conditions for such a transfer, and in particular the material means needful to carry out the revolution in his whole system of agriculture which is necessarily bound up with it.[1]

The qualifications were important. It was not suggested that Russia could by her own efforts by-pass the stage of bourgeois capitalism and reach socialism by the direct path, transforming the communal institutions of her feudal past into the communal institutions of her socialist future. What was suggested was that the proletariat of the advanced countries, having victoriously achieved their own revolution, would be able to carry backward Russia with them into socialism without Russia having herself had to tread the capitalist path ; and there was nothing illogical about this conception once Europe was regarded as a unit. Marx himself made no public pronouncement at this time. But that he endorsed Engels's view was shown two years later in a letter addressed to a Russian journal in reply to an article criticizing him as anti-Russian. The reply denied that he had ever prescribed " a general path to which all nations are fatally destined ", and summed up with a negative, but revealing, verdict :

> If Russia continues to travel on the path which she has been following since 1861, she will be deprived of the finest chance ever offered by history to a nation of avoiding all the ups-and-downs of the capitalist order.[2]

The issue was soon to be complicated by the emergence in Russia of a vigorous group of young Marxists, which, splitting away from the *narodniks* and in diametrical opposition to them, condemned the rural commune as a mere feudal survival and preached the need for the development of capitalism in Russia as the prelude to a proletarian revolution. The leaders of this movement, Plekhanov, Axelrod and Vera Zasulich, left Russia in the late eighteen-seventies and in 1883

[1] Marx i Engels, *Sochineniya,* xv, 261.   [2] *Ibid.* xv, 375-377.

founded the Liberation of Labour group in Switzerland.[1] The members of this group assumed and continued to assume that the orderly scheme of revolution laid down in the *Communist Manifesto* applied to all countries and that socialism could be reached in Russia only through the intermediate stage of bourgeois capitalism. It caused some bewilderment that this scheme should apparently be set aside by one of its authors. In February 1881 Vera Zasulich wrote to Marx asking for a clarification of his view on the Russian peasant commune. How embarrassing the enquiry was to the ageing Marx is suggested by three variants of a long draft reply which remained among his papers. In the end he rejected them all, and contented himself with a brief letter explaining that the analysis in *Capital* based on western conditions, where communal property had long disappeared, was not applicable to Russia, where such property still survived in the form of the peasant commune. He expressed the conviction that " this commune is a point of support for the socialist regeneration of Russia ", but added cryptically that, " in order that it may function as such, it would be necessary to remove the harmful influences to which it is exposed on all sides and then guarantee to it normal conditions of free development ".[2] Neither in 1877 nor in 1881 did Marx mention the main qualification attached to Engels's admission of 1875 — the hypothesis of a victorious proletarian revolution in western Europe. But this omission was remedied in the following year, when Marx and Engels jointly signed the preface to a new Russian translation of the *Communist Manifesto* and included in it their last joint utterance on Russian affairs :

> The question now is : Can the Russian commune — this already, it is true, much impaired form of primitive collective land tenure — pass over directly into the highest, communist form of land tenure ? Or must it, on the contrary, undergo the same process of decay which has determined the historical development of the west ?
>
> The only possible answer to this question at the present time is as follows. If the Russian revolution serves as a signal for a workers' revolution in the west, so that the two complement each other, then contemporary Russian land tenure may be a starting-point for communist development.[3]

The study of these texts suggests the conclusion that Marx and Engels in their later years — and Marx perhaps even more than Engels — were impelled by a human desire to satisfy enthusiastic *narodnik* supporters to place more faith in the potentialities of the Russian commune

---

[1] See Vol. I, p. 4.
[2] Marx i Engels, *Sochineniya*, xxvii, 117-118 : the rejected drafts are *ibid.* xxvii, 677-697.
[3] *Ibid.* xv, 601.

than was justified either by Russian conditions or by any reasonable interpretation of the *Communist Manifesto* or of *Capital.* Marx died in 1883. Capitalism continued to develop in Russia, and with it the strength of the Marxist group. The *narodniks,* caught in the blind alley of terrorism, began to lose influence. Plekhanov in a series of brilliant articles and pamphlets pressed home the argument that the peasant commune could develop only into bourgeois, not into communist, forms of social organization, and that "bourgeois-peasant socialism" could not be the road to communism; and at the founding congress of the Second International in Paris in 1889 he made the challenging claim that "the Russian revolution will triumph as a proletarian revolution or it will not triumph at all ".

The great Russian famine of 1891 once more threw the agrarian problem into lurid relief. The disaster could be attributed just as easily to the disintegrating influences of capitalism on the peasant commune as to the inherent backwardness and inefficiency of the communal system. But, whatever the diagnosis, it was plain that historical processes were at work which could not be reversed. Engels beat a quiet retreat from the concessions which he and Marx had made to the *narodniks* ten and fifteen years earlier. The retreat was registered in a letter of February 1893 to the old *narodnik* Danielson, who had written to denounce the advance of capitalism as the cause of the famine. Engels was in no mind to deny the evils of capitalism. But this was no longer the point. The opportunity of avoiding them, if it had ever existed, had been missed. The peasant commune had become part of the " dead past ", and Russia could not escape her capitalist destiny :

> History is the most cruel of all goddesses. She drives her triumphal chariot over heaps of corpses, not only in war, but also in times of " peaceful " economic development.[1]

This grim pronouncement restored Russia to a normal place in the revolutionary scheme of the *Communist Manifesto.* The gleam of hope which Marx and Engels seemed to have held out of a privileged path to salvation was extinguished; and when in the following year Engels, on the occasion of a republication of his article of 1875, once more reluctantly took up the challenge, he repeated, without any formal change of position but with a marked change of emphasis, that " the initiative in such a transformation of the Russian commune can come not from itself, but exclusively from the industrial proletariat of the west ", and that " agrarian communism, surviving from a primitive order of society, has never produced of itself anything but its own

[1] *Ibid.* xxix, 206.

disintegration ".[1] When Lenin began to write in the eighteen-nineties, he whole-heartedly followed Plekhanov's polemic against the *narodniks* and made the development of capitalism in Russia his main theme. But some of the old arguments were to reappear many years later, and in a very different setting, in the controversies about " socialism in one country " and the collectivization of agriculture.

Whatever differences might arise about the path by which the goal was to be reached, Marx and Engels never wavered on one cardinal point : collective large-scale agriculture was an indispensable condition of socialism. It was because the *narodniks* seemed to offer this condition that their theories had been momentarily attractive. In the last year of his life, Engels returned to the west in a long article on " The Peasant Question in France and Germany ", and attempted to answer a puzzling question. He argued that the bourgeois revolution, while it had freed the peasant of western Europe from his feudal status and obligations, had none the less worsened his material and moral situation by depriving him of " the defence of the self-administering commune of which he was a member ". He had been exposed to the full blasts of capitalist exploitation and been transformed into " a future proletarian ". Why then did the peasant generally regard social-democracy, the party of the urban proletariat, as his worst enemy ? This was because social-democrats inscribed in their programmes a policy of nationalization of land which seemed to the peasant to threaten him with the loss of what little land he had.

Engels drew a sharp distinction between small and large proprietors, the former predominating in France and western Germany, the latter in Mecklenburg and East Prussia, with other parts of Germany in an intermediate position. As regards the small owners he frankly stated the dilemma : " We can win over quickly to our side the mass of small peasants only if we make them promises which we notoriously cannot keep ". These promises would be, in effect, to release them from rent payments and mortgages and guarantee them the ownership of their land in perpetuity. Social-democrats could not consistently advocate a policy tending to perpetuate a system of small ownership which contradicted the principles both of socialism and of efficient production. But they need not take the offensive against the small peasant :

> In the first place . . . we foresee the inevitable ruin of the small peasant, but are in no case called on to hasten it by our intervention.
> Secondly, it is equally obvious that when we win state power, we shall not think of forcibly expropriating the small peasant (whether with or without compensation does not matter), as we shall be compelled to do with the large landowners. Our task in relation

[1] Marx i Engels, *Sochineniya*, xvi, ii, 387, 391-392.

to the small peasants will consist first of all in transforming their private production and private ownership into collective production and ownership — not, however, by forcible means, but by the method of example and by offering social aid for this purpose.[1]

As regards large and medium-sized estates employing hired labour, socialists were naturally more interested in the labourers than in the proprietors. But, even as regards the proprietors, it was not so much a question of destroying them as of " leaving them to their own fate " ; for they already faced certain ruin from the competition of a more highly developed capitalist agriculture in the form of imports of trans-Atlantic grain. In any event, the break-up of large estates was not the socialist aim : the large proprietor was, according to his lights, a more efficient producer than the small peasant. As long ago as 1850 Marx, advocating the nationalization of land as part even of a bourgeois revolutionary programme, had proposed that " confiscated property should remain the property of the state and be converted into workers' colonies, tilled by associations of the rural proletariat which would thus enjoy all the advantages of large-scale agriculture ".[2] Engels now argued that, just as large-scale capitalist industry was ripe for the transition to socialized industry, so the large capitalist estate could become the socialist collective farm :

> Here the transformation of capitalist cultivation into social cultivation has already been fully prepared and can be carried out at once, exactly as, for example, in the factory of Herr Krupp or Herr von Stumm.

Moreover this large-scale socialized cultivation would serve as a model to the small peasants of the advantages of large-scale cooperative enterprise.[3]

The final legacy of Engels in the peasant question was thus a renewed insistence on the principle of large-scale agriculture as a necessary ingredient of socialism, a suggestion that large-scale capitalist estates were ripe for direct conversion into socialist state farms, and an attempt to lead the small peasant proprietor along the inevitable path of collective ownership by methods of persuasion rather than by those of constraint. These ideas formed the background of the agrarian policies of all social-democratic parties for the next twenty years, though they did little to mitigate the lack of sympathy felt by the majority of peasants for these policies.

[1] Lenin (*Sochineniya*, xxiii, 308) was afterwards to quote this passage in defence of the policy of conciliating the " middle peasant " (who in Russian conditions corresponded to Engels's " small peasant " — the small-holder working for himself without hired labour).

[2] Marx i Engels, *Sochineniya*, viii, 487.   [3] *Ibid.* xvi, ii, 441-461.

NOTE D

WORKERS' CONTROL ON THE RAILWAYS

THE issue of " workers' control " as it presented itself on the railways was anomalous in two respects. In the first place, all the main Russian railways were state-owned before the revolution, so that the conception of a control exercised by the workers over enterprises still operated, subject to that control, by their capitalist owners did not apply. Secondly, the railwaymen's union, the largest and most closely organized of Russian trade unions, was unique in including clerical and technical as well as manual workers, so that the practical difficulties which arose elsewhere when " workers " tried to take over factories, were not here in evidence. Fortified by these advantages, the railwaymen presented to the Soviet Government on the first day of its existence a formal challenge which could not be evaded or postponed. The railwaymen's union entrusted the management of its affairs to an executive committee of some forty members (the " All-Russian Executive Committee of Railwaymen " or Vikzhel) of whom, at the time of the October revolution, two are said to have been Bolsheviks, two *Mezhraiontsy*, and one a non-party Bolshevik sympathizer ; the rest were Right and Left SRs, Mensheviks and independents.[1] Like most trade unions in which the skilled workers had a predominant voice, the railwaymen's union was radical rather than revolutionary. From the moment of the October revolution Vikzhel took over the administration of the railways on its own account and acted as an independent power. In short, it played the rôle of a mammoth factory committee exercising "workers' control ". It recognized no political authority, and no interest other than the professional interest of the railwaymen.

The challenge was offered in the most open and dramatic form on the day after the October revolution at the second All-Russian Congress of Soviets. At the second and last session of the congress on October 26/November 8, 1917, Kamenev had read out the list of the new all-Bolshevik Sovnarkom, in which the post of People's Commissar for Communications had been left " temporarily unfilled ". At the end of the proceedings a delegate of Vikzhel demanded a hearing, which was

---

[1] The sources for the composition of Vikzhel are quoted in Bunyan and Fischer, *The Bolshevik Revolution, 1917–1918* (Stanford, 1934), p. 153.

refused him by Kamenev from the chair. This led to " noise in the hall " ; and " after prolonged negotiations " it was agreed that the delegate should be allowed to make a statement. He then read a declaration drafted earlier in the day by Vikzhel. Vikzhel adopted " a negative attitude to the seizure of power by any one political party " ; announced that, pending the formation of " a revolutionary socialist government responsible to the plenipotentiary organ of the whole revolutionary democracy ", it would take charge of the railways and that only orders issued by it would be obeyed ; and threatened, in the event of any attempt to apply repressive measures to railwaymen, to cut off supplies from Petrograd. To this broadside Kamenev could make only a formal reply insisting on the sovereign authority of the All-Russian Congress of Soviets. Another railwayman from the body of the hall denounced Vikzhel as " a political corpse " and declared that " the masses of railway workers have long ago turned away " from it. But this statement was still too remote from the facts to make much impression.[1]

The attitude of Vikzhel went beyond workers' control as commonly conceived : it was syndicalism in its most extreme form. Nevertheless Sovnarkom was powerless. The railways remained in the hands of Vikzhel ; and two days later an ultimatum threatening a general railway strike [2] compelled the Bolsheviks to enter into negotiations with the other socialist parties for a coalition government. The negotiations dragged on, and led to the resignation of a group of Bolsheviks who thought that Lenin and Trotsky were taking too stiff a line.[3] But, after the deadlock seemed complete, negotiations were taken up again in the All-Russian Congress of Peasants' Deputies which met in Petrograd on November 10/23, 1917. Here, five days later, the agreement was reached which admitted three Left SRs to Sovnarkom : the agreement was endorsed by Vikzhel, and a former member of the committee filled the vacant post of People's Commissar for Communications.

The compromise with Vikzhel was uneasy, and proved even less durable than the government coalition. An all-Russian congress of the railwaymen's union was in session at the time of the meeting of the Constituent Assembly and, at the insistence of Vikzhel, passed by a small majority a vote of confidence in the assembly. This was intended, and recognized, as a challenge to the Bolsheviks and to the government. The Bolsheviks had now, however, tried out their ground and were ready to meet defiance by action. The rank and file

[1] *Vtoroi Vserossiiskii S"ezd Sovetov* (1928), pp. 87-90.
[2] Bunyan and Fisher, *The Bolshevik Revolution, 1917–1918* (Stanford, 1934), pp. 155-156.
[3] See Vol. 1, pp. 108-109.

of the railwaymen were more sympathetic to the Bolsheviks than the moderates who controlled Vikzhel. The defeated minority seceded from the congress and formed a rival railwaymen's congress of its own ; and this congress, having listened to a long political address by Lenin,[1] created its own executive committee (known, by way of distinction, as Vikzhedor) consisting of 25 Bolsheviks, 12 Left SRs and 3 independents. The new congress and its executive committee at once received official recognition from Sovnarkom ; and a member of Vikzhedor, Rogov, became People's Commissar for Communications. It remained to make the new régime effective. To this end the Soviet Government now proceeded to invoke the principle of workers' control in order to undermine the authority of Vikzhel over railway employees. A regulation of January 10/23, 1918, probably the most frankly syndicalist measure ever included in Soviet legislation, entrusted the administration of every railway line to a Soviet elected by the railwaymen of that line, and general control over all Russian railways to an All-Russian congress of railwaymen's deputies.[2] This new organization built up from below served to destroy the efficient and hostile Vikzhel and to substitute the shadowy but friendly Vikzhedor. But it did not become, and could not become, an effective instrument for running the Russian railways. When the Brest-Litovsk crisis was over, and it was once more possible and urgent to return to issues of domestic organization, the Soviet Government at length took the matter in hand. A report to VTsIK from the People's Commissar for Labour dilated eloquently and in detail on the " disorganization and demoralization " of the Russian railways.[3] This was the prelude to a decree of Sovnarkom of March 26, 1918, which gave to the People's Commissar for Communications " dictatorial powers in matters relating to railway transport ". The functions of the all-Russian congress of railwaymen were apparently limited to the election of the members of the commissar's collegium ; these elections were subject to confirmation by Sovnarkom and VTsIK, and the powers of the collegium were limited to an appeal to the same two organs against the commissar.[4] The decree, drastic

---

[1] Lenin, *Sochineniya*, xxii, 226-242. The congress sat simultaneously with the first All-Russian Congress of Trade Unions in January 1918 ; but no relations seem to have been established between the two congresses, and it is significant of their relative strength and importance that Lenin found time to address the railwaymen's congress himself, but sent Zinoviev to speak for the party at the trade union congress.

[2] The regulation was published in the official journal of Narkomput' ; extracts in translation are in Bunyan and Fisher, *The Bolshevik Revolution, 1917-1918* (Stanford, 1934), pp. 653-654.

[3] *Protokoly Zasedanii VTsIK 4ᵍᵒ Sozyva* (1920), pp. 44-45.

[4] *Sbornik Dekretov i Postanovlenii po Narodnomu Khozyaistvu* (1918), pp. 820-822.

though it seemed, was not difficult to defend and justify. " When I hear hundreds of thousands of complaints," said Lenin at VTsIK, " when there is hunger in the country, when you see and know that these complaints are right, that we have bread but cannot transport it, when we meet mockery and protests from Left communists against such measures as our railway decree " — and the speaker broke off with a gesture of contempt.[1]   The railways were a microcosm of Russian industry.   They were, as Lenin said later, a " key " of the economic situation.   The policy adopted in dealing with them was the prototype of industrial policy as a whole.   Workers' control successively served two purposes.   It broke up the old order that was hostile to the revolution ;   and, when pursued to its own logical conclusion, it demonstrated beyond possibility of contradiction the need for new forms of control, more rigid and more centralized.

[1] Lenin, *Sochineniya*, xxii, 490.

LIST OF ABBREVIATIONS

Comintern = Kommunisticheskii Internatsional (Communist International).

Glavk(i) = Glavnyi(ye) Komitet(y) (Chief Committee(s)).

Glavkomtrud = Glavnyi Komitet Truda (Chief Labour Committee).

Goelro = Gosudarstvennaya Komissiya po Elektrifikatsii Rossii (State Commission for the Electrification of Russia).

Gosplan = Gosudarstvennaya Obshcheplanovaya Komissiya (State General Planning Commission).

GUM = Gosudarstvennyi Universal'nyi Magazin (State Universal Store).

Kombedy = Komitety Bednoty (Committees of Poor Peasants).

Narkomfin = Narodnyi Komissariat Finansov (People's Commissariat of Finance).

Narkomprod = Narodnyi Komissariat Prodovol'stviya (People's Commissariat of Supply).

Narkomput' = Narodnyi Komissariat Putei Soobshcheniya (People's Commissariat of Communications).

Narkomtrud = Narodnyi Komissariat Truda (People's Commissariat of Labour).

Narkomzem = Narodnyi Komissariat Zemledeliya (People's Commissariat of Agriculture).

NEP = Novaya Ekonomicheskaya Politika (New Economic Policy).

RSFSR = Rossiiskaya Sotsialisticheskaya Federativnaya Sovetskaya Respublika (Russian Socialist Federal Soviet Republic).

Sovkhoz = Sovetskoe Khozyaistvo (Soviet Farm).

Sovnarkhoz = Sovet Narodnogo Khozyaistva (Council of National Economy).

Sovnarkom = Sovet Narodnykh Komissarov (Council of People's Commissars).

SR = Sotsial-Revolyutsioner (Social-Revolutionary).

STO = Sovet Truda i Oborony (Council of Labour and Defence).

Vesenkha   =Vysshii Sovet Narodnogo Khozyaistva (Supreme Council of National Economy).

Vikzhel   =Vserossiiskii Ispolnitel'nyi Komitet Soyuza Zhelezno-dorozhnikov (All-Russian Executive Committee of Union of Railwaymen).

VTsIK   =Vserossiiskii (Vsesoyuznyi) Tsentral'nyi Ispolnitel'nyi Komitet (All-Russian (All-Union) Central Executive Committee).

TABLE OF APPROXIMATE EQUIVALENTS

1 arshin	=2 ft. 4 ins.
1 chervonets (gold)	=1 £ sterling (gold).
1 desyatin	=2·7 acres.
1 pud	=36 lbs.
1 sazhen'	=12·7 cubic yds.

END OF VOL. II